INTIMATE ✤ POLITICS

Marriage, the Market, and State Power
in Southeastern China

Harvard East Asian Monographs 265

INTIMATE ✌ POLITICS

Marriage, the Market, and State Power
in Southeastern China

Sara L. Friedman

Published by the Harvard University Asia Center
Distributed by Harvard University Press
Cambridge (Massachusetts) and London 2006

© 2006 by the President and Fellows of Harvard College
Printed in the United States of America

The Harvard University Asia Center publishes a monograph series and, in coordination with the Fairbank Center for East Asian Research, the Korea Institute, the Reischauer Institute of Japanese Studies, and other faculties and institutes, administers research projects designed to further scholarly understanding of China, Japan, Vietnam, Korea, and other Asian countries. The Center also sponsors projects addressing multidisciplinary and regional issues in Asia.

Library of Congress Cataloging-in-Publication Data

Friedman, Sara.
    Intimate politics : marriage, the market, and state power in southeastern China / Sara L. Friedman.
      p. cm. -- (Harvard East Asian monographs ; 265)
    Includes bibliographical references (p.) and index.
    ISBN 0-674-02128-2 (cl : alk. paper)
    1. Women—Government policy—China—Hui'an Xian. 2. Women—China—Hui'an Xian—Social life and customs. 3. Women—China—Hui'an Xian—Social conditions. 4. Marriage—China—Hui'an Xian. 5. Sexual division of labor—China—Hui'an Xian. 6. China—Social policy. 7. China—Ethnic relations—Political aspects. I. Title. II. Series.
    HQ1236.5.C6F75 2006
    305.40951'245--dc22

                                        2006004089

Index by David Prout

♾ Printed on acid-free paper

Last figure below indicates year of this printing
16 15 14 13 12 11 10 09 08 07 06

for Gardner

Acknowledgments

The process of researching and writing this book would not have been possible without the generous support and inspiration provided by many individuals and institutions. The project began as a doctoral dissertation at Cornell University under the guidance of Steve Sangren, Kath March, Beth Povinelli, and Sherm Cochran. Their assistance over the years has been immensely valuable, and this book and the research on which it is based benefited in numerous ways from their careful instruction and probing questions. During my years at Cornell, courses with John Borneman, Vivienne Shue, and Viranjini Munasinghe also shaped my thinking and enabled me to explore different ways of approaching the nation-state, socialist politics, and intimate life.

My fieldwork in China from 1995 to 1997 was funded by the Committee on Scholarly Communication with China and the Wenner-Gren Foundation for Anthropological Research. Follow-up trips in 1998 and 2000 were supported by a Lam Family Travel Grant from the Cornell University East Asia Program and a Cornell Mario Einaudi Center Travel Grant. Subsequent research in 2002 was funded by a Grimm Fellowship for Travel in Asia from Washington University. I am grateful to all of these sources for their support and interest in my work and for enabling me to return to Hui'an on a regular basis. The writing of my dissertation was made possible by a National Science Foundation Graduate Fellowship, a Woodrow Wilson Dissertation Grant in Women's Studies, and a Cornell Women's Studies Program Dissertation Fellowship.

I began to turn the dissertation into a book while I was a postdoctoral fellow at the Fairbank Center for East Asian Research at Harvard University. I am grateful to the Center and its director, Liz Perry, for providing me with a space to think and write free from the demands of both graduate school and teaching. I learned much in that year from friends and colleagues who read my work and engaged in critical discussions on all manner of topics. Special thanks are due to Brian Axel, Eileen Chow, Sandra Hyde, Ann Marie Leshkowich, Felicity Lufkin, Liz Perry, Elizabeth Remick, Cathy Silber, Chris Walley, Rubie Watson, Woody Watson, Rob Weller, and Marty Whyte. My colleagues at Washington University created a welcoming and stimulating environment that enabled me to write most of the book while also embarking on a new teaching career. Lara Bovilsky, John Bowen, Lou Brown, Letty Chen, Geoff Childs, Patrick Eisenlohr, Bret Gustafson, Bob Hegel, Ahmet Karamustafa, Fatemeh Keshavarz, Rebecca Lester, Andrew Mertha, Linda Nicholson, Shanti Parikh, Laura Rosenbury, Rachel Roth, Rich Smith, and Jim Wertsch made my years in Saint Louis both happy and productive, and I thank them for their support. At Indiana University, I have had the good fortune to join a vibrant academic community that has made the task of completing the book all the more pleasurable. I am especially grateful to Kon Dierks, Helen Gremillion, Stephanie Kane, Scott Kennedy, Sarah Knott, Ethan Michelson, Marissa Moorman, Susan Nelson, Scott O'Bryan, Radhika Parameswaran, Sarah Phillips, Heidi Ross, David Shorter, Marvin Sterling, Jeff Wasserstrom, Brenda Weber, and Jeanne Sept for welcoming me into their midst.

Over the years many people have strengthened the manuscript through their close readings of chapters, and I hope that they will see their efforts reflected in this version. Many thanks to Larry Barnett, John Bowen, Rob Culp, Thamora Fishel, Susan Hangen, Julie Hemment, Lisa Hoffman, Jennifer Hubbert, Suad Joseph, Scott Kennedy, Smita Lahiri, Tamara Loos, Ethan Michelson, Beth Povinelli, Jeff Wasserstrom, Erik White, and Li Zhang. Erik Mueggler and David Shorter stepped in at critical moments and offered to read the entire manuscript, and I am indebted to them for their generosity. The two anonymous reviewers for the press offered incisive comments that helped me clarify the focus of the book and strengthen its arguments. Tom Lyons produced several of the wonderful maps that I used in the dissertation, and I have adapted those here. Mike Hollingsworth beautifully redrew the map of Shanlin at a moment's notice. Katherine Lawn carefully copyedited the manuscript, and Cheryl Tucker of Harvard's Asia Center Publications Program offered invaluable editorial assistance and guidance. David Prout did an excellent job on the index.

Some material from Chapters 2 and 7 appeared previously in article form (Friedman, 2004) and it is reprinted here with permission of the Association for Asian Studies. Sections of the Introduction and Chapters 2 and 3 were published in an earlier article (Friedman, 2005), and they are reprinted with permission from the American Anthropological Association.

The research on which this book is based was carried out with the assistance of many people and institutions in China. At Xiamen University, the Overseas Education College and the Foreign Affairs Office initially facilitated my research and my institutional affiliation. Guo Zhichao of the Anthropology Research Institute took me under his wing and gave generously of his time and resources in arranging contacts, finding sources, and answering innumerable questions. My debt of gratitude to him is immeasurable. Lan Daju accompanied me to archives, debated anthropological and feminist theory, and offered his own insights into Hui'an culture. Zheng Zhenman was always available during my visits to Xiamen for discussions about Fujian culture and history, pushing me to think more critically about my research conclusions and methods. Lin Baoqin and Qiu Suhua taught me the language skills necessary to conduct my research in Minnan dialect. Many thanks to Qiu Laoshi in particular for patiently explaining the nuances of Hui'an dialect and local folk songs. Both she and Yang Zijing provided homes away from home, offering places of respite from the hectic pace of fieldwork. Return trips to Xiamen would not have been the same without the friendships of Jan Engsberg, Mila Tan, Stephanie Koenig, and Cynthia Brokaw.

The staffs at the Fujian Provincial Party Archives and the Fujian Provincial Library provided valuable assistance during my brief sojourn in Fuzhou in the fall of 1996. I would also like to express my appreciation to Guo Nujing for opening her home to me and making my stay in Fuzhou a much more pleasant one than it would have been without her.

Of course it is to the people of Chongwu and Shanlin that I owe my greatest debt. I thank Wang Feng and Cai Yongzhe for sharing their knowledge of Hui'an and Chongwu with me; Wang Minghui and her family for offering companionship and a second home in town; and finally Cai Xueping for her patient assistance, which proved invaluable to my research. To all the villagers of Shanlin who welcomed me into their lives and homes, good-naturedly submitting to endless (often frustratingly ignorant) questions, I express my heartfelt gratitude. I truly wish I could name you individually. To my A Beh and A M, this project would never have been possible without you. Thank you for taking me in and treating me as one of your own, even when times were rough.

These acknowledgments would not be complete without thanking the many people who have enriched my life over the years. The love and understanding of my parents, Ellin and Bill Friedman, have helped me persevere despite the often long distances that separated us. Stuart Friedman, Jennifer Friedman, Dorothy Weiner, Ruth Drosdek, Cindy Krieger, Janet Paskin, Betsy and Henry Judson, and Barbara and Jerry Nosanchuk continually remind me of the joys of close-knit families and friendships in ways both large and small. I have dedicated this book to Gardner, whose careful reading and willingness to debate the fine points of everything from grammar to theory have strengthened my research and writing at every turn. He daily renews in me appreciation for the joys of learning and growing together.

S.L.F.

Contents

Table, Maps, and Figures — XIII
Note on Romanization and Transcription — XV
Introduction: Intimate Politics — 1

PART I: "THE HUI'AN WOMAN" AS FEUDAL SUBJECT

1 Industrious Women and the Changing Meanings of Labor — 31
2 Fashioning Liberated Socialist Subjects — 67

PART II: INTIMATE LIFE IN THE POST-MAO ERA

3 Marriage, Intimacy, and Late-Socialist State Power — 107
4 The Ties That Bind — 136
5 Stone-Carving Factories, Youth Culture, and the Lure of Consumption — 168

PART III: THE PRODUCTION OF DIFFERENCE

6 Ethnicity in Drag: Mass Media, Tourism, and the Politics of Representation — 197
7 Symbolic Citizenship in a Civilized Nation — 230
   Epilogue — 248

APPENDIX

Propaganda Folk Songs and Protest Poetry — 257

REFERENCE MATTER

Notes 269
Works Cited 301
Character List 325
Index 333

Table, Maps, and Figures

Table

1	Women's average age at first marriage and length of postmarital separation	112

Maps

1	Eastern Fujian and Taiwan	2
2	Hui'an county and Chongwu township	20
3	Shanlin village	22

Figures

1	New housing in Shanlin	23
2	Village housing plots	24
3	Female construction worker	34
4	Young woman repairing fishing nets	57
5	Transporting stones for house building	58
6	Stone polisher at work	60
7	Middle-aged woman posing in the gin'a headpiece	76
8	An elderly woman wearing the hairstyle and hair ornaments similar to those adopted after the gin'a was banned	87
9	Woman in her thirties wearing the hoegin and lueh'a	88
10	Hulin worship case	149
11	Funeral procession	158

12　Bride escorted by her dui pnua during her wedding
　　procession　　　　　　　　　　　　　　　　　　　　　　160
13　Wearing the young traditional hoegin and blue, cropped
　　top　　　　　　　　　　　　　　　　　　　　　　　　　174
14　Young traditional dresser with new style shirt　　　　　176
15　Young women in new style attire　　　　　　　　　　　177
16　*Minsu huakan* cover　　　　　　　　　　　　　　　　203
17　Black-and-white photo of "real" Hui'an women　　　　204
18　Black-and-white photo of "real" Hui'an women　　　　205
19　Rebuilding a village ancestral home　　　　　　　　　　214
20　Statue of "the Hui'an woman" in the Chongwu
　　statue park　　　　　　　　　　　　　　　　　　　　　225
21　Villa built to overlook the village harbor　　　　　　　252

Note on Romanization and Transcription

Throughout the book I have chosen to retain the distinction between the primary language of my fieldwork, Minnan dialect (also known as Hokkien), spoken in southeastern Fujian province and Taiwan, and China's national language, Mandarin. Most transcriptions are in the language in which the speech was conveyed to me. Exceptions include official terms or statements and excerpts from written texts; these I generally transcribe in Mandarin. Mandarin terms are romanized according to the *pinyin* system and are denoted by italics. Minnan terms are romanized according to the system developed by the Chinese Dialect Research Office at Xiamen University's Chinese Language and Literature Research Institute (see the *Putonghua Minnan fangyan cidian* [1982]). All Minnan expressions are displayed in this Franklin Gothic font to distinguish them from Mandarin terms. With the exception of well-known public officials, I have used Minnan pseudonyms for all personal names. All place-names, both real and fictitious, are in Mandarin for greater accessibility.

Hui'an residents speak a version of the Quanzhou subdialect, often described locally as a "salt-water accent" (giam zui kniu). Their speech displays several lexical and phonological variations on standard Minnan (which in the People's Republic of China is based on the language of the Xiamen area). In my transcriptions I have generally standardized these variations so as to make them more accessible to Minnan speakers. I have chosen not to include Chinese characters for folk-song transcriptions because several of the characters used to represent spoken Minnan are not standardized (either within

Taiwan and Fujian or between them) and not all of them are familiar to those who read Mandarin. In the Character List I include the characters for Mandarin equivalents in parentheses when necessary. This decision may leave speakers of Minnan and Mandarin equally frustrated, but I hope my translations and the guidelines I provide below will prove helpful to both groups.

Because most English-language scholarship that includes Minnan text has employed a Taiwanese romanization system, a few explanatory points are in order.

> The doubled consonant gg indicates a prenasalized voiced velar stop (as in ggeh for moon). *Bb* indicates a prenasalized voiced labial stop (as in bbing for bright and bbi for beautiful).
>
> Nasalized pronunciations are indicated by an *n* placed directly before the vowel, as in gnia (to be afraid, to fear) and bbnia (name).
>
> A final *p*, *t*, *k*, or *h* indicates a short rising or falling tone, as in bat (to recognize, to know) and sok (speed).
>
> Linguists designate eight tones in Minnan dialect. I have chosen not to indicate tones in the text.

INTIMATE ✾ POLITICS

Marriage, the Market, and State Power
in Southeastern China

INTRODUCTION ✼ Intimate Politics

In the summer of 1994, I visited a family I had met the previous year who lived in an eastern Hui'an village I call Shanlin. The oldest daughter in the household, Bbingden, was twenty-six at the time and had been married to her fisherman husband for five years. One evening during my visit, Bbingden's mother-in-law suddenly entered the family courtyard, her sandals churning up dust as the sound of rubber on tile announced her arrival. She had come to ask Bbingden to spend the night with her son. Bbingden's sister turned to me as the older woman walked past and commented, "She'll refuse to go," adding that Bbingden would use me as an excuse to explain why she could not traverse the few village paths that led to her husband's home. Sure enough, Bbingden soon appeared out of the lengthening shadows, her headscarf and headpiece tidily in place and her cropped top neatly buttoned down the side. She grabbed my arm and pulled me through the back door and into the street, walking briskly to escape her mother-in-law.

Bbingden's behavior that evening was not out of the ordinary, nor was it a performance put on for my benefit. Bbingden's female kin and peers commented frequently on the fact that in five years of marriage Bbingden had visited her husband only a few times. As was typical among married women in this community, Bbingden would not live with her husband until she bore a child. In order to avoid becoming pregnant she did her best to refuse her mother-in-law's visitation requests, acquiescing only at the one time of year when all married women were required to spend the night in their conjugal homes, the

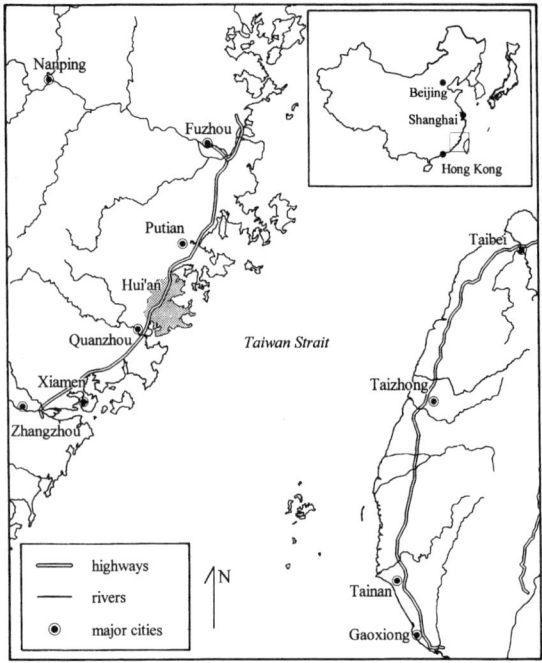

MAP 1: Eastern Fujian and Taiwan

Chinese New Year. Such reluctance was expected of new (and even not so new) wives; it was a crucial element of the extended natal residence marriage (*chang zhu niangjia*) customs for which this coastal region of southeastern China was known (see Map 1).¹ These customs initially interested me because they differed so dramatically from the standard form of rural Han Chinese marriage with which I was familiar, where women married into their husbands' families as adults and took up immediate residence in their conjugal homes and villages.

Intimate Politics explores the very practices that have constituted eastern Hui'an residents, women in particular, as an uncomfortable anomaly among China's majority population, rural Han. Together with unusual female dress styles, atypical divisions of labor between men and women, and powerful same-sex networks, extended natal residence marriages have long distinguished the villages in the eastern part of Hui'an county (also known as Huidong) from other rural Han communities. Yet this book is not simply a study of how wives such as Bbingden have refused to live with their husbands, why women have generally performed all of the heavy manual labor in these communities, or how female sartorial styles have differed so dramatically from typical Han peasant garb. I also ask what such practices have come to mean in a post-1949 socialist order that has incorporated forms of marriage, labor, and dress into a developmental scale extending from the primitive to the civilized. The ranking of peoples along this scale and the reformist interventions such ranking demanded were part of a wholesale effort to remake Chinese society by replacing its "feudal" elements with liberated socialist ideals and practices. As various state actors became involved in the intimate aspects of Huidong women's lives (from where they slept and ate to what they wore, where they contributed labor, or with whom they formed emotionally compelling bonds), their official models of progress and civility were challenged by the diversity of local practices and the active commitments of local residents. These politicized entanglements have generated what I call "intimate politics," a form of embodied struggle in which socialist civilizing agendas have been formulated, contested, and, in some cases, transformed through the bodies and practices of local women.

As I trace the contours of these intimate politics in eastern Hui'an, I move from the state-sponsored social and economic reforms of the Maoist decades immediately following China's socialist revolution in 1949 to the market-based "reform and opening" (*gaige kaifang*) that has characterized the post-Mao era from the late 1970s into the new millennium. The experiences of eastern Hui'an residents in this latter period of what I term "late socialism" attest to the continued influence of Maoist reform campaigns and the systems of meaning they introduced while, at the same time, they make all too apparent the contradictions such legacies now engender. Market reforms have expanded economic opportunities in the region and have given residents access to urban and Taiwanese cultural trends and consumer goods. Yet those same market forces have also created new expectations for productivity, consumption, and social "openness" that require villagers to search for an acceptable middle ground between high socialist ideals and new understandings of intimacy, progress, and civility.

These contemporary struggles take place in the context of a more diffuse form of state power that is less overtly top-down and less broadly intrusive than modes of state control found under the Maoist regime, at times working in concert with and at other times in conflict with market forces and consumer desires. This new configuration of state and market is manifested quite strikingly in changing government attitudes toward the symbols of local difference. The very practices that were attacked in Huidong villages under high socialism as emblems of "feudal backwardness" are often now, in a market economy, precisely those that officials, media producers, and emerging entrepreneurs aspire to sell to predominantly Han consumers as exotic local "appeal." This process of commodification has had significant consequences for Huidong women, as local cadres and businessmen have begun to promote the region through ethnic tourism and cultural festivals that highlight the distinctive attire and even the marriage practices of female residents. The marketing of regional culture has meant that young women's repeated efforts to overcome their designation as "feudal" and "backward" have often stumbled on a newly commodified ethnic terrain in which they can be marketed as desirable objects of an exoticizing Han gaze. How such women are to define a progressive identity for themselves given this fraught position at the crossroads of socialist civilizational hierarchies and market forces constitutes the larger question addressed by the chapters to follow.

Socialist Reforms and Alternative Marriage Practices

Ethnic identification in modern China has been very much a state affair and especially so after 1949 when the socialist regime molded China's diverse human landscape into 56 different nationalities.[2] Beginning in the 1950s, the Chinese Communist Party (CCP) widely promoted an image of a harmonious, multiethnic Chinese nation (*Zhonghua minzu*), masking the new nation's hierarchical principles and often violent exclusions in a rhetoric of equivalence. Yet the majority Han quickly claimed the top rung of this national hierarchy; as the 92 percent of the population "who metonymize[d] the nation" (Williams, 1989:439), they made Han synonymous with Chineseness itself. Although the residents of eastern Hui'an were officially classified by the socialist regime as Han, they failed to fully display the markers of civilization associated with this privileged stratum.

Women's distinctive marriage practices, adornment styles, and labor patterns established the gendered ground on which they were repeatedly likened to a vast array of "backward" minority groups. This anomalous position within an increasingly rigid ethnic-cum-civilizational hierarchy meant that Huidong villagers came to be seen as simultaneously Han and yet not-quite-Han.[3] Accordingly, the intimate politics that defined the first two decades of the Maoist era were further motivated by the party-state's desire to reaffirm the Han status of Huidong residents and to shore up the evolutionary principles on which this civilizational hierarchy rested.

The mass reform campaigns carried out in eastern Hui'an in the 1950s and 1960s sidestepped the question of ethnic differences between Huidong residents and other Han Chinese by glossing such differences in a civilizational discourse of developmental stages. State reformers consistently defined local women as evolutionary oddities mired in a backward, oppressive state identified by the signifier "feudal." In so doing, they drew inspiration not only from the Stalinist criteria for ethnic identification used by state ethnographers across China,[4] but more importantly from a model of marital evolution introduced by the nineteenth-century American anthropologist Lewis Henry Morgan. Morgan (1964) assigned forms of marriage to levels of technological advancement, creating an evolutionary scale that correlated marriage and family organization with material life. His approach coincided nicely with the materialist theories then being developed by Karl Marx and Friedrich Engels, and Engels (1972) incorporated Morgan's theory of marital evolution into his attack on private property and its subjugation of women within a patriarchal family based on female monogamy. Morgan's model in its Marxist form subsequently inspired the CCP to emphasize marriage as a key feature defining a particular group's evolutionary status (see McKhann, 1995:43–44; Tong, 1989).

As outside work teams (*gongzuo dui*) composed of cadres from across the county and even the province entered Huidong communities in the early 1950s implementing new land and family reforms, their members quickly focused on local marriage practices as the linchpin in a cultural complex that distinguished Huidong from surrounding Han areas. These practices were attacked by reformers, who viewed them as part of an array of feudal customs that had to be eliminated in order to establish a new socialist society. State campaigns identified women as the bearers of cultural difference and civilizational inadequacy in the region and hence reforms targeted women almost exclusively: cadres urged wives to live with their husbands immediately after marriage and strove to eradicate related customs of underage and arranged marriage that they argued encouraged women to delay conjugal residence. Reformers also worked to simplify female dress and headpiece styles (seen as unnecessarily extravagant and as obstacles to productivity and conjugal intimacy) and struggled to disband the all-female networks that were perceived as a cause of high suicide rates among young women. Ultimately, however, although these reforms produced lasting changes in some aspects of women's physical appearance, they achieved less immediate results in suicide reduction and only temporary "gains" in marital reform. As Bbingden's experience attests, young Huidong wives continued to live apart from their husbands well into the 1990s.

Despite the limited impact of state reforms on many features of local practice, these campaigns were successful in introducing an official discourse that encouraged many of the men and women I knew to depict themselves and their behavior in strikingly negative terms. As recently as the 1990s, they applied the derogatory signifier "feudal" to everything from a young wife who refused to visit her husband to a style of headpiece so heavy and elaborate that it hindered a woman's ability to work in the fields or prevented her from lying down in bed with her husband (and therefore engaging in sexual relations with him). In other words, the discursive force of socialist reforms created a powerful system of meaning through which local residents came to understand and evaluate their own practices. Even with the end to many intrusive state interventions in the current market-reform era (1979 to the present), this system of meaning has continued to influence how Huidong villagers perceive and experience these contested domains of social life, even as their practices have begun to change.

When I first visited the region in 1993 and 1994, and when I began eighteen months of research in the Huidong village of Shanlin in 1995, I was unaware of this history of state intervention. What struck me initially were the similarities between many of these local practices and women's postmarital natal residence patterns and sisterhood bonds found elsewhere in Han China. I had first learned of eastern Hui'an through reading accounts of "delayed transfer marriage" (*bu luo fujia*) in the Pearl River Delta region of southern China. Women from certain parts of the delta maintained natal residence after marriage and generally sought to avoid sexual relations during conjugal visits in order to prevent pregnancy and maintain ideals of chastity and purity (Sankar, 1978; Siu, 1990; Stockard, 1989; Topley, 1975). These delta women also developed sisterhoods through which they shared religious teachings focused on preserving bodily purity and encouraged one another to resist their husbands' sexual advances. Women's access to personal income through silk work further inspired forms of resistance to delayed transfer marriage itself, such as providing funds for a husband to purchase a concubine or refusing to marry altogether, a late-nineteenth- and early-twentieth-century practice of sworn spinsterhood that coincided with the growth of industrial silk filatures in the region.[5]

Although the literature on the delta region certainly demonstrates that the complex of practices I found in eastern Hui'an was not unique, particularly in areas with similarly ambiguous and fluid ethnic identities (Siu, 1990), nonetheless the fact that these practices still existed in Huidong through the late twentieth century is rather striking. Delayed transfer marriage and marriage resistance gradually died out in southern Guangdong, succumbing to the economic ravages induced by the worldwide silk market crash of the 1930s, the upheavals produced by the Japanese invasion, and the resulting migration of many spinsters to Hong Kong and Singapore.[6] Similarly powerful sisterhood relationships and delayed conjugal residence in an area of southern Hunan where women communicated via their own script had also largely disappeared by the second half of the century (Silber, 1994). I am not denying that married women throughout Han China have continued to find ways to maintain ties with their natal families (Judd, 1989), but in no region other than eastern Hui'an have I been able to document for the contemporary period a similarly widespread and institutionalized practice of postmarital natal residence and all-female networks.[7]

As a result of these comparisons, I initially perceived Huidong marriage customs as remarkably tenacious and unchanging. Here,

I thought, I had discovered an example of women's persistent resistance to patriarchal and patrilineal family arrangements. Yet I quickly came to realize that this image of a female utopia and the sense of stasis on which it rested were deceptive. Not only had extended natal residence marriage and its related customs come under attack from state actors as early as the 1940s and throughout the Maoist decades, but in the 1990s such practices were beginning to change in even more dramatic and contested ways. What was producing these changes? Why were they emerging in the relatively relaxed atmosphere of the post-Mao era with its opening to the outside world and apparently diminished state control, instead of during the period of high socialism when officials had seemed so committed to altering the social and cultural landscape of the region?

As I trace these transformations both in the lives of the people I worked with and in the manner in which their practices were represented by and to others, I explore several related, but still somewhat poorly understood, features of rural life in socialist and late-socialist China. In the process, I hope that readers will come to appreciate what is both familiar and distinctive about life in eastern Hui'an as compared to other parts of China or the larger socialist world. To begin, what has been the role of state campaigns and different state actors in defining and transforming the everyday lives and intimate practices of rural residents? How do the experiences of Huidong villagers—men and women, old and young—force us to rethink previous assumptions about the object of socialist governance and the relationship between intimate life and socialist liberation (*jiefang*)? Two, how have the interventions of socialist reformers and market forces shaped local identities in the Maoist and post-Mao periods? In particular, how has the figure of "the Hui'an woman" constructed over time by both state officials and media producers come to define outsiders' perceptions of Huidong women? How do young Huidong women today challenge that figure as they seek to create new definitions of self free from the feudal attributes of the past? Finally, what do these struggles tell us about changing constructions of difference in socialist and late-socialist China and the power such constructions have to inspire prejudices as well as opportunities? How do discursive productions of difference—formulated in contexts ranging from government reports and propaganda folk songs to newspaper articles and popular television programs—perpetuate the ambiguous ethnic and civilizational status of Huidong residents, and how does such ambiguity itself engender powerful material consequences by, for instance, guiding state-determined labor allocations or the path of tourism development?

In responding to these questions briefly below and more fully in subsequent chapters, I foreground the complex struggles over sameness and difference that have shaped intimate politics in eastern Hui'an. State reform campaigns, media portrayals, and the self-depictions of Huidong villagers were not based exclusively on ethnic hierarchies or status distinctions between peasants and urbanites. Instead, they were characterized by complex interweavings of ethnic, gender, cultural, and native-place differences that have influenced how outsiders have aspired to represent and transform this coastal region, as well as how locals have attempted to counter such representations and construct their own identities. The legacies of these contests persist in Shanlin even today, in the reflections of villagers themselves and in new state campaigns that continue the project of disciplining and civilizing unruly, rural, and most often female subjects.

The Intimacy of State Power

The power of the socialist regime to transform intimate practices in eastern Hui'an has been far from absolute. Instead of a singular state, unified in intent and method, what we find in the case of Huidong is a state apparatus riddled with internal contradictions and diffuse interests, peopled by multiple actors dedicated to what have often been conflicting goals. These actors have included groups as diverse as outside work teams, local cadres (male and female), village militiamen and -women, local and urban intellectuals, and new socialist institutions such as mass campaigns, literacy schools, and, more recently, family planning teams. Thus rather than viewing the state as a unified entity or agent that exists above society, dictating its every move, I have found it helpful to consider the state as a set of normalizing practices oriented toward the production of particular kinds of political subjects (Abrams, 1988; Connell, 1990; Li, 1999; Mitchell, 1991).[8] This approach, influenced both by a Gramscian focus on class power and hegemony and by the Foucaultian concept of governmentality, traces the emergence of a distinctly modern form of state power that works through creating and normalizing citizen-subjects who ultimately come to govern themselves (Hansen and Stepputat, 2001:2–5)—citizen-subjects who are, as Foucault put it, "subject to someone else by control and dependence, and tied to [their] own identity by a conscience or self-knowledge" (1983:212, 1991). As Corrigan and Sayer astutely argue in their study of English state-formation: "The enormous power of 'the State' is not only external and objective; it is in equal part internal and subjective, it works through us. It works above all through the myriad ways it collectively and individually (mis)represents us and variously 'encourages,' cajoles, and in the final analysis forces us to (mis)represent ourselves" (1985:180).

The "internal and subjective" dimensions of state power are critical to understanding the connections between Huidong women's intimate relations and practices on the one hand and socialist visions of liberation and civilization on the other. We often regard intimacy as an acknowledgment of humanity through the mutual recognition it generates between two individuals engaged in intense personal relations (Benjamin, 1988; see also Giddens, 1992).[9] Yet intimate relations also require a broader context of recognition—one defined by such social and political entities as the community, the courts, or the nation-state. At times, even ostensibly liberal, multicultural societies refuse to recognize the intimate choices of certain disempowered groups (such as women and minorities) and in so doing deny them the very humanity that intimacy acknowledges (Berlant, 1997, 1998; Grayson, 1998; Povinelli, 2002b; Wiegman, 2002). Seen from this perspective, intimacy produces affective ties that constitute the grounds for incorporating (or refusing to incorporate) these individuals and groups into a larger chain of national inclusion: as Lauren Berlant suggestively notes, intimacy "poses a question of scale that links the instability of individual lives to the trajectories of the collective" (1998:283).

Reformers' efforts to transform Huidong women's intimate practices as part of producing them as new kinds of socialist subjects confirm the powerful role that intimacy plays in enfolding individuals and individual bodies (sexed, raced, unusually adorned, intensely laboring) into a national imaginary. The sense of intimacy I am invoking here is broader than that used in studies of Western multicultural societies, necessarily so given the Confucian and socialist underpinnings of the twentieth-century Chinese countryside that both heightened attention to gendered roles, activities, and spaces and aspired to erase those very differences through an overarching concern with labor and productivity (Yang, 1999). On the one hand, reformers sought to redefine not only families, households, and the affective ties that linked members of domestic units (Y. Yan, 2003) but also embodied symbols of civilizational status such as sartorial styles and the kinds of labor performed by men and women. On the other hand, some intimate relationships were heralded as critical to the process of socialist construction, whereas others were denied recognition and denounced as counterproductive, even dangerous.[10] For instance, reformers actively undermined close same-sex bonds among Huidong women (known colloquially as dui pnua ties),[11] yet simultaneously worked feverishly to foster "feelings" (*ganqing*) in local marriages. Whereas female homosociality was judged feudal and backward, conjugal intimacy was deemed critical to cultivating the liberated subjects who would ultimately constitute the more encompassing intimate community of the socialist nation. Fostering these new forms of intimacy was not an end in itself, but a step (albeit an important one) in making Huidong women into proper subjects for an emerging socialist nation.

Subjectivity and the Figure of "the Hui'an Woman"

The protracted process of creating liberated socialist subjects in eastern Hui'an pivoted on the production of a particular image of local society defined by certain constitutive practices and figures. These intimate practices—of marriage, labor, dress, and same-sex ties—were clearly gendered in that they were inscribed on or enacted through the bodies of local women. As a result, the figures produced by the reformist discourses and civilizing interventions of state actors were also gendered female, the most prominent example being the figure of "the Hui'an woman" (*Hui'an nü*). This figure emerged discursively from the work team reports, county and provincial Women's Federation documents, and propaganda folk songs of the high socialist era. It should not be confused with the actual women who lived through this period and its reformist campaigns but instead exemplified one possible subject position among others.[12] Women could (and often did) contest that position, although to varying degrees.

"The Hui'an woman" represented a temporary or potential state, what Stuart Hall has called "the category, the position where the subject—the I of ideological statements—is constituted" (1985:102). As such, this figure was not a fixed or singular identity that fully defined how Huidong women perceived themselves, but it did bear the imprint and therefore the power of official discourses on women's liberation and socialism's civilizing impact (Moore, 1994:4; Trinh, 1997).[13] "The Hui'an woman" came to encapsulate virtually all that was attacked as feudal, backward, and oppressive in Huidong communities, from women's residence patterns and labor obligations to styles of dress and same-sex relationships. As a striking example of the more general category of feudal subject, "the Hui'an woman" was set in contrast to the idealized subject of the new socialist era, the liberated socialist citizen. Dressed all in black, with a heavy, awkward headpiece constraining her movements and obscuring her face, "the Hui'an woman" both displayed and enacted the oppressive features of the old order—in her appearance, her "abnormal" conjugal relationships, and the ease with which she took her own life. If we think of subjectivity as a process of self-construction over time, we can begin to understand how different generations of Huidong women at different points in their lives might have contested how "the Hui'an woman" represented them and their practices, forging a sense of themselves as liberated socialist women through a dialogue with that figure.

"The Hui'an woman" constituted a site for the articulation of a variety of characteristics condemned under the new socialist order. These characteristics became keywords in the regime's civilizing project; invested with perlocutionary force, terms such as "feudal" (honggian), "closed" (bbo kaihong or bbue tong), "nonprogressive" (bbo kaihuat), and "unscientific" (bbo kohak) spread from official circles to the realm of common speech. Their widespread use in contexts ranging from everyday social interactions to official state pronouncements and propagandist folk songs created multiple arenas in which individual men and women contended with the categories set up by the post-1949 regime as they struggled to establish new identities in an emerging socialist order.

When state reformers identified young women in Huidong villages with "the Hui'an woman," they subsequently provided set explanations for why women refused to live with their husbands or why they committed suicide in groups. As the products of feudal restraints, close-mindedness, oppressive family arrangements, or overly demanding same-sex bonds, these practices came to be understood predominantly through the semiotic frameworks created by the socialist regime. Even when the actual conditions of women's and men's lives contradicted such explanations, work team members, local cadres, and higher-level government officials continued to frame the problem of Hui'an society as one of "feudal oppression" (ignoring, for instance, the extent to which socialist policies might have encouraged wives' continued postmarital natal residence or strengthened all-female networks, both outcomes I discuss in subsequent chapters). Over time, these terms became the means through which not only state actors but also villagers themselves began to explain and represent their practices, even as women frequently resisted reformers' efforts to alter those very patterns of behavior.

By the time I conducted research in Shanlin in the mid-1990s, one would have expected this language of high socialism to have gone the way of communes, Mao suits, and such anachronistic terms of address as "comrade." Yet throughout the years I spent in Shanlin, I was struck by the frequency with which villagers used these terms in everyday conversations to describe their ways of life. When talking about their worship of popular deities, such as Mazu or Guanyin for instance, women and men openly defined such practices as "superstition" (bbesen), acknowledging the term's derogatory connotations while simultaneously supporting and engaging in worship on a regular basis. When commenting on women's past refusal to live with their husbands, men young and old often attributed such behavior to the fact that women were "close-minded," "feudal," or "not progressive." As I discuss in Chapter 7, a young woman in the 1990s who expressed reluctance to visit her husband or socialize with a fiancé might find herself accused by peers of "being feudal," like women who continued to wear the hoegin, the headscarf and headpiece that now symbolized local attire. In many cases, this manner of depicting local practices and figures was enacted by individuals born long after the reformist decades of the Maoist era. How was it, then, that Shanlin residents continued to represent themselves through signifiers introduced by the early socialist regime at the same time that many of the people I knew openly rejected those very formulations of their identity? What were the consequences of these contradictions for the many young women who were striving to establish a more progressive identity for themselves?

Put simply, subjectivity was not merely a process; it was also a struggle, one conducted on highly contentious ground. If in the past women had predominantly been defined by the backward signifier "feudal," then young women in the 1990s had to struggle against that subject position as they worked to create an image of themselves as appropriately open (kaihong) and progressive (huat dian) participants in a new, market-reform era. The contested nature of this process became apparent to me shortly before the Chinese New Year in 1996, when the mother of the family with which I lived sent me to "call for the bride" (gio sin Iniu)—to summon her second son's wife, A Hong, for a conjugal visit—because her son had just returned from several months at sea on a merchant marine vessel. Already married for three years at this point, 23-year-old A Hong continued to reside in her natal home, having yet to bear a child. Although she and her husband had clearly cultivated an independent relationship (as evidenced by the fact that he had gone to her house immediately upon returning to the village), her mother-in-law nevertheless chose to err on the side of caution by sending me to urge her to come spend the night. I arrived at A Hong's natal home that blustery, winter evening to find her sitting in her bedroom with a female companion, chatting and knitting under a dim light. The moment I entered the room the other woman asked immediately whether I had come "to call for the bride," and when I replied innocently that I had, she burst out laughing. A Hong then patiently explained to me that it was not necessary to call for her. Unlike older generations of women, she did not have to wait to be called but would visit her husband on her own initiative. In carving out a newly defined progressive status for herself, A Hong explicitly contrasted her actions with what she characterized as the feudal orientation of her elders: "Now if we want to go [visit our husbands], we just go. Before it was very feudal, but it's not anymore."

Although "the feudal" was purportedly a feature of a past social order (as A Hong's companion's outburst made so clear), A Hong's use of the term showed how it continued to shape the boundaries of possible and acceptable behavior in the present, particularly for young women. In other words, this language also functioned metapragmatically: it both pointed to a prior moment in which Shanlin women had been defined as feudal, backward subjects *and* constituted a present context in which both that subject position and all that it said about local practices were being challenged (see Silverstein, 1976, 1985). The continued use of socialist language in the 1990s thus reflected the extent to which the civilizing impulses of state socialism still influenced, albeit not without contestation, how different Shanlin residents experienced their own practices and actively worked to change them.

Although the transformations of the post-Mao era have greatly expanded the horizons of young women's activities and opportunities, the persistent power of socialist figures (such as "the Hui'an woman") and signifiers (such as "feudal") structures that expansion in ways that often produce new risks and dilemmas. This picture runs counter to popular portrayals of late-socialist Chinese society in which China's recent opening to foreign investment and cultural trends, coupled with liberalization of the market and decreased central government control, are viewed as encouraging a liberating transition to both a more prosperous and a more open society. Without denying the new freedoms and improved standards of living enjoyed by Shanlin residents since the 1980s, I also heed the cautions issued by postsocialist scholars such as Katherine Verdery who warn that these periods of transformation have many possible outcomes, not all of them necessarily improvements over the socialist past (1996:15–16). Market forces often impose their own forms of discipline through patterns of production and consumption that create new social hierarchies and often unrealizable or highly contested social expectations.

This post-Mao period of "opening up," to borrow James Farrer's phrase, has engendered new dilemmas and inequalities in both urban and rural China, especially for women, the working classes, migrants, and ethnic minorities (Erwin, 2000; Farrer, 2002; Gillette, 2000; Makley, 2002; Mueggler, 2001; Schein, 2000; H. Yan, 2003; Zhang, 2000). Several of these recent studies emphasize heightened pressures on women of disparate backgrounds as they encounter an increasingly commodified and consumer-driven sexual environment, one defined by sexual openness and a competitive marriage market in which women are expected to improve their lives and insure their futures through marrying up the social hierarchy. Rarely in these accounts, however, do we find a similarly contentious and politicized history of intimate life that continues to influence young people's efforts to transform their intimate relations in the reform era.[14] Young Shanlin women such as A Hong have sought to redefine themselves and their abilities through precisely those domains of intimate practice singled out by early socialist reformers as the sources of women's oppression (marriage, dress, labor), but they have done so in ways that also subject them to new standards for consumption and mixed-sex socializing and that frequently contravene still-powerful expectations of female modesty, frugality, and diligence. The process of creating new visions of self thus becomes a struggle over many possible subject positions, some ghostly shadows of a past signifying system and others the product of ostensibly liberating forces but imbued with disciplinary power and social consequence nonetheless.

The Production and Power of Difference

As they strove to transform the representations of themselves and their practices long promoted by state reformers and local officials, young Shanlin women in the 1990s confronted a powerful interweaving of ethnic, gender, and place-based difference. These diverse constructions of difference have coalesced in the post-Mao period in such a way as to perpetuate the ambiguous position of Shanlin residents in a national order, once again linking anxieties about their intimate practices to debates over the civilizational standing of the national body. As discussed above, the figure of "the Hui'an woman" has constituted one site for establishing hierarchies of difference. I have found it helpful to regard this figure as an example of what Hall calls a "condensed social position," one in which different "systems of reference" articulate with one another at certain historical moments (1985:111, 1996:39–41). During the Maoist decades, this figure signified much that was feudal, backward, and oppressive in local society and therefore had to be eradicated in order to forge a new socialist order. The constructions of difference salient in that period defined "the Hui'an woman" according to distinctions between liberated and oppressive marriages, open and closed consciousness, and productive and unproductive labor. In the post-Mao era, by contrast, the figure of "the Hui'an woman" has condensed around the commodification and "feminization" of ethnicity (Schein, 2000), the skills and resources valued in a market economy, and new standards of civilization and culture promoted by state-sponsored "socialist spiritual civilization" campaigns. This more recent condensation has not simply replaced an earlier Maoist vision, however; instead, Shanlin women find themselves enmeshed in the conjuncture of these very different subject positions and the systems of meaning they bring with them.

These constructions of difference build on a series of binary oppositions: feudal/socialist, backward/civilized, rural/urban, wasteful/productive, and ethnic/Han. Far from being natural divisions already existing in the social world, binary oppositions such as these are the products of particular political, cultural, and socioeconomic orders that divide up social life and identities along opposing lines, even as those lines are frequently breached.[15] By fixing the parameters of difference, official binaries limit the range of identification possibilities available to various groups; they function as what Ralph Litzinger terms "forms of representational violence" (2000:137). In other words, more than simply restricting the horizon of possibility, binary differences also disadvantage certain groups in both symbolic and material ways.

By acknowledging that identities are constructed out of "the intersection of systems of difference" (Abu-Lughod, 1991:140), we move closer toward understanding such linkages between difference and power. At the same time, we must also take into account how certain groups (as well as segments within those groups) are actually made to see themselves as different in specifically unequal terms (Spivak, 1985).[16] Although repeated state reform campaigns defined

Huidong women as "other" in relation to the socialist nation, their experiences of otherness have not remained static over time and have produced different consequences across generations of village women. During the period of high socialism, socialist propaganda and state reformers characterized Huidong women as emblems of feudal backwardness, fixing them in a temporally and developmentally a priori state vis-à-vis the civilized socialist nation. In the post-Mao era, by contrast, media producers and tourism entrepreneurs have identified local women with exotic, ethnic difference, as still less advanced than the "civilized" Han but capable of inclusion in the late-socialist nation through the marketability of that exoticism. These late-twentieth-century celebrations of difference demand that local women assume a role with which they do not identify, one that aligns them with the devalued element in the Han/non-Han binary and constitutes them as objects to be gazed upon and voyeuristically consumed.[17]

Despite the pervasive inequalities that characterize these contexts, I do not want to suggest that hierarchies of difference have rendered Huidong residents completely powerless objects of subjectification or that they have produced a fixed, unchanging other within Huidong communities. Women cadres of various generations (and the men related to them through marriage or birth) often claimed that they were more open and advanced than their subordinates; village men overwhelmingly defined themselves as more progressive, urbane, and scientific than village women; and young women who had begun to dress in urban attire frequently depicted those who continued to wear local dress as feudal and backward in both their thinking and practice. In my interactions with Shanlin residents, I found them actively engaged in the production of diverse local identities, often in reference to what Louisa Schein has called a "mobile" other (2000:232), one who shifts as groups within the community displace the negative stereotypes of local women onto yet other segments of local society.[18] The displaced hierarchies I saw emerging within Huidong communities in many ways parallel the hierarchies of difference that shape struggles at the level of the nation-state, where the Han majority aspires to produce itself as the pinnacle of civilization through contrasts with its internal others, national minorities (Gladney, 1994b; Schein, 1997), or where intellectuals, urbanites, and officials seek to constitute a civilized Chinese nation in opposition to "peasant backwardness" (Cohen, 1993; Flower, 1997; Kipnis, 1997). These multiple struggles over how to define and evaluate difference culminate in recent campaigns to foster national subjects who are at once socialist and civilized. In Chapter 7 I examine one such effort to call into being this civilized socialist citizen, the mid-1990s' movement to "build socialist spiritual civilization" (*shehuizhuyi jingshen wenming jianshe*).

The place of Shanlin residents within this national order is far from stable. Despite claiming an official Han status, their distinctive social and cultural practices align them with marginalized, ethnic others—those seen as constituting the backward, uncivilized underside of an idealized Han nation. At the same time, their growing prosperity in the reform era also distinguishes them from rural residents of the interior who are the presumed locus of the "peasant backwardness" that has ostensibly prevented China from realizing its destiny as a modern nation-state. As I show in the chapters to follow, although the figure of "the Hui'an woman" condenses the multiple forms of difference produced by both Maoist and post-Mao civilizing projects, it does not fully determine the identities subscribed to by all Huidong women. Within this figure we find the gender, ethnic, and native-place divisions that undermine a unified vision of the Chinese nation.

Shanlin: A Village in Flux

As I sat in the Fujian provincial archives in the fall of 1996, poring over sometimes barely legible copies of the 1950s' work team reports that first lodged this image of "the Hui'an woman" in my head, I was struck by a common refrain with which many of the reports began. Emphasizing the geographic isolation of a poverty-stricken Huidong region, they repeatedly painted an image of a self-enclosed physical landscape that blocked the liberating winds of socialism. This landscape was depicted as mirroring, even reinforcing, the oppressive social world the report authors had been sent to eradicate. Reading such accounts more than forty years after they were written, I reflected on how dramatically the physical contours of Huidong had changed, as newly paved roads now linked many

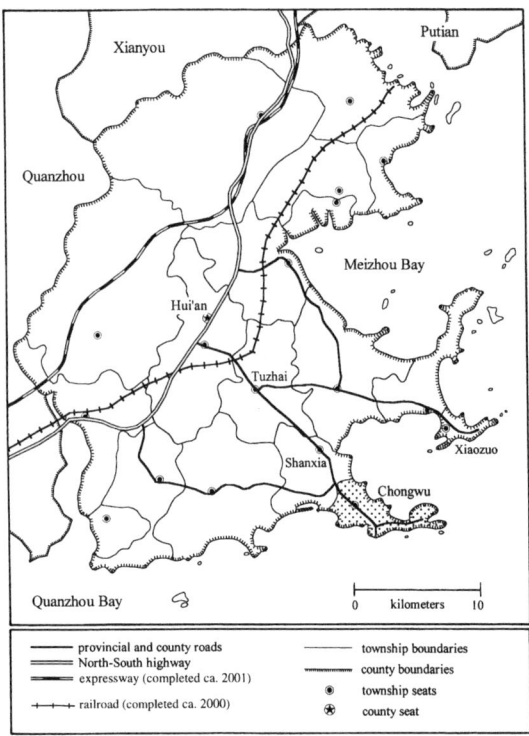

MAP 2: Hui'an County and Chongwu Township

villages to the main highway that traversed the region, funneling people and goods from the county seat and other provincial cities to this coastal area and back again.

As one travels eastward from Hui'an's county seat, the land branches into two peninsulas that subdivide as they extend into the Taiwan Strait like pincers on the crabs local fishermen catch in coastal waters (see Map 2). Prior to the socialist period, I was told, many of these outermost pincers had been only tentatively connected to the mainland by thin strips of land that were often submerged at high tide. Although post-1949 cadres had built up these isthmuses, the outlying areas remained for socialist reformers the most entrenched sites of feudal practice.

Shanlin is located on one such strip of land in the coastal Huidong township of Chongwu. Hui'an itself was the last county created in Fujian's Quanzhou prefecture, its establishment dating to the year 981 in the Song dynasty (Chen and Wang, 1992:25; Clark, 1991:54). Chongwu, the eponymous township seat, was established as a Ming dynasty military garrison only in 1387, its coastal location making it an ideal site for defense against bandits and pirates.[19] With the garrison came the first major influx of Han settlers into the eastern part of Hui'an county; these immigrants included military households, officials, and commoners. The legacy of this settlement history continues to be felt today, for contemporary residents of Chongwu town do not practice many of the customs found in the township's villages.

As one of the larger of seven major villages in Chongwu township,[20] Shanlin was renowned in the Mao era for its skilled fishermen and substantial fleet of fishing boats. Despite the comparative poverty of those years, village residents often spoke proudly of their past accomplishments and the considerable resources owned by the village collective. During the tense decades from the 1950s to the 1980s, however, the region's proximity to Taiwan also meant that little investment was made in infrastructure or industry along the coast. With the introduction of market reforms in the 1980s, local officials began to look beyond fishing and agriculture in an effort to develop the region's economic base. By the early 1990s, a burgeoning stone-carving industry in Chongwu employed many young women and men from the township's villages. Industrial jobs and the service industries that accompanied them largely enabled Shanlin youths to avoid the patterns of out-migration found in communities further inland. The village's multigenerational population thus made it a valuable site for studying diverse reactions to the new marriage, courtship, and socializing practices of the post-Mao era.

Changes in the local economy have gone hand-in-hand with transformations in the physical layout of Shanlin itself as the center of community life has shifted to recently built sectors. The older part of the village lies on the slope of one of two mountains that loom over the coastline, hence its designation as the "upper village" (see Map 3). Many of the houses in this upper sector date back several generations; although few of the original wood-frame houses remain, most have been rebuilt using locally quarried granite. Densely

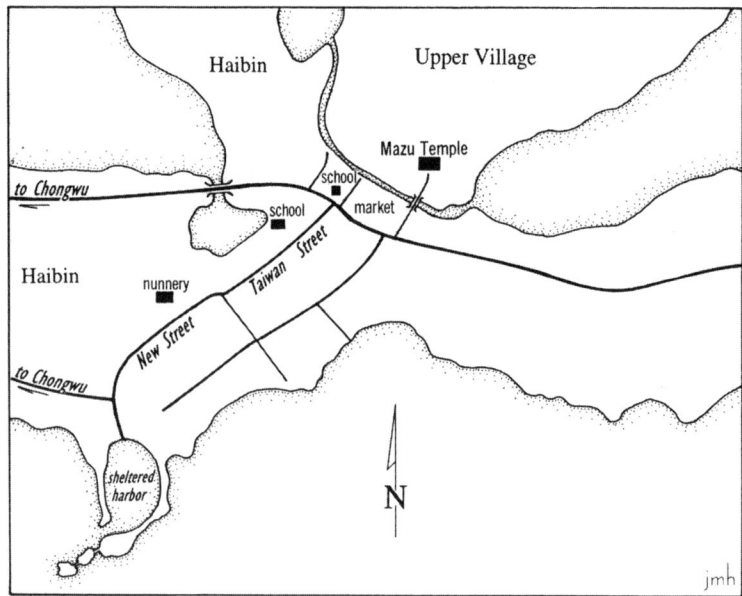

MAP 3: Shanlin Village

constructed on a one- or two-story model, these homes traditionally housed stem or even extended families. The landscape of the upper village, crisscrossed by narrow paths that open onto shared wells and courtyards, is dotted with ancestral homes (zoocu), the focal sites for lineage branch activities, funerals, and ancestor worship.[21] The Mazu temple is also located in this part of the village; it was rebuilt in the 1980s following its partial demolition and use as a nursery and at times public canteen from the Great Leap Forward (1958–1960) through the Cultural Revolution (1966–1976). With the exception of the two vegetarian nunneries that have relocated to newer neighborhoods, these sites constitute the principal centers for much of Shanlin's communal life.

By the late 1970s and early 1980s, population pressures forced village cadres to develop housing in the flat plain that lay between the two mountains, land that had previously been used for farming. This plain extended southwest from the market area that lay at the base of the upper village, finally meeting the ocean on the far side of the peninsula. A new road was built running from the village marketplace (where it was named Taiwan Street) down to the ocean (at the half-

FIG. 1: New housing in Shanlin (photograph by the author, 1996)

way point it became New Street). In the late 1980s, an enterprising assistant party secretary mobilized village women to build a sheltered harbor at the southernmost end of this road, an engineering feat that shifted the center of village fishing from a small harbor on the eastern coast to this newly developed sector of the village.[22] As stone-carving factories began to spring up to the west of the harbor in the 1990s, this area slowly emerged as a burgeoning economic center.

In the 1990s, the land on both sides of Taiwan and New Streets was divided into housing plots, and homes two, three, and even four or five stories high soon covered the landscape in all directions (see Fig. 1). In contrast to the household organization that had predominated in the upper village, these homes primarily housed nuclear or stem families. Having a separate housing plot significantly enhanced young men's marriageability in the reform era, and this trend contributed to the growth in nuclear family units in the village (see also Yan, 1997). Social pressures such as these also made housing-plot distribution a hotly contested issue as availability declined and prices soared. A 100-square-meter foundation plot in the mid-1990s cost 50,000 *yuan*, a considerable sum for most villagers whose yearly household income might average between 10,000 and 30,000 *yuan*. With better transportation access, plot planning, and the potential

FIG. 2: Village housing plots (photograph by the author, 1996)

for running water, these newer sectors of the village were becoming increasingly desirable among all but the elderly members of the community (see Fig. 2).[23]

The "reform and opening" policies of the post-Mao era have also had a significant impact on villagers' movements beyond both township and county borders. From the mid-1950s through the late 1970s, Shanlin, like other rural communities in Maoist China, was isolated from regional marketing and social networks that had linked it to Taiwan, Southeast Asia, and other areas along China's southeast coast (see also Chan et al., 1984; Friedman et al., 1991; Parish and Whyte, 1978; Shue, 1988). The past two decades, by contrast, have witnessed the renewal of these pre-1949 lines of trade and communication, reintegrating Shanlin residents into provincial networks as well as more far-flung business and kinship ties.

Lying only a few kilometers from Chongwu town and some twenty kilometers from Hui'an's county seat, Shanlin is thickly embedded in a coastal social and economic universe that extends from the booming special economic zone of Xiamen in the south of the province to the provincial capital, Fuzhou, in the north. With the village connected by two (only recently paved) roads to the township and from there to Hui'an city and Fujian's main north-south highway, residents of all ages travel fairly frequently beyond the village proper. Many go to Chongwu town to shop, attend junior middle school,[24] carry out business with the township government, work in stone-carving factories, or visit one of the many temples and nunneries. Small business owners in Shanlin travel regularly to Hui'an city and beyond to order and transport stock; sick villagers visit hospitals in Hui'an, Quanzhou, or as far away as Fuzhou; and others travel to nearby cities for pleasure, business, or to see kin who have moved away. My own research took me along similar routes as I followed older women on visits to relatives in neighboring villages and on pilgrimages to temples along the coast; accompanied young women on shopping expeditions to Hui'an, Quanzhou, and Chongwu; and visited stone-carving factories across the township with village workers.

Shanlin's coastal location has also facilitated villagers' integration into a transnational regional economy encompassing Taiwan, Japan, and Hong Kong. Local stone-carving factories now produce headstones and grave-site adornment primarily for export to Japan, local fishermen increasingly fish on Taiwanese-owned fishing boats, and the catch from both deep-sea and coastal fishing is often destined for markets in Hong Kong, Taiwan, and Japan. Many village families have renewed ties with close kin resident in Taiwan, and several have members who visit the island yearly and often work informally while they are there.[25] Satellite antennas give villagers access to Taiwanese television, providing much-desired Minnan-language television programming to complement the Taiwanese radio stations that have long been accessible from the Fujian coast. In addition, Minnan-language popular music and music videos flow freely across the Strait, offering Shanlin youths images of love, romance, and heartbreak to compare with their own marital experiences and desires (see Gold, 1993; and Chapter 3). These popular-culture channels reinforce the outward orientation encouraged by renewed economic ties and contribute to the creation of a coastal world in which villagers look as much toward Taiwan for their visions of the future as toward urban centers in China proper.

Outline of the Study

Like all ethnographies, mine is a partial account, conditioned in large part by my own status and interests as well as by fluctuations in Sino-U.S. relations over the course of my research. Particularly during the tense months in early 1996 leading up to Taiwan's presidential election, Shanlin's coastal location put me in a sensitive and often difficult position, as U.S. warships stood ready to intervene should the cross-Strait conflict escalate into overt military engagement.[26] Villagers' willingness to open their personal lives to me contrasted sharply with my limited access to formal statistics and official voices. My understanding of economic and political transformations in the region came largely through historical documents and informal interviews with retired officials and local entrepreneurs, material I supplemented with villagers' accounts of life in different eras, my own observations of economic developments and government campaigns, and my experiences visiting stone-carving factories and working in a village fish-processing factory for several months. If in this book I privilege the voices and experiences of women over those of men, it is in part because of my greater access to women during my research due to my own status as a young, unmarried woman. But this privileging is intentional as well; it represents my effort to allow Shanlin women to speak for themselves while also acknowledging my own role as organizer and presenter of their voices (Wolf, 1992). In this manner, I offer this book as a different view of, and in some cases a corrective to, previous depictions of Huidong women and their place within a socialist order premised on hierarchical visions of civilization, liberation, and progress.

The chapters that follow move between the socialist reforms of the Mao era and the many transformations taking place during the high tide of marketization in the 1990s. Some periods in this span of roughly 50 years are covered more thoroughly than others; for instance, despite my repeated questioning, villagers were generally reluctant to discuss the Cultural Revolution in great detail, but they were more than happy to go on at length about the 1950s and early 1960s. The diverse array of sources and methodologies required by this broad scope will become apparent to the reader as I draw on archival documents, life histories, folk songs, and the observations, interviews, and daily life experiences that constitute the foundations of ethnography. The following two chapters in Part I introduce the concepts and events that lie behind my notion of intimate politics by examining early socialist civilizing policies, reform campaigns, and gendered formulations of labor and value. In Part II, I explore the implications of those politics for personal struggles and intimate attachments in the post-Mao era, focusing on marriage and courtship, same-sex networks, and new work and leisure patterns. Part III turns to questions of representation and the production of difference through an analysis of post-Mao media images, tourism development, and the effects of contemporary socialist civilizing campaigns. Despite the shifts in time periods and sources among the three sections, I continue to weave an analysis of discourse and lived experience through all of the chapters.

The three parts of the book can also be read as different treatments of intimacy and state power. Part I shows how the development of socialist state power in China after 1949 hinged on redefining conjugal and same-sex intimacy and embodied practices of labor and dress as part of creating new socialist subjects. Part II turns to the new intimacies produced by the intersection of market reforms and state reproductive regulation. It outlines a more diffuse mode of state power that promotes forms of romantic love, opposite- and same-sex bonds, and consumption proper to the goals of economic development and population control and improvement. Part III shifts our focus to the level of the nation and asks how representations of intimate relationships and embodied practices incorporate villagers into the larger intimate public of the nation-state. Ethnic imagery and identity, new state civilizing campaigns, and different modes of labor and dress forge a new basis for enfolding individual subjects into the national body. Read together, the three sections examine the role of intimate practices in the formation of a socialist Chinese nation, moving between the specific features of one region and the anxieties and tensions found in communities across China's vast landscape.

PART ONE 〰 "The Hui'an Woman" as Feudal Subject

CHAPTER ONE 🖎 Industrious Women and the Changing Meanings of Labor

The industrious, frugal, virtuous Hui'an woman (*qinlao jianpu xianhui de Hui'an nü*)
—Inscription at the base of a statue of "the Hui'an woman" erected by the Chongwu township government in 1998

When I arrived in Shanlin in the fall of 1995 for my first extended period of fieldwork, I began to acclimate myself to the community by taking long walks through the village each day. Some days I turned left out of the courtyard of the family home where I lived and then left again onto the cobblestoned path that traversed the eastern edge of the market area. Holding my nose as I crossed over the murky canal at the base of the upper village, I selected one of the many dirt and stone paths that wove around the homes clustered on the gradually sloping mountainside. Life in the upper village was very much a public affair. Through open doorways I glimpsed mothers and grandmothers caring for young children; fishermen sitting in courtyards, picking through outstretched fishing nets to remove bits of seaweed and broken remnants of the day's catch; women washing clothes and dishes next to neighborhood wells; men leaning with bored expressions against the cool stone of their doorways, some unemployed, others in between stints on a Taiwanese fishing boat or merchant marine vessel; and young people enjoying a rare day off from a stone-carving factory because a shipment of uncut stone had been delayed. On the path I often passed housewives returning from the market with bright yellow baskets balanced on the ends of their bamboo shoulder poles.

If I made my way farther up the mountain, the terrain grew steeper and the number of people I encountered gradually diminished. I would eventually reach a more level area at the top of the mountain where elderly and middle-aged women grew peanuts and sweet potatoes in neat rows. Because the land was not terribly fertile, during the planting and growing season I might find myself trailing behind a row of women carrying large wooden buckets filled with nightsoil or water that they used to coax the leafy green plants into growing in inhospitable soil. Having insisted a few times on carrying well water for my host family, I knew how heavy those buckets were, and I marveled at the women's ability to manage them with grace along the steep, uneven mountain path.

Had I not seen these plots with my own eyes, I might have taken much longer to learn that some Shanlin women still worked the land. None of the women in the cadre household where I lived engaged in agriculture, although they had as recently as a decade earlier. By the mid-1990s, many families received supplies of sweet potatoes and peanuts from relatives who lived in villages with more arable land, whereas others simply purchased their staples in the market. The plots that did remain were cared for almost exclusively by older women; only occasionally did I catch a glimpse of a woman in her twenties or thirties working a plot on the mountain or tending the plants growing in an empty housing plot in the flats. This shift away from agriculture had freed young women to engage in other forms of labor that were emerging with market reforms, such as stone polishing in the many factories that now dotted the township. Certainly, as the statue inscription quoted above proclaimed, Hui'an women were still "industrious," but the form that industry took and the meanings attributed to it had begun to change dramatically.

If, rather than turning left out of my doorway, I instead walked straight, I would find myself on a new, unpaved road that cut through the maze of housing plots and half-built homes in the plain that stretched southward from the village market. This road paralleled Taiwan Street and offered views of the backs of the newer homes and shops that lined the eastern side of the thoroughfare. Here, in the midst of tightly packed earthen foundation beds marked off by low stone walls, I often came across crews of female construction workers engaged in what was known in village parlance as "little labor" (sio gang)—hauling by hand heavy blocks of granite and loads of sand and dirt or mixing concrete and mortar with long-handled hoes. Whereas the women on these crews did the heavy manual labor of carrying, lifting, and transporting, their male overseers directed the placement of stone slabs, laid floors or brick walls, and raised roofs.

As I walked along the road one sunny October day in 1995, I was hailed by a group of women in their thirties and forties, their brightly colored tops and headscarves flapping in the wind. They were carrying stone slabs from one work site to another and then, with carrying poles balanced carefully across their shoulders, slowly transporting the slabs up a rickety wooden plank to what would become the second story of a house. Resting from their labors, they peppered me with a familiar set of questions about what I was doing in Shanlin, where I came from, and who I was living with in the village. Noticing the camera bag slung across my chest, they asked me to take their picture. One member of the group insisted on posing alone. Standing amid the dust of the building site with her carrying pole balanced over her shoulder and one leg propped up on a stone slab, she stared proudly into the camera (Fig. 3).

Although the context is different, the woman's proud pose bears striking similarities to the statue of "the Hui'an woman" that I visited on a return trip to Shanlin in the summer of 1998.[1] This stone figure, a full twenty meters in height, towered above the community; as the very embodiment of female strength, diligence, and local sartorial appeal, it was adorned in local garb and held a bamboo hat in one hand and a gathered fishing net in the other. With a clearly muscled body, the figure literally embodied the values of labor and hard work that had defined villagers' lives during much of the socialist period and that were reiterated in the inscription at the statue's base. At first I was struck by the anachronistic quality of this monument to the heroines of socialist realism. When I compared the statue to my photograph of the construction worker who posed for me that fall day, however, I began to reconsider what labor meant to different generations of Shanlin residents and how women might have both embodied and contested these socialist ideals through their own labor practices. The ability to engage in productive labor,

FIG. 3: Female construction worker (photograph by the author, 1995)

to suffer physical deprivation and even bodily pain, has been a key feature of stock images of "the Hui'an woman" produced since the 1950s. As hardworking, diligent, and frugal, "the Hui'an woman" reflected socialist values that linked labor participation to socialism's promise of gender liberation. At the same time, however, this figure also underscored the ways that the region's unusual gender divisions of labor have constituted Huidong women as anomalies among their Han counterparts.[2] When seen in this light, the statue's celebration of women's laboring bodies also served to redefine unconventional labor practices so that they conformed more closely to images of the Han socialist citizen.

This chapter traces that history of labor and gender liberation in Shanlin with several goals in mind. It seeks to contribute to a growing feminist literature that probes more deeply into precisely how the socialist regime transformed women's labor experiences and the value of their labor. Moreover, it asks how the distinctive complex of intimate practices in eastern Hui'an affected the meanings attributed to women's work, given the unusual distributions of tasks between women and men. It also shows how women of different generations wove tales of labor and suffering into their own accounts of marriage and explains how labor practices supported the region's postmarital residence patterns. Finally, the chapter examines how market reforms have altered long-standing gender divisions of labor and created new forms of work and prosperity for both women and men in Shanlin.

In seeking to understand the transformations and upheavals experienced by different generations of Shanlin women, I have separated them into cohorts defined loosely by age and more precisely in terms of their labor and marital histories. In a broader sense, then, these cohorts have emerged from the particular political moments during which women came of age, and they reflect how those moments shaped their experiences of work, family, and self (Rofel, 1999:7, 21–22). I begin with labor because it was key to a host of other intimate transformations—changes in marriage customs, the composition and strength of same-sex dui pnua ties, modes of socializing and consumption, and, to a certain extent, how Huidong women have been represented by and to others. I do not mean to suggest, however, that labor was the sole causal factor producing these other changes; in fact, as the chapters in Part II show, changes in all of these domains have emerged from a complex interweaving of forces—at once economic, political, social, and cultural.

Men Fished, Women Farmed—Oh, How We Suffered!

Gender divisions of labor in Shanlin have historically followed a somewhat atypical pattern for rural Han China. A local expression frequently repeated in both popular accounts and scholarly works attributes greater shoulder strength to women and greater arm strength to men. This ethno-physiological claim justifies women's responsibility for agricultural, household, and manual labor and men's responsibility for what is seen as the more skilled, but also physically taxing, work of fishing (e.g., Zhou, 1992:87–88). Women's control over agriculture distinguished Huidong from most other areas of rural China in the early twentieth century. In his rural surveys conducted nationwide from 1929 to 1933, John Buck found that women's share of agricultural tasks ranged from virtually none in certain areas of China's north to roughly 30 percent in the double-cropping rice regions of the south (Davin, 1979:117–118; Jacka, 1997:23–24). In none of the villages surveyed by Buck, moreover, did women perform all of the agricultural labor.[3]

Like other communities in eastern Hui'an, Shanlin in the first half of the twentieth century was quite poor, with only minimal gradations in wealth within its population. Men engaged in the backbreaking work of rowing nonmechanized boats into the Taiwan Strait or as far north as Zhejiang province to engage in deep-sea fishing, using hand-thrown nets and fishing lines. Wealth during this period was calculated in terms of boats; families with the resources to purchase their own vessels hired other village men to fish on them for a meager wage, often in cooperation with the owners themselves. Those men disenchanted with the opportunities at home engaged in small-scale trade with Taiwan or sought their fortunes farther south, emigrating to Hong Kong and what are now Singapore and Malaysia. For village men at least, Shanlin's coastal location linked it to a regional fishing and trading economy that extended beyond the nation's borders.

Women, by contrast, remained on the land. If their families owned agricultural plots, women worked the sandy soil to grow sweet potatoes and peanuts, the region's primary crops. Those without their own plots might rent from kin or other villagers or cultivate lands on the periphery. In addition to the household work of cooking, cleaning, gathering kindling, and fetching water, women also provided much of the subsidiary labor related to fishing: pulling in nets from the shore, repairing fishing nets, and transporting and selling the day's catch. Prior to marriage and childbirth, a woman's labor was organized by her family of birth, and the value of a daughter's labor likely encouraged her family to support her postmarital natal residence. Once a married daughter bore a child and moved in with her husband, her labor transferred to her conjugal family. During the period between marriage and childbirth, women faced labor demands from both sets of kin, and conjugal visits were often structured around the busy planting and harvesting seasons.

In their recollections of the decades prior to 1949, older Shanlin residents emphasized the overarching poverty of the times and the bitterness of their lives and labor. Their accounts are punctuated by depictions of the destruction wrought by the Japanese when they came ashore briefly in the late 1930s, destroying crops and burning fishing boats; by memories of illnesses and siblings who died as children; and by references to the upheaval and chaos of the 1940s when bandits and warring factions wreaked havoc on the county. The experiences of Shanlin native Bbokli, an energetic woman in her late fifties at the time of my research, are representative of those of many in this cohort of women and men whose childhoods were defined by the early deaths of parents, adoption and alternative family arrangements, and the hardships associated with households containing only one adult male. Bbokli's life of hard work continued even when I knew her in the mid-1990s, a time when if her family had been better off she could have rested from her labors and enjoyed her grandchildren. Instead, many of our conversations took place while picking sweet potatoes in the plot she cultivated near her home in the upper village or while sitting in her stone courtyard untangling the fishing nets used by her husband and elder son. Unlike many Shanlin families in which the younger generation of men no longer went to sea, Bbokli's two adult sons continued to fish: the elder on a coastal boat he rented with six other men and the younger for a Taiwanese boat captain.

Bbokli was born to a family in the township seat, but her birth parents died when she was only a month old, possibly in one of the cholera epidemics that swept through the region. A mere 40 days after her birth she was adopted by a woman in Shanlin. According to Bbokli, this woman had adopted her on behalf of the woman's son and daughter-in-law because the latter was already 27 years old and had not yet borne a child or shifted to conjugal residence. This kind of adoption was a common tactic employed by mothers-in-law faced with a recalcitrant daughter-in-law, and the practice continued throughout the socialist period and into the post-Mao era until the population policy made such adoptions difficult, although not altogether impossible. Bbokli's presence would force the daughter-in-law to assume conjugal residence (in order to care for the baby), and, if the family was lucky, Bbokli would also "usher in a younger brother."

The situation in Bbokli's adopted family was a bit more complicated than it appeared at first glance, however. The woman who adopted Bbokli was not Bbokli's adopted father's birth mother. His mother, like Bbokli's, had died young, and he had been raised by his paternal aunt (his father's younger brother's wife). This aunt had arranged his marriage and thus stood in the position of mother-in-law to the woman who would become Bbokli's adopted mother. The aunt had just given birth to a baby boy when she adopted Bbokli, and she nursed Bbokli together with her own son. As soon as Bbokli was weaned she was cared for by the aunt's oldest daughter, a young woman who had married but not yet shifted residence. Only when Bbokli's adopted mother herself bore a son and needed help with child care did Bbokli begin living and eating with her adopted parents (and later with four more younger brothers and sisters). At that point, as she recounted to me, she was a mere four or five years old.

In the past when I was small, my father single-handedly supported eight of us [literally "fed eight mouths"]. One person supported eight others. . . . He didn't earn any money, no money. In the past my father rowed a small boat [that went out to meet the larger boats when they returned from fishing and for a fee transported the catch to shore]. I also went with him and suffered hardship, rowed with him. In those days we ate only two meals. . . . There wasn't enough to eat. I went with my mother early in the morning to carry nightsoil up the mountain [to fertilize the crops]. I went with her into the mountains to gather grass and kindling and wouldn't return until dark. There wasn't enough to eat in those days, not enough to eat.

Bbokli went on to describe how as a young girl she also hired herself out to work for the owners of local net boats, pulling in nets laden with fish from the shore for only a modest wage. Defining her childhood through the socialist narrative genre known as "speaking bitterness" (*suku*), Bbokli named her oppression using tropes of suffering inculcated in her young adulthood, reiterating how bitter (gankoo) those years were, plagued by hunger and dire poverty. Socialist cadres had urged Chinese to speak bitterness as a means of acquiring awareness as socialist subjects. Through articulating their experiences of suffering, Shanlin residents of Bbokli's generation were to recognize themselves not as unfortunate individuals but as victims of class antagonism and exploitation. For women such as Bbokli, however, class deprivation was inseparable from the suffering they had experienced as women. By speaking bitterness, therefore, they simultaneously constituted themselves as gendered subjects whose understanding of embodied capacities and intimate life choices frequently diverged from the class narratives articulated by official actors (Anagnost, 1997:29-35; Rofel, 1999:137-148).

Bbokli defined the kind of work she did as a child as zue gueh (*zuo huo*), a term that referred specifically to manual labor—physically exhausting, important for family survival, and yet unable to generate much-needed income. Although Bbokli did engage in some wage labor, poorly remunerated though it was, she minimized her contributions to her family's livelihood by employing a term implicitly opposed to the kind of work performed by her father. In depictions of their youth, both men and women of Bbokli's generation emphasized their father's role as the sole supporter of the family. Fathers had to support often large numbers of dependents (literally "feed" so many "mouths"), a burden they were seen to bear on their own as the primary cash-generators for the household.

Because Huidong was not a rice-growing region, income from fishing was necessary if families were to purchase rice in the markets. Bbokli's assessment of women's work as manual drudgery does not deny the fact that she and her mother labored intensely in the pre-1949 era, but it does invoke an implicit contrast with men's work, seen not only as demanding but also as potentially income generating. Influenced by a socialist ideology that defined this period by its harsh suffering and marked inequality, Bbokli portrayed her childhood experience of work as an embodiment of bitterness and emphasized her inability to improve the lives of her family members. In this manner, she reaffirmed women's labor participation at the same time that she minimized its productive potential. Only men, it seems, could actually "feed" the family, and many men struggled to achieve even this basic goal.

Liberating Women by Liberating Their Labor

As an adult, Bbokli went on to replace her mother-in-law as a small-team leader and to assume a number of other low-level cadre positions in Shanlin. One would think that her official capacities would have encouraged her to draw a clear line between the suffering of her childhood and the improvements in village life brought by the 1949 Communist victory known as Liberation. Yet as we harvested sweet potatoes one November day in 1996, I asked Bbokli what had happened at Liberation and was rather surprised by her response: "Liberation was Liberation, there was nothing to eat. When we were children there was nothing to eat, [life] was bitter." Bbokli would have been roughly nine years old when the Communists came to power, certainly old enough to recognize any improvements in her family's livelihood. Was she simply confusing the time before and after 1949, subsuming both periods into her difficult childhood? Or had Liberation in fact not ushered in memorable progress in the quality of life in Shanlin, particularly for women?

When the Communists took over Shanlin in 1949, they brought with them an approach to women's liberation honed through years of struggle in the rural base areas of Jiangxi and Yan'an. Adopting an orthodox Marxist approach enshrined in Engels's *The Origin of the Family, Private Property, and the State* (1972), the party encouraged women's participation in socially recognized productive labor as the primary means of achieving equality with men. Deng Yingchao, vice-head of the All China Women's Federation, argued in 1953 in her work report to the Second National Congress of Women, "'Ten years of practice has proven that mobilizing the masses of women to participate in production is the basic key to improving equality between men and women and to achieving the thorough liberation of women'" (quoted in Evans, 1998:7). The limitations of this approach, including the double burden it created for rural women who also remained responsible for housework and child care, have been well documented elsewhere (Andors, 1975; Davin, 1979; Johnson, 1983; Thornborg, 1978; H. Yan, 2003). Here I am interested in the particular construction of labor—and by extension gendered labor—that emerged from this much heralded association between socially recognized production and women's liberation.

Collectivizing the Economy

Across most of rural Han China, the liberation of female labor required that cadres and work teams promote women's active participation in agricultural work. Gail Hershatter's research in rural

Shaanxi suggests that in some parts of the country poor women had engaged in farming prior to Liberation, although they did so ostensibly out of necessity, contravening normative ideals that encouraged them to identify proper womanhood with "inside" work (2000:81–83). In these cases, Liberation did not so much transform the kinds of tasks women performed as redefine the meaning and value of that labor so that experiences previously associated with deprivation and hardship came to be identified with ideals of socialist womanhood (Hershatter, 2002). In eastern Hui'an villages, it was not only poor women who worked in the fields but in fact virtually all women. Work team reports and government documents describing implementation of the 1950 Marriage Law and land reform in Huidong acknowledged that women did not have to be coaxed into productive labor because they were already present in the fields. What cadres did face was an unconventional gender division of labor that had to be redefined as Han and socialist and that had to be made to serve other goals such as marital reform.

Land reform itself was a comparatively mild process in Shanlin due to the absence of landlords in the community, the relatively small proportion of arable land in the region, and by extension the secondary role of agriculture in the village economy. Because boats defined wealth in Shanlin, cadres assigned class labels according to boat ownership instead of land ownership. From 1950 to 1952, households were classified as fishing laborers (*yu gong*), poor fishermen (*pin yu*), middle fishermen (*zhong yu*), rich fishermen (*fu yu*), or fishing capitalists (*yuye zibenjia*) depending on the number of shares they owned in boats and whether they fished for themselves or were forced to sell their labor to others.[4] As a result of this classification system, collectivization proceeded in Shanlin along two separate tracks: fishing collectivization for men and agricultural and manual labor collectivization for women.

According to retired cadres who had presided over collectivization in Shanlin, the absence of existing models for collective fishing meant that their initial efforts followed those in agricultural communities. Mutual-aid teams, cooperative groups that fished in one or occasionally two boats, were formed in Shanlin as early as 1950 and 1951.[5] Because teams had access to low-interest or interest-free loans from banks and credit unions, they were able to upgrade outdated equipment and repair damaged boats, leading to significant increases in production and earnings. As a result, they became an increasingly desirable form of labor cooperation among village men. By 1953, Shanlin boasted nine mutual-aid teams with 172 members; one year later the number of teams had grown to fifteen and total membership to 293 (Chongwu, n.d.).

In 1955, cadres encouraged fishermen to organize lower producers' cooperatives (*chuji hezuoshe*) composed of two to five boats, and by the end of that year roughly 80 percent of all fishermen in Shanlin had joined one of the village's eleven cooperatives. The following year ushered in a significant political shift as Shanlin joined with the neighboring village of Haibin to form a joint administrative village (*xiang*). This political transformation coincided with the transition to advanced producers' cooperatives (*gaoji hezuoshe*), with one cooperative shared by the two villages and two maintained separately. Only at this point did all productive resources revert to collective ownership: decision making shifted out of the hands of fishermen to a cooperative steering committee (*weiyuanhui*) and representative committee (*daibiaohui*), and men found themselves assigned to boats regardless of choice or past practice.[6] When in 1958 Shanlin became part of the township-wide Fei Yue People's Commune, Shanlin and Haibin further unified their political and economic structure by forming a single production brigade (*da dui*).

The transition to producers' cooperatives also led to a gradual homogenization of the location and type of fishing. Whereas prior to Liberation and during the early stages of collectivization individual boats had made their own decisions about where to fish and for how long, now most able-bodied men (including teenagers) were sent to the Zhoushan fishing grounds off the coast of Zhejiang province to fish for ribbon fish (*daiyu* or beh hi). These expeditions lasted for seven to eight months, creating a mass exodus of adult men from the village.[7] The absence of young men for most of the year frequently made it difficult for recently married couples to bear the children who would require a wife to assume conjugal residence. The requisite conjugal visit at the New Year holiday nicely coincided with the boats' return to the village, and yet shy young wives often refused to sleep with husbands whom they viewed as strangers. As the next chapter will show in greater detail, at the same time that socialist reformers struggled to eradicate postmarital separation, cadres simultaneously instituted economic arrangements that sent young men and increasingly young women out of their communities for months and even years at a time.

Collectivization of agriculture in Shanlin was instituted a few years after that of fishing, beginning in 1953 with the formation of mutual-aid teams that combined 20 to 30 households to share labor. Plots initially remained in the hands of their original owners, and each household reaped the harvest from its own fields. In 1954, when cadres organized women into lower producers' cooperatives, 20 percent of their harvest was turned over to the cooperative and the rest distributed to members. With the shift to advanced producers' cooperatives in 1955, members received half their share of the harvest according to work point distribution and half based on their allocation of basic grain rations (*ren kouliang*).[8] Land was now completely dissociated from individual household ownership, and women simply performed the labor assigned to them by the cooperative. As a result, it was not uncommon for nonresident wives to refuse visitation requests from their mothers-in-law at busy planting and harvesting times because farming was no longer the responsibility of the household alone.

Beginning in 1957 and 1958, collectivization also spread to the forms of heavy manual labor and construction work performed by women. As the Great Leap Forward (1958–1960) gathered steam, unmarried women and nonresident wives across eastern Hui'an increasingly found themselves assigned by their production teams to labor on public works projects outside of their home villages. These projects represented the hallmark of the Great Leap pledge to rapidly increase China's production output and catapult the country into the standing of an industrialized nation. They involved investments in irrigation, transportation infrastructure, water conservancy, and land reclamation. Although accounts from other parts of China differ in their assessment of rural women's participation in public works projects, in Huidong there was little doubt that women would constitute the majority, or even the sum total, of the workforce on irrigation and construction projects (see Davin, 1979:138; Diamant, 2000:251; Huang, 1989:62, 66; Huang, 1992:88; Ruf, 1998:103–105; Thornborg, 1978:586). The gender divisions of labor in eastern Hui'an had historically defined manual labor as women's work, making women the "natural" targets of official efforts to fill labor quotas. Because most able-bodied men were fishing in Zhoushan for much of the year, moreover, women were the only group available to participate in these projects on a regular basis.[9]

The first massive labor projects in the region were carried out from roughly 1957 until 1960. They included the building of a major reservoir just west of Hui'an county and north of Quanzhou city (the Wutan or Hui'an Women's Reservoir),[10] irrigation canals feeding off the reservoir, a railroad bed for the main Jiangxi–Xiamen line, and smaller reservoirs in the region. In my interviews with village women who had worked on these projects, I was struck by the fact that many were sent directly from one site to the next, sometimes not returning to their natal villages for a year or two at a time. For instance, Bbokli described how she was first sent to Datian in western Fujian to help build the railroad bed there. After six months, she was transferred to Luoyang to dig an irrigation canal, and from there to Wutan Reservoir. A mere sixteen or seventeen at the time, Bbokli recalled how all the women her age cried to go home, but they were not permitted to leave. Gguathua, a few years Bbokli's senior, was also sent to Datian for roughly four months in 1957, and after returning to her natal village she was dispatched immediately to Wutan Reservoir for another four or five months. Following her stint at Wutan, she was assigned to work on the Luoyang irrigation canal and finally on the Dadan Reservoir southwest of the township. In total, she worked outside of her natal village from ages nineteen to twenty-three.

These construction projects required such demanding physical labor that nearly 40 years later women still recalled in great detail the hardships they had experienced. Shanlin native A Di was sent to the Wutan Reservoir for ten months in 1958 and 1959. She first worked as a cook, feeding the women as they came in from their shifts, day and night. As recently as the mid-1990s, A Di could vividly recount the arduousness of the construction tasks, for there was little machinery and most of the digging was done by hand. Dirt and stones were carted in by truck and then boat, but the women had to carry the materials to their work sites and lay them out by hand. After working as a cook, A Di was assigned to row the boats back and forth across the growing reservoir, transporting building materials. By 1959, she recalled, work had reached a fevered pitch and they were forced to work overtime, sometimes through the night with no rest, particularly when inspection teams visited the site.

Many women who had been assigned to build these public works argued that they were not free to return home when they chose; those who did run away often faced village struggle sessions and were denied access to the public canteens where villagers ate during the Great Leap period, effectively forcing them back to their work sites. Yet, at the same time, some accounts suggest that a system of labor strategizing did exist under high socialism, one in which such factors as cadre connections, class status, and personal circumstances likely played significant roles. A Di ran away from Wutan in 1959 and stole back to Shanlin because her mother was ill. Unlike other women, she was not forced to return to work and later refused brigade calls to serve as a midsize-team leader on the Luoyang irrigation project. In the end, she was assigned her mother's former low-level cadre position in the social order division of the brigade and taught in the village nursery school. In 1960, Bbokli was summoned to join the first group of Shanlin women ever to fish on the boats going up to Zhoushan. In her frank, blunt style, Bbokli recalled, "I didn't go. I thought about this one point. [You're] calling us women to go fish, and there won't be any place for us to take a shit. It will be deathly embarrassing. I didn't want to go." Women's participation in fishing lasted only that one season, and thus Bbokli successfully avoided joining the men at sea.[11] Her experience and that of A Di suggest that despite the general portrayal of grueling labor assignments, in fact some women faced more bitter work than others.[12]

What was the relationship between this large-scale mobilization of female labor in Huidong and local norms of postmarital separation? If prior to collectivization women's labor contributions had encouraged families to support their married daughters' continued natal residence, did collectivization of agricultural and construction labor undermine local marriage practices or further support them? The mobilization of large numbers of young, unmarried, or childless married women to work on labor projects far from home was itself a product of women's extended natal residence after marriage and patterns of surname and village exogamy. Married women's continued presence in their natal communities prior to childbirth, like the residence of unmarried women who were not expected to assume conjugal residence for many years to come, made their labor both physically and socially available to their natal production teams. Removing such women from their communities for long periods of time would not threaten the social fabric of the village and family as it might if wives customarily had resided with their husbands immediately upon marrying.[13] Women's engagement in work outside their natal communities also fit neatly with their own desire to delay conjugal residence, for they viewed residence in their husbands' homes as a loss of freedom and the beginning of even heavier workloads.

Gguathua, who worked on public works projects for four years, had married into Shanlin from another village in the region two years prior to her first labor assignment at Datian. As a result, she spent many of her early married years living and working outside the region. Not surprisingly, she did not give birth to her first child until the age of 25, two years after she returned to her natal village and eight years after she married. In A Di's case, her time spent outside Shanlin perhaps inspired her to divorce her first husband. A Di initially married a Haibin man in 1957 when she was seventeen, but within a year she was sent to the Wutan Reservoir. Sometime between her wedding and her return from Wutan in 1959 she initiated divorce proceedings. A Di told me about her marital history casually one afternoon while we were visiting with her oldest daughter-in-law (who was also A Di's sister's child). When I asked A Di why she had divorced her first husband, she refrained from commenting on her motives and merely smiled when her daughter-in-law jumped in and attributed A Di's decision to "feudal constraints" (honggian sokbok).[14] In the absence of A Di's own commentary, it is difficult to know for certain why she initiated the divorce, but her extended absence from the brigade might very well have strengthened her resolve to leave her husband. In any case, her divorce request was quickly granted, and soon after she was introduced to a Shanlin man from a minor surname group (himself twice divorced) who she agreed to marry. Even though at that point A Di was working in Shanlin, she did not begin living with her second husband until four years later when her mother-in-law adopted a son for the childless couple. A Di then went on to bear five sons of her own.

These examples suggest that collective work assignments might have extended already lengthy periods of postmarital separation by making it more difficult for couples to become acquainted and to foster the kinds of intimacy that would lead to pregnancy and childbirth. In other cases, separation itself might have emboldened women and men to seek divorces from unsuitable spouses at a time when, as most villagers recalled, divorces were granted without much fuss by the commune. A Di's husband attributed his first two divorces to the fact that his wives never came to visit, a result perhaps of women's diminished sense of labor obligations to their conjugal families with collectivization. Moreover, at the same time that collective work assignments limited opportunities for cultivating conjugal intimacy, they also strengthened the same-sex dui pnua bonds that reformers in the early 1950s had worked so hard to undermine. Even the youngest participants, some only eleven or twelve years old when they first left home, joined public works projects under the watchful eyes of not only natal family kin but also fellow dui pnua.

Under the mantle of socialist collectivization, then, officials normalized the atypical gender divisions of labor in eastern Hui'an by hailing the women who participated in these projects as paragons of socialist virtue. Celebrating women's labor contributions, county officials in 1959 renamed Wutan Reservoir Hui'an Women's Reservoir (*Huinü shuiku*).[15] In a 1964 statement commemorating the building of the reservoir, the Hui'an County Party Committee credited socialism with transforming these women "from the slaves of the old society" into "masters of the country" (Zhong Gong Hui'an Xian Wei Bangongshi, 1964:1). Instead of attacking Huidong women's labor patterns as Han anomalies linked to unusual marriage practices, these officials praised women's spirit of diligence and their ingenuity in overcoming adversity and credited them with transforming a drought-stricken landscape into a river of rice and grain. Overwriting intimate bodily capacities with socialist tropes of self-sacrifice and gender liberation, they proclaimed that "the completion of Hui'an Women's Reservoir is a glorious chapter in Hui'an women's participation in socialist construction, marking a new period in the lives of Hui'an women—with their heads raised high and shoulders squared, they have daringly and tirelessly built a new socialist era!" (1964:6; see also "Hui nü song," 1963).

Eating and Speaking Bitterness

Despite such celebratory moments during the flush of socialist exuberance in the late 1950s and early 1960s, Shanlin women in the 1990s looked back on the collective era with mixed emotions. Together with their male counterparts they spoke longingly of the egalitarian ethos that pervaded those decades and the commitment of both cadres and villagers to social order and community spirit. Nonetheless, they were also clear-eyed about the demands made on them and their bodies. Shanlin women who had toiled in collective fields or on public works projects used the expressions "to labor" (zue gang) or "to put out labor" (cut gang) to describe their activities, both of which highlighted the intensive manual nature of their work. Women of this cohort depicted in great detail the physical hardships they faced and the poor conditions under which they worked, all of which they portrayed using tropes of bitterness and suffering. Unlike official accounts from the collective era that praised Hui'an women's socialist spirit in the face of primitive work conditions, Shanlin women's recollections of the period emphasized the pain they suffered, agonizingly recounting the long distances over which they transported heavy loads, the lack of adequate tools and machinery, and the unfamiliarity of life in the mountains where they were sent to cut down bamboo and build the railroad bed. Their use of the phrase "putting out labor" also evoked their lack of control over work assignments and their sense of alienation from the fruits of that labor. One "put out labor" for the production team, a collective unit that allocated that labor where it was needed. Rewards were minimal, either mediated by the work point system or occasionally, as on public works projects, remunerated through a meager wage.

The system of collective rewards created a hierarchy of tasks and skills that re-enshrined gender divisions of labor in a manner that largely devalued the work performed by women. Male-dominated fishing occupied the pinnacle of the collective hierarchy both because of its critical contribution to village livelihood and because of the combination of physical and skilled labor it demanded. Shanlin residents described this prioritization through reference to a hierarchy of basic grain allocation. Deep-sea fishermen received a state-subsidized allotment of 45 *jin* of rice a month, and those fishing along the coast 28 *jin*.[16] Women and children engaged in agriculture or manual labor, by contrast, received a mere ten to fifteen *jin*.[17] As in the pre-1949 era, without men's earnings from fishing, families were unable to purchase enough rice to feed themselves. Moreover, during the three-month sweet potato season, women were not given any rice rations, only a distribution of sweet potatoes or sweet potato flour.

In their recollections of this period, women attributed the considerably smaller grain rations allocated to women's work to the secondary status of agriculture in the collective economy, a devaluation that also shaped women's own interpretations of their work. A Di proclaimed to me one afternoon that prior to the current market-reform era, women were "useless" (bbo diong yong) because they "had to go earn useless money." This sense of uselessness was expressed quite frequently by women of A Di's cohort; despite living through an era when their labor had been celebrated by the collective for its contributions to building socialism, these women acknowledged that such ideological recognition failed to translate into material rewards. By establishing fishing as the primary source of income and access to rice, the system of work point allocation and rice distribution reaffirmed a gender division of labor that inherently favored the kinds of work performed by men. Unlike in agricultural communities where collectivization often transformed the gendered allocation of tasks or, at the very least, revalued women's labor, in Huidong a fishing-based economy insured the continued devaluation of women's contributions in very real material ways.

Shanlin women who had reached adulthood in the 1950s and early 1960s surprised me with how critical they were of the high socialist years, using the trope of bitterness inculcated through speak-bitterness campaigns and local folk-song traditions to portray not only the presocialist feudal past but also their ostensibly liberated lives under Mao. As they wove accounts of labor burdens into personal marital histories and experiences of state marriage reform campaign, some even singled out the collective features of labor mobilization as explanations for women's suffering. One such account has long stood out in my mind. It was told to me by Ggimlan, a woman in her mid-fifties who had grown up in the neighboring village of Haibin and was a childhood dui pnua of the mother in my host family. When I first asked Ggimlan to talk about her youth, she chose to tell me the story of her patrilateral cousin who she referred to as her older sister:

> There was one time, our older sister was thirty-eight and hadn't yet given birth.... She really didn't like to go [to her husband's home], really didn't like it. In the end, though, she had to go. Otherwise, if her labor power [lolik] wasn't transferred she couldn't receive her grain ration. She had married into Houyang from Haibin. In those days they wouldn't distribute [her ration], in those days the plots were all divided up. If you didn't have a plot you didn't get a distribution. If you didn't have a household registration then you weren't given a plot. It was like that. Her mother-in-law was insistent about urging her [to shift residence]. And then she really went, she went to put out labor for the production team. Our sister Siulan was really honest.

Despite Siulan's efforts to avoid visiting a husband Ggimlan portrayed as fierce and violent, the demands of a collective labor system left her with little choice in the end. Ggimlan ultimately blamed this system for her sister's premature death. Less than a year after Siulan moved to Houyang, she died a horrible death in a tragic accident. She had been standing on the stone ledge overlooking the village latrine as she ladled nightsoil into a bucket to fertilize the fields. The stone was old and it broke under her weight. As Siulan fell into the latrine she grabbed for the remaining ledge, but the stone slab slid on top of her, trapping her underneath. Only after the villagers dug out the heavy stone were they able to extricate Siulan, and by then she had already suffocated. "You know," Ggimlan added in a low voice, "that is the worst kind of suffering. If she hadn't gone [to her husband's village], she wouldn't have been killed."

Ggimlan's account, like those of other women of her generation, offers a stark critique of the high socialist era and the demands socialism made on women's bodies and intimate relationships. Her story interweaves labor expectations with state efforts to change local norms of postmarital separation, showing how cadres put pressure on women in various ways to reject local marriage customs. Yet by defining their experiences through tropes of bitterness, suffering, and uselessness, women of this cohort refused their seamless incorporation into a socialist nation characterized by selfless labor and struggle. Even as they expressed pride in their abilities, they identified as useless subjects, distancing themselves from collective efforts to mobilize their labor and claim them as self-sacrificing socialist workers. By preserving a norm of postmarital separation, moreover, this generation of women maintained their anomalous position in a socialist civilizational order organized as much around how one married as how one labored.[18] Their combination of socialist heroism with adherence to "backward" marriage customs reinforced a tenuous relationship to socialist labor ideals and perhaps even encouraged women such as Bbokli to describe Liberation not as an end to bitterness but as merely a passing moment in its ongoing cycle of production (see also Hershatter, 2002:58–59).

Politics or Production?

The famine that followed the Great Leap Forward in the early 1960s led to a reorganization of the collective and a redistribution of gendered labor in the community.[19] Beginning in 1962, Shanlin officials implemented policies designed to inject individual incentive into a stagnating economy by giving villagers more control over the means of production and the fruits of their labor. Public canteens closed down, and villagers again earned a combination of work points and basic grain rations. Fishing yields grew rapidly in the 1960s as individual production teams contracted with the brigade for a guaranteed level of production value (*chan zhi*), spurred on by increased mechanization, improved technology, and better training for fishermen.[20] Women devoted more time to agricultural production and the cultivation of ocean products such as seaweed as they were freed from labor obligations on public works projects. Brigade officials also established workshops that produced rice noodles and fishing nets in an effort to absorb the labor of newly resident village daughters-in-law.

The radical leftist ideology of the Cultural Revolution descended on Shanlin in 1966 when the Cultural Revolution Revolutionary

Committee assumed control of the production brigade, displacing the previous leadership and dividing the community into two opposing political factions. The first two years of the Cultural Revolution saw a fervent commitment to both revolution and production, with fishing yields peaking in 1967 at 157,245 *dan*, for an average yearly income of 756 *yuan* per fisherman (Chongwu, n.d.).[21] Following that year, however, the political situation quickly deteriorated into chaos and conflict; production was no longer emphasized over politics, and many members of the faction associated with the pre–Cultural Revolution leadership were banned from participating in the large-scale expeditions to the Zhoushan basin and were forced to eke out a meager living from coastal fishing. The effects of this political upheaval were clear in plummeting production rates and the brigade's failure to meet yearly production targets. By 1975, fishing yields had dropped to 67,677 *dan*, and average yearly income per fisherman to a mere 253 *yuan* (Chongwu, n.d.). Villagers who lived through the period overwhelmingly recalled the poverty of those years, with the families of those in politically suspect categories suffering the most acutely—some surviving only on the sweet potatoes their children stole from collective fields.

The Cultural Revolution decade also witnessed a new wave of female labor mobilization as young women were sent to the Huangtang area in the west of the county to farm unsettled lands or to a nearby township to build a sea embankment that would connect a low-lying peninsula to the mainland.[22] Women from across eastern Hui'an went to Huangtang from roughly 1967 to 1972 for lengths of time varying from several months to one or two years. Conditions were not as strict in this later phase as they had been during the Great Leap Forward; younger women who had worked at Huangtang or on other projects recalled that they were free to return home for periodic visits, most commonly at the New Year holiday. In Huangtang women planted sweet potatoes and rice, and after the harvest the brigade transported any surplus above their own needs back to their home communities.

Despite the chaos of the Cultural Revolution, Shanlin experienced a steady growth in population over the decade, leading to demands for new housing and thus a gradual decline in the amount of village land available for agriculture. These shifts perhaps explain why young women were dispatched to cultivate arable land elsewhere in the county, particularly now that other contract-based forms of production had been denounced as revisionist by the new leadership. Their labor mobilization was also justified in ideological terms quite similar to those that inspired the large-scale movement of urban youth "sent down" to the countryside in the 1970s. Many Shanlin women who had gone to Huangtang recalled a propaganda folk song from the period that invoked ideals not unlike those used to galvanize their urban counterparts: sacrifice for the larger good, obedience to Mao Zedong, and commitment to the socialist battle.

This folk song, titled "Ten Send-offs of Little Sister to Huangtang," reinforces the ideological and practical motivations for sending young women away to farm sparsely settled regions of the county in order to increase grain production.[23] "Ten Send-offs" begins by urging villagers to follow Mao Zedong's call to set off for Huangtang. It exhorts the young woman addressee to do her part for the socialist battle by producing grain and sending it home for consumption. She is told she must not waver in her commitment to Mao, the benevolent leader who has wisely guided her and her country on the path to socialism, or to political work more generally. Her contributions are depicted as both ideological (supporting the socialist cause) and practical (feeding her community and cultivating undeveloped lands). Although the song acknowledges that the young woman might long for home and family, it simultaneously urges her to suppress those emotions and devote her efforts to the more important tasks at hand.

"Ten Send-offs" literally calls the eastern Hui'an countryside into being by naming sites at each stage in the young woman's journey. It recreates this physical landscape not through local meanings or histories but through the ideological imperatives of the Cultural Revolution that demanded self-abnegation in the service of collective goals. This self-denial was also gendered in specific ways that made young women once again its "natural" target. By adopting "little sister" as its form of address, the song enacts the perspective of a paternalistic leader in the guise of an older brother. Although it effects the fusion of state and society that Claude Lefort argues is so central to totalitarian projects such as the Cultural Revolution, it does so through cloaking the socialist nation in the garb of the patriarchal family. In other words, the song does not merely fuse a generic self into what Lefort calls "the great communist 'us'" or "the People-as-One" (1986:290); it enacts that fusion through reference to a gendered familial hierarchy in which a young woman's subservience and obedience to her family (personified by her older brother) translates into her devotion to socialism and the socialist nation (personified by Chairman Mao). In this case, the "little sister" is not distinguished by her unusual marriage or residence patterns; instead, she is hailed as a socialist youth who, despite the radical egalitarianism of the period, is advised to sacrifice her own needs to the demands of traditional age and gender hierarchies.

The end to the Cultural Revolution with the fall of the Gang of Four in 1976 put a stop to this mobilization of female labor for public works outside the region. As several members of the pre–Cultural Revolution leadership resumed control of the brigade, they initiated new projects aimed at rebuilding the local economy and rejuvenating an environment ravaged by the excesses of the Great Leap Forward. Even low-level female cadres were rehabilitated during the late 1970s, and Bbokli spoke proudly of the months she spent on the east mountain overseeing the planting of trees to replace those cut down to fuel village iron works during the Great Leap. Younger women returned to cultivating seaweed in collective plots along the shore, tasks now linked in propaganda folk songs to the new goals of the post-Mao leadership.

Shanlin native Siokden reached adulthood during this period of economic rebuilding in the late 1970s. As a teenager she worked on collective seaweed plots organized by the brigade together with other women her age. They eased the boredom of their tasks by singing propaganda folk songs structured along familiar tropes like the months of the year. Although her memory of the songs had faded in recent years as she struggled to raise a family and assist her husband with his coastal fishing, Siokden was able to reconstruct for me a relatively complete version of one such song. Organized around the production tasks at hand, the song's content was primarily political, intended to repudiate the ideological extremes of the Cultural Revolution and to salvage the reputations of key leaders such as the recently deceased Zhou Enlai. Praising the newly installed post-Mao leadership and their more pragmatic economic policies, the song strikes a careful balance between the excesses of the past and the production demands of the present. The country's new direction is reaffirmed most strongly in the third stanza:

In the third month we must harvest the seaweed;
The leadership of Chairman Hua is so wise;
The Third Plenum rules the country [and] all under heaven is stable;[24]
The entire nation welcomes [the reforms].

At the same time that the women of Siokden's generation were being reeducated in a careful balance of post-Mao reforms and collective production, village men were also moving away from collective fishing and experimenting with new contracting arrangements. Under the "contracting everything to the household" (*da bao gan*) system, Shanlin implemented a test contract case in late 1978 using nine deep-sea fishing boats (the brigade received only a few fixed payments, and all remaining proceeds were allocated by the boat itself). Due to the success of the test case, the contract system was extended to the entire brigade in 1979, and in 1980 a few fishermen began to build new boats for themselves and to fish in local waters instead of joining the fleet that continued to go north for much of the season. The year 1983 witnessed an even more dramatic revision of the contract system when the brigade calculated the value of its boats and contracted them out to 40 boat technicians. The technicians had five to seven years to repay the brigade and controlled all earnings above a few fixed payments, using a work point system based on individual performance and overall yields to compensate the fishermen (CWZZ, 1996:92).

Contracting produced a steady increase in fishing output and value throughout the 1980s, and technological improvements to the boats made fishing safer and more productive. At the same time, however, contracting gradually divested the brigade of its own collective resources, leaving it—as many villagers described in the 1990s—an empty shell, a mere shadow of its former glory. By 1992, the village fleet had stopped its yearly expeditions to the Zhoushan basin due to overfishing and pollution in the area and local boats' inability to compete with the more technologically advanced Zhejiang vessels. The end to these expeditions led to a visible decline in Shanlin's fishing industry, forcing young men to seek employment in other forms of fishing or in newly emerging land-based occupations.

Reform-Era Economies

As market reforms were gradually implemented in Shanlin in the 1980s and 1990s, they opened up a range of occupational opportunities previously unimaginable in a collective economy organized around fishing, agriculture, and manual labor. This diversification has simultaneously transformed gender divisions of labor in the region and the gendered value of different tasks, enabling some young women to create a more empowering relationship to their own productive capacities. Today that empowerment results not from socialist ideals of gender liberation but from the material and social benefits generated by access to substantial wage income. By the same token, the end to state allocation of labor and the introduction of new skills demanded by a market economy also disadvantage villagers with limited access to education and financial resources. The result is a village society in which all aspire to new forms of consumption and more comfortable lifestyles, but in which a social landscape of general poverty is gradually being reconfigured along increasingly disparate lines of wealth and status.

Even after sweet potato and peanut plots were contracted out to individual households in 1982, agricultural cultivation continued to decline in Shanlin, in large part due to the construction of new homes and other buildings on previously arable land.[25] As men moved out of large-scale fishing in the late 1980s and 1990s, growing numbers of them took up coastal fishing for crabs and other seafood, products increasingly in demand on the domestic and international markets. Some women therefore have continued to work in fishing's subsidiary occupations, mending fishing nets (see Fig. 4), unloading and transporting boat equipment, and selling the remaining catch from coastal fishing in the village market. Because coastal fishing was highly sensitive to the tide schedule, fishing rotated around the clock, exhausting household members particularly during the important crab season in the late winter.[26]

The move away from agriculture and the decline in fishing have freed up female labor for a range of other forms of employment

FIG. 4: Young woman repairing fishing nets (photograph by the author, 1994)

emerging in the reform era. Beginning in the early 1980s, large numbers of young Shanlin women began to work for wages on construction sites both within the village and elsewhere. Many migrated south along the coast to the new special economic zones of Xiamen and Shenzhen to perform the same kinds of construction labor that their mothers had performed on public works projects during the Mao era, now building apartment buildings and high-rises instead of dams and railroad beds. Others remained in Shanlin, transporting heavy blocks of granite as they worked for stone quarry managers or building contractors (see Fig. 5). Although the pay was quite minimal during the early reform era, often as low as 1 to 3 *yuan* per day, participation in wage labor gave young women the opportunity to visit urban centers (unlike their elders who had been sent to remote rural areas) and to accumulate personal funds. Even if they only spent such earnings on clothing and adornment, women of this cohort spoke proudly of their ability to acquire independent purchasing power.

As market forces took off in the late 1980s and early 1990s, women of different age groups also began to move into new lines of employment, some of which involved working together with men

FIG. 5: Transporting stones for house building (photograph by the author, 1995)

or male kin, or at least in similar occupations. A variety of privately owned shops sprung up around the village, ranging from tiny neighborhood stores run by elderly women or men, to fruit stalls, dry goods stores, fashionable clothing shops, tailoring establishments, and large wholesale distributors presided over by savvy businesswomen and -men in their twenties and thirties. By the mid-1990s, Shanlin enjoyed a booming consumer economy that had spread out from the market area to newer sectors of the village. This expanding consumerism also knit Shanlin residents ever more tightly into a regional universe encompassing the township and county seats, as well as more far-flung provincial cities. Whereas older villagers recalled having to walk the few kilometers to the township (then commune) to attend political meetings during the Maoist years, by the 1990s a burgeoning transportation sector offered multiple transport options for those seeking goods or services farther afield. It was not uncommon for husband-and-wife teams to purchase a three-wheeled covered truck and jointly run a transport service between the village and the township seat or for women in the roughly 20-to-40 age group to drive such vehicles independently. Of the several different kinds of vehicles traversing the township's roads in the mid-1990s, only motorcycle taxis remained the exclusive domain of men.[27]

Beginning in the early 1990s, a significant shift occurred in the structure of young female and male labor within Shanlin and Chongwu township more generally. In March 1992, Chen Xinxing, the township party secretary, traveled to Japan to explore the possibility of expanding the township's stone-carving industry to include the production of headstones and other grave-site adornment for export to Japan. The early reform era had already witnessed a significant expansion in stone-carving workshops in the township, from 16 in 1985 to 34 by 1989, yet all relied on male labor and hand-carving techniques.[28] Headstones and other grave-site pieces required polishing of the stone in addition to carving, both of which were now mechanized processes. Young men monopolized the carving and cutting sectors as they abandoned fishing for more desirable land-based occupations.[29] Polishing, however, became the domain of young women.

By 1993, the year following Party Secretary Chen's trip, the number of headstone factories alone in the township had grown from 1 to 59.[30] As new and existing enterprises purchased the machinery necessary to produce headstones, they opened the way for widespread growth in female labor participation. Of the 8,287 workers in the industry in 1993, over 50 percent were women (CWZZ, 1996:123). The number of women working in the industry remained relatively stable through the rest of the decade at roughly 4,000 across the township.[31] Although the majority of factory women worked as stone polishers, some began to move into artistic forms of relief carving done in small workshops.

Headstone factories employed the largest number of workers overall (as many as several hundred per factory), as well as the majority of women (roughly 70 percent of all workers in these factories were young women in the 15 to 25 age range). They also offered the steadiest employment. After completing a short apprenticeship, stone polishers worked on a piecework basis, with remuneration varying in accordance with the style of piece, the variety of the stone, and the type of polishing machinery used (see Fig. 6). Average earnings ranged from 1,000 to 2,000 *yuan* per month, a figure that remained constant through 2002. Even when wage levels dropped to

FIG. 6: Stone polisher at work (photograph by the author, 1995)

500 to 700 *yuan* per month due to increased industry competition or declining demand, such wages continued to compare favorably with those in other employment sectors. Shop assistants, accountants, cashiers, and women who worked in other industries earned an average monthly salary of 400 *yuan* in the mid-1990s. Women who served in the lowest rungs of the village government bureaucracy earned a mere 50 *yuan* per month, whereas those who labored on construction projects or mended fishing nets received a daily wage of 20 *yuan*, without the assurance of steady work.

Young Shanlin women's experiences of factory labor in the 1990s offer several compelling contrasts to what have generally been portrayed as rather gloomy and oppressive industrial opportunities for Chinese women in the reform era (Gao, 1994; Jacka, 1997; Lee, 1998; Rofel, 1999). Unlike rural women from the interior of the country, they do not have to migrate to urban areas or special economic zones in search of higher wages; in fact, the wages they earn in local factories most often surpass those offered in the light industries that dominate the export sector. Nor do their wages necessarily compare unfavorably with those of their male counterparts. Unlike during the collective era, the kind of work assigned to men is not remunerated at a consistently higher rate than that assigned to women, although men do tend to dominate the managerial positions that give them access to annual or semiannual bonuses.

Shanlin women's participation in factory work also differs from that of rural women elsewhere in China in regard to their marital status. Due to a norm of postmarital natal residence in Huidong communities, women do not stop factory work upon marriage. They remain in the workplace after marriage as before, turning their wages over to their mothers. An increasing number even resume work following childbirth if they can arrange for acceptable child care. The high wages women earn in these factories make continued work a desired option for their conjugal families, particularly because such profitable labor does not require migration out of the community.[32]

As stone carving shifted the township's economic base from overall dependence on a declining fishing industry, it simultaneously created a skilled labor force in the township composed of both women and men. Factories draw on a township-wide labor supply, and the crowds of dusty bicyclists lining the township's roads at dawn and dusk provide ample evidence of this daily commute. Shanlin's two largest headstone factories employ several hundred workers, from both within and outside the village. These enterprises represent the success stories of the reform era, riding the high tide of exports to Japan and foreign investment from Taiwan, Hong Kong, Malaysia, and Japan. And as the chapters in Part II illustrate in greater detail, stone-carving factories have also profoundly affected young people's courtship and marriage practices, undermining long-standing patterns of conjugal avoidance and postmarital separation.

Now Women "Can Eat Just Like Men"

The recent diversification of Shanlin's economy has created a new economic hierarchy in the community. No longer does fishing occupy the pinnacle of the economic structure; by the 1990s, it had been devalued in many villagers' eyes to the status of "useless" labor because of the considerable physical hardship it entailed and the extended periods of work outside the village it required. With the end to the mass expeditions of the collective era and the sale of the village fleet, most fishermen have been forced to work as wage laborers for local captains, on boats with international licenses that fish for tuna in Micronesia, or, increasingly, on Taiwanese fishing vessels.[33] As a result, the stone-carving industry has gradually replaced fishing as the occupation of choice, linking skill with income generation to a much greater degree than fishing ever could. Stone carving and polishing resemble fishing, however, in that they forge this link without altogether eradicating the value of physical labor. When a group of ten young women traveled to the far northern province of Heilongjiang in 1996 to polish stones in a factory managed by a village businessman, those who earned the highest sums were widely praised in Shanlin for their ability to "eat bitterness" in such an arctic climate. In this situation, the attribution of bitterness functioned as a sign of admiration, highlighting the substantial income generated by these women's willingness to endure physical hardships. Many earned over 20,000 *yuan* in an eight-month period (and a few as much as 50,000 *yuan*), more than many villagers' yearly household income.

This reevaluation of manual and skilled labor has also reconfigured gender divisions of labor in Shanlin. No longer are women relegated solely to manual forms of work, for as stone polishers they, too, now bask in the glory of being identified as valued skilled laborers (cf. Rofel, 1994:243; Lee, 1998). The title of this section conveys appreciation for women's improved status through a paraphrase of a comment I overhead made by an elderly Shanlin woman. Observing a mother preparing a hearty soup of meat and fish for two of her daughters who had just returned home from working in stone factories, the elderly neighbor acknowledged the daughters' substantial contributions to the family's income with the aside, "now [they] can eat just like men." This family had four daughters in their late teens and early twenties, all of whom worked in some aspect of the stone-carving industry. Aside from their father's wage of 1,000 *yuan* per month earned on a local fishing boat and the small income their mother generated from her tiny shop, the daughters' earnings supported the family and enabled their brother to continue his education.

The identification of stone carving and polishing as skilled work was also conveyed through the language that villagers used to refer to work in stone-carving factories. Unlike the terms zue gueh and zue gang employed in earlier periods, villagers in the 1990s used the expression zoh sit (*zuo shi*) to refer to factory work and nonmanual wage labor more generally. These terminological distinctions reflect more than different types of activities; they also give meaning to labor through situating it in specific political, social, as well as economic contexts (Zhang, 2000:186–187). Zoh sit is one of many expressions that convey the need for initiative, planning, and skill in the market economy. In contrast to the Mao era when villagers' labor was organized for them by the collective, the post-Mao period has witnessed an intense focus on the role of the individual in achieving personal and familial economic success. In Shanlin, this emphasis on applying one's talents emerged most saliently in the concern that individuals take the initiative to develop a tao loo or occupation.

Whereas finding a tao loo was cause for concern among virtually all sectors of the population, it was especially pressing for young women who lacked many of the skills necessary to advance in a market economy. Those who chose not to work in the stone-carving industry or to perform manual labor often found themselves frustrated by a saturated small-business market and a lack of education that hindered their ability to branch out into other lines of work. Geographic immobility also curbed aspirations, particularly if a conjugal family obstructed a young daughter-in-law's efforts to look for work opportunities outside of the region. In discussions among themselves, young women often voiced these concerns by drawing attention to the ways they felt disadvantaged by the demands of a market economy, formulating their own visions of desirable work in response.

One April evening in 1996, Siubbin swung open the heavy metal gate and pushed her three-wheeled taxi into the courtyard of the family home where I lived during my research. She was tired after a long day of driving back and forth between Shanlin and the township seat, and she was eager to complain about her limited earnings to all who would listen. The two daughters in the family, the oldest of whom was Siubbin's sister-in-law, quickly engaged her in conversation in the cool darkness of their first-floor bedroom, adding their own tales of employment woe to Siubbin's laments. Bored with sitting in her taxi all day, Siubbin was considering switching to construction work. Upon hearing her plans, the younger sister, A Den, retorted that manual labor only brought in 20 *yuan* per day, a paltry sum in comparison to earnings from driving a taxi. But Siubbin and A Den's older sister, Bbingden (who herself ran an only modestly profitable fruit shop), agreed that manual labor was simple and straightforward, and guaranteed a minimum of a few hundred *yuan* in earnings per month. Siubbin argued that it was in fact more arduous to drive a car than to perform construction labor. She straightened her headscarf in a tiny mirror propped up against the bars of the window and then turned to A Den and commented on the ease of her work as the owner of a wholesale business: sitting in her shop all day, A Den did not get dirty running around outside and could simply wait for the money to come to her. As A Den protested that her business had declined precipitously in recent months, Siubbin countered, "You have culture, a good head, whatever you do will make good money!"

Siubbin and Bbingden's depiction of manual labor as being desirable because of its simplicity draws attention to the stressful aspects of work in the reform era. The expansion in work options and the ability to change jobs when needed or desirable could be confusing and anxiety provoking for villagers accustomed to state allocation of their labor. Because there were many more work opportunities in the 1990s, there were also many more chances to fail. No one form of employment was guaranteed over the long term, and earnings fluctuated with shifts in the local and transnational regional economy. In Siubbin's eyes, A Den was more competitive in this marketplace because she had "culture," meaning that she had gone to school for a few years and had been able to maintain a basic level of character recognition and Mandarin-language skills through her business venture. Moreover, as Siubbin noted, A Den had a good head. She was well known in the village for her sharp mind and tongue and for her shrewd ability to maximize profits from her wholesale shop through risky, but judicious, participation in rotating credit associations and through high-interest loans to other villagers. In comparison with Siubbin and Bbingden who had very little formal education, A Den did indeed benefit from the skills needed to make money in the reform era.

Although these three women did not explicitly mention the need for a tao loo, their analysis of current work possibilities and their underlying assumption that one could switch jobs if desired conveyed an image of work as something that one sought out and planned for in order to maximize earnings or to insure stability and a stress-free lifestyle. These elements of intent and initiative were largely missing from older women's recollections of both the pre-1949 and collective eras, although A Di's acknowledgment that she had avoided being sent back to work on irrigation projects suggests that even within the limits imposed by the collective structure some strategizing did take place. The changing meanings attributed to the categories of manual and skilled labor in the reform era have created new standards of desirable work, making manual labor appealing for its straightforward simplicity while also reinforcing the connection between skilled labor and income-earning potential. No longer are women necessarily disadvantaged in this emerging hierarchy solely by virtue of their gender, moreover, as increasing numbers earn considerable sums in the industrial workplace. Yet as the worried tone of A Den, Siubben, and Bbingden's conversation implied, like women across China they also faced the double-edged sword of the market in which "freedom of mobility joins freedom of discrimination, and opportunities blend with insecurity" (Z. Wang, 2000:64).

Conclusion

In their comments on life in the current market economy—both the opportunities it offers and the new limitations it imposes—older villagers frequently described the emergence of a society remarkably similar to that of the pre-1949 Nationalist era. They pointed to growing inequality within the community, corruption and the excesses of official power, and the absence of neutral parties to settle disputes or aid the disadvantaged. Against this picture, they held up the 1950s and 1960s as a time of relative equality and social order, when cadres labored together with the people and shared in their common poverty. Yet, despite their nostalgia for the egalitarian ethos that suffused the decades of high socialism, Shanlin women persisted in underscoring the suffering and bitterness they experienced under collective labor assignments. Instead of extolling the collective era as a time when their labor was valorized by the party, they described themselves as useless, devalued by a collective labor hierarchy that solidified preexisting gender divisions of labor and enshrined the superiority of male-dominated fishing.

The trope of labor has not completely disappeared in reform-era Shanlin, nor has it simply been relegated to the dustbin of "socialist nostalgia" (Rofel, 1999:131). The stone-carving industry redefines the link between skilled labor and income-earning potential in a manner that continues to valorize hard work and even suffering. With their ability to participate in both highly remunerated skilled jobs and simple manual labor, Shanlin women themselves play an active role in redefining the meanings of intimate bodily capacities associated with production and the generation of wealth. In the process, they also contribute to redefining village social spaces in ways that create new possibilities for marriage and courtship practices. Many of these changes build on a longer history of marriage and family reforms in the region, and I turn to this dimension of intimate politics in the next chapter.

CHAPTER TWO 🦋 Fashioning Liberated Socialist Subjects

When CCP cadres first entered Huidong villages in the early 1950s, they were surprised to discover many wives residing in their natal communities and contributing labor to their birth families instead of to their conjugal ones. These practices were unsettling to officials accustomed to typical Han marriage patterns in which wives immediately shifted their residence and labor to their husbands' homes and families. Enforcing postmarital conjugal residence became a major component of the CCP's program of women's liberation in eastern Hui'an and was coupled with efforts to change the ways women adorned themselves and formed close bonds with one another. Under the mantle of eradicating feudal oppression, these reform initiatives aspired to "sculpt the body politic" (Cott, 2000:5) of the new socialist republic by reshaping women's bodies and intimate attachments.

It was only several months into my research that I became aware of this history of state reform campaigns in eastern Hui'an. As I spent more time with older Shanlin residents, I frequently heard them describe how outside and local cadres had tried to force married women to live with their husbands and how officials had effectively banned the intricate headpieces worn by married women. Elderly and middle-aged villagers often recited for me fragments of songs and slogans that conveyed the reformist message of state actors, together with local songs that expressed women's resistance to both marriage and mass campaigns. Armed with a basic understanding of these early reform initiatives from interviews and folk songs,

I decided to venture into provincial and county party archives to see whether I could gain access to the official side of the story. I was amazed to find a wealth of material on early socialist campaigns and Nationalist-era cultural-reform movements in Fujian province, some of which specifically targeted Hui'an marriage customs. Using what I learned from work team reports, exchanges between government bureaus, policy statements, and general campaign reviews, I returned to Shanlin to interview retired cadres and other villagers who had been activists in the campaigns of the 1950s and 1960s or, conversely, the subjects of them. Based on these interviews and archival materials, this chapter examines how post-Liberation reform campaigns formed part of a larger effort to build a new socialist society through transforming women's intimate practices and relationships, most notably those of marriage, bodily adornment, and same-sex bonds.

My analytic aims here are twofold: to analyze the content and power of the language used by state actors to characterize local practices and to evaluate the effectiveness of the reform campaigns themselves. Unlike their Nationalist predecessors (Friedman, 2002), socialist reformers had the support of national initiatives such as the 1950 Marriage Law and the implementation efforts that followed its promulgation. These state-sponsored campaigns aimed to eradicate the oppressive vestiges of a feudal marriage system and to replace them with socialist marriages premised on free consent and mutual feeling. Approaching marriage as the core of a larger feudal complex, reformers in eastern Hui'an focused on connections between postmarital natal residence and women's adornment styles, labor patterns, close ties with other women, and penchant for taking their own lives. Although transforming local marriage customs was key to overturning this complex, changes in all these domains were necessary if cadres and work teams were to refashion Huidong women into appropriately liberated Han socialist subjects.

The Power of Language in Socialist Societies

Scholars of socialist societies have often emphasized the vital role of language in the party-state's project of transforming popular consciousness. In her study of official literature and histories published by intellectuals and bureaucrats in socialist Romania, Verdery (1991) calls attention to the myriad ways that socialist regimes have made use of language in their attempts to revolutionize mass consciousness and redefine forms of subjectivity. Yet, as Gal and Kligman argue in their analysis of gender and socialism in Central Europe, the discursive power of the state is often insufficient to transform citizens' established ways of thinking and identifying themselves. In fact, they suggest that people only come to "recognize themselves" when political discourses are integrated with everyday practices (2000:117) or, as Hall contends, when "ideas ... connect with a particular constellation of social forces" (1996:43; emphasis in original). When the CCP came to power in China, it, too, sought to popularize a language of revolution that would act on the consciousness of the population by literally enacting divisions between the old society and the new (Dirlik, 1989). Although in eastern Hui'an this state discourse quickly became integrated into local ways of speaking, its impact on actual behavior and forms of identification was less apparent. Whereas Huidong residents learned to depict customs such as extended postmarital natal residence as backward and oppressive, they were less inclined to change those customs, despite heightened campaign rhetoric and increasingly intrusive state interventions. This emerging disjuncture between the discourse of state actors and local practice requires that we look more critically at the "project of rule" in high socialist China and ask how or, rather, whether rule was accomplished in the manner claimed in the writings and statements of early socialist officials (Li, 1999; see also Corrigan, 1994).

The discourse of cultural reform in Huidong centered around the derogatory signifier "feudal" (*fengjian*), a term applied to a range of pre-1949 social, political, and economic relationships and practices. Feudal constituted what Michael Schoenhals has called a "formulation" (*tifa*), a formalized element of discourse that was created and reproduced through the writings and pronouncements of state representatives with the goal of producing "consequential effects upon the feelings, thoughts, and actions of people" (1992:5). Like J. L. Austin's "perlocutionary acts," formulations "do things" through the effects of language, in principle creating change through language itself (1975:109). As a marker distinguishing the oppression of the old society from the liberating force of the new, feudal functioned as a powerful sign of what was to be struggled against and eradicated in the process of building a socialist society.

The term feudal was not new to post-1949 China nor did it derive its meaning solely from a Marxist stage theory of history. Centuries of indigenous debates over effective statecraft had weighed the merits of a feudal system of decentralized administration against the centralized bureaucracy long favored by China's imperial rulers (Min, 1989:89–136).[1] In the early twentieth century, feudal became associated with local forms of power that "threatened a new ideal of a national reunification under a strong central state" (Fitzgerald, 1996:160; see also Duara, 1995:158–60). By the late 1910s and 1920s, this sense of political "disunity" was gradually linked to cultural backwardness and under the influence of a Marxist theory of social evolution feudal was granted a place in a historical march toward modernity. Reformers of all stripes struggled to overthrow the feudal elements of the old society in order to create a strong, unified, modern nation-state (Fitzgerald, 1996:159–167).

The association of feudal with cultural backwardness was firmly fixed by the time the Communists came to power in 1949. Once qualified with the adjective, a particular custom was effectively connected to the oppressive past and, in keeping with the goal of revolutionizing Chinese society, set up for eradication. Mao himself had argued that awakening the individual from the stupor of feudalism was necessary to liberate the nation as a whole from the bonds of imperialism (Fitzgerald, 1996:93–94). Adopting the rhetoric of anti-feudal struggle, socialist reformers affirmed this dual goal: by liberating individuals from feudal practices and beliefs they would create the "awakened" socialist citizens necessary to make China into a strong socialist nation, free from the clutches of imperialist power and bourgeois ideology. The mass campaigns carried out in eastern Hui'an also affirmed the extent to which these feudal dispositions were perceived as written on and through gendered bodies. Creating liberated socialist subjects required working on the body and its intimate capacities; for Huidong women this meant reshaping not only their capacity to labor but also their physical appearance and their bonds with husbands, conjugal kin, and nonkin women.

Extended Natal Residence Marriage and the Nationalists' Rhetoric of Reform

Efforts to root out cultural backwardness in eastern Hui'an had begun even prior to the CCP's victory in 1949 with Nationalist government efforts to reform the practice of extended natal residence marriage (ENR). ENR likely came to the attention of Nationalist authorities because of its connection with underage marriage, a practice the government had long attacked as the source of a weakened Chinese race and nation.[2] After multiple requests from the provincial-level Social Affairs Bureau (*Shehui chu*), the Hui'an county government finally, in October 1943, submitted a set of "Procedures for Prohibiting Backward Marriage Customs" in the county.[3] The report outlined the specific practices to be eliminated by the government and the methods for doing so. Addressing the distinctive features of local marriage customs, it stated quite bluntly: "After marriage, women are absolutely forbidden from assuming extended natal residence. If [a married woman] must return to her natal home for special reasons, she cannot reside there for more than six days." Subsequent articles laid out explicit methods for monitoring this prohibition. Parents were ordered to report a married daughter's visit to the local headman. If a wife overstayed her six-day limit, the headman was empowered to act on behalf of the husband's family and urge or, if necessary, force her to return. The county government was required to send civil servants on periodic trips across the countryside to make household checks. If they discovered an improperly resident married woman, they had the power to arrest her and send her to the township government office for disciplining.

Additional articles addressed a further "evil" (*e xi*) of local society explicitly linked to the practice of ENR, the prevalence of collective suicides among young women. The county procedures required that parents observe specific housing arrangements when married daughters came to visit. Daughters were not "to stay overnight with other women so as to prevent the women from getting together and forming inappropriate thoughts [*jieban wei fei zhi niantou*]." A later article clarified these "inappropriate thoughts" as the intent to commit collective suicide by drowning. Without explaining the connection between ENR and collective suicide or providing any details on the frequency or nature of the latter, the procedures then called upon a number of local figures to take part in the now-joined battle against these two social ills. Police and ward officers were charged with destroying the goddess temples (*shen nü miao*) understood to foster a superstitious mentality among local women (which presumably encouraged suicide). The Women's Association was to assist in this task by spreading propaganda, rectifying women's lives and customs, and establishing literacy classes to advance female education. Granting an important role to civil servants and gentry families, the procedures called on these local elites to set an example for the rest of the population and threatened violators with severe punishment.

On paper at least, the county government appeared committed to eradicating the "backward custom" of ENR and its perceived, but unexplained, counterpart, collective suicide. Yet subsequent documents reveal that the fight against ENR continued to occupy the minds of provincial and even national bureaucrats, suggesting in fact that ENR had not been eradicated from the Hui'an countryside and that the perception of the practice as "backward" and "evil" had spread to higher levels of the bureaucracy. In a September 3, 1948 communication from the national Ministry of the Interior to the Fujian provincial government, the ministry noted that "according to reports, women in said province's Hui'an county return to their natal homes four days after their wedding and without the happy [occasion] of pregnancy must not move again to their husband's home."[4] It continued to explain, where prior documents had not, the mechanism through which ENR was understood to encourage suicide (although less clearly why it was collective in nature). Because most women "are mired in this backward custom [ENR] and cannot bear their spiritual suffering," they commit collective suicide by drowning.[5] The ministry added that this "backward custom" violated principles of humanity and undermined social order, requiring both urgent educational measures and stringent prohibition. The provincial government itself took action by including ENR in a series of customs prohibited in its 1948 document, "Detailed Regulations for Implementation Procedures to Prohibit Undesirable Customs Among the People."[6] These regulations charged police and township and local headmen with rigorously investigating cases in which married women observed the "evil custom" of remaining in their natal homes.

This series of government reform initiatives built on an earlier spate of campaigns and outcries by local intellectuals in eastern Hui'an. Inspired by the reformist ethos of the 1919 May Fourth Movement, these movements from the 1920s and early 1930s included ENR in attacks on a range of local customs, including women's elaborate sartorial and headpiece styles, marriage by purchase, gambling, opium smoking, superstition, extravagant weddings and funerals, and armed lineage feuds.[7] One author, writing in a Chongwu township magazine published by local intellectuals, described ENR and collective suicide as "evil habits" that were "nothing other than the behavior of a barbaric people" (YXGMM, 1934). This rhetoric identifying ENR with evil, backward customs aligned local intellectual interests with the reformist goals of government officials; at the same time, it also made many intellectuals into vehement critics of government inaction. By December 1948, Hui'an students at Xiamen University were openly attacking the county government's failure to enact viable reforms. One writer in the left-wing newspaper *Luoyang daobao*, published by the university's Hui'an native-place association, openly accused the county government and local elites of ignoring both the Ministry of the Interior's and the provincial government's orders to eliminate ENR and other "unhealthy" customs: "Our long-serving county magistrate, local gentry, and even Women's Association have, at the most, discussed [the problem of ENR], issued orders, or merely boasted in the newspaper. [We] have yet to see [them take] any real actions" (Zhi, 1949:9).

Nationalist bureaucrats and local intellectuals alike viewed ENR as a custom crying out for reform, and yet neither group succeeded in implementing its espoused program. In its most severe form, ENR was understood to encourage mass suicides among young women and to weaken patriarchal power in the family by undermining husbands' control over their wives. The rhetoric used against ENR identified it with a host of other backward practices that were seen to threaten China's ability to constitute itself as a modern nation-state with appropriately civilized, enlightened citizens. Although the rhetoric itself would change once the CCP came to power, the underlying goal of creating modern, productive, now socialist citizens out of the Huidong masses continued as state reformers directed their attention to eradicating the remnants of a despotic past.

Dressing for the New Nation

One of the first reforms propagated by the new communist government in eastern Hui'an focused on transforming women's headpieces, hairstyles, and sartorial patterns. Work teams and local cadres joined together in enacting the transition from the old society to the new through the bodies of village women, removing what they perceived as the corporeal vestiges of feudal oppression. Work team reports described Huidong women as literally weighed down by the burden of elaborate headpieces, shackled by heavy silver bracelets, and reluctant to sleep with their husbands for fear of disturbing intricate hairstyles. The costs required to maintain these styles also came under attack as the party began to promote ideals of thrift and industriousness.

Government documents espoused the need to educate women (and villagers in general) about the benefits of "changing dress" (gai zong) and eliminating wasteful ornamentation, and they called on cadres to teach women to associate sartorial reform with the wholesale elimination of the old society.[8] A 1952 work team report from the Dong Zhou base area in eastern Hui'an attacked the local custom of "combing up the hair" as a remnant of feudal ignorance and excessive consumption:

The education in ignorance [provided by] feudal society has made women believe that they cannot work like men, that they can only dress up for the benefit of others. During the period of Nationalist reactionary rule, women had already exchanged the long topknot for a short one. [Yet] up through Liberation, women still adorned themselves with trivial, heavy, and cumbersome silver ornaments. These silver ornaments require considerable sums [to purchase] and adornment requires much time. At the same time, this [practice] perpetuates an ignorant consciousness. Therefore, there was a period in the past when women were mobilized to change their attire, when women were made to carry out sartorial reform. But forceful methods were used [instead of] resolving the problem from [the level of] thought. Women still feel: "Men are men, women are women. Changing attire makes men and women indistinguishable. It won't do [*bu cheng yangzi*]." Thus women today continue to comb up their hair. Propaganda has yet to achieve effective results. This reveals the level of ignorance in the thinking and consciousness of women from this locale.⁹

In the villages of Chongwu township, reformers also identified extravagant adornment styles with extended natal residence marriage customs and restricted labor productivity. Shortly following Liberation, local officials initiated a campaign to eliminate the gin'a, a long, black headpiece extending out as far as one foot in front of the face, along with the intricate hairstyle and ornaments that accompanied it (see Fig. 7). There were two forms of the gin'a: an elaborate version and a simplified style for everyday wear. Women wore the elaborate gin'a on their wedding day, when participating in auspicious rituals, and when visiting as guests. They decorated it with silver flowers and a wide array of colorful ribbons and other ornaments. They combed their hair in an intricate bun that extended out from the back of the head, held in place by silver hairpins. The simpler form of the gin'a used fewer decorative ornaments and substituted bamboo hairpins for silver. It was worn by married women after they began to reside in their husbands' homes. Both styles also included a long piece of black cloth attached just above the forehead that could be let down to conceal the face (Chen and Shi, 1990:199–200).¹⁰

According to retired cadres in Chongwu, reformers attacked the gin'a on a number of fronts. They focused on the sheer weight of the headpiece and decorative ornaments (roughly 7 to 8 pounds) as well as the fact that married women refused to sleep with their husbands at night for fear of disturbing their elaborate hairstyle. One Shanlin cadre recalled, "[Women] had it so hard. They couldn't turn over [*fan shen*], [their lives were so] bitter. With Liberation, we wanted to change and eliminate this unreasonable system." The cadre's use of the expression "turn over" is pivotal here because it succinctly links two underlying premises of headpiece reform. In its more literal meaning, "turn over" refers to the fact that women could not physically turn over when lying in bed because of the elaborate headpiece. Elderly village women vividly described for me how, if they did lie down in bed with their husbands, they were forced to sleep sitting up against the headboard or on their side. Moreover, lying down easily disturbed the hairstyle and ornamentation, making a woman's immodest behavior (the fact that she had slept with her

FIG. 7: Middle-aged woman posing in the gin'a headpiece (photograph by Jiang Changyun; Chen and Shi, 1990: n.p.; reproduced by permission of the publisher)

husband) apparent to all. By eradicating the gin'a, the government sought to eliminate one of the many factors that encouraged women to avoid conjugal visits.[11]

The figurative meaning of "to turn over" is equally as evocative here. In the Communist's new language of revolution, turning over meant emancipation, literally the throwing off of the shackles of feudal society and the constructing of a new order built on equality, access to the means of production, scientific thought, and democratic politics (Hinton, 1966:vii). Turning over required eliminating the class oppression experienced by Chinese peasants as a whole and, in the case of eastern Hui'an, the gender oppression faced by women specifically. By eradicating "this unreasonable system" of female headpieces, newly established officials sought to liberate women from the general bitterness of feudalism and the specific bitterness of local adornment styles. Their efforts underscore significant gender differences in what were ostensibly mass movements to cultivate new socialist citizens, confirming Tina Chen's insight that "as a nodal point in the interplay between citizenship, the politics of nation-building, and gender-formation, clothing [and adornment more generally] participated in the creation of socialist citizens to populate the new nation" (2001:144).

The physical weight of the gin'a and the costly silver and gold ornaments favored by village women also drew criticism from the new government for other reasons. The Dong Zhou report emphasized that women believed they could not "work like men" and only "dressed up for the benefit of others," thereby intensifying the need to eliminate elaborate styles in order to promote women's active participation in productive labor. When interviewed in the mid-1990s, elderly Shanlin women stressed that the cumbersome size and sheer weight of the headpiece had made it extremely difficult to perform the tasks required of them as "proper" daughters-in-law (carrying heavy buckets of water from the well, cleaning, and laboring in the fields). Accordingly, by freeing married women from such an exacting style of adornment, cadres simultaneously sought to achieve two related goals: liberating women's labor power and encouraging their immediate conjugal residence upon marriage.[12]

Marriage Law Campaigns

Efforts to remake women's physical appearance were soon paired with marriage and family reforms directed more specifically at the region's distinctive marital practices. The 1950 Marriage Law was implemented in Hui'an through a series of campaigns that peaked from 1952 to 1953 and then subsided as rural collectivization moved to the forefront of state policy in the mid-1950s. In addition to attacking what were defined as the widespread ills of the feudal marriage system,[13] these campaigns quickly focused on the distinctive nature of local marriage customs, most notably the practice of extended natal residence. As early as September 15, 1950, a report from the county government to the province described in vivid detail the unusual marriage problems found in eastern Hui'an communities:

Only when fortune and luck have it that a woman becomes pregnant [and] is about to give birth will she return to her husband. If she has not given birth, then [she] will continue to follow the custom of extended natal residence until the great age of thirty- or forty-plus years. Only then will this evil phenomenon slowly be eliminated.[14]

Bemoaning this undesirable situation, the report's authors lamented the fate of men and women married for five or even six years who failed to recognize one another in public because they had spent so little time together.

This document, issued just months after the initial promulgation of the Marriage Law, outlined a framework for including ENR under the purview of Marriage Law implementation. It did not merely add ENR to the existing litany of feudal customs, but framed it as a particularly "backward," "awful," and even "evil" practice, one that required outright and immediate eradication. The report also raised the question of why such a custom had persisted over the ages, concluding: "This of course is the evil result of feudal power and women's continuous devaluation and oppression under Nationalist rule." By claiming for the new communist government the commitment to overturning such a practice, the authors of the report drew a clear line between what they decried as the oppressive, feudal society of the Nationalist era and the new society put in place by the Communists, simultaneously highlighting the socialist regime's implementation of policies that the Nationalists had addressed largely on paper. Marital-reform campaigns, by extension, would also demonstrate the regime's ability to carry out these efforts at a much more intimate level through intervening in residents' personal and familial desires surrounding conjugality.[15]

In 1952, the provincial court and provincial Women's Federation jointly sponsored a Marriage Law and judicial reform campaign in Hui'an county. The movement was first conducted in August 1952 in two base areas in the county, both of which practiced ENR. From mid-September to mid-October, it was extended to a total of seven districts, Chongwu being one of them.[16]

The various reports compiled from the 1952 movement vigorously attacked the feudal custom of ENR. The Dong Zhou base area draft report argued, "The retention of feudal customs exposes the barbaric rule and fetters that the old marriage system inflicts on youth, particularly on women. Extended natal residence is the concrete expression in this locale of the feudal marriage system's oppression and fettering of young men and women" (Dong Zhou, 1952). The report then went on to highlight the marital conflicts such customs produced:

The phenomenon of extended natal residence is widespread. Aside from married women who have already given birth or adopted daughters-in-law who reside virilocally, married women maintaining extended natal residence account for almost 100 percent of the marriages in the base. This is a result of feudal arranged marriages [which] create poor feelings among couples. When the rule of the husband's authority [*fuquan de tongzhi*][17] is added to this, it arouses women's hatred of men. Therefore, they give no heed to men's pulling and dragging, their beating and cursing, and refuse to return to their husbands' homes. (Dong Zhou, 1952)

According to this passage, a couple's lack of "feelings" (*ganqing*) for each other played a key role in women's reluctance to assume conjugal residence. A result of arranged matches and, as noted elsewhere in the report, a persistently young age at marriage, the absence of marital affection figured prominently in reformers' distinctions between backward feudal marriages and enlightened socialist ones. By advocating marital self-determination and mutual affection, Marriage Law campaigns emphasized the importance of *ganqing* in constituting a form of marriage radically different from that imposed by an oppressive feudal system.[18] As I discuss in greater detail in the next chapter, this emphasis on feelings would continue to shape young people's vision of ideal marriages well into the 1990s, even as the link between *ganqing* and socialist liberation grew increasingly attenuated.

Like headpiece styles, moreover, the problems posed by ENR were depicted as encompassing a wider set of issues than simply feudal thought and oppression. The Summary report for the 1952 movement raised further consequences of the "abnormal relations among men and women" produced by persistent ENR customs in the region. Because couples did not live together, it argued, they were unable to establish feelings for each other, producing strained marital relations that further undermined social order, health, and reproduction:

Men engage in wild visiting of prostitutes and gambling, breaking up families and scattering members. For instance, among the fishermen in the fifth district's Chongwu and the fourth district's Xiaozuo townships, over 10 percent go on wild visits to prostitutes because their wives maintain extended natal residence and they cannot live a happy life, [leading] to depression and loneliness. Because of this, they become infected with venereal disease, which seriously affects their own health and that of their descendants. (Summary, 1952; see also Lin, 1981:259)

In addition to causing social upheaval and damaging their husbands' reproductive health, women's refusal to shift residence was also depicted as having a deleterious effect on production and consumption. A 1953 report by the provincial Women's Federation quoted the men in Hui'an's Zhengdong administrative village as follows: "Before the home was not like a home. Therefore, [we] took our earnings and went whoring, gambling, drinking. If our wives return, we will willingly work ourselves to death."[19] Accounts of reunited couples repeatedly emphasized both parties' renewed commitment to productive labor and their more judicious use of household resources, and propaganda folk songs extolled the contributions of freely chosen marriages to a happy and productive family life (see also Glosser, 2003:191–193).

ENR further hampered women's labor participation by miring wives in competing family loyalties. The Summary report emphasized that nonresident wives faced a double burden because natal families sought to retain their daughters' labor power after marriage and conjugal families made labor demands on nonresident daughters-in-law. Another work team document from the 1952 movement lamented: "During the busy agricultural season, [nonresident married women's] natal family fields must be planted and they must also go to their husbands' homes to help out. Their waists ache and their backs are sore from exhaustion. In all there are no benefits in it for them."[20]

By suggesting that ENR created a problem of ambiguous loyalties for nonresident married women, these early reports provide a basis for understanding why later cadres responded so negatively to daughters-in-law who refused to contribute labor to their conjugal collectives prior to shifting residence. Official documents and propaganda reaffirmed the state's view that married women's "proper" obligation was to their husbands' families through such simple rhetorical conventions as using the verb "to return" when referring to a wife's shift to marital coresidence. One returns to a place to which one belongs, therefore use of the phrase "to return to the husband's home" (*hui fujia*) implied that married women belonged in their husbands' homes, not with their natal families. "Women, Return to Your Husbands' Homes" (*Funü hui fujia*), a propaganda folk song from the marriage reforms of the 1950s, made this point explicitly by adopting the voice of a married woman enlightened by socialist campaigns. The first two verses are as follows:

I advise us women that we must put all in order[21]
Each one of us must understand,
Extended natal residence has no base
The husband's home is our base area [*genjudi*].

I advise us sisters to recognize clearly
Returning to [our] husbands' homes is glorious
We must aid and respect one another
To build feelings between husband and wife.

This song urged wives to reside with their husbands in order to build happy, productive families. In official documents, state reformers reaffirmed the goals conveyed through this song by portraying in great detail the deleterious consequences of wives' continued natal residence, specifically as it affected family unity, reproduction, and, most importantly, productive labor. From reformers' perspective, married women often refused to contribute labor where they should (to their conjugal families), and their continued absence purportedly forced their husbands into dissolute habits. By quoting rural men's discontent with ENR customs, the party simultaneously reconfirmed its commitment to poor peasant men even while, as in this folk song, it advocated conjugal residence as a means of liberating women from feudal oppression.

Collective Female Suicide

The third focus of CCP reforms during the first half of the 1950s was the problem of unusually high female suicide rates in eastern Hui'an, a problem exacerbated by the collective nature of many suicides, which involved anywhere from two to five or six young women at a time. Throughout Chinese history, suicide has been one of the few acts available to women to escape unhappy or oppressive marriage and family situations (Wolf, 1975). Collective suicides have been much less common in China than individual deaths, however, except for the areas of the Pearl River Delta where delayed transfer marriage and sisterhoods prevailed (Sankar, 1978:43–48; Stockard, 1989:118–121).[22] In the early 1950s, female suicide rates rose across the country as Marriage Law implementation came into conflict with traditional gender roles and patrilineal family ideals. In Hui'an, the prior existence of high collective suicide rates encouraged reformers to identify female suicide itself as a problem to be eradicated through Marriage Law campaigns.

The Nationalist-era county proposal for eliminating ENR linked it directly to collective female suicide but lacked a detailed discussion of the specific causes for the collective aspect. The proposal merely hinted at the role of close, same-sex relationships among women (dui pnua ties). Post-1949 documents make this connection more explicit. The 1950 report from the county to the provincial government highlighted the critical role of dui pnua in deterring women from visiting their husbands or assuming joint residence:

When a woman returns to her natal home after marriage, her intimate, bosom sisters [dui pnua] will come to grill her and hold a tête-à-tête, asking all manner of questions. If a woman remains at her husband's home for a few extra days, she will be ridiculed and mocked by these bosom sisters: "Now that you have a husband, [you've] forgotten [us] and reject [your] own natal family." Therefore, although some women are willing to live with their husbands, they fear that people will criticize and mock them, and thus they are ashamed to move to their husband's home. (Report, 1950)

This emphasis on "feudal chastity," work team reports concluded, created an abnormal social environment in which "women place a greater weight on sisterly feelings [*jiemei qing*] and view good relations with their husbands as shameful" (Disbanding, 1952; see also Lin, 1981:256, 258–259; Lin and Lin, 1992:248–249). Dui pnua ostensibly drew young women away from their proper orientation to conjugal families and reproductive (as well as productive) labor, in part through reinforcing the value of same-sex intimacies over heterosexual unions.

How did this situation lead women to commit collective suicide? According to official documents, high suicide rates resulted from a combination of feudal ideology, oppressive marital conditions (intensified by a norm of ENR), and a strong sense of obligation to fellow dui pnua. A 1953 provincial report argued that "Hui'an women use suicide as the 'most glorious' and 'most moral' way of opposing the feudal marriage system."[23] Because of a "superstitious" belief in a better life after death, reformers contended, women viewed suicide as a more desirable option than persistent suffering in this world (see also the folk song "The Twelve Miseries" in the Appendix). These ideological and material pressures, so report authors argued, were exacerbated by close dui pnua ties that encouraged collective suicides. Reports often included sample scenarios to explain this connection. A woman ridiculed by her fellow dui pnua for displaying "good feelings" for her husband might suggest collective suicide as a means of reaffirming her commitment to her dui pnua. Or, a woman unhappy with her own marital or family situation might appeal to fellow dui pnua to join her in committing suicide. In some cases, a particular suicide was attributed to a "suicide wave" spreading through a community. It was precisely this kind of direct or indirect pressure from same-sex peers, government and work team reports suggested, that encouraged collective female suicide in Hui'an.

The collective nature of female suicide provoked attention and concern across the socialist bureaucracy. Charts listing suicides and their causes represent a veritable palimpsest of official reactions to female suicide, with the various written responses added by different readers offering a glimpse into the concerns of 1950s' officialdom. Readers repeatedly underlined the phrase "collective suicide" (*jiti zisha*) when it appeared in specific entries or jotted down the character "collective" (*ji*) in the margins. The explanations for collective suicides frequently attributed them to the presence of "feudal sisterly affection" (*fengjian jiemei qingyi*) among the participants, assigning impetus for the suicide act to one member in particular (although not always to the same individual in different recordings of the same incident).[24] In this manner, both the documents and the marks left by their readers blamed dui pnua ties for exacerbating an already oppressive marital and familial environment and for encouraging multiple deaths among young women.

If we place CCP concern with collective female suicide in the context of attacks on ENR, we can discern other reasons why its collective nature might have preoccupied both local and higher-level officials. On the one hand, these deaths (like ENR and cumbersome headpieces) deprived the region of a major source of labor power: as one report asserted, "these young and vigorous women provide effective strength for the front line of production. Their deaths, in wave after wave, cause incalculable damage to society's productive force and a loss of national wealth" (Disbanding, 1952). On the other hand, as I argue in Chapter 4, collective suicides reaffirmed young women's primary commitment to nonkin women of their generation as opposed to spouses or to natal and conjugal kin. These same-sex commitments—emotionally intense but reproductively moribund—reinforced local norms of chastity that encouraged women to delay (and sometimes avoid altogether) consummating heterosexual unions. CCP attacks on ENR revealed how the state had struggled to balance its commitment to women's liberation with equally compelling support for rural men and patrilineal families. Like ENR, collective female suicide (and the dui pnua bonds it affirmed) undermined familial control, in this case by depriving conjugal families of hard-won wives and further offspring and natal families of filial respect and material support. Draping itself in a mantle of what was undoubtedly sincere humanitarian concern, the party sought both to prevent young women from taking their own lives and to stabilize families and reinforce patrilineal imperatives.

Implementing the Reforms

The rhetoric of the documents quoted above and those like them reveals a party-state dedicated, at least on paper, to overturning what it perceived as some of the worst abuses of the old system. In practice, state actors deployed a wide array of methods and new institutions as they began to enact reforms. By defining the persistence of local headpiece and sartorial styles, marriage customs, and female suicide as problems of feudal thought, reformers committed themselves to a program of rule rooted in education and enlightenment. In cases such as headpiece reform, they combined this program with more forceful methods that achieved results but at a cost.

Three newly established institutions in village society worked together to transmit the language and program of socialist reform to the larger population and to cultivate an enlightened group of women who would lead the way in enacting reformed practices. As early as 1951, Shanlin's new communist government established a nightly women's class (hulu ban) to improve literacy rates and transmit political propaganda. By 1952 and 1953, the class had grown into a full-scale People's School (bbin hao) composed of several sections and upwards of one hundred students, virtually all of them women.[25] Although the school focused primarily on literacy, it also taught mathematics and accounting, agricultural skills, sanitation, music, and politics. According to Tiamzai, an elderly Shanlin man who had taught in the People's School for many years, these last two courses met twice a week and constituted an important avenue for ideological training in the benefits of new reforms. Teachers in the politics class instructed students about destroying the old customs and initiating the new, focusing in particular on reforming dress and headpiece styles and encouraging married women to reside with their husbands. The music class solidified these efforts by teaching folk songs imbued with strong propagandistic messages.

Among a mostly illiterate female population, folk songs vividly conveyed the new ideas of social reform in a manner accessible to a large sector of the community. Eastern Hui'an had a rich tradition of folk songs, including the popular "bitterness songs" (koo gua) sung by women that served as a precursor to the "speak bitterness" narratives introduced by the socialist regime. In keeping with Mao's position that propaganda "should make use of local dialects and should be put into words that local people without a high level of education could understand" (Holm, 1984:6–7), local cadres and work team members adapted many of these songs to fit the ideological needs of the times, preserving their melody and basic structure while infusing them with new political content.[26] Both reworked and newly composed songs were taught in a range of forums, from formal schools to mass meetings. They were sung aloud by village cadres, militiawomen, and Youth League members, some of whom recalled using megaphones to project their voices from village rooftops. The more than seventy songs that I collected in Shanlin utilize a number of different themes and musical styles. They employ mnemonic devices based on tropes like the months of the year, the days of the holiday season, or numbered progressions, all reinforced by the use of rhyme and repetitive phrasing. Their content reflects issues prominent in the 1950s and 1960s, such as encouraging marital and family reform, decrying the harmful effects of the gin'a, promoting collective labor, and advocating support for Taiwan's reunification and opposition to U.S. imperialism.

The new People's Militia (bbin bing) served as another institution for conveying CCP propaganda on current reform movements. Young women activists joined the militia and participated in nightly village rounds and even defense exercises along the coast. As part of their duties, female militia members were required to attend the People's School. By participating in the militia and the school, young women were exposed to the party's reformist messages and were expected to pass them on to the people. Women who displayed an exemplary record in school and militia duties were selected to join the village (and later brigade) government and the Women's Representative Committee. Those who demonstrated good leadership skills were encouraged to join the Youth League and party. Women cadres represented the final link in the propaganda chain. They both mobilized women to follow the dictates of reform campaigns and served as models for other village residents.

How did state reformers make use of these new institutions in implementing reform programs? In the case of headpiece reform, the Shanlin village government deployed a combined strategy of thought education and forceful intervention, an integrated approach that the Dong Zhou base report lamented was missing in reform efforts conducted in that area. Cadres used women's classes to convey the message that removing the gin'a was essential to women's liberation and their full participation in productive labor. Sutgoo, a Shanlin resident in her mid-seventies, recited for me a propaganda folk song taught to village women at the height of the anti-gin'a campaign:

> The People's Government is really something
> No longer do we comb up our hair but wear it in a bun
> With our gin'a removed, we are free and easy
> With flowers in our hair, oh so pretty.[27]

FIG. 8: An elderly woman wearing the hairstyle and hair ornaments similar to those adopted after the gin'a was banned (photograph by the author, 1995)

Other women and men recounted songs that reaffirmed the need to change local adornment styles so as to conform sartorially to the expectations of a new era. These propaganda messages sought to instill in this generation a commitment to overturning the old society through casting off forms of bodily adornment depicted as awkward, unattractive, and ultimately oppressive.

Reformers combined this educational approach with direct intervention in women's lives, forcibly stripping the gin'a from the heads of those who continued to wear it. According to a former Shanlin official who had helped organize the first campaign in 1951, local cadres posted sentries at the major intersections leading in and out of the village. If a woman from another village tried to enter Shanlin wearing the gin'a, the sentries would remove it from her head before allowing her to enter. Similarly, Shanlin women were prevented from leaving the village wearing the gin'a. This method effectively reached the sectors of the female population most likely to wear the headpiece: married, but nonresident, wives off to visit their husbands in other villages and all married women who set out to visit other villages or participate in auspicious rituals. Many an elderly Shanlin woman described for me how the government liter-

88   FASHIONING LIBERATED SOCIALIST SUBJECTS

FIG. 9: Woman in her thirties wearing the hoegin and lueh'a (photograph by the author, 1996)

ally "tore" (tiah) the gin'a off women's heads and forced them to cut their hair and wear it in the simple bun described in the folk song above (see Fig. 8). They also recalled the backlash produced by these forceful measures, as some women resorted to suicide rather than removing their headpieces, too ashamed to expose their faces and heads outside of their natal communities.

In general, this combination of thought education with direct intervention achieved rapid and dramatic effects. Within several years the CCP had effectively banned the gin'a in Shanlin, and village women gradually replaced it with the much simpler hoegin, the headscarf and headpiece frame worn into the 1990s, and the lueh'a, a broad-rimmed bamboo hat painted a bright yellow with contrasting accents (see Fig. 9). And yet subsequent sartorial reforms were less successful in producing lasting changes. Beginning with the Great Leap Forward and the establishment of the commune system in the late 1950s, the government used work points to regulate other features of women's dress. Young women were encouraged to adopt trousers in place of low-waisted, loose, cropped pants; by the 1960s the commune even dispatched teams of seamstresses to sew these trousers in the villages (Wang, 2002:30). Women were also urged to cut their hair and wear it in braids, donning army caps instead of the hoegin. Those who refused to change their attire or hairstyle were not permitted to attend meetings and demonstrations in the commune center, activities for which villagers received work points if they participated. By barring women who failed to conform sartorially, the commune manipulated the work point system to fulfill noneconomic goals. Village women who had participated in such activities recalled that in those days the government "controlled us through work points." At the same time, however, they admitted to frequently ignoring sartorial demands, simply changing back to their old style of dress once they returned to the village (Wang, 2002:30). Well into the 1990s, women of this generation continued to wear distinctive forms of local attire, including the hoegin and low-waisted, loose, cropped pants.

The government adopted an even broader approach to marital reforms, one that focused on educating cadres as well as the masses. Cadre meetings were held at all levels to transmit the principles of the Marriage Law and to help cadres overturn their own established ways of thinking and acting. A series of meetings for the masses were also held, directed specifically at women, the elderly, and youths (Summary, 1952). In these gatherings, cadres sought to teach people to distinguish the feudal marriage system from the new socialist order and to give voice to the suffering they had experienced in the oppressive marriages of the past. Older villagers were to be shown "that it was reasonable to call on their daughters to go to their husbands' homes and to have their daughters-in-law return" (Dong Zhou, 1952).

In order to extend the scope of the movement to reach those women without the time to attend such gatherings or classes at the People's School, village cadres organized propaganda teams that traveled around the community performing plays and singing folk songs. In Shanlin, groups of cadres and militiamen and -women were assigned to different sectors of the village where they would hold meetings with household members to teach them about the "evils of the feudal marriage system" and encourage them to adopt new, reformed marriage customs. Soelu, a former head of the Shanlin women's militia, recalled that the Marriage Law Movement "began with propaganda. Afterward, the work was taken up by the militia." The People's Schools, People's Militia, and local cadres worked in concert to transmit the message of reform to the people. In the words of one retired female cadre in Shanlin, propaganda troupes went to "release those who had been fettered" by the old society.[28]

Villages and townships throughout the county designed their own initiatives to encourage married women to cohabit with their husbands. Many locales relied on women cadres to lead the way in setting an example for the masses. A Ggin, who had served as the chair of the Shanlin Women's Representative Committee and the head of the women's militia in the early 1950s, confirmed this approach: "Women cadres were more advanced, their level was higher. [When] they weren't working they resided at their husbands' homes, occasionally visiting their natal families." The 1952 Summary report further noted that women cadres often took responsibility for mobilizing other women to live with their husbands. It cited the example of Hu Zhu administrative village in today's Tuzhai township where the women's representatives took the name list of the entire administrative village and divided it up among themselves, taking the initiative to urge all nonresident wives to shift residence (Summary, 1952).

As part of this high tide of activism, administrative villages engaged in mass send-offs and receptions for women who had agreed to live with their husbands. Based on statistics from 6 districts and 75 administrative villages in the county, the Summary report claimed that 6,884 of the 7,846 women who maintained extended natal residence pledged to return to their husbands' homes during the 1952 campaign. The administrative villages put on plays, showed slides, and held drum performances to send off their daughters and welcome their daughters-in-law.

Yet not all accounts depicted such a rosy picture of successful reform. Retired women cadres in Shanlin recalled that it was often difficult to convince villagers to accept the ideas presented in marriage-reform propaganda, young women usually being the most resistant. A folk song from the 1950s written by an unknown Shanlin resident vividly depicts the conflicts that took place between those who espoused the propaganda of the new order and those who continued to hold fast to the old ways. The antiphonal song began with a man's stanza:

> [I] advise our women that they must owe a debt [live with their husbands, contribute labor to their conjugal families, bear children]
> Now with Liberation [they should] change their headpiece
> If they come [to their husbands' homes], none of that feudal style
> The neighbors near and far will talk.

In response to these demands, all of which supported the local sartorial and marriage reforms of the early 1950s, the woman responded:

> [I] advise you, good sir, not to mention [this] again
> Our persons are free at this young age
> Our customs are all this style
> It's not that we don't owe a debt.[29]

Refusing to accept the demands of the new era, the female interlocutor presented postmarital natal residence as an accepted local practice, one that had persisted over time and would continue despite the Communists' reform efforts. Officials were certainly aware of the obstacles they faced in trying to change such customs, and documents from the period are replete with admissions of failed attempts or limited results. As early as 1952, the Summary report acknowledged the need to safeguard women's residence shift by creating favorable living conditions for new daughters-in-law once they moved to their conjugal homes. It called on local cadres to organize discussion groups in which women who had pledged to shift residence could voice their fears and concerns.[30] Exhorting cadres to arouse the masses and throw off the bonds of "feudal thinking," the report also reminded cadres that they would have to alleviate women's fears in order to achieve campaign goals.

Cadres faced considerable pressure to eradicate ENR in large part because of its perceived contribution to high female suicide rates. Work teams across the county struggled to break up groups of young women who had made pacts to commit suicide together. Reports described the signs that cadres and work team members were to look for as they sought to determine whether a group of women planned to take their own lives and offered guidelines for how work teams were to infiltrate such groups and transform their thinking (see Disbanding, 1952). They repeatedly cited the number of suicide groups successfully disbanded and the number of women saved from premature death. Yet such documents simultaneously included figures on recent suicides, demonstrating the persistence of the problem despite work teams' concerted efforts to put an end to female suicides. By 1957, provincial reports claimed that suicides resulting from marital problems had declined across the province, returning to pre–Marriage Law levels by 1956.[31] A 1957 report from the Hui'an Democratic Women's Federation, however, noted the continued presence of collective suicide groups in the county and documented at least 82 cases of female suicide county-wide for the first half of the year alone.[32] Despite work team interventions, therefore, female suicide clearly remained a serious problem in Hui'an, a persistent sign that CCP campaigns to liberate women had achieved only mixed results.

By 1953, Marriage Law implementation nationwide had taken a conservative turn, and cadres were urged to retreat from the more aggressive methods some had employed in previous campaigns. As Kay Ann Johnson argues in her study of the Marriage Law, "The goals of the [1953] campaign had become essentially informational, trying to eradicate popular fears and misconceptions about the Marriage Law while making the new legal rights of women and youth better known to them and better enforced by the courts and local cadres when people sought to use them" (1983:145). In Hui'an, a Marriage Law Implementation Month conducted in March of that year focused renewed attention on education and thought work as work teams sought to eliminate the concerns and misunderstandings they argued had arisen in the course of the 1952 social-reform movement.[33] They directed their efforts toward educating the masses in the principles of the law and showing them that the Marriage Law was not intended to force couples to divorce or wives to live with their husbands. According to one report:

In Song Lin administrative village, during the half month of social reform last year [1952] 26 couples divorced, creating a harmful influence. [The masses] thought that if [reform] came again there would be [widespread] divorce. . . . Women who maintained extended natal residence feared that this time they would be forced back to their husbands' homes. . . . Several women . . . ran away to hide in the mountains or in relatives' homes. (Basic Summary, 1953)

Under the influence of this final campaign to implement the Marriage Law, cadres backed away from the more interventionist methods adopted in previous campaigns, shifting primarily to an educational course of action. Although this approach aspired to consolidate the principles enshrined in the law, it also meant that many of the underlying conditions supporting local marriage customs would remain in place and in some cases they were strengthened by the collectivization campaigns that were to follow.

How Effective Were the Reforms?

One of the major obstacles to successful reform was the cyclical nature of the campaigns themselves. As many Shanlin villagers who lived through the 1950s and 1960s argued, the movements came in waves, one high tide followed by another. The ebb and flow of state interventions encouraged young women and their elders to ignore or only minimally comply with cadre and work team demands with the knowledge that once a campaign ended, life would return to normal. Tania Li has described similar reactions to state development programs in Indonesia as the product of "an intimate, sometimes cynical knowledge of the limits of state capacity to deliver on promises" (1999:316; see also Herzfeld, 1997). A corresponding familiarity with socialist reform campaigns drew Huidong residents into an emerging national community organized around the rhythms of official propaganda and mass movements, while their repeated experience of campaign limits simultaneously inspired skepticism toward the very policies designed to produce that national body. As a result, basic elements of the traditional marriage system in eastern Hui'an remained in place, although there were widespread propaganda statements to the contrary.

Understanding this contradictory outcome requires that we look more closely at the impact of the Marriage Law itself. Feminist scholarship on the Marriage Law has been divided between studies that conclude that the law ultimately shored up the patrilineal family and patriarchal privileges (Croll, 1981; Johnson, 1983; Stacey, 1983) and those that find women—especially peasants and members of the urban working classes—taking advantage of the new liberties enshrined in the law and divorcing in high numbers (Diamant, 2000). As seen in the example of A Di and her husband discussed in the previous chapter, some men and women in eastern Hui'an certainly benefited from the more liberal attitudes toward divorce advanced by Marriage Law campaigns, at least during the 1950s. Yet not all elements of the feudal marriage system were so readily overturned. As I document in the next chapter, Shanlin youths married at relatively young ages throughout the Mao era, although the period prior to the Cultural Revolution witnessed later marriages than the decades that followed, more likely as a result of poverty than effective state enforcement. More importantly, parents and matchmakers continued to arrange marriages, granting young people very little say in their marital futures. At most, women and men were shown a picture of their future spouse or were allowed a quick glimpse of the other person and then granted a nominal right to refuse the match based on his or her appearance. Many Shanlin residents who married after 1949 claimed that the Marriage Law's emphasis on marital freedom and self-determination had little impact on local practice other than the brief wave of divorces in the 1950s. Young people's ability to meet and choose their own spouses was further hampered by persistent prohibitions on same-surname marriage, which, when coupled with a norm of patrilocal residence, forced most women to marry out of their natal villages into communities populated by other surnames. Only a few youths married within Shanlin prior to the 1980s, and it was the rare individual who freely selected his or her own spouse.

All of these factors—underage, arranged, surname-exogamous, and patrilocal marriages—supported the continued practice of ENR customs within the region by creating conditions that made women unwilling to reside with their conjugal families. This situation was further exacerbated by general cadre reluctance to implement the Marriage Law, a problem repeatedly criticized in government documents and work team reports throughout the early 1950s.[34] Thus not only did cadres fail to eradicate the feudal practice of ENR, but they were unable to change many of the underlying conditions that supported ENR and made it appealing to young women. For those women who had developed "feelings" for their husbands, the inability (or unwillingness) of cadres and work teams to alter the general environment of dui pnua and societal disapproval left such women with little opportunity to live with their spouses prior to childbirth.

As Marriage Law implementation gave way to collectivization campaigns, new pressures emerged that also worked against effective marital reform. Collectivization often reinforced traditional patrilineal kinship structures and patrilocal residence patterns in the countryside, limiting the scope of marital change originally envisioned by the CCP (Croll, 1981:187; Diamond, 1975). The particular gender divisions of labor in eastern Hui'an that I described in the previous chapter intensified these conflicts, pitting new marriage ideals against efforts to collectivize the economy. Both agricultural collectivization and the extended length of fishing expeditions and public labor assignments diminished the number of occasions on which young wives would or could visit their husbands. These economic changes in turn perpetuated local marital practices and, in some cases, further lengthened periods of postmarital separation.

At the height of the Great Leap Forward in 1959, a young man from the joint Shanlin-Haibin cooperative wrote a letter to the Hui'an County Women's Federation protesting some of the marital problems that had arisen with collectivization. He raised two objections:

1. In the old period, upon reaching the busy agricultural season women who had married out would return to their husbands' homes to help out. Now that the cooperative has been established, [women] say that these fields belong to the state [*shi gong jia de*] and [they] don't come.

2. Nowadays we male youths frequently change fishing grounds. We go for over a year, and women frequently go to the reservoirs to perform labor. There are few days for both parties to meet. Added to this, women rarely come to their husbands' homes. In one year they come less than twenty days. This means some youths are unable to establish feelings [for one another] even though they have been married for five or six years. It means both parties bear the burden of very large thought problems. We bear great resentment against changing fishing grounds.[35]

This letter succinctly summarizes two of the ways that collectivization encouraged and even strengthened existing ENR practice. Collectivization of the fields meant that nonresident married women no longer felt obligated to contribute labor to their husbands' families during the busy agricultural season as they had when plots were farmed by individual families, and as a result there were fewer occasions on which wives felt compelled to visit their husbands. Furthermore, under the commune system both young men and women were sent out of their villages to work for extended periods, thereby limiting the amount of time that both spouses would actually be resident and available to visit with each other.

The letter writer frames the intensification of ENR practice as both a practical issue (collective ownership of fields, labor assignments outside of the village) and a persistent ideological problem. He continues his critique by asking the Women's Federation the following: "Comrades, why is it that under the leadership of the current People's Government the existing problems are of a greater scale than during the old period?" Stepping back from overt criticism of government policy, he adds, "The Great Leap Forward of our motherland is correct. [But] young people also want a little optimism. Only [in this manner] will this thought problem not exist for youths." One senses that the young man's continued references to thought problems merely soften his otherwise scathing critique of collectivization policies. By drawing attention to the contradictions that had emerged between economic and marital policies, he showed quite clearly that marriage reform had taken a backseat to collectivization efforts. Rather than eliminating ENR, the commitment to collectivization had further entrenched women's refusal to contribute labor to their husbands' families and had set up additional obstacles to a couple's ability to develop marital "feelings."

Controlling Women's Labor

Collective organization of labor need not always undermine marital reform, however, as we saw in the case of Siulan, Ggimlan's older sister, who was forced to move to her husband's village in order to labor in collective fields and receive her state-allocated grain ration. By the time of a renewed campaign in the 1960s to encourage Huidong women to reside with their husbands, cadres had begun to make use of their control over women's labor, residence registration, and grain rations to enforce postmarital conjugal residence. The "Women, Return to Your Husbands' Homes" (*Funü hui fujia*) campaign took place under the auspices of the nationwide Socialist Education Movement (1962–1966), which was designed to rectify "unhealthy tendencies" that had emerged in the countryside during the years following the disastrous Great Leap Forward (Baum and Teiwes, 1968:12; Meisner, 1986:289). In keeping with Socialist Education goals of consolidating the collective economy and promoting production, the "Women, Return" campaign devoted considerable effort to facilitating newly resident wives' participation in collective production in their conjugal villages.

The campaign began in 1964 with teams of local cadres, female Youth League members, and militiawomen fanning out across the Chongwu commune. Their mission was to track down young wives who had yet to reside with their husbands' families and encourage them to assume conjugal residence. Also referred to by Shanlin villagers as the movement to "Transform established habits and social customs" (*Yi feng yi su*) and as part of the campaign to "Destroy the four olds, establish the four news" (*Po si jiu li si xin*), this reform effort mobilized the socialist institutions employed in earlier Marriage Law campaigns. This time, however, movement leaders placed greater emphasis on insuring that married women remained in their conjugal homes. As authors of the 1966 summary report by the Woman-Work team of the Hui'an Socialist Education Working Group argued:

Sending married women back to their husbands' homes is not the conclusion of the work. It is the beginning of the even more difficult task of consolidation. Some women return to their husbands' homes and stay two or three nights as expected, then run back to their natal homes. Some wander all over, influencing the leadership's centralized fulfillment of collective production.... Each brigade ... [should] set up a small leadership group to consolidate the return to the husband's home, earnestly strengthening leadership.[36]

Many of the middle-aged women I interviewed in Shanlin had themselves been either targets of this campaign or activists in promoting conjugal residence. They described in great detail the steps taken to guarantee married women's continued residence in Shanlin. Bbilei was in her teens when the movement began. As a member of her production team's Youth League, she was dispatched to summon nonresident daughters-in-law from other villages. Bbilei described how when the women arrived in Shanlin, they refused to eat, sleep, or even speak. Brigade cadres organized nightly study classes for newly arrived wives in order to educate them about socialism and the benefits of coresidence with their husbands. The classes conveyed the message that living with one's husband was part of the spirit of "cultural revolution" necessary to destroy the "four olds" and to bring an end to feudalism more generally (Woman-Work, 1966). More importantly, attendance was taken at each session and those who missed classes were immediately investigated by the brigade. In this manner, the meetings not only provided key ideological education but also enabled cadres to monitor the residence patterns of village daughters-in-law.[37]

Village women who participated in the movement also emphasized that the brigade arranged work for newly resident wives. They were assigned to harvest seaweed, dye sails, braid fishing lines, transport stones, and collect firewood on the mountainside. The brigade set up rice noodle factories to employ young wives and inducted a select few into the brigade militia. According to Soelu, then a prominent female cadre, "only [by our arranging work] would they stay. [We] began with the collective, [and the wives] slowly got used to it."

The collective economy enabled local cadres to organize work for these new village members as part of facilitating their integration into the community. Thus no longer was women's labor viewed as a latent force to be freed through social reform and ideological education, but as in Siulan's case it served as a means to encourage young women's permanent settlement in their conjugal villages. With this goal in mind, the brigade also arranged collective meals so as to prevent daughters-in-law from refusing to eat in their conjugal homes. Through a combination of work and study activities, cadres insured that women only had to return home to sleep.[38] As one former activist phrased it, newly resident wives could now "reside at their conjugal homes with their minds at rest."

This renewed emphasis on consolidating married women's residence in their husbands' homes raises several intriguing questions about what interests state reformers had in promoting conjugal coresidence in eastern Hui'an, particularly at a time when urban couples might be assigned to work units in different cities and parts of the country. The goals of creating stable family relationships and providing peasant men with sexual access to their wives continued from the earlier era of Marriage Law implementation. It was the institution of the collective economy, however, that both required and facilitated further state intervention in Huidong marriages. Neil Diamant (2000:255) argues that across China cadres found it difficult to manage married women's movement between their natal and conjugal homes because such unstable residence patterns disrupted the distribution of work points and grain rations. Although Huidong collectives had access to married women's labor when they were resident in their natal villages, the possibility that such women might leave at any time also undermined cadres' control over a reliable labor force. At issue was not labor productivity per se; rather, the "Women, Return" campaign reflects a more compelling concern with controlling labor. The party expected that a married woman direct her labor toward her conjugal family and community (recall the discussion above on government documents' use of the verb "to return"), and when local marriage practice contravened such expectations reform campaigns adopted measures that made use of collective control over labor, residence, and grain rations in order to undermine those customs. In short, the collectivized economy at once increased the need for state access to women's labor and strengthened cadres' ability to enforce women's conjugal residence through controlling their labor.

Villagers' evaluations of the campaign's success ranged from positive appraisals, claiming that virtually all of the women encouraged to return during this period eventually bore children and settled with their husbands, to more critical accounts documenting resistance to joint residence and wives' rapid return to their natal homes once the campaign ended. Soehua, herself an object of campaign mobilization efforts, represents the second category. Soehua married into Shanlin from a village on the far side of the commune in 1965 at the height of the movement. She was seventeen years old at the time. As we sat on her balcony 30 years later discussing this momentous campaign, Soehua described how once she married, members of the Shanlin Youth League and its party branch secretary came to urge her to shift residence. She recalled that all of the nonresident wives in her natal village were quite young at the time and did not want to move. Although they were instructed to sleep at their husbands' homes, Soehua claimed that many women snuck off to the homes of other kin in the village. If they had no relatives of their own, they avoided staying with their husbands by spending the night at a dui pnua's relative's house. Soehua recounted the various kinds of work the brigade arranged for new daughters-in-law such as herself to tie them to their conjugal village. Yet at the same time she noted that when nightly study meetings tapered off, she and other young wives abandoned their work responsibilities and returned to their natal villages.[39] None of them, she asserted, wanted to live with their husbands' families: "We didn't accept [the idea of residence shift]. At seventeen years old, we mostly didn't come." In-laws were required to report on whether their daughters-in-law had in fact resided with them. If a wife refused to move, Soehua recalled, the brigade wrote a big character poster stating that she had opposed the policy and failed to return to her husband's home. They posted one on the door of her natal home and one at her conjugal home. Soehua downplayed the effectiveness of such measures, however, asserting that "everyone saw it as, well, not mattering at all. [They] didn't pay attention to it." By contrast, other village women recalled how Shanlin cadres went in search of wives who had fled back to their natal homes, sometimes forcing them to return to Shanlin in the middle of the night.

Like many of the Shanlin residents I interviewed about the campaign, Soehua argued that a majority of the new wives mobilized to shift residence simply returned to their natal families after the campaign if they had not yet become pregnant. Soehua herself did not move permanently to Shanlin until she gave birth to her first child in 1971. Another female Youth League participant recalled that when she married in 1967, she continued to reside in her natal home, the campaign having ended by that time due to the onset of the Cultural Revolution. In sum, the recollections of village women and retired cadres reveal a mixed picture of campaign success: although some wives did settle in Shanlin as a result of the campaign, it is likely that equal numbers returned to their natal villages at the earliest opportunity. Perhaps if the Cultural Revolution had not produced such upheavals in local governance, the campaign would have continued and joint residence would slowly have become part of village practice. Instead, ENR remained the norm in Shanlin and the other villages of eastern Hui'an throughout the Cultural Revolution decade and into the post-Mao era. As an elderly Shanlin woman proclaimed to me quite definitively in 1996: "[Coming to one's husband's home] without having yet given birth is called coming [as part of] 'transforming established habits and social customs.' [Coming] after giving birth is called coming [because one] should."[40]

Conclusion

What are we to make of these repeated state efforts to reform sartorial practices, marriages, and dui pnua relationships in eastern Hui'an? As the statement quoted above from an elderly Shanlin woman reveals, villagers quickly absorbed the language of reform conveyed by state actors, new socialist institutions, and local activists. As late as the 1990s, retired cadres and members of the masses alike reproduced this language in their daily speech and in their recollections of the Maoist era, describing local marriage customs, dress styles, and female suicide as "bad," "feudal," "superstitious," or "unscientific," and women's thinking as "fettered" or "shackled" and therefore in need of "liberation."[41] Yet again, as the foregoing quotation nicely demonstrates, the adoption of this language did not necessarily translate into changes in intimate practices: shifting residence after giving birth to one's first child is what one "should do"; shifting residence prior to that time is the forced result of political campaigns such as that to "transform established habits and social customs."

Scholars of socialist societies, including Verdery and Schoenhals, have argued that language has served as a powerful tool in the partystate's program of transforming the consciousness of the people. Verdery turns to Bakhtin's concept of authoritative discourse to emphasize the power of this official language that, in Bakhtin's words, "we encounter ... with its authority already fused to it" (Bakhtin, 1981:342). Yet Bakhtin also suggests that authoritative discourse does not necessarily determine behavior because its rigidity undermines its ability to transform thought and practice (1981:343). For that purpose Bakhtin proposes the concept of an internally persuasive discourse, one that "is affirmed through assimilation, tightly interwoven with 'one's own word'" (1981:345). An internally persuasive discourse is inherently transformative because of its ability to awaken independent consciousness and enable a separation from authoritative discourses. What Verdery and Schoenhals see in the discourse of the socialist party-state is an authoritative discourse that strives, albeit often unsuccessfully, to become an internally persuasive discourse.

My analysis in this chapter suggests, moreover, not only that authoritative state discourses failed to become internally persuasive with regard to intimate life, but also that they failed to become socially persuasive. Reformers' inability to translate repeated campaigns and propaganda into lasting changes in villagers' intimate practices derived in many ways from their inability (or perhaps unwillingness) to transform the underlying social conditions that made those practices desirable and, some women might argue, even necessary. Despite its claims to have overturned the old feudal order and to have replaced it with a new socialist society, the CCP (like its Nationalist predecessor) was unable to eliminate many of the basic features of that old order, which meant that the new society rested on a shaky foundation indeed. The language of revolution and reform in many ways remained *merely* an authoritative discourse precisely because the party-state was unable or unwilling to change the underlying conditions that would have made ENR and, to a certain extent, female suicide less appealing. By ultimately reverting to an economistic concern with transforming the relations and means of production, the CCP retreated one step further from a more encompassing approach to social change.

In the next section, I examine how many of the changes sought by state reformers in the 1950s and 1960s have begun to materialize in the post-Mao era. The conditions contributing to these transformations differ dramatically from the state-directed reform campaigns of the Mao era, which relied heavily on propaganda, socialist models, and even coercion. In the 1990s it is the unintended effects of diverse state policies, from market reforms to family planning, that have created an environment in which such changes are desired and accepted by a large segment of the population. This is not to say that the language of reform advocated by the party-state has simply disappeared. In fact, it is by contrasting their own behavior with the feudal practices and thinking of older generations that young women and men today strive to produce themselves as open and progressive subjects of the market-reform era.

PART TWO Intimate Life in the Post-Mao Era

CHAPTER THREE ✺ Marriage, Intimacy, and Late-Socialist State Power

The intensive, yet ultimately ineffective, reform campaigns of the 1950s and 1960s provided a powerful point of reference for Shanlin villagers in the 1990s as they debated the dramatic transformations in marital practices emerging in the second decade of post-Mao market reforms. Soehua, the woman who disparaged the achievements of the 1960s' "Women, Return to Your Husbands' Homes" campaign, later in our conversation observed to me that couples "today have changed greatly, they have progressed. Nowadays, even before having a child they talk on the phone, page each other. Women go [to their husbands'] on their own. Now things are good, [couples] are very open." Soehua's evaluation of contemporary marriage and courtship practices reveals a new appreciation for open relationships, one that again contrasts feudal customs and women's reluctance to visit their husbands with progressive attitudes toward mixed-sex socializing and the cultivation of "feelings" between spouses. Although premised on a continued norm of extended natal residence marriage, Soehua's comments suggest that this norm coexists with a degree of open interaction unimaginable in the marriages of her generation.

Everywhere I looked in the mid-1990s, it seemed, young couples were getting together in private and public in ways unheard of a mere five or ten years prior. They were sitting together in family courtyards, chatting on the phone, paging each other, walking along the beach, catching the bus to the township or county seat, or even riding together on motorcycles and mopeds—all scenes that indicated a kind of intimacy and physical familiarity rarely acknowledged in relationships among older villagers. If younger couples were more open, as Soehua claimed, did that mean their ties were now based on love and feelings, the very sentiments promoted by state reformers of decades prior? Did freely chosen matches in fact liberate village youths, as those very reformers had claimed? Or did they also enmesh them in new expectations, those shaped by changing standards for male-female relations as well as new state regulatory processes?

As I struggled to make sense of the new forms of courtship and marriage I saw emerging during my research, I could not help but compare them with the past marriages I had heard of from older villagers such as Soehua. Men and women alike regaled me with vivid accounts of brides who had refused to join their husbands in bed, choosing instead to spend the entire night standing against a wall or sitting in a chair. Others told of young wives who, when faced with the requisite conjugal visit at the New Year holiday, waited until late at night to make the trip and then busied themselves with household chores, eventually fleeing back to their natal homes in the early morning hours so as to escape their husbands' overtures. These scenarios seemed to offer little opportunity for developing the kinds of intimate attachments young people in the 1990s so desired in their marital relationships.

In many ways, villagers in their late teens and early twenties at the time of my research were caught between two marital worlds: that of their older siblings and parents in which marriages were arranged and feelings were cultivated only years later (if at all) and that of a reform-era environment in which ideals of progress and openness were inspiring not only national goals of economic development and international trade but also, as Soehua argued, new forms of courtship and marriage. Some members of this cohort had acquiesced to arranged matches, but they sought to redefine those relationships by "cultivating feelings" (bueyong gamzing) prior to the actual marriage. Others broke off arranged engagements; some went so far as to divorce undesirable spouses or found themselves divorced by dissatisfied partners. These actions, many contended, freed village youths to choose their next spouse on the basis of mutual affection and compatibility. Soehua may have been thinking of her youngest son when she commented on the current state of village marriages, for his experiences reflect this renewed attention to choice and feelings. At age 15 he had broken off an engagement arranged by his parents and then became acquainted with several other young women, but he chose not to marry any of them. His father finally introduced him to the daughter of a friend, and the couple began to spend more time together. After three months they decided to marry, and the wedding took place in 1998, when Soehua's son was 23 and his wife 22. Soehua's daughter-in-law gave birth to her first child a mere two years after the wedding. Even prior to childbirth, moreover, she spent much more time in her conjugal home than had wives of many previous generations.

In this chapter I examine how young people in Shanlin envisioned and enacted the marital freedoms they claimed were available to them beginning in the mid-1990s. At the same time, I also ask how parents, in-laws, peers, older villagers, and new forms of state power have continued to shape and even limit those freedoms, particularly for young women. At first glance, changes in local marriage practices appear to follow a familiar global pattern whereby industrialization and wage income lead to greater spousal choice and an attendant emphasis on romance and love (e.g., Shorter, 1977). The actual situation in Shanlin, however, is more complex than this modernization narrative conveys. Yan Yunxiang (1997) argues that conjugality has gradually "triumphed" over patriarchal family arrangements in rural China not because of economic reforms but largely due to changing definitions of the ideal family and intergenerational shifts in power relations within families. Although these family dynamics have played an important role in Shanlin, they are not sufficient to explain changes in how youths now envision and form their marriages. For that we must look as well to different kinds of state intervention in eastern Hui'an and new governmental aims. What young people saw as greater individual control over their marriages was also produced by an unusual convergence of previous marital reforms with the market forces and new state regulatory processes emerging in the 1990s. In other words, while the post-Mao era in general was characterized by the retreat of official actors from many domains of intimate life, in Shanlin young people's marital ideals and intimate attachments continued to display the imprint of state power.

Feudal Dispositions and Marriages Without Feelings

Despite the repeated efforts of early socialist reformers to reshape extended natal residence marriage to make it conform to ideals of liberated socialist partnerships, the marital experiences of Shanlin women and men up through the early 1990s attested to the limited impact of such reforms. Certainly the 1950s and 1960s had witnessed a few significant changes: some individuals were granted the opportunity to see their future spouse prior to marriage and give their approval for the match, perfunctory though that approval might be; officials were more likely to enforce procedures for marital registration, requiring couples to sit together for an engagement photo (something most women recalled as a terrifying experience rather than as an opportunity to become better acquainted with their future husband); and divorces were at least possible in the 1950s, although how socially accepted they were remains difficult to discern. As we saw in the previous chapter, however, by the 1960s officials seemed more committed to enforcing women's conjugal residence than to upholding principles of free spousal choice. The mandatory classes held for women in the mid-1960s taught shy young wives to identify conjugal residence with service to the people, urging them to shed their backward ways and move in with their husbands. The Cultural Revolution brought an end to these marriage reform campaigns as the Cultural Revolution Revolutionary Committee turned its attention to promoting leftist ideology and rooting out remaining class enemies. Although some villagers who came of age in the late 1960s and 1970s recalled breaking off engagements for political reasons, they did not describe marriage itself as a concern of the Cultural Revolution leadership, as it clearly had been for an earlier generation of officials.[1] Cultural Revolution matches continued to be arranged by parents and matchmakers, were largely surname and village exogamous, and involved postmarital separation periods of five to six years on average.

The rise of the post-Mao leadership in the late 1970s and 1980s brought few changes to these trends. When reflecting on marriages formed during this period, Shanlin residents in the mid-1990s often described them as "black marriages" (oo hun) because they took place when couples were too young to wed legally and were not registered with the village government. Marriage at ages 15 and 16 was not uncommon for women in the 1980s, as the economic boom produced by market reforms enabled families to accumulate the resources needed to marry off their children, and many were doing so at increasingly younger ages.[2] The average age at marriage for Shanlin women in the 1980s was a mere 16.8 years (see Table 1), well below the new legal age of 20 set in the 1980 Marriage Law. Although growing numbers of young women were marrying within Shanlin itself, they were still acquiescing to arranged matches, usually to men they had never spoken with or had only glanced at from afar, at ages often younger than those of their mothers and grandmothers.[3] With their energies now focused on rebuilding the local economy and introducing new forms of production and ownership, local cadres paid scant attention to these illegal marriages and the long periods of postmarital separation that followed them. Despite a 1985 county government resolution calling on officials to strictly enforce bans on underage and arranged marriages and to implement marital registration, my findings from Shanlin show that such campaigns did little to curb the black marriages of the period (Hui'an County Government Resolution 303, 1985).[4]

In their recollections of this not-so-distant past, villagers focused on a set of behaviors associated with a new bride: how she hid her face with her headscarf or bamboo hat, how she spent the requisite night at her conjugal home sitting in a chair or standing against the wall so as to avoid joining her husband in bed, or how she went hungry rather than eating together with her husband's family. These behaviors were attributed largely to young wives' feudal dispositions; as women who were pai se—embarrassed, ashamed, shy—or who feared being made to feel this way (gnia pai se), they displayed these dispositions through expected patterns of shyness and avoidance.

Sutgoo, an energetic woman in her mid-seventies, had taken a shine to me on one of my first trips to Shanlin, and whenever I visited her in her slightly run-down two-story home in the upper village she eagerly regaled me with tales of life in the Huidong villages of her youth. On one such occasion I asked Sutgoo whether she would allow me to tape her narrative, and with an impish grin on her deeply lined face she readily agreed. Pausing to press tea and some dried fruit on me and my research assistant, she then pro-

Table 1
Women's Average Age at First Marriage and Length of Postmarital Separation

Year married	Average age at first marriage	Separated for 1–3 years (%)	4–6 years (%)	7–9 years (%)	10+ years (%)	Total number of marriages
1923–49	17.7	24	45	21	10	42
1950–57	18	7	43	36	14	14[a]
1958–66	18.2	10	65	25	0	31
1967–76	17.8	26	45	27	2	51
1977–89	16.8[b]	17	36	29	6	120[c]
1990–93	17.9	22	14	2		49[d]
1994–97	22.2	60				15[e]

[a] I speculate that my *n* for this cohort is small because many couples who married during these years may have divorced due to Marriage Law campaigns. When I asked for marital histories, respondents may have reported the marriage that lasted, not their initial marriage. Women's average age at first marriage during this period conformed to the legal age of 18 as specified in the 1950 Marriage Law.

[b] This average remained constant even after the legal marriage age was raised to 20 in 1980. Only in 1989 did I begin to see a trend toward conformity with the 1980 Marriage Law. Four out of the sixteen women whose marriages I documented for that year married at 20 or 21; the remaining twelve ranged in age from 15 to 19.

[c] There are fifteen marriages in this cohort for which I have no data on residence shift. One woman remarried after being widowed, one shifted residence after many years of childlessness, eight women divorced, and five women had yet to shift residence when I took their marital histories.

[d] There are thirty women in this cohort for whom I have no data on residence shift; this gap makes the percentages only provisional. Twenty-one women had not yet shifted residence by the time I completed my research in 1997 or had marriage trajectories that I was unable to follow during subsequent visits. Ten marriages subsequently ended in divorce.

[e] My *n* for this cohort is small because many of the marriages that took place during this period were second marriages, following earlier divorces. Five of the women whose marriages I recorded for this period either had yet to shift residence by the time I completed my research in 1997 or had marriage trajectories that I was unable to follow on later visits. One woman had divorced within the first three years of marriage.

SOURCE: Data collected through a 1996 survey of 41 randomly sampled village households and interviews conducted in Shanlin primarily from 1995 to 1997. Includes both women who were born in and those who married into Shanlin.

ceeded to describe in vivid detail her own generation's fear of interacting with men who were not close kin, highlighting the social repercussions of such interactions:

We feared, feared those men.... In the past, we were afraid of a man, afraid, not like people today. People today will joke around together, and laugh. ... We'd never dare to do that in our day! ... When we lived at home—sixteen, seventeen years old, seventeen, eighteen—our parents would beat us if we said one word to a boy. They would say that men and women were supposed to keep their distance, that [a woman] should never speak to a man. That's the way it was back then.

Like Soehua, whose reflections began this chapter, Sutgoo explicitly contrasted the culture of fear that permeated male-female relations in her day with what she perceived as the casualness and ease that characterized contemporary interactions. As her husband sat nearby making tea and chiming in with added details, Sutgoo recounted how she had been married off at the young age of fifteen to a complete stranger. She spent the first five days following the wedding in her mother-in-law's house where she sobbed unceasingly, refusing to be comforted by the neighborhood women who reminded her that she would soon return to her natal home. When her younger brother arrived in Shanlin bearing gifts from her natal family, Sutgoo begged him to stay with her, and on the fifth day after the wedding the two siblings rode together in the bridal sedan chair for the trip back to their village on the other side of the township.[5] On subsequent conjugal visits, Sutgoo traversed the township on foot, entering a community populated almost entirely by strangers. Only five years later did she settle in Shanlin after giving birth to her first child (she would go on to have a total of eight, three of whom died in childhood).

How recently had the picture Sutgoo and Soehua painted of contemporary marriages so different from their own become a reality? The experiences of Siuden, a slight yet feisty Shanlin native who married in 1986, provide a valuable example of how little had changed for women even in the first decade of post-Mao market reforms. Siuden was married at age seventeen to a village youth selected for her by her parents. Her husband was an adopted child, a status that made him less desirable as a spouse because villagers assumed that he would not maintain close ties with his parents into adulthood or benefit from their support. Nonetheless, Siuden had her first child four years into the marriage—a relatively standard period of post-marital separation in Shanlin—and began residing with her husband immediately thereafter. When I met Siuden in 1995, she was living in a rented home in the older section of the village, together with her husband and their three children. Far from content with their living situation or her husband's ability to provide for the family (he liked to drink and gamble away his meager earnings), she eagerly recounted for me the fear she had experienced on her wedding night when she first met her husband: "I was sitting on the bed and refused to face him, turned away. It was night, the doors were all closed. I didn't know him at all." Having married a man from her own village did not make Siuden any more comfortable with her husband, and she avoided him as best she could: "If I went to the harbor and ran into him, my heart would begin to pound. I was scared to death. If he was with a group of men, I would run away as fast as I could." "In those days," she continued, "it was like that. Everyone was afraid, everyone was pai se."

The intertwining of fear, shame, and avoidance in Siuden's narrative is precisely what earlier reform campaigns had sought to replace with liberated thinking and a new norm of conjugal intimacy. And yet in Siuden's account, such sentiments were not simply reflections of internal states (feudal or closed consciousness), as was so often claimed by state actors, but were literally embodied—something Siuden emphasized when she slammed shut the door of her house to recreate for me the physical shock of fear and isolation she had experienced on her wedding night. By refusing to face her husband when he sat next to her on the bed, Siuden had expressed her own properly shy disposition and desire to avoid further physical intimacy. Like older women, she adopted an almost formulaic manner of articulating her fears of marriage and men in general, reinforcing an association between an expectation of pai se behavior and a form of marriage in which young brides wed virtual strangers. Women of all ages frequently described how they had refused to visit or sleep with their husbands during their early married years, a practice reflected in the common expression of sexual innocence, "I didn't know him." Fear of sex likely played a role in such refusal, as did the desire to maintain the appearance of propriety in their self-presentation to me. But many wives sought to avoid sexual relations with their husbands precisely because pregnancy put an end to the freedom of natal residence so cherished by young women.

Siuden went on to describe the labor demands she faced from her husband's family, demands that made her all the more reluctant to agree to conjugal visits:

Before when our mother-in-law came to call us, we would run far and wide. I didn't want to go. . . . We had to carry water, sweep the floors, wash chairs and tables. . . . In the fourth month[6] we had to help water and fertilize the sweet potato crop, carry night soil. I went about twice a year, once at New Year's and once during the fourth month. If they didn't come to call me, then I wouldn't go. At New Year's they didn't have to call us, everyone had to visit. But I would wait until eleven o'clock to go, then after midnight I would run home. Just carry some water, sit on the bed for a while, and then go back.

These requests for sex and labor led many young women to fear conjugal visits, and they eluded them as best they could, whether by fleeing at first sight of an approaching mother-in-law or by performing a minimum number of required tasks and then escaping at the earliest acceptable moment. Even in the 1980s and early 1990s, natal families generally supported such efforts not only because they were an expected feature of local marriages but also because families benefited from their daughters' household labor and from the wages young women had begun to bring home from construction work and, later, stone polishing. Conversely, women who engaged in what was seen as immodest behavior found themselves subject to social sanctions and ridicule from dui pnua, kin, and neighbors. Perhaps for this reason many young wives refrained from informing family members and same-sex peers when they first became pregnant—pregnancy being a sure sign that they had slept with their husbands—preferring instead to make their condition known by following certain ritual proscriptions or by letting their bodies do the talking for them.[7]

Not all villagers, however, expressed the same reactions to community expectations of shyness and avoidance on the part of new brides. By the 1980s, high socialist ideals of liberated marriages were gradually becoming interlaced with a new discourse of marital desires and intimacy influenced by the rapidly commodified and individualistic environment of the market-reform era. Young men were the first to seize on this convergence, dissatisfied as many of them were with the lack of intimacy in established norms of marital practice.

When Zinzai married in 1984 at age nineteen to a Shanlin woman two years his junior, his marriage had been arranged by a matchmaker and the auspicious wedding date selected by his father. Zinzai recalled how he had initially refused to return home for the wedding, forcing his father to travel to Xiamen where he had been doing construction work to escort him back to the village. The couple met for the first time on their wedding day. Despite his wife's reluctance to join him in bed or even look him in the face, Zinzai maintained that he sought to persuade her of his good intentions on the rare occasions after the wedding when she did acquiesce to conjugal visits while struggling (sometimes angrily) to break through her fear. Depicting himself as more open-minded than other young men because of the time he had spent in the city, he recounted his experience of these visits for me during a series of interviews in the winter of 1997:

Ah, sometimes it was cold. I could see how she suffered and it made me angry. I would say to her, "Anyway, it doesn't matter if you sleep, if you won't sleep [at least] sit on the bed, it's warm. It doesn't matter." But she didn't dare. She just stood there so cold that she was shivering and her nose was running. I was so angry that I couldn't sleep.

Zinzai's early frustrations with his wife permeated his recollections of their tense initial years of marriage. His vivid depictions of how she shivered through the cold night as she stood alone to avoid joining him in bed reinforced an image of the feudal young wife whose aloofness, shyness, and fear of physical contact were often difficult for new husbands to accept. Building to a fevered pitch, Zinzai responded angrily to his wife's distance: "I was so angry that I didn't want to pay any attention to her. I called out to her with good intentions, not with any ulterior motives, nothing. But in those days, no one's thinking was open, village women weren't open-minded. They all were afraid of being ashamed or embarrassed."

In Zinzai's account, openness functions as the antithesis of feudal dispositions marked by shame, embarrassment, and fear. Although feudal clearly retained its connotation of backwardness, by the 1980s and 1990s it no longer signified all that had to be rejected in the name of building socialism. Instead, as ideals of openness flourished with market reforms, feudal assumed a new kind of relevance as a benchmark against which to measure the progressiveness of contemporary marriage practices. As one middle-aged Shanlin man asserted to me in 1996, "[No one] is feudal in this era of openness." He then proudly described how his recently married son and daughter-in-law visited one another and even spent the night together without parental prompting. Young people now emphasized "being open" in their marital practices as part of realizing a form of courtship and marriage they deemed appropriate for the more liberal society ushered in with market reforms. Their aim in enacting this form of conjugal intimacy was not earlier state goals of socialist liberation and heightened productivity but a vision of heterosexual compatibility and attraction that dovetailed with newly integrated industrial workplaces and leisure activities (see Chapter 5).

Open Marriages

What was it about Shanlin marriages beginning in the mid-1990s that made them no longer feudal, in short, that made them look increasingly like the liberated marriages advocated by socialist reformers 30 to 40 years prior? As Zinzai related his tale of early marital woes to me, he recalled how his wife had repeatedly refused his invitations to watch a movie together or visit the burgeoning city of Xiamen, how "she didn't dare." Listening to this depiction of herself more than a decade later, Zinzai's wife, A Lan, was outraged: "In those days, who did things like that? It wasn't like nowadays. Now they go all over the place even before marriage, they stay in hotels together."

A Lan's outburst sheds light on several of the dramatic changes in courtship and marriage that have taken place in Shanlin in the years since her wedding. In contrast to young wives (and often husbands) who were pai se, who did not dare to speak directly to their spouses, much less eat or venture out in public with them, young couples in the 1990s were actively cultivating relationships based on feelings and shared activities. "Staying in hotels together" was obviously one of the more contentious of these activities, and it represented a striking change from the behavior of the new bride who refused to join her husband in bed so widely depicted in Maoist work team reports or portrayed for me by older villagers.

The vision of open, progressive marriage aspired to by contemporary Shanlin youths rested on several key features. Although many young couples marrying in the mid-1990s had acquiesced to arranged marriages, they sought to infuse those relationships with the intimacy attributed to freely chosen matches. The fact that women and men were marrying at increasingly older ages gave them more time to "cultivate feelings" prior to and immediately following marriage and, as I discuss in Chapter 5, a greater sphere of youth socializing inspired by mixed-sex workplaces gave them the space in which to do so. As young people incorporated new social freedoms into existing patterns of marriage and courtship, they began to generate the feelings earlier state reformers had deemed so critical to liberated socialist marriages.

A Den, the savvy businesswoman I introduced in Chapter 1, was the youngest daughter in a local cadre family. Like her older sister and two older brothers, she had been betrothed in her childhood to another village youth. A Den had very little, if any, contact with this young man until 1995 when she was 21 years old. In part because her father was an official and in part because her fiancé was the nephew of a prominent village businessman, there had been no talk of marriage before the couple began to approach the legal marriage age (now 20 for women and 22 for men). The local government had begun to strictly enforce the legal age in 1994, requiring couples like A Den and her fiancé who were the same age to delay marriage until the man had turned 22.

Prior to that time, however, A Den's fiancé began to stop by her home to visit, an event that initially sent A Den's mother scurrying to gather several of her dui pnua to sit with the couple and encourage easy conversation. I myself joined in many of these short and awkward visits, noticing how a usually confident and outspoken A Den became shy and subdued as her dui pnua engaged her fiancé in casual banter. After several months, the couple began to visit by themselves, chatting together in the back room of A Den's shop until late in the evening or speaking regularly on the telephone. When Amway sales became popular in the summer of 1996, A Den asked her fiancé to take her on his motorcycle to a meeting in a neighboring village. Over time the couple ventured out in public more frequently, although A Den was quick to deny these outings, claiming that such talk made her feel pai se.

In the fall of 1996, shortly after A Den's fiancé's twenty-second birthday, the couple made a trip to the county seat to register their marriage. Legal recognition (together with access to independent income) emboldened them to venture beyond the village borders, and on several occasions during my time in Shanlin they traveled together to Chongwu, the county seat, and the nearby city of Quanzhou, even staying overnight in hotels. This was the kind of behavior that so outraged A Lan, Zinzai's wife, for according to her it took place before marriage itself. Although A Den and her fiancé were legally married in the eyes of the state, they had not yet received the social recognition bestowed by a wedding ceremony. In local dialect, legal registration was known simply as "becoming engaged" (ding hun), a stage distinct from marriage (giat hun), which was marked by the appropriate wedding ritual and the social passage it performed. Yet this distinction was becoming increasingly irrelevant to growing numbers of Shanlin youth who used the recognition provided by legal registration to engage in the kinds of behavior associated with marriage, most notably emerging in public together, traveling outside the village, and, in some cases, even sleeping together (see also Yan, 1996:193, 2002). Women who spent the night with their husbands generally did not take up permanent residence in their conjugal homes but adapted the practice of conjugal visits to fit an earlier stage in the marriage process.

This move away from the conjugal avoidance practiced by pai se brides in the past meant that young wives in the mid-1990s were becoming pregnant and shifting residence much sooner than their predecessors, and some brides were already pregnant on their wedding day. Elders were more likely to condone such behavior, moreover, for they feared that with strict enforcement of the legal marriage age and a continued norm of postmarital separation in the community young people would be old by the time they had children and would face economic hardship as they approached middle age without support from the next generation.[8] Therefore, as village youths began to socialize and even engage in sexual relations prior to and immediately following marriage, members of the older generation rarely criticized these new patterns because they increased the likelihood of earlier pregnancy and coresidence. A Den's mother offers a good case in point here. Although she professed to me that she had been much too embarrassed to speak directly to her husband, not to mention to sleep with her head at the same end of the bed as his, she saw nothing wrong with A Den socializing with her fiancé. In fact, she actively encouraged such behavior and was quite distraught when, at one point in their courtship, A Den's fiancé appeared to show interest in a woman who worked with him at a local stone-carving factory (the misunderstanding was quickly resolved by a visit from A Den's future mother-in-law). Some of the older woman's eagerness stemmed from the fact that her future son-in-law was widely recognized as a good catch (he was quite handsome, made a very good salary as a factory manager, and stood to benefit from his close relationship with his entrepreneur uncle), and more frequent visits on his part signaled to her that a wedding might be imminent. By the same token, she was also keen to see her younger daughter safely settled in a marriage, particularly given A Den's unpredictable temperament and advanced age (22 was still considered quite old by the senior generation).

The growing acceptance of these new courtship and marriage trends was reflected in the fact that of the fifteen couples whose first marriages I recorded for the period from 1994 to 1997, slightly more than half bore a child and moved in together within three years of their wedding (see Table 1). Despite her mother's worries, A Den gave birth to a baby girl a little over a year after her 1997 wedding and began residing first with her husband and his extended family and later in the couple's own spacious villa constructed on the plot adjacent to his uncle's home. Unlike both her mother and her older sister, Bbingden, A Den displayed few of the pai se behaviors long attributed to Shanlin wives: she began to socialize with her husband long before they registered with the government or held a wedding ceremony, she traveled with him beyond the village borders, and, perhaps most significantly, she went on her own accord to spend the night with him prior to their wedding and immediately afterward.[9] Yet unlike women a few years her junior who were increasingly open about engaging in these behaviors, A Den was careful to present an appearance of modesty, despite her actions. When her peers urged her to treat them to a meal in celebration of her registration, she refused, at first denying that she and her fiancé had registered with the government and only later, under much duress, agreeing to treat a small group of dui pnua at a nearby restaurant. A Den was also quick to dispel rumors that she was sleeping with her fiancé/husband, and she often made a point of returning home at the crack of dawn and immediately opening her shop in order to maintain an appearance of propriety (although she grew more relaxed as her wedding approached). When she became pregnant, she refrained from informing her natal kin and closest dui pnua. Only when she could no longer hide the signs did A Den admit her condition, and for much of her pregnancy she (like other modest wives) remained inside her natal family's compound so as not to be seen in public.

A Den had agreed to an arranged match, but she knew her husband relatively well by the time they married and successfully skirted the obstacles and conflicts that arose during their courtship. For many other couples, however, the process was not as smooth. Some, like Soehua's son, were able to break off undesirable matches arranged in their childhood, particularly as growing numbers of parents acknowledged that children were no longer willing to accept such arrangements. Others agreed to arranged marriages but then divorced. As the rate of broken engagements and divorces soared in the 1990s, young people expressed an even greater commitment to finding a spouse with whom they were compatible and could "cultivate feelings," and many argued passionately against the suffering they experienced by being forced to marry at too young an age.

As my research assistant and I walked the muddy paths of Shanlin in the late winter of 1996 in search of villagers who could recite for us the propaganda folk songs of the Maoist era, we stumbled upon A Ping's dry goods shop. Invited in by a mutual friend who was knitting together with A Ping, I was struck immediately by her beauty and the subdued air of sadness that surrounded her. A Ping still wore local attire in those days; her headscarf made from one of the newer synthetic fabrics then favored by young women set off her fine features and pale skin. Eager to be of assistance, A Ping offered to introduce us to a neighbor who she claimed had a beautiful singing voice and still remembered many of the older songs.

We never met A Ping's neighbor that day but instead sat for hours in the drafty, sparsely furnished main room of her parents' house with its granite walls only partly covered with plaster and decorated with faded calendars from local fishing companies. A Ping seemed quite young to me, and as we chatted I became confused by her references to her mother, father, and grandparents because each title appeared to encompass multiple individuals. It slowly dawned on me that A Ping was married, and therefore that her references to kin included members of both her natal and her conjugal families.[10] At that point A Ping was almost twenty years old, the same age as my research assistant from the township. Yet she had already been married for four years to a young man who lived on the opposite side of the village in a large, well-appointed house—much nicer, in fact, than A Ping's natal home. By rights A Ping should have been satisfied with the match: her husband was relatively well educated by village standards, he was essentially an only son (his younger brother was severely disabled), and his father owned one of the boats that fished for tuna in the South Pacific, at the time a profitable enterprise. I was familiar with A Ping's conjugal family because her older sister-in-law, a divorcée, sewed clothing for village women who wore local attire and was active in a local group of observant Buddhists. After meeting A Ping, however, I began to see their family affairs in another light.

A Ping had originally been engaged to a boy from another village in the township, the son of one of her mother's childhood dui pnua. At age thirteen, she decided that she wanted to break off the match, and after some wrangling her mother finally agreed.[11] In the ensuing years, according to A Ping, her parents were flooded with engagement proposals, but she refused them all. When she turned sixteen, her father's dui pnua came to propose a match with his nephew, and under acute pressure from all her family members A Ping reluctantly agreed to the match. Shortly afterwards, however, she decided yet again that she wanted to break off the engagement, but this time her mother refused to give in. Instead, A Ping's mother agreed to the pending wedding date selected by the groom's family, all without informing A Ping. As A Ping persisted in her plans to end the engagement, then, her mother and mother-in-law busied themselves with wedding preparations. A Ping recounted for me this period in her life not long after we first met:

My mother, she didn't let me know [that I was to be married], didn't let me know. Only when the day neared did she tell me. She told me and I refused. My mother said, "No, then let's see what you can do about it!" She said, "You've already accepted the money from people [the bride-wealth], what are you going to do?" Just like that. I wouldn't take their money. I wanted to return it, to take back this gold. When I went over, they were in the midst of frying cakes [in preparation for the wedding exchanges]. They thought that I wanted to marry, . . . that I was so happy that I rushed over to their house. I didn't know how to respond. So I said, "It's true, I want to marry. . . . Otherwise why would I rush over to your house?" Just like that. I had wanted to return the gold and tell them that I wasn't getting married. . . . I didn't know how I was going to give them back the gold! So I just brought it back home with me.

Despondent after this incident, A Ping refused to notify her dui pnua of her impending marriage, and in the end one of her close dui pnua made the wedding procession arrangements for her. Afterward, when faced with the reality of her marriage, A Ping initially tried to make the best of it, at one point even agreeing to meet secretly with her husband so that they could become better acquainted. By the time I met A Ping in 1996, she still felt that she did not really know her husband since he had been away for much of their marriage, fishing on his father's boat. Despite her efforts to "cultivate feelings" in the relationship, A Ping continued to bemoan the bitterness produced by her arranged marriage. Much of that bitterness seemed to stem from her contentious relationship with her mother-in-law, who, A Ping claimed, treated her as an outsider and frequently demeaned her in public (although on several occasions during my time in Shanlin A Ping also admitted that her in-laws had paid for her medical care and had even accompanied her to the county seat to see a doctor for a persistent foot injury).[12] In that first year we spent together, A Ping regularly mentioned her desire for a divorce but acknowledged that her parents, although supportive in principle, would not permit her to initiate the divorce request, for to do so would cost the family too much in compensation money.[13] Resigned to her difficult state of affairs, A Ping summed up her mood of despair one cold winter evening when I stayed over at her home: "So now I just have to wait; nothing will change until [my husband] returns [from fishing overseas]. We are really hurt by this arranged marriage, and so young. I just want to find someone with whom I can get along, someone I can talk to."

A Ping frequently argued that the most important thing to look for in a marital relationship was the presence of feelings between the two people, something that had to be cultivated over time through regular interaction and thus was lacking in her own marriage. Like A Ping, most young people in Shanlin opposed the early marriages that they argued prevented them from having the opportunity to become acquainted with potential spouses and establish compatibility. In many cases, however, they espoused more equivocal views on arranged marriage. Like young Taiwanese women in the 1960s who "were not eager to assume the responsibility of choosing the person they *would* marry" (Wolf, 1972:101–102; emphasis in original), young Shanlin women in the mid-1990s also recognized that initiating their own marriages might place them in a potentially dangerous and fragile position, particularly if the marriage failed and they later required parental support (see also Hoodfar, 1997:61–65). As A Ggiok, an outspoken, nineteen-year-old stone polisher argued,

Having parents arrange the marriage is better. . . . If parents engage us and then we complain "Oh, our parents arranged a bad engagement," we can divorce if we want to. If we find our own spouse and it turns bad and we want a divorce, then our parents will say, "At the time, you yourself wanted [the match]." This is to say that your parents won't let you [get divorced], right? . . . We have to think this way. Parents should decide some and we ourselves should decide some. Parents can't let us decide it all.

In fact, several of the parents I knew actively sought out potential partners for their divorced or yet-to-be-engaged children, claiming that young people did not know how to look for an appropriate spouse. In the end, however, they admitted that the decision as to whether to marry that person ultimately rested with the younger generation.

In A Ping's case, perhaps it was her acquiescence to her arranged match that encouraged her natal family to support her when relations with her conjugal kin broke down. Like growing numbers of young people in the mid-1990s, A Ping had begun to socialize in mixed-sex groups and to attend gatherings at restaurants and karaoke parlors, sites that were not yet widely accepted for youth leisure activities. Although she was married, her nonresident status and her husband's extended absence from the village enabled her to create a social life fairly similar to that of her unmarried peers. Unlike those peers, however, A Ping faced disapproving comments from her mother-in-law and elder sister-in-law, both of whom were quick to complain about the young men who stopped by her village shop each evening or her outings to morally questionable consumer sites. A Ping sought to mitigate their criticisms by defending her propriety, even to the point of adopting a more modest approach to conjugal visits. Although her husband was not resident in the village, A Ping was still expected to spend the night at his home on certain festival days. Rather than initiating those visits herself as most young wives did by the mid-1990s, A Ping chose instead to wait for her mother- or sister-in-law to summon her. That her mother-in-law did come to call for her reflects the older woman's own commitment to a pattern of conjugal visiting premised on an earlier norm of pai se brides, one that was rapidly disappearing from the community.

Despite A Ping's conciliatory efforts, her conflicts with her female conjugal kin soon escalated into more public battles, and her mother-in-law went so far as to accuse her of engaging in immoral behavior (a not-so-subtle reference to prostitution). When A Ping's husband finally returned to the village in 1997, he bowed to pressure from his mother and suddenly informed A Ping that he wanted a divorce. Divorce negotiations quickly deteriorated into open hostility between the two families, however, and A Ping's grandfather refused to accept the modest payment (5,000 *yuan*) initially offered by her conjugal family; it failed, so he argued, to compensate A Ping "for the loss to her reputation" (bbnia snia e sunsit) after so many years of marriage. As negotiations stalled, A Ping found herself in a state somewhere between being married and single. When I next saw her a year later, the divorce had yet to be settled.

On my first day back in Shanlin in the summer of 1998, I sat with A Ping in the doorway of her dry goods shop as she recounted for me the details of her divorce. Pale after a year of repeated illnesses, A

Ping listlessly picked up her knitting and then put it down again, all the while complaining, "I'm such a mess" (ggua ziok'e lang luan'a). With the divorce negotiations drawn out for so long, she had been unable to leave the community to find more profitable work. Given her liminal status, her mother had cautioned her that "people would say [she] was running off with someone else." Feeling trapped and under constant surveillance, A Ping proclaimed that the next time she married, it would be to someone who lived far away from such prying eyes.

The Freedom of Romantic Love?

Once A Ping's divorce was finalized and she had begun to look for a new spouse, she was more committed than ever to selecting that person herself. A Ping had repeatedly argued that choosing one's own spouse was fundamental to a marriage based on love and feelings. Like other young people in Shanlin, her own understanding of love was increasingly influenced by a diverse array of forces, including exposure to transnational mass media. Movies playing in the village theater or available on video compact discs often depicted romantic encounters along with the typical martial arts or gangster fare; the movie *Titanic* was quite well liked by A Ping and her cohort. Popular singers from China, Taiwan, and Hong Kong crooned sentimental lyrics in Mandarin and Minnan, conveying themes of emotional fulfillment and self-realization long denied under the collective focus of state socialism (Gold, 1993; Yang, 1997a). In addition to the daily music-video hour broadcast on township television, young people also gained access to popular songs and videos through personal video compact disc and karaoke players, a now standard component of dowries.[14] Music videos often included scenes of lovestruck couples wandering hand in hand, staring dreamily into each other's eyes, or of rejected lovers mournfully contemplating their loss. Like other tales of tragic love, these songs and videos "set a tone and provide[d] a model for interpreting or framing events in people's romantic lives" (Abu-Lughod, 1986:258; see also Yan, 2002:37–38).[15] Even illiterate young women who could not read the stream of characters flowing across the bottom of the television screen knew many of these songs by heart.

Yet A Ping's emphasis on free spousal choice also had roots in another moment, the marriage reform campaigns of the 1950s. In response to my questions about how to define a love marriage, Shanlin men and women in the 1990s generally agreed with A Ping that having the opportunity to select one's spouse constituted the precondition for romantic love (dam luan ai, luan ai, or aizing). This precondition harkened back to the calls of earlier socialist reformers who had advocated "free love" (*ziyou lian ai*) as an integral component of the "free marriages" (*ziyou jiehun*) appropriate for liberated socialist subjects, marriages that were not arranged but were freely chosen. Despite reservations about the bourgeois connotations and individualist ethos of romantic love, reformers nonetheless urged couples in Huidong villages to "build feelings" (*jianli ganqing*) and "build love" (*jianli aiqing*) as part of realizing socialist ideals (Dong Zhou, 1952).

This association between "free love" and "free marriage" had created a strong conceptual link between love and free spousal choice, despite the dearth of opportunities throughout the Maoist decades and even in the early post-Mao years to realize that connection in practice. By the mid-1990s, this precondition for romantic love was beginning to have a broader impact in Shanlin as romantic ideals gained greater purchase: it effectively placed romantic love out of the reach of many young people who had already acquiesced to arranged marriages, regardless of whether they had begun to "cultivate feelings" or were actually content with the match. For members of this group, the emphasis on free choice created an ideal of freedom at the same time that it excluded them from a definition of romantic love limited to specific behaviors and desires.

Take the case of Gianyong, a Shanlin man in his late teens who was engaged to one of A Ping's younger sisters. Neither Gianyong nor A Ping's sister was overtly unhappy with their arranged match; in fact, they socialized together frequently, and Gianyong was a regular guest at A Ping's natal home. Nonetheless, Gianyong himself argued that because the match was arranged, it prevented them from attaining romantic ideals. During a birthday gathering I attended for Gianyong's older sister, I overheard a guest joke with him about his relationship with his "girlfriend," referring to A Ping's sister, the future spouse selected for him by his now-deceased grandmother.

The Minnan term "girlfriend" (lu ping iu) was relatively new in village parlance, a word explicitly associated with mutual affection, love, and free choice.[16] Instead of acknowledging A Ping's sister as his "girlfriend," however, Gianyong quickly retorted, "Someone you've been betrothed to is *not* a girlfriend [kit'e m'si lu ping iu]; a girlfriend is someone you find on your own [lu ping iu si gagi gnia'e]." Thus, despite the two being obviously fond of each other, Gianyong refused to identify his fiancée as his "girlfriend" precisely because their match had been arranged and not freely chosen. The forcefulness of his retort reinforced the fact that romantic love signified more than freedom and personal autonomy; romantic ideals also contained their own forms of obligation, in this case created by a model of socialist marriage ostensibly liberatory in nature.

We can see, then, how an earlier state vision of liberated socialist marriages rooted in choice and feelings assumed powerful proportions in young people's understanding of romantic love in the 1990s, precisely at a time when media messages and leisure activities reinforced those romantic desires. In adopting expectations of romance and rejecting the feudal expression of pai se behavior, however, young men and women encountered a structure of romance characterized by new demands and expectations (see Collier, 1997:103–104). The desire to create relationships based on choice and feelings required that young people take more individual responsibility for their marriages, something that was increasingly possible as parents retreated from arranging matches. Yet such expectations often overlooked the importance of future parental support and community opinion, as well as the influence of new forms of state power that now regulated youths' marital behavior more stringently than ever before.

The Regulatory State

It was state reformers in the 1950s who had introduced an emphasis on feelings and free choice as a way of combating Huidong's feudal marriage customs and fostering the conjugal intimacy fundamental to the creation of liberated socialist subjects. Yet it was their counterparts in the 1990s who were making the realization of those ideals, together with new governmental aims, possible. As Table 1 shows, starting in 1994 young women consistently began to marry at or above the legal marriage age, at 22.2 years on average. In contrast to prior decades, particularly the 1950s and 1980s when state reformers were unable to make such enforcement an established feature of local governance (despite two national marriage laws), the 1990s witnessed a renewed campaign to make Huidong society "legible" (Scott, 1998; Diamant, 2001). Officials once again began registering marriages and monitoring couples' ages, now not as part of Marriage Law campaigns but in order to implement new regulations on marriage registration and family planning that stemmed from efforts to control population growth. Focused on limiting fertility and planning births, the national population policy had the ancillary effect in Shanlin of rationalizing and expanding local bureaucratic power. By refusing to intervene in the black marriages (below the legal age, not registered with the government) that constituted the norm throughout much of the 1970s, 1980s, and early 1990s, local officials had in essence failed to achieve the goals of late marriage and childbearing deemed critical to successful population control (see Greenhalgh, 1993:228). A new policy push in 1994 led to a crackdown that effectively linked marriage procedures to fertility regulation.[17]

No longer able to ignore bureaucratic requirements and simply marry their children when they pleased as had A Ping's parents, Shanlin residents found themselves faced with a strict list of registration procedures to follow.[18] First, parents had to confirm that their child's age in the village register (*hukou*) was in fact correct, a complicated task given that most villagers calculated age according to the Chinese reckoning system (*xusui*) whereby a child was considered one year old at birth and acquired another year immediately following the Chinese lunar new year. Some parents preparing for upcoming weddings found that they would have to wait an additional year, or even two, precisely because the government calculated age by the exact birth date (*zhousui*). Once age was established, the couple had a joint photo taken, another key element of marriage registration established in principle as early as the 1950s. Armed with a document from the village government attesting to their residence and ages, the engagement photo, and a sum of money, couples then set off for the township or county seat. As part of registration procedures, the woman was subject to an ultrasound examination to determine whether or not she was pregnant. If cleared, the couple was finally given a marriage license (*jiehun zheng*) and a birth-permission certificate (*zhun sheng zheng*), both necessary if they were to have a child.

Enforcing registration has clearly allowed state actors to extend their regulatory reach over both individuals and society more generally, elaborating a mode of governance organized around the production and disciplining of bodies and populations, or what Foucault (1978) termed "biopower." Yet, if we focus exclusively on the ways that marital registration has made Huidong society "legible" to the late-socialist regime, we miss other, equally important, consequences of that process. By enforcing the legal marriage age and registration protocols, officials have also provided village youths with the time and recognition needed to reshape their marital experiences and expectations. Young people themselves argued that waiting to marry enabled them to wrest marital decision making away from parents and elders and to cultivate relationships based on mutual compatibility and affection. At the same time, however, marriage has once again become part of a larger program of societal transformation, inviting officials back into villagers' intimate lives as they monitor the age of their younger charges and the reproductive capacities of village daughters-in-law.

Another outcome of this growth in marriage bureaucracy and official monitoring of women's fertility has been the redefinition of local conceptions of marriage. In my discussion of A Den's courtship, I noted that villagers referred to marital registration as "becoming engaged," distinguishing it from the wedding ceremony that in their eyes signified marriage. The enforcement of marital registration was beginning to blur this distinction, however, so that the marriage process bore less and less resemblance to earlier social and ritual forms. Now that parents were more reluctant to engage their children, prior stages of initial betrothal (kit) and ritual confirmation (deh dnia) were rapidly disappearing from the community, replaced by the simple and increasingly meaningless distinction between engagement/registration on the one hand and marriage/wedding on the other. Although the timing of the wedding ostensibly depended on the financial resources of the groom's family and the auspicious date they had selected, in fact it was now subject to the legal requirements imposed by official registration. Surprisingly, though, the ceremony itself and the ritual exchanges that accompanied it received little attention from officials. Unlike the 1980s when the county government had sought to curb the rising costs of bridewealth and increasingly extravagant weddings, the 1990s witnessed ever more elaborate weddings, with little state interference.[19] Officials, it seemed, were less interested in controlling the *content* of wedding rituals than in redefining their *significance*, particularly to the extent that the latter reflected the state's ability to regulate fertility. As I show in the next chapter, this separation of ritual content from its political and economic import would quickly affect all sectors of village society as families and young people struggled to meet the growing costs of wedding celebrations and the gift exchanges associated with them.

As state regulation expanded once again into these intimate domains of villagers' lives, it produced effects that spilled out beyond the bounds of that regulatory sphere. The behaviors made possible by the enforcement of marital registration began to take on a life of their own in Shanlin. As officials and older villagers gradually accepted the practice of conjugal visits once a couple had registered with the government, that convention began to spread to couples too young to register, whose sexual activity fell outside the regulatory gaze of the state.[20] Young people were slowly forming relationships prior to reaching the legal marriage age, and not all of them culminated in marriage. Even when those relationships involved sexual intimacy, local officials had no recourse to controlling or monitoring the fertility of the women involved, precisely because state conceptions of sexuality focused exclusively on reproduction within marriage (Friedman, 2000). Only if an underage woman became pregnant would officials intervene. In short, despite expanding and intensifying bureaucratic control, new state efforts to regulate marriage (and through it fertility) have produced a range of unintended consequences, some of which reinforce the power of state actors to shape intimate life and others that undermine related policy aims such as population control.

The Limits of Choice

When A Ping wrote to me in 1999 to tell me that she had found a new boyfriend among her coworkers at a local stone-carving factory, she again emphasized the prominence of feelings and choice in her decision: "Two or three coworkers pursued me, but I didn't accept them. [My boyfriend] pursued me for a long time and treated me very well. He is very sincere about feelings, so I chose him" (personal communication, December 20, 1999). By the time A Ping sent me this letter, she and her boyfriend had already registered their marriage at the township government office, and A Ping had begun living with him and his family. Before their relationship was socially acknowledged by a wedding ceremony, moreover, A Ping was several months' pregnant with their first child.[21]

By privileging feelings and rejecting the conventions of extended postmarital natal residence, did A Ping achieve happiness and security in her new marriage? Listening to her in the summer of 2000 as she recounted for me once again the story of how she had met her new spouse, I could not help but recall the warnings of other young women who had cautioned against the volatility of feelings and the dangers they posed to women. In actively "cultivating feelings" in their marriages, couples ran the risk that such feelings might dissipate or be destroyed. Many of my interlocutors acknowledged this risk by reflecting on the negative effects of having "too much feeling" or being on "too good terms" with a fiancé or spouse. Because a couple with feelings for each other often spent more time together, a husband or fiancé was more likely to lose interest in the relationship or the couple might begin to fight regularly, consequences that frequently led to divorce.[22] By declaring feelings through such behavior as socializing prior to marriage or making conjugal visits without being summoned, young women also ran the risk that a desire for intimacy might ultimately undermine their marital stability.

Although young women recognized these shortcomings in creating marriages based on feelings, they also admitted that young men no longer had interest in women who were unwilling to socialize prior to marriage or to visit their husbands once married. Eager to reject the feudal dispositions signified by agreeing to an arranged match or behaving in a pai se fashion, young women felt pressured to make themselves desirable to their male counterparts not only by enhancing their looks but also by becoming socially available. As Lila Abu-Lughod (1990) found in her study of young Bedouin wives, this emphasis on conjugality, while freeing women from extended family discipline, potentially enmeshes them in new webs of expectation and control that make them more dependent on one individual, their husbands. When relations with husbands break down or fail to live up to romantic expectations, young wives often find themselves with few options or places to turn for support.

By the time of my last visit to Shanlin in the summer of 2002, A Ping was firmly established in her conjugal home; her son was over a year old, and she had been living with her husband, her brother-in-law and his wife, and her mother-in-law for two years. Yet, on this visit, A Ping seemed more unhappy than ever. Unlike two years prior when she had painted an exuberantly happy picture of her marriage, now A Ping was willing to acknowledge its shortcomings. Only after their marriage did she discover that her husband was deeply in debt as the result of a gambling habit. Her mother-in-law had recently begun to pressure them to move out of the family's crowded house and find a place of their own, but A Ping complained that they had no money to do so because virtually all their earnings went to pay off her husband's debts. She sighed and looked distressed, admitting that for a time before her son was born she had even considered leaving her husband and returning to Shanlin. Yet she could not bear the thought of what other villagers would say about her if she did.

By choosing her own spouse, becoming pregnant before the wedding, and residing with her husband immediately, A Ping found herself with few options. Her own mother helped out as best she could, giving the couple money to pay off the interest on their debts and covering A Ping's gift-exchange obligations in Shanlin. It was obvious from A Ping's laments that day, however, that her natal family would not be willing to support her and her child if she were to leave her husband for good. Nor would she face particularly bright remarriage prospects, given her twice-divorced status and the fact that she had already borne a child (and a son at that), thereby raising questions about whether the government would permit her to have another. A Ping's experiences reveal how the private conjugal intimacy that market reforms appear to have fostered becomes interwoven with a form of public intimacy in which women's sexual activity, marital fidelity, and reproductive potential are subject to strict government scrutiny and community monitoring. Or, to put it another way, although young people now view conjugal intimacy as directed toward their own personal needs and desires, that intimacy is simultaneously enabled by and woven into a new collective project of producing a properly managed and "high quality" population.[23] Young women in particular are closely attuned to these powerful linkages between intimacy and regulation, as they incorporate the disciplinary effects of community opinion and family planning policies into their own marital calculations. Whereas free choice and feelings had enabled A Ping to move beyond the expectations of pai se brides that had characterized extended natal residence marriages of the past, they had also enmeshed her in new constraints—increasingly rigid definitions of what constituted open and progressive marital behavior together with expanding state control over marriage and women's reproductive capacities.

Conclusion

Emily Honig and Gail Hershatter perceptively noted that in 1980s' China, "young people courted and married in a society that did not speak with a unified voice about love" (1988:122). A similar diversity of views characterized Shanlin well into the 1990s. My persistent questions about love and marriage in the reform era often elicited the response, "It's not romantic love, it's chaotic love!"[24] Yet others like Soehua and Sutgoo clearly pointed to what they saw as the progressive, free, and open nature of contemporary relationships. These conflicting reactions mirror the contradictory experiences of young women and men who have struggled to create a social world in which choice and feelings might constitute established features of local marital practice. By constructing feelings as free and being pai se as feudal and restrictive, young people perpetuated earlier reformist visions of liberated socialist marriages. Yet they did so in a rapidly changing environment in which market forces, media images, and new leisure and consumer activities were transforming those very marital ideals and the courtship practices used to achieve them.

As they sought to redefine themselves as open and progressive actors in the post-Mao era, Shanlin youths struggled with the construction of marital emotions popularized through earlier marriage reform movements. Contemporary concepts of love, pai se, and feelings displayed what L. A. Rebhun (1999:207) terms a "palimpsestic quality," evoking multilayered discourses of collective socialist liberation, productivity, and women's embodied resistance to labor and sexual demands, as well as individual desires and personal fulfillment. These multiple layers reveal how the very experience and expression of marital emotions are shaped by changing social and economic conditions; by the same token, they also alert us to the political configuring of intimate life and the key role of marriage in a broader state disciplinary project aimed at producing the liberated subjects of a new socialist order.

Ironically, despite powerful Maoist state critiques of feudal wives and marriages "without feelings," only in the post-Mao era have large numbers of Shanlin youths begun to cultivate marriages based on feelings and choice. The space in which to forge these new relationships is a product of diverse and somewhat contradictory forces, including the socializing opportunities provided by mixed-sex workplaces and new bureaucratic interventions aimed at regulating marriage and fertility. This diverse legacy has had powerful consequences for young women who remain attuned to the nuances of societal expectations and parental support as they seek to establish new marital practices, all the while cognizant of the commanding gaze of state actors on their bodies and sexual activities. Their experiences and those of their male counterparts suggest the presence of a continuing struggle in reform-era China over the very meaning and consequences of marriage and intimate attachments.

CHAPTER FOUR 🌿 The Ties That Bind

The growing popularity of romance among Shanlin youths has intensified their desire for intimacy in their marriages. In the past, conjugal intimacy was hindered by a number of forces, from arranged matches, village exogamy, and collective work assignments to wives' pai se dispositions and ostensibly feudal close-mindedness. But same-sex peers were also accused of obstructing marital intimacy by holding young women to expectations of conjugal avoidance. In the 1950s, many work team reports went so far as to claim that the sisterly feelings fostered among such peers undermined the power of feelings in marriage, thereby subverting reformers' efforts to build liberated socialist marriages. These accounts presented same-sex intimacies as a counterproductive force, in effect denying female homosocial bonds any place in the larger intimate community of an emerging socialist China.

Within Shanlin, however, these same-sex or dui pnua relationships have constituted something quite distinct from the "counterintimacies" decried by early socialist reformers. Lauren Berlant and Michael Warner (1998) have coined the concept of counterintimacy to describe intimate forms that take shape outside of normative spaces such as kinship, the domestic arena, property relations, or even the nation. For Berlant and Warner these are nonstandard intimacies, some of a sexual nature, that have virtually no "institutional matrix" to which they can lay claim (1998:558–559, 562). Thinking about dui pnua bonds as one such example of counterintimacy enables us to appreciate the challenges that same-sex relationships posed to socialist notions of intimacy; at the same time, dui pnua also introduce significant cultural differences into the bases for intimacy and normativity outlined by Berlant and Warner. Dui pnua intimacies are at once physical and emotional without being narrowly (if at all) sexual. Nor are they intrinsically nonnormative; in fact, male and female dui pnua are regularly incorporated into village social, economic, and ritual life, supporting patrilineal kinship networks and creating alternative (but no less accepted) webs of relatedness. But as the critiques leveled against dui pnua networks by early socialist reformers made all too clear, there have been contexts in which female dui pnua bonds have been defined as nonnormative, where they have been made "counter." By looking more closely at what makes dui pnua ties into counterintimacies, we can better appreciate how Shanlin women have defined and experienced their intimate same-sex relationships and how at certain moments those bonds have been perceived as threatening to a particular social or political order.

On a hot October day in 1995 I accompanied a very pregnant Bbingden as she rested in her bedroom in her parents' home. I had been showing her a set of photographs published in a book about eastern Hui'an, and she had eagerly pointed out several women she recognized. She then reached into the side drawer of the wooden desk next to her bed and pulled out a picture of herself with a group of young women taken seven or eight years earlier when they were in their early twenties. Describing them as her "dui" (short for dui pnua), Bbingden added that the group had been close since they were children. When I asked whether she still saw them regularly, Bbingden replied, "They've given birth, married out. They don't have time."

Perhaps thinking ahead to the approaching birth and her eventual move to her husband's home, Bbingden then proceeded to describe how her dui pnua had played important roles in the ritual confirmation of her marriage: they had sent her off on the first day of her wedding and had returned on the third day to escort her back to her natal home. When Bbingden finally gave birth two months later, her dui pnua again came forward to visit her in the hospital or at her husband's home where she spent her postpartum month. They arrived laden with gifts of money, children's clothing, and gold jewelry to adorn her daughter, sometimes with their own children in tow. Soelan, a dui pnua with whom Bbingden continued to maintain a very close relationship, accompanied her throughout much of this time and even spent the night with her in the cold, drafty bedroom Bbingden reluctantly occupied in her mother-in-law's house.

As dui pnua are woven ritually into the fabric of community and family life, they shore up norms of patrilineal kinship and married women's patrilocal residence, even as they interlace such norms with same-sex intimacies and nonkin social networks. In this sense, dui pnua bonds are themselves accepted and expected relational forms in Huidong communities. And yet in the midst of this normalcy, there are moments when dui pnua ties have been singled out by state reformers and villagers alike for undermining a desired social world. As I outline the contours of this important relationship for Shanlin women, I pause to consider two contexts in which dui pnua are not so readily incorporated into a normative order: one, during the early socialist period when, as we saw in Chapter 2, a woman's dui pnua were accused of sapping affective energy from her marital relationship and encouraging joint suicides; and two, during the current market-reform era when ever-expanding dui pnua networks are blamed for excessive gift exchanges and increasingly burdensome ritual demands. Drawing attention to these moments when dui pnua bonds become detached from their institutional moorings and are denounced as counterintimacies reveals how dui pnua intimacy itself is produced and how it differs from the intimacy forged in heterosexual relationships and patrilineal kinship.

The Problem of Definition

A basic definition of dui pnua might read something like this: dui pnua are same-sex, predominantly nonkin and same-age cohort relationships formed by groups of women or men.[1] They usually originate in childhood (although that is changing more recently) and tend to incorporate peers from one's own village—neighbors, classmates, workmates, and sometimes children of a parent's dui pnua. For women, dui pnua initially include a core group of two or three girls and then expand over the life cycle as a woman's social contacts increase and she engages in a wider range of school and work activities. Among women who came of age prior to the post-Mao market reforms, dui pnua were generally cohesive units that did not change significantly after a woman reached her early teens. For younger women, however, diverse schooling and employment opportunities have produced divergent dui pnua trajectories, transforming dui pnua into egocentric networks that overlap but are not always identical from one woman to the next. Today, the formation of dui pnua relationships is not ritualized in any way, nor is it clear that dui pnua regularly formalized their bonds in the past.[2] Unlike the sisterhoods and sworn spinster communities previously found in the Pearl River Delta region of southern Guangdong, dui pnua do not have physical spaces that they can claim as their own (Sankar, 1978; Stockard, 1989). No girls' houses or spinster houses dot the Huidong landscape; instead, dui pnua might sleep together at one member's home or, in the past, in collective sites such as the women's militia barracks or the rudimentary dormitories provided for those sent to labor on public works projects.

This definition falls somewhat flat, however, when compared with the excitement and affect that infused women's voices when they talked to me about their dui pnua relationships. Younger women spoke proudly of the number of dui pnua who accompanied them on their wedding day; their elders grew animated as they recalled the activities they had engaged in with fellow dui pnua and the secrets they whispered to one another as they shared a bed at night. There was certainly more to dui pnua intimacy than the roles these peers played at weddings, births, and funerals, important as those ritual occasions were to village women and men. What made dui pnua different from other village ties, particularly those organized around agnatic and affinal kinship bonds?

When compared with the rich vocabulary found in other parts of Han China for describing same-sex, nonkin relationships, the term dui pnua is striking for its neutrality. Whereas Qing courtesans or Republican cotton-mill workers modeled their bonds on biological sister ties or mother-daughter relations (Mann, 1997:139–140; Honig, 1985), Huidong women adopted a kinship- and gender-neutral term most readily translated as "companion." And whereas young women in the area of southern Hunan known for its distinctive women's script (*nüshu*) formalized their nonkin, same-sex matches as "old sames" (*laotong*) or "sworn sisters" (*jiebaizimei*) (Silber, 1994), women in Huidong villages adopted naming conventions that identified their bonds with those of their male counterparts. Yet the neutrality of the term has not prevented Shanlin women from distinguishing their dui pnua ties from other kinds of relationships; in fact, they were quick to define dui pnua as being qualitatively different from patrilineal kin, even as they were often inconsistent in how they characterized that difference.

Shanlin women frequently contrasted dui pnua with a group of patrilineal kin they described as "one's own people" (gagi'e lang, also known as cindong), those individuals related in a male descent line through a woman's father or husband. "One's own people" share the same ancestral home and in principle trace descent from a common ancestor. Before villagers began building new homes in the flats, they often resided in or around these ancestral homes, making "one's own people" also one's closest neighbors. Although patrilineal kin groups grew more residentially dispersed in the post-Mao era, they developed closer ritual and economic ties as the government relaxed restrictions on lineage activities and worship. Commemorative celebrations for a lineage-branch god's birthday and collective efforts to rebuild a crumbling ancestral home provided occasions for reaffirming a conception of "one's own people" as those who were part of oneself, constituting a collective self juxtaposed to a collective other.

But what has this conceptualization meant in practice for women whose relationship to the category of "one's own people" has always been mediated through men? Prior to marriage, women define their gagi'e lang as the patrilineal descent group traced through their natal grandfather and father. Despite their internalization of this identity, women's membership in the category is in fact only temporary. After marriage and residence shift, they transfer their gagi'e lang to the husband's patriline, yet once again they are considered outsiders and achieve full membership through a male, in this case their sons. In the extended natal residence marriage region, moreover, the period of transition from one group to another is drawn out by virtue of a married woman's continued residence in her natal home prior to the birth of her first child. During this period, women are theoretically identified with both groups, although they and their families (both natal and conjugal) often strategically manipulate this coexisting membership in order to negotiate demands for time and resources.[3]

One might speculate that women form dui pnua ties as a reaction to their marginal status in patrilineal kin groups. Such a conclusion would make dui pnua merely derivative of a particular mode of kinship, however, an assumption undermined by the absence of similar nonkin ties among women in most of rural Han China. Furthermore, male dui pnua perform many of the same roles as female dui pnua (offering companionship, emotional support, and ritual assistance) and dui pnua networks work in many of the same social and ritual contexts as kin, features that support the conceptualization of dui pnua as a social relation on analytic par with kinship. For women, moreover, dui pnua provide an alternative and perhaps equally compelling sense of community, one built not on the symbolics of shared physical substance and common descent but on a particular understanding of intimacy as realized through emotional support and daily practice (cf. Smith-Rosenberg, 1975; Weston, 1991:107–116).

Despite women's tenuous connection to patrilineal kin groups, they consistently identified dui pnua as outsiders when compared with gagi'e lang, who were considered insiders. Biological sisters provided the most common point of reference: whereas sisters were "one's own people," dui pnua were clearly nonkin and thus outside of that privileged circle. This distinction is quite striking when we compare dui pnua once again with nonkin, same-sex bonds found elsewhere in China. Biological sisters did not serve as a relevant model for dui pnua as they had for Shanghai factory workers or Qing courtesans, nor did nonkin intimacies provide inspiration for biological kin as they did for sisters and cousins in the *nüshu* region who adopted the language of sworn sisters in letters to new brides (Silber, 1994:61). Yet Shanlin women were often inconsistent in their interpretations of how sisters differed from dui pnua. The degree and type of intimacy attributed to these two groups could vary dramatically, depending on the particular context or individual. When I asked a group of women in their early thirties to whom they felt closer, a dui pnua or a sister, one woman replied immediately, "Of course sisters are closer." Upon further discussion, however, the group acknowledged that not all women were closer to their sisters than to dui pnua. During their teenage and young adult years, the two sisters in my host family rarely, if ever, spoke directly to one another, worked, ate, or socialized together. They both had dui pnua, however, with whom they slept together at night, shared intimate thoughts and experiences, exchanged clothing, lent money, and even traveled outside the village. In this case, their dui pnua relationships clearly superseded the sibling tie in closeness and level of shared activity.

It is in part the fluid nature of kinship itself that makes it difficult to pin down the differences between dui pnua and kin. In Shanlin, the constructed nature of kin relations quickly becomes apparent when one recognizes that "blood" ties are merely one component of a complex social domain that also includes intricate forms of adoption (such as Bbokli's adoptive family, described in Chapter 1), ritualized bonds with fictive ancestors, and sworn relationships modeled on the parent-child tie (known in local dialect as kue). Market reforms have made villagers reliant on various kinds of kin relations in order to maximize their resources and social connections, and as young people increasingly marry within Shanlin, matrilineal and affinal kin have come to play more important social and economic roles (see also Yan, 2001). Dui pnua have a place within this heterogeneous web of relatedness not as substitutes for kin but instead as part of a broad realm of intimacy and obligation that encompasses many different relationships. In this sense, dui pnua ties force us to look beyond kinship in order to comprehend the range of intimate bonds that draw Shanlin villagers together.

The Production of Intimacy

Differences between dui pnua and biological sisters or patrilineal kin become more apparent when we look at how same-sex intimacy is actually produced. In describing fellow dui pnua as intimate companions, women used the adjective cin, which in its various cognate forms has a range of meanings applicable to both kin and nonkin bonds. Cin connotes genealogical closeness, emotional intimacy, even affection—qualities that were applied in different contexts to both groups.[4] Whereas its use in reference to dui pnua most commonly emphasized emotional closeness and mutual support, when attributed to kin, cin usually referred in a more abstract manner to the degree of genealogical closeness. In the case of dui pnua bonds, intimacy was something that had to be produced; among kin, it was often seen merely as a function of the genealogical tie. The use of cin to evoke same-sex intimacy also distinguished dui pnua relationships from marital bonds whose emotional depth was signified by the presence or absence of feelings.

When I asked Shanlin women to describe what made dui pnua such intimate companions, they tended to focus on two main components of the relationship. One was a sense of emotional closeness and compatibility, as seen in portrayals of dui pnua as women "who you are fated to be with" (wu yan'e) or "who know your heart" (di sim'e). This sense of intimacy revolved around the ability to share thoughts and secrets, such as those involving marriage and even sexual relations. Dui pnua offered emotional support during the difficult and often turbulent early years of marriage, prior to childbirth and its requisite shift to conjugal residence. This construction of dui pnua intimacy as the exchange of personal thoughts and experiences most closely approximates scholarly interpretations of close friendships and emotional bonds among Euro-American women, which tend to stress the use of emotional language as the major signifier of intimacy (Smith-Rosenberg, 1975). When recounting their dui pnua relationships for me, however, Shanlin women also emphasized a second component of intimacy, the kinds of joint activities they engaged in with fellow dui pnua. This conception of intimacy as engendered by certain forms of practice introduces an image of the dui pnua bond as one that must be produced and then reaffirmed over time.

In Shanlin, eating together and cooking for someone are activities that signify the existence of an intimate relationship, especially among family members or between a husband and wife. Older villagers often described the initiation of a second marriage by saying that a man "went to eat with" a particular woman, an expression I learned to interpret only after repeated questioning. Moreover, a wife might express her desire for a divorce by stating that she would no longer cook for her husband.[5] Nonresident married women employed the refusal to eat with their husbands' families as one means of eluding the claims of a marital tie and denying feelings of intimacy with their husbands and in-laws.⁶ When I asked young women why they were reluctant to live with their mothers-in-law, virtually all mentioned the fact that they "did not dare to eat their fill" in their husbands' homes. Only after A Hong, the second daughter-in-law in my host family, gave birth to her first child did she regularly join the family for meals. Serving herself a small bowl of watery rice gruel, she ate quickly and then rose immediately to help with the dishes. Her older sister-in-law urged her to stay seated and eat more, but she claimed to have satisfied her hunger.

Given this context it is striking that dui pnua frequently mentioned eating together as an important feature of their relationship. In contrast to most guests who politely refused offers of food or newly resident daughters-in-law who were reluctant to join conjugal kin at the same table, the dui pnua I knew were quite comfortable eating in one another's homes. They also shared delicacies and nutritious foods and even cooked for one another. In so doing, they assumed roles of reciprocal nurturing that presumed, by the very nature of such activities, a degree of intimacy not found among more genealogically distant kin or in other village ties.⁷ In addition to eating together, dui pnua frequently slept together at night and shared clothes, activities that also fell within the culturally recognized sphere of intimate behavior. Hence, they literally enacted their closeness through engaging in specific kinds of shared activities.

The relationship between Bbingden and Soelan that I mentioned above exemplifies this kind of intimacy. Both women were in their late twenties in the mid-1990s and had been dui pnua since their teenage years. They met when Soelan, who had once run a shop up on the mountain, came down to purchase stock at the wholesale store managed by Bbingden's sister. When Soelan's family built a new house down the road from Bbingden's natal home, the two women began to sleep together every night. On my first visits to Shanlin in 1993 and 1994, the second story of Bbingden's natal home had not yet been completed, and so I joined them in the old-fashioned canopy bed they occupied in one of the downstairs bedrooms. A few months before my arrival in 1993, they had opened a fruit shop together in the front of Bbingden's house. Although Soelan usually returned to her parents' house for meals, she occasionally ate together with Bbingden's natal family or brought over favorite foods to share with Bbingden in the shop.

When I returned to Shanlin in the fall of 1995, I found both Bbingden and Soelan noticeably pregnant with their first children, Bbingden after many years of marriage and Soelan after divorcing her first husband and marrying a man from a village on the other side of the township seat. At the end of the year, both women gave birth to daughters, a mere month apart. Bbingden went into labor first, and during her postpartum month she frequently asked Soelan to keep her company at her husband's house. Only after Soelan gave birth and moved to her husband's village did the two women cease to spend their nights together. Throughout much of their adolescence and early adulthood, in other words, they maintained an intimate relationship by sharing culturally meaningful activities (eating and sleeping together, sharing a business venture) and by confiding in one another their desires, fears, and experiences.

This sense of intimacy is by no means a recent product of the reform era. Both women who married before 1949 and those who married soon after the Communists came to power often compared the strong emotional bonds forged with fellow dui pnua (notably not biological sisters) to their weak ties with husbands considered strangers for several years following marriage. Folk songs dating to those periods are replete with depictions of the care and companionship provided by dui pnua, which starkly contrast with the heavy workloads, loneliness, and suffering experienced by young wives resident in their conjugal homes.

The popular bitterness song titled "The Twelve Miseries" offers a compelling example of this genre. Written in the 1950s by two Shanlin youths, it speaks in the voice of a young married woman who expresses her hatred for her husband and his family, meanwhile bemoaning her bitter fate. In the fifth stanza of the song, she laments:

> The fifth misery is this wretched fate
> At times my body is not at peace
> There are no zue dui [dui pnua] to care for us[8]
> Leaving me to suffer my entire life.

The absence of fellow dui pnua to care for women when they visit their husbands or after they shift residence is a prominent theme in this lament genre. Another song, of unknown authorship, describes the twelve months of the year and the visits a young bride makes to her conjugal family during each month. The song vividly depicts the labor demanded of her in different seasons and her sense of despair and suffering at each visit. In the second stanza, the young woman mourns:

> The second month brings the wintry crab season
> Arriving at their home to perform long labor
> Tears stream down and my eyes redden
> There are no zue dui to care for us.

Faced with heavy work burdens and the loneliness and bitterness brought on by living among strangers, young wives in these songs longingly recalled the care and support offered by fellow dui pnua. Bitterness songs thereby reinforced the emotional intimacy of same-sex bonds even as they acknowledged the power of marriage and conjugal residence to render those ties asunder.

The strength of dui pnua ties was also reflected in their power to forge links in death as in life. As we saw in Chapter 2, post-1949 socialist reformers were quite concerned about joint suicides among dui pnua and the threat such deaths posed to marital stability in the region. Subsequent Chinese-language scholarship on Huidong has looked anew at these suicides. In an often cited article, Xiamen University professor Jiang Bingzhao attributes women's group suicides to oaths sworn among fellow dui pnua that emphasized their desire to continue their bonds in death as in life: "Although we were not born together, we will die together. You must not wrong me, I must not wrong you" (1989:194). Jiang's account and the reports penned by early post-1949 work teams confirm that groups of dui pnua did form suicide pacts and take their lives together, even on rare occasions as late as the 1980s.[9] For these authors, collective suicides attested to the nonnormative nature of dui pnua relations and the tragedies they produced for natal and conjugal families alike. Here I am interested in how the particular construction of dui pnua intimacy facilitated the continuity of such bonds after death in ways that also reintegrated same-sex networks into normative social institutions.

One feature of collective suicides rarely discussed in the existing literature is the extent to which they affirmed the power wielded by dui pnua over one another. In other words, group suicides were more than destructive events; they were also performative acts that enacted the intimacy and obligation inherent in the dui pnua bond. Many of the reports written by 1950s' work teams sent to disband suicide groups in Huidong emphasized that only one young woman in any group desired to commit suicide, but that she successfully convinced her fellow dui pnua to join her in death. Shanlin residents in the 1990s attributed women's tendency to commit suicide to their "thin skin" and feudal thinking, describing women as quick to take their own lives following disputes or perceived attacks on their reputations.[10] They characterized such deaths as impulsive and unnecessary; young women in those days, villagers often claimed, "would go and die for nothing." I suggest that we consider how those collective suicides, rather than simply being "for nothing," also affirmed the collective power of the dui pnua bond. The power of dui pnua intimacy created an obligation that not only transcended the desire to live (as expressed in the saying quoted by Jiang above) but also superseded women's commitment to their natal families and future conjugal ones.

By the time of my research in the mid-1990s, this power was reproduced in life cycle rituals and forms of female worship that reaffirmed the bonds between living and deceased dui pnua. At the same time that suicide validated the ties among dui pnua who died together, it also created new obligations between the living and the dead that women satisfied through innovations on existing forms of social practice. For instance, young women in the 1990s often paid homage to deceased dui pnua who had taken their own lives or otherwise died young by cleaning their graves and placing graveside offerings during the annual Tomb Sweeping Festival (*qing ming jie*). The right to sweep a grave was customarily limited to individuals in the category of the deceased's "own people," but under these circumstances dui pnua assumed the status of kin in performing the ritual.[11] Moreover, young women regularly visited the parents and grandparents of deceased dui pnua, especially during holiday times. Some attributed persistent physical ailments or misfortune to the fact that they occasionally failed to make such visits, suspicions often confirmed through consultation with a spirit medium. Others distributed ritual gifts to the families of deceased dui pnua when they married or gave birth, just as they would have were the dui pnua still alive. The powerful ties between the dead and living were reconfirmed (and in some sense put to rest) when the fiancé of a woman who died before marriage himself prepared to marry. He first invited her dui pnua to a meal, prior to which the group traveled the route from her natal home to his house, just as they would have for a wedding procession. Only three days later could the man marry his new bride, having first completed his obligations to the dui pnua of his deceased fiancée.

The spirits of dui pnua who have taken their own lives belong to the category P. Steven Sangren terms "remembered ghosts," nonkin who have died violent deaths and are remembered because of their untimely and unnatural end. Sangren argues that remembered ghosts are considered particularly powerful (*ling*) because they mediate the opposing forces of *yin* and *yang*. They are *yang* because they are remembered (as opposed to forgotten ghosts), but their status as nonkin also defines them as *yin* in relation to ancestors (Sangren, 1987:144–146). The power that deceased dui pnua—as members par excellence of this anomalous category—exercise over their living counterparts is expressed in a female-centric form of worship known as hulin worship, which placates the spirits of individuals who have died unnaturally or prematurely, thereby converting them to a more *yang* state.

The spirits of deceased dui pnua often inflict their memory on their living counterparts through instigating illness or family misfortune. In the case of married women who have shifted residence, this spiritual intervention commonly appears in the form of an illness afflicting either themselves or their children. Women frequently turn to local spirit mediums to resolve such problems, and mediums in turn often blame these disturbances on the spirit of a woman's deceased dui pnua. They instruct the woman to install a small wooden figure of her dui pnua in a hulin worship case. These cases are kept separate from the main household altars located in public living spaces; they are found in bedrooms or other private rooms in the house and are installed only by married women who have taken up conjugal residence (see Fig. 10). In addition to figures of deceased dui pnua, the cases often contain figures representing a woman's conjugal (and occasionally natal) kin who died young,

FIG. 10: Hulin worship case (photograph by the author, 2002)

spouses or kin from a previous life (in the Buddhist cycle of death and rebirth), or generic spirits representing women and men who died in childhood or before marriage. The distinguishing feature of this kind of worship is that it appeases the spirits of individuals or categories of individuals who cannot be worshipped as ancestors because they have died without descendants or spouses.[12]

Most of the dui pnua worshipped in hulin cases or remembered through rituals and visits to the deceased's parents have died by suicide, one of the most common forms of violent death in Chinese society, particularly for women (Lee and Kleinman, 2000; Wolf, 1975). Bloch and Parry describe suicide as "the supreme example of 'bad' death," by which they mean that "the suicide acts for himself alone, and loses for others his regenerative power" (1982:16–17). By extension, they argue that death by suicide eliminates any possibility of individual rebirth or renewal for the community as a whole, a conclusion echoed by Lee and Kleinman in their analysis of suicide in China: "Whatever the individual motives involved, suicide represents a rejection of everything in society on the level of cultural production, and compels the members of society to doubt its core values" (2000:223). The case of dui pnua worship, however, suggests that such examples of "bad" death might in fact offer renewal (or at least affirmation) to a community, but one differently conceived.

The inclusion of the spirit of a deceased dui pnua in a hulin case redirects the power of the spirit to the welfare of the worshipper, a fellow dui pnua. In this case, the power that women attribute to deceased dui pnua reinforces and reenacts the intimacy experienced when such individuals were still alive. Moreover, unlike most of the other figures included in the hulin case, deceased dui pnua do not stand in a kinship relation to the worshipper; their social ties travel through dui pnua networks and extend the protective power of the spirit to the nuclear families of each individual worshipper. In cases where several dui pnua worship the same spirit, those links cross the boundaries of patrilineal kin groups, natal ties, and even villages. Thus the power of deceased dui pnua as realized through hulin worship and other forms of remembrance undermines the insider/outsider distinction so prominent in comparisons between living dui pnua and kin. In fact, this worship suggests an alternative conception of community to the hierarchical, cross-generational patrilineal unit usually reaffirmed through death ritual and ancestor worship (Sangren, 1987; Watson, 1982), one organized around predominantly nonkin, female dui pnua ties.

Only two days remained before the one-month birth or sang'geng celebration for A Peng's second granddaughter, and she was frantic with preparations. Without a minute of her own time to spare, A Peng asked me to make the trip to a village nunnery where the senior nun would worship on her behalf. The focus of this worship was not the gods who resided on the family's household altar (A Peng would worship them herself). Instead, the nun would recite before the goddess Mazu the names of the figures in A Peng's hulin case, requesting peace and prosperity for the growing family. As A Peng issued rapid-fire instructions that cold February morning, she told me to write down a list of the spirits in her case (as she herself was illiterate). Consulting with her dui pnua A Bbi, who was helping with preparations, A Peng enumerated seven figures, four of whom were generic names for individuals who had died prematurely or spouses from a previous life and three of whom were people A Peng had known. I prepared a bag of oranges as an offering, spirit money, and incense and then set off on the short walk to the nunnery.

The senior nun was not in when I arrived, having been summoned to a meeting at the village government office intended to solicit contributions for a new junior middle school. When she returned to the nunnery, having committed 10,000 *yuan* to the project, she rested for a few minutes before listening patiently to my request. Rising and approaching the Mazu altar in the center of the nunnery's cavernous main hall, she threw divination blocks to determine whether A Peng's list was complete. When the god replied in the negative, she asked me to phone A Peng for the two missing figures. After writing out the list again, she had me read it aloud to her and two other women waiting there to worship. The three personal names were instantly recognized by the two onlookers, both of whom were roughly the same age as A Peng although they did not hail from Haibin, A Peng's natal village. When I said "A Ggin," one of them commented, "that is [A Peng's] older sister." Loo Wna was A Ggin's dui pnua, and the two had committed suicide together, they added. The third, Gnualan, was married to someone they couldn't recall, and they thought that she too had drowned herself on the same occasion. Although the two onlookers had not known the three deceased women personally, they were well aware of their power as spirits and A Ggin's reputation had spread among women of this generation in both Shanlin and neighboring Haibin.

Having worshipped with A Peng on many occasions, I had come to learn that she was not the only woman to have installed a figure of A Ggin in her hulin case. A Peng's dui pnua from her native Haibin had also installed her, as had A Ggin's own dui pnua, who were several years their senior. Just a month earlier, A Peng's dui pnua A Bbi had been talking to me about her relationship with A Peng when she brought up the subject of A Ggin. A Ggin had been quite pretty and bright, A Bbi recalled, but after her marriage she was often reluctant to visit her husband. Only many years later did she give birth to a son, and even then she drowned herself in the reservoir together with her dui pnua. A Bbi wasn't sure why A Ggin had taken her own life, but she confirmed that A Ggin's spirit was very powerful and that many women from Haibin worshipped her. Given that few women of this generation had married within Haibin, their worship united them in a female community that extended across the township's many villages. In fact, one Haibin woman who had married into Shanlin was widely known for being possessed by A Ggin's spirit, and as a result she was often visited by other Haibin natives who regarded her as a powerful spirit medium. In 2002, I learned that this community of middle-aged worshippers, united by dui pnua and natal village ties, had begun to expand across generations, as one or two instructed their newly resident daughters-in-law to install A Ggin in their hulin cases as well.

The Everyday Practice of Dui Pnua *Intimacy*

Certainly not all dui pnua reaffirmed their bonds through death and worship; most produced same-sex intimacy in much more mundane ways as they labored together and offered mutual support in daily life. Although women of all ages described a dui pnua as someone they did everything with, the Nationalist, Maoist, and post-Mao eras provided different frameworks for these everyday activities, with the result that the composition and scope of dui pnua bonds fluctuated as well. Elderly women emphasized that work patterns in their youth had prevented them from interacting with fellow dui pnua during the day, leaving them only the evening and nighttime hours to gather with their peers to chat, knit, and sleep together, often five or six to a bed. Despite the socialist government's efforts to disband dui pnua networks in order to prevent joint suicides, the shift to collectivized labor in the mid-1950s provided a new basis for creating and maintaining dui pnua ties. Girls and young women began working together on collective plots, in newly developed fish hatcheries and seaweed beds, and on public infrastructure projects. These work environments, together with new socialist institutions such as People's Schools and People's Militias, expanded the realm of shared dui pnua activity and the intensity of group interaction.

The dui pnua experiences of A Peng and A Bbi are indicative of these changes. Both were part of a substantial group of women who married into Shanlin from neighboring Haibin in the 1950s and 1960s at the height of collectivization. Of the original five members of their dui pnua, A Peng, A Bbi, and Ggimlan had maintained their ties into middle age. They had known one another since they were roughly eleven years old, when, as A Peng recalled, they "were together all the time." If one of their families needed help with some work, their dui pnua would come to offer their labor. As children, the group slept together in the same bed every night and spent many of their daytime hours together as well. From ages eleven to thirteen they attended the noon literacy school established by the brigade. In their mid-teens, they were sent to build an irrigation canal in a township south of the county seat and remained there for two full years. When they returned to Haibin, they were assigned to raise seaweed together in the ocean plots bordering the village.

Ggimlan married first, at age seventeen, and A Bbi followed a year later. When they were nineteen, A Peng and Ggimlan were sent to harvest bamboo in western Fujian, while A Bbi went with other young women to catch squid in the waters off Shantou. After returning to Haibin they resumed their joint work cultivating seaweed. When A Bbi's husband's family began building a new house in Shanlin, A Bbi brought her dui pnua with her each night to help with the construction. A Bbi did not move permanently to Shanlin until the age of 22, however, when she gave birth to her eldest son. She was the first of their dui pnua to have a child, and A Peng and Ggimlan continued to visit her regularly in Shanlin before they too shifted residence.

The joint activities of these three dui pnua were more varied and extensive than the patterns of dui pnua interaction described by elderly village women. As I argued in Chapter 1, the shift to a collective economy meant that young women's labor was no longer organized by their families but by the production brigade. This shift increased the possibility that groups of dui pnua might work together during daytime hours, whereas they had engaged in separate, family-organized labor in the pre-1949 era. Moreover, the mobilization of women to work on long-term public infrastructure projects also strengthened dui pnua ties and enabled groups of young women to maintain their same-sex networks even when they were not resident in their natal villages. Ironically, it was these very same patterns of labor organization that young men had argued hindered the development of conjugal "feelings," weakening marital bonds while strengthening dui pnua relationships.

The different marriage patterns of various generations of Shanlin women also influenced their ability to maintain dui pnua ties after taking up conjugal residence. The bitterness songs quoted above lamented young wives' inability to sustain strong dui pnua ties after moving to their conjugal homes. Older women often reminded me that dui pnua "go their own way after having children," and even Bbingden had suggested that the demands of housework and child care left married women little time to visit with fellow dui pnua, especially when such visiting required trips to other villages. Yet for A Bbi, A Peng, and Ggimlan, the fact that they had all married into the same village enabled them to preserve their dui pnua circle after giving birth. The unification of Haibin and Shanlin into a single production brigade had solidified ties between the two communities, producing a flurry of intrabrigade marriages that facilitated the perpetuation of women's dui pnua relationships.

When A Peng and her husband built a new house down in the flats in the 1980s, A Bbi came daily to help carry loads of sand and dirt. When an important event took place in one of their families, the other dui pnua would help cook and prepare or would send a child or grandchild over with needed supplies. By the time of my research, this group of women had reached middle age and thus were free from child-care responsibilities of their own. A Bbi often slept at A Peng's house after a late night of chatting or watching television. When A Peng's daughter and daughter-in-law gave birth, A Bbi accompanied A Peng to the hospital in the county seat and helped with cooking and housework after they returned. A Peng later went with A Bbi and her daughter-in-law for the latter's prenatal visit at the county hospital. The two women intervened in each other's family disputes, and A Peng even served as matchmaker for one of A Bbi's sons, a role performed by male dui pnua as well. They were known across the community for their regular visits to spirit mediums and their travels to temples throughout the region. Ggimlan seemed to have dropped out of the cycle of daily contact by this time in their lives, yet she participated in larger outings such as informal pilgrimages to worship at distant temples.

Despite their more variegated labor activities within the collective economy, this group of dui pnua remained centered on childhood ties formed in their natal community. For women such as Siokden who came of age in the late 1970s (see Chapter 1), the shift from a collective to a market economy offered them even greater opportunities to diversify their dui pnua networks as they moved from cultivating seaweed beds, working collective sweet potato plots, and attending People's Schools to joining construction teams in nearby urban centers and engaging in wage labor within Shanlin itself. Because many of these women were now marrying within their natal communities, they were able to maintain these larger networks after marriage and childbirth, if they so desired.

The Tomb Sweeping Festival in 1996 dawned clear and warm, a welcome respite from the cold rains that had persisted through much of the early spring. There was a festive air in the village market as villagers purchased foodstuffs, incense, and spirit money to use in offerings at their ancestral homes and at family grave sites high up on the mountain. I ran into Siokden as she was returning from her ancestral home; she would soon set off to worship on her husband's boat docked in the harbor, and she invited me to join her and another woman whose spouse fished together with him. The fishing boat was small, roughly ten meters in length, and it rocked back and forth in the wind as Siokden placed her offerings in the front hold and lit incense before retreating to the rear to burn coarse sheets of spirit money. After gathering up the offerings, we walked to several small temples and shrines along the coast where fishermen had placed the bones of corpses they had found at sea or that had washed up on the beach. These were dangerous, even dirty, sites, Siokden warned me, and she and her companion hastily lit incense and burned spirit money to appease the wandering souls before moving on as quickly as possible. On our way back to her house, I asked Siokden whether the other woman was her dui pnua. She hesitated for a moment, and then described her as a friend, adding that they had only met as adults after the woman married and moved to the east side of the village near Siokden's conjugal home. As for her dui pnua, Siokden added, she probably had several hundred from the different activities she had pursued over time. Adding them up, she counted over a hundred dui pnua in total.

It was not unusual for women Siokden's age and younger to claim such large numbers of dui pnua, even when they no longer maintained regular contact with them. Surely they were exaggerating, I thought to myself, comparing Siokden's initial claim of several hundred dui pnua with her final count of roughly one hundred, itself quite substantial when compared with the dui pnua networks of older women such as A Peng that rarely exceeded seven or eight members. Of course, Siokden had gone on to describe how she invited only ten or so close dui pnua to accompany her on her wedding day, knowing that none of them would refuse. The numbers had further decreased over time as some failed to give a gift when she had a baby or refused to contribute labor when her mother-in-law built a new house, all recognizable ways of signaling that they had grown apart and did not want to keep up the relationship. By 31, Siokden reflected, she no longer maintained close ties with many of her childhood dui pnua.

Although Siokden married within her natal village, the demands of child rearing and her husband's coastal fishing left her little opportunity to sustain her dui pnua relationships into adulthood. For women a few years younger, such as Bbingden and Soelan, an even greater diversity of wage labor and business possibilities enabled some to preserve their dui pnua networks even after bearing children. Once Bbingden and Soelan had finished their postpartum recoveries, they resumed work in their fruit shop, with Bbingden returning to virtually permanent residence in her parents' house and Soelan either commuting to Shanlin on a daily basis or living with her parents for weeks at a time. In mid-1997, they moved the shop to a stall in the village market and invited a third dui pnua (also a new mother) to run the business with them. When I returned to Shanlin in the summer of 1998, the three women were still working together, spelling one another in order to attend to child care or household duties. By 2000 the third dui pnua had opened her own stall, and Soelan and Bbingden had moved their shop back to its original location. Even after Bbingden gave birth to a son in 2001, Soelan continued to run the store for both of them. She regularly purchased food and clothing for Bbingden and her children, and Bbingden reciprocated by cooking daily meals that her daughter carried over for Soelan to eat while she worked. When I stayed with Bbingden and her husband in their new home in 2002, Bbingden frequently described how Soelan had cared for her during her difficult second pregnancy and had even lent her money to finish construction on the house. Although the two dui pnua had given birth and shifted residence (in Soelan's case moving to another village entirely), they were able to maintain their dui pnua ties through participating in a joint business venture and continuing to feed and clothe one another.

Ritual Reaffirmation and Contestation

Although work and marital experiences play a critical role in the formation and perpetuation of dui pnua networks, life cycle rituals fully integrate same-sex ties into a world of patrilineal kinship, patrilocal residence, and conjugal reproduction. During funerals, birth celebrations, and weddings, dui pnua act more like kin than at any other time. By the same token, their increasing presence in some of these rituals, particularly weddings, has also inspired new critiques that identify changing forms of dui pnua intimacy with growing ritual burdens in a cash economy. As gift exchanges and ritual expectations place increasingly heavy demands on families and individuals, dui pnua ties have once again come under scrutiny, this time for raising the costs of social obligations to levels that many villagers are hard-pressed to meet.[13]

Girls are educated in dui pnua ritual obligations from a young age, something I learned as I watched A Peng and A Bbi weave such teachings into their daily routines with their four-year-old granddaughters. After A Bbi arrived at A Peng's home bright and early one summer morning with her granddaughter in tow, A Peng called for her own granddaughter, who lived in the east wing of the extended family's sprawling home. Instructing the girl to play with her guest, A Peng added, "afterwards when you get married the two of you can go together [in the wedding procession]." A little while later, after she and A Bbi had caught up on gossip, A Peng called the children over for breakfast, telling them to sit nicely and eat together. As the girls began to sip their steaming rice porridge, A Peng offered a final comment—addressed as much to A Bbi as to the children—that when they grew up they could become dui pnua and go together to send off their parents and grandparents when they died.

One sign of Shanlin's aging population was the funerals that took place on a weekly, at times even daily, basis over the course of my research. As A Peng's instructions indicated, when a parent or grandparent died, dui pnua were expected to participate in the funeral procession that wound from the deceased's ancestral home, through the center of the village, and up to a burial plot located somewhere on the mountainside above the upper village.[14] Close dui pnua helped

FIG. 11: Funeral procession (photograph by the author, 1996)

with specific tasks during funeral preparations and accompanied the mourner during the rituals that preceded the funeral itself. Once a burial date was selected, they distributed funeral paraphernalia to the mourner's extended dui pnua network and collected a small sum of money from each participant to offset the cost of the funeral.[15] Pieces of coarse muslin, hand towels, or handkerchiefs were carried or worn during the funeral procession and identified for onlookers the participant's relationship to a specific primary mourner. The colors of decorative yarn and types of fabric used in funeral cloths and attire marked degrees of genealogical closeness in the relationship between the mourner and the deceased.[16] As a result, the ability of mourners to marshal large numbers of kin and dui pnua was made evident to those observing the funeral procession through the items participants wore or carried as they followed the coffin on its final journey through the community (see Fig. 11).

The increasing elaborateness of funerals in Shanlin, with families holding gongdik ceremonies to guide the deceased's soul on its way to the underworld and hiring opera troupes and marching bands to perform during the procession and after the burial, was not itself a function of the number of dui pnua who participated, although a substantial dui pnua presence certainly displayed for onlookers a mourner's social capital. With weddings, however, there was a more direct correlation between the expansion of dui pnua networks and the ritual burdens shouldered by young people and families alike. Whereas prior to 1949 a bride had been carried in a sedan chair on her wedding day without any kin or dui pnua to accompany her, after Liberation brides were required to walk to their conjugal homes and one or two dui pnua served as escorts. There was little feasting or gift giving during the high socialist decades; at most a dui pnua would be served a simple bowl of rice noodles before setting off on her return journey. Beginning in the late 1970s and early 1980s, however, these escorts were treated to tea and snacks provided by the groom's family, and marital gift exchanges gradually became more elaborate. As Siokden recalled when describing for me her own wedding in 1983, a dui pnua who participated in a wedding was expected to present the bride with a small monetary gift, usually only a few *yuan* in those days. On the second day of the wedding, the bride's dui pnua returned to visit her in her conjugal home, this time bringing her delicacies such as lean pork or pig liver that they cooked themselves (by the 1990s, however, most dui pnua simply purchased foodstuffs for the bride). On each of these occasions, the groom's family prepared bags of candy to send back with the bride's dui pnua. On the third day, one or two close dui pnua accompanied the bride as she made the rounds of her husband's village to serve tea to his patrilineal kin. When the bride returned to her natal home that afternoon, she again brought bags of candy from her husband's family to distribute to dui pnua, natal kin, and neighbors.

By the 1990s, young women were marrying with as many as 50 or 60 dui pnua in their wedding processions. Decked out in their best attire, dui pnua traveled by foot or bus from the bride's natal home to her conjugal one and protected her from the onslaught of firecrackers set off by the groom's dui pnua as the bridal procession approached his house (Fig. 12). Serving tea and snacks to this entourage was no longer sufficient; now a family marrying in a daughter-in-law was expected to treat her dui pnua to a banquet on the afternoon of the wedding in addition to sending them off with bags of candy, fried cakes, and fruit when they departed. When Bbingden's next-door neighbor was preparing for her oldest son's wedding in January 1997, she argued that it was this distribution of ritual gifts

FIG. 12: Bride escorted by her dui pnua during her wedding procession (photograph by the author, 1997)

that made the event so expensive. The groom's family traditionally sent the bride's family several baskets filled with food and clothing as part of the wedding exchanges, but the quantity had increased dramatically in recent years. Her future daughter-in-law's family had originally asked for twelve loads (each load was two baskets), but two days before the wedding the neighbor was in Bbingden and Soelan's fruit shop complaining that the family now wanted two more loads of fruit. In addition, the bride had initially requested seventy bags of candy to distribute to her dui pnua, but now she had raised it to seventy-five. On the day of the wedding, moreover, the groom's family scrambled to assemble five additional bags for extra dui pnua who had accompanied the bride, forcing the women to stand around waiting uncomfortably as the bride's aunt negotiated with the groom's family.

We can see how the expansion in the size of dui pnua networks has increased the burden on families marrying in a daughter-in-law. In addition to hosting the bride's dui pnua, many families now also hold banquets for the dui pnua of the groom as well as those of his father and brothers. These expenses, when added to the costs of hosting patrilineal kin and fulfilling gift-exchange obligations, make weddings a daunting prospect for many village families. Unlike Mayfair Yang (2000) who finds in this ritual economy an empowering archaic logic that undermines capitalist principles of production and exploitation, Shanlin residents expressed more ambivalent responses to their newfound ritual freedom. Rather than celebrating what Yang terms "economic hybridity," they were more likely to critique the burdens of ritual expenditure, deploying long-standing socialist rhetoric to attack what they saw as wasteful extravagance (poodiong lionghui). Bbingden's neighbor ultimately spent over 30,000 *yuan* on her son's wedding, with the gift bags presented to the bride's dui pnua and natal kin accounting for roughly a third of that sum. And she still had a second son to marry off in the future.

As village youths reached adulthood in the mid-1990s, the growing size and changing composition of their dui pnua networks also added to their own financial burdens as their peers began to marry and give birth in increasing numbers. By working in stone-carving factories, running shops, or participating in new kinds of leisure activities, young women and men had greater opportunities to meet not only fellow villagers but also peers from across the township. As they incorporated these new social contacts into existing modes of same-sex sociality, they further altered basic premises about dui pnua intimacy, longevity, and mutual obligation.

A Ping, whose marital experiences I described in the previous chapter, claimed to have over one hundred dui pnua, and she proudly recounted for me the contexts in which she had formed these bonds. She started with the earliest group, those she had met when her family built their house in the flats in the early 1980s. She was only "a little thing" then and spent most of her days with this core group of four dui pnua. As time went on, she began to contract out orders to knit sweaters for export and met more young women from the neighborhood as a result. At age seventeen she started polishing stones in a township factory, where she encountered women from villages across the township. She also moved to the nearby city of Quanzhou for a year to work in a factory there. After returning to Shanlin, she opened up a dry goods shop in the village and continued to knit for export. At each of these stages, A Ping explained, her circle of dui pnua expanded accordingly.

A Ping's experience of building a dui pnua network was rather typical for women of her generation. Such large numbers necessarily created a hierarchy of closer and more distant dui pnua, something A

Ping herself described. Moreover, the fact that young women were forming many of these dui pnua ties in their teenage years meant that they faced ever-expanding gift obligations once their peers began to marry and have children. Many women in their teens and twenties confessed that they felt pressured to display their social worth by marshaling as many dui pnua as possible to participate in their weddings. As one unmarried woman admitted to me, if she didn't invite very many dui pnua to accompany her when she married, then people would say that she didn't have any. Young women gathered along village streets to observe wedding processions and were quick to judge the number of dui pnua accompanying the bride. This social competition, coupled with young women's access to more substantial cash resources, made ritual exchanges increasingly burdensome.

During the winter of 1996, A Ping complained repeatedly about how overwhelmed she was by her gift demands; over the next three months she would have to accumulate roughly 2,000 *yuan* to meet dui pnua gift needs for weddings and upcoming births. The income from her dry goods shop fell far short of such an amount, and she frequently had to borrow money from her mother to fulfill her ritual obligations.[17] Dui pnua intimacy for her was now marked not only by shared activities and emotional support but also by the material contributions that shored up these bonds and insured their longevity. As A Ping and many other women reminded me, failure to participate in these exchanges (known colloquially as to deh lang, meaning literally "to follow" or "to go along with others") would signify a rejection of the intimacy and obligation inherent in the dui pnua tie.

A Ping listed for me the precise amounts she would have to present to specific individuals in the ensuing months. Her required gifts for village dui pnua who were soon to marry fell into two main categories: women who had attended her wedding and those she had met after she married. There were three brides in the latter group, and each required a gift of 50 *yuan*, the going rate in the mid-1990s (for close dui pnua, 100 *yuan* was the norm). For women who had accompanied A Ping when she herself married several years earlier, the expected gift was significantly less. As she explained it, she only had to present an increment above the gift that woman had given her. Because all three of the women on A Ping's list who fell within this category had presented her with a gift of 5 *yuan* on her wedding day, she only had to return a gift of 10 *yuan*, an acceptable increment above the initial gift.

The addition of an increment above the original amount obscures the compulsion to return inherent in the gift by both its difference and its deferral (Bourdieu, 1977:5; Mauss, 1990). As Pierre Bourdieu argues, the delay in the return of a gift, perhaps one of several years, further draws out the sense of obligation between the two parties (1977:6–7). Young women in the 1990s faced a greater sense of obligation overall due to the large number of dui pnua relationships they formed and a compressed apex of gift giving created by shorter intervals between marriage and childbirth. At the same time, however, the increasingly volatile nature of dui pnua relations potentially altered the terms of the exchange relationship itself. Because dui pnua networks had begun to fluctuate so dramatically over time, with additions and subtractions occurring apace throughout the period in which young women married and gave birth, there was no guarantee that a dui pnua today would be a dui pnua tomorrow. More importantly, she might not have been a dui pnua yesterday, in which case the money an already married dui pnua gives her on her wedding day will never be returned.

These fluctuations have increased the likelihood of incomplete cycles of exchange, introducing the uncertainty that Bourdieu finds so central to the perpetuation of exchange practices. Bourdieu attributes this tension to the individual strategies and collective forms of misrecognition that undergird gift exchanges. Among Shanlin residents of A Ping's generation, by contrast, uncertainty was also fostered by local cadres' recent enforcement of the legal marriage age. This enforcement produced an artificial division in the marital ages of young women belonging to the same generational cohort, with the result that as dui pnua networks expanded over time, there was a greater possibility of one-sided gift giving and, hence, ultimately of the failure to maintain dui pnua ties after marriage and childbirth.

The gift obligations faced by young women like A Ping were further compounded by changing perceptions of what categories of people required such gifts and thus implicitly by transformations in the very composition of dui pnua networks and the kind of intimacy they created. As A Ping enumerated the individuals for whom she would have to provide gifts, I was struck by her inclusion of a group of friends (ping iu) from Chongwu, the township seat, who would soon marry. Three of these friends were men and two were women.[18] Because these individuals were from the township seat and not the village, she included them in the more generic and less intimate category of friends rather than in the category of dui pnua.

In a conversation we had when I returned to Shanlin in the summer of 1998, however, A Ping referred to another young woman as her Chongwu dui pnua. Surprised, I asked her how someone from Chongwu town could be a dui pnua: Weren't dui pnua supposed to come from Shanlin or at least from another village in eastern Hui'an? She concurred with my definition but added that she used the term dui pnua because if she said friend, people might assume that the person was male. Faced with such a situation, she would have to qualify the term by adding that it was a "female" friend. To say dui pnua was much simpler. Perhaps more sensitive to community opinion after her divorce, A Ping intentionally gathered a broader range of relationships under the rubric of dui pnua so as to insure social acceptance. Her rhetorical move constituted a prophylactic measure that tacitly acknowledged the not-quite-acceptable nature of relations with nonkin men and the power of village gossip.

In so doing, however, A Ping introduced an interesting twist in the concept of dui pnua and same-sex intimacy. As young women began to socialize with people from outside the village and with men, the category of dui pnua potentially became more flexible. It could expand to include residents of other locales, even individuals who otherwise would be classified as friends. Or, as happened in the case of a village funeral I attended, dui pnua remained limited to women of the village and new categories emerged, such as "factory friend" (gang iu). The deceased's daughter was only in her twenties and had been working in local stone-carving factories for several years. In the funeral procession, the daughter's dui pnua carried funeral paraphernalia appropriate to their relationship with her (mourning cloths tied with red and green yarn), whereas her factory friends wore black armbands and carried white hand towels, both of which were recognized as more generic funeral items. In contrast to A Ping's rhetorical inclusion of a Chongwu "friend" in her dui pnua network, this young woman ritually distinguished dui pnua from relationships formed in the workplace, thereby reinforcing the association of dui pnua with long-term, intimate, same-sex village ties.

The fact that A Ping used the term dui pnua to avoid confusion over the sex of the person from Chongwu also reflected a certain level of ambivalence among young women about their relationships with nonkin men. One village woman in her thirties, in the midst of describing the differences between her generation of dui pnua and youths today, argued that "before we didn't dare to speak to men [or] to go out together with them." She claimed, by contrast, that some dui pnua groups in the 1990s included both women and men. A Ping's decision to use the term dui pnua so as to avoid suspicion that an individual might be male suggests that village women of her age cohort did not so readily include men in their conceptualization of dui pnua. Yet insofar as the boundaries of dui pnua networks were potentially flexible, they indicated the possibility of a move toward mixed-sex dui pnua groupings in the future. In fact, A Ping also included a young man from the village in the gift-giving list she described to me in 1996. Because he planned to treat a mixed group of men and women to a meal at a restaurant a few days following his wedding, she felt compelled to give him 50 *yuan*. Although not yet ready to define him as a member of her dui pnua, she nonetheless placed him in the category of gift-receiving individuals, a group previously composed only of dui pnua and female kin.

Conclusion

Throughout much of the twentieth century dui pnua ties offered support and solace to young women as they negotiated the transition to adulthood. By the end of the millennium, young women reaffirmed their intimate bonds with fellow dui pnua through engaging in a wide array of shared activities. These included some that were easily recognizable to older women, such as accompanying new brides during the lonely and often frightening first days of marriage, and others that had emerged in the more open environment of the post-Mao era, such as socializing together with a dui pnua's fiancé or husband. Regardless of age, however, women consistently contrasted their relationship to patrilineal kin groups with dui pnua ties. Although they offered conflicting interpretations of the differences between kin and same-sex peers, they regularly acknowledged that dui pnua intimacy, unlike the genealogical closeness of kinship, had to be forged through both practice and emotional bonds. Prior to the reform era, marriage and residence shift could put an end to these intimate ties, particularly if young women married into different villages. The growing trends of marriage into the same village and of village endogamy have given younger dui pnua more opportunities to maintain their ties into their adult years. This potential for longevity, however, has also provoked greater anxiety about dui pnua permanence and has introduced the possibility that the refusal to meet gift obligations or labor requests might signal a desire to end such an intimate bond.

At the same time that dui pnua are incorporated into a normative social world, they redefine that normativity by affirming same-sex intimacies and same-generation groupings that differ significantly from forms of social organization based on patrilineal kinship. The inability to fully incorporate dui pnua into a kinship-based community order becomes most obvious at precisely those moments when dui pnua come under attack, whether for undermining the conjugal bonds necessary to the reproduction of patrilineal kinship or for making the rituals that integrate women into their conjugal families increasingly costly for families and young people alike. The counterintimacies that dui pnua represent in those contexts expose the challenges that same-sex intimacy poses to a hierarchical, heterosexual world of patrilineal kinship. Part of that challenge emerges from the very different image of intimacy contained in and enacted through dui pnua bonds, even as such intimacy, too, must adapt to meet the demands of a market economy.

The next chapter looks more closely at how market reforms have begun to redefine both same-sex and cross-sex intimacies through the emergence of industrial work sites and new forms of socializing and consumerism. It focuses on the role of stone-carving factories in introducing such activities and in turn examines how labor patterns and dui pnua ties now shape young people's social lives in an era of greater monetary resources and an increasingly prominent youth culture. Rather than viewing these changes solely as liberating for young women, I probe the ambivalence and uncertainty underlying young women's engagement in new leisure activities, responses intensified by villagers' perceptions of stone-carving factories, restaurants, and karaoke parlors as spaces spawning disorderly social and sexual relations.

CHAPTER FIVE 🍃 Stone-Carving Factories, Youth Culture, and the Lure of Consumption

A few days before the start of the Chinese New Year holiday in 1996 an air of excitement and anticipation began to permeate the village, despite the chilling rain and rapidly dropping temperatures. One morning A Hua, a Shanlin woman in her mid-twenties, invited me to accompany her when she went to the stone-carving factory where she worked to pick up her final paycheck before the holiday. A Hua's workplace was located in an industrial zone on the eastern edge of the township seat. She had been polishing headstones there since the factory had opened two years prior, but unbeknownst to both of us at the time, she would soon cease working after becoming pregnant with her first child. The factory was owned by a man from a village on the far side of the township with a long tradition of stone carving—the very area, in fact, that A Hua had married into nine years earlier when she was only sixteen.

As we passed through the metal gates and entered the courtyard, we found groups of young women and men milling around waiting for the factory accountant to arrive with their wages. The women workers were predominantly from Shanlin and neighboring Haibin, A Hua informed me, and like her most adopted local dress styles and sported long headscarves. I was struck by the carefree and casual atmosphere of the courtyard scene. Although many workers were chatting and laughing in same-sex groups, they often broke off to engage in easy banter with members of the opposite sex. Pairs of young women linked arm in arm strolled around the courtyard, stopping periodically to talk with the cashiers at the desk or to respond to joking comments from clusters of young men with cigarettes dangling from their lips. According to A Hua, these interactions were not unusual in the factory setting, and on multiple occasions I had observed male and female workers socializing with one another as they waited for a delayed shipment of stone or for the cutters to finish before they could begin their carving and polishing tasks. Stone-carving factories had created an integrated work environment that, as I argued in Chapter 1, was largely unprecedented in the region.

As these casual interactions spread from the factory floor to village shops and family courtyards, they spawned a flourishing youth consumer and leisure culture premised on new kinds of same-sex and mixed-sex socializing. In this chapter, I examine three forms of consumption and socializing that emerged or expanded dramatically in the mid-1990s, with particular attention to the youth practices they have fostered and to novel modes of forging intimate relationships. In so doing, I continue an analytic thread woven throughout this part of the book, one that compares the effects of market forces with earlier marriage-reform campaigns and rural collectivization in order to explain why some configurations of state and economy have been more successful than others in transforming intimate relationships in Shanlin.

In addition to underscoring the liberatory impact of market reforms, I also analyze villagers' often conflicting responses to this new youth culture and to the consumer spaces that have emerged in the 1990s. Although Shanlin residents regularly pointed out the myriad ways in which their lives had improved in the post-Mao era, they also acknowledged the many drawbacks of a market economy: the pressure of too many choices, insecure job futures, the demand for new skills, and ever more burdensome gift-exchange obligations. Beyond these general concerns, young women also faced constraints and dilemmas that were a function of both their age and gender. On the one hand, their access to considerable wage income and new leisure sites empowered them to socialize casually with both men and fellow dui pnua while also exploring possibilities for marital relationships. On the other hand, young women simultaneously faced growing uncertainties about what constituted proper consumption, ritual etiquette, and female morality, especially as they began to venture into social spaces marked by commodified sexual encounters.

Stone-Carving Factories as Chaotic Spaces

By the mid-1990s, large headstone factories such as the one in which A Hua worked were recognized by village and township residents as the primary source of economic growth in the region. Together with workshops that produced smaller pieces of grave-site adornment, companies that ordered and transported uncut stone, and businesses focused on the trade and finance components of the industry, these factories contributed substantially to the health of the local economy. As many Shanlin residents noted to me when reflecting on the industry, "if the factories go bad, then everything goes bad." Within the village, factory workers and managers supported a variety of businesses, from clothing stores and hair salons to tailor shops, restaurants, and building contractors. When stone-carving orders dropped, other sectors of the economy felt the pinch along with the workers.

Villagers' reactions to the industry's impact on young people and their social relations were more mixed, however. Some saw the casual mixed-sex encounters fostered by these workplaces as positive developments that enabled young couples to overcome long-standing patterns of arranged matches and conjugal avoidance. Others emphasized what they perceived as the disorderly or chaotic effects of such interactions, drawing direct connections between frequent mixed-sex socializing and a rising incidence of broken engagements, divorces, and extramarital affairs among youths in their late teens and twenties. Factories were clearly more than production sites; they were also social spaces that generated particular modes of interaction that young people identified with post-Mao aspirations of openness and progressiveness. In this sense, villagers subscribed to French theorist Henri Lefebvre's (1991) approach to social space as a productive force, for they viewed factory spaces as active generators of practice and meaning rather than as simply passive containers for human behavior, even though they frequently disagreed about how to evaluate the results of that productive process.

Mixed responses to stone-carving factories and their social consequences often emerged in the ways that villagers talked about space and spatial configurations in the region. Stone-carving factories originated in the western part of the township, an area with an established history of artisanal stone carving and thus a strong base for developing mechanized processes in the reform era. When complaining about the decline in marital stability and sexual morals among contemporary youth, both older Shanlin residents and younger critics attributed the origins of this social decay to those communities heavily populated by stone-carving factories. For them, the villages on the far side of the township had inspired youth trends that infiltrated more conservative places such as Shanlin. At the same time, however, by the mid-1990s many residents of those communities enjoyed a higher standard of living than Shanlin villagers, and some had grown quite wealthy from opening their own factories. Young women in search of potential spouses often spoke eagerly of marrying into one of those villages in hopes of achieving a more prosperous future.

Such conflicting responses to this industrial geography extended into the factory space as well. During one of the many conversations we had whenever he returned to Shanlin from his international shipping job, A Dam, a well-educated village man in his late twenties, attributed the rising divorce rates in the region to the existence of "too narrow a social space," referring specifically to the gossip that emerged from stone-carving factories where men and women came into frequent contact. For instance, he explained to me, a man learns that his girlfriend has been seen spending time with a male coworker. When he overhears others talking about her, "his face suffers, and it disturbs his internal equilibrium." At this point, A Dam continued, the man loses his ability to make judgments, and any feeling between the couple is destroyed. Perhaps reflecting on his own pending divorce (which, as far as I knew, had no connection to stone-carving factories), A Dam then concluded that a man in this position would have no choice but to divorce his wife or break up with his girlfriend.

Young people who actually worked in the factories, however, saw these spaces quite differently. One winter evening in 1996 I sat chatting with Bbinghui, the nineteen-year-old assistant in A Den's wholesale shop. One of A Den's dui pnua stopped by and, not finding her in, stayed to visit with us before returning home. This woman was widely known as a successful stone polisher, and she herself bragged about the several thousand *yuan* she brought home to her mother each month. Bbinghui, unmoved by her boasts, began to muse aloud about the social ills that had arisen in Shanlin in recent years, accusing the men and women who worked in stone-carving factories of divorcing or finding other lovers in growing numbers. A Den's dui pnua was quick to retort, arguing vociferously that she spent her time at the factory working hard to earn a good wage, not relaxing and talking with men. She presented an image of the factory as a place of work, where one labored to earn income, rejecting Bbinghui's depiction of factories as social spaces that gave rise to chaotic influences.

Women who worked as stone polishers were invested in defining factories not as chaotic sites but as spaces that produced socially valued products, whether those be high wages or more progressive relationships between men and women. Even young women such as Bbinghui who at one point in their lives criticized the "chaos" engendered by the factory environment often later sought work as stone polishers, lured by the promise of substantial earnings and the opportunity to expand their social circles. Within a year of our conversation, Bbinghui quit her job in A Den's shop and began polishing stones in a Shanlin factory. When I last saw her in 2002 she was still working in the factory, despite having married into neighboring Haibin and given birth to a baby girl.

As these accounts attest, stone-carving factories have come to occupy a highly contested position in village society, one intensified by the industry's increasingly crucial contributions to village social and economic life. By creating a mixed-sex work environment, factories challenged long-standing gender divisions of labor that had separated nonkin women and men into different work spaces and forms of labor. Although critics' depictions of mixed-sex factories as chaotic spaces certainly reflected a perceived rise in divorces, affairs, and broken engagements, they also pointed to growing anxieties about the impact of market reforms more generally, anxieties easily expressed through this new arena of economic life that differed so dramatically from those of the past.[1] Casual encounters between men and women spread from the shop floor to new leisure sites and developed into a youth culture fed by access to wage income and the consumption activities available in a market economy. Through engaging in these new consumer and leisure practices, village youths have been able to redefine their expectations for mixed-sex and same-sex relationships, but not always without consequence. For young women, factories, shops, restaurants, and karaoke parlors were also potentially sites of social and sexual excess, their impact on a woman's reputation made more uncertain by rapid changes in collectively recognized standards for female morality. This uncertainty created an ever-shifting moral topography of youth socializing and consumption that made navigating the intimate spaces and practices of the reform era an increasingly fraught endeavor for young village women.

Zng Tik *or Dressing Fashionably*

Goods, Elisabeth Croll argues, have become significant vehicles through which social groups refashion themselves in post-Mao China, especially in the case of the "rehabilitation of the category 'female'" (1997:6; see also Freeman, 2000:chap. 6; Miller, 1994:221). Both urban and rural women have appropriated fashion, jewelry, and cosmetics to create a new image of womanhood freed from the drab attire and unisex models espoused in the Mao era. Many studies of former socialist societies have shown how centralized production and distribution systems suppressed the production of consumer goods and frustrated consumer desires (Verdery, 1996). With market reforms, then, come much-desired commodities that, as Croll suggests, contribute to the cultivation of new identities, including feminine identities (see also Davis, 2000). The history of socialist sartorial reforms in Huidong communities has meant that young women's renewed attention to bodily adornment must be evaluated in more complex terms than simply the rehabilitation of femininity. Although sartorial practices no longer overtly link women's bodies with political subjectivity (as they did during both the 1950s and the Cultural Revolution), that history continues to inform intergenerational struggles over dress that now focus more explicitly on local standards of beauty, appropriate expenditures, and women's moral-cum-sexual rectitude.

Young working women in the mid-1990s enjoyed access to considerably more personal income than did their elders. Although those working in stone-carving factories usually claimed to give their

FIG. 13: Wearing the young traditional hoegin and blue, cropped top (photograph by the author, 1997)

entire salary to their natal families, many also admitted to keeping a portion for their own use or to regularly asking their mothers for spending money. Those in less profitable lines of work usually retained the bulk of their earnings for themselves.[2] Across the board, young women emphasized the mobility and freedom they felt they had achieved though access to personal funds. They were free to buy what they desired, whether that be clothing, foodstuffs, cosmetics, music tapes, or even consumer electronics. Wage earning also increased their physical mobility, enabling them to take trips outside the village, "to go out and walk around" (cut ki gnia gnia ze), rather than remain confined to the home for lack of money. As was the case among young women who began laboring for wages on construction sites in the early reform period, working women in the 1990s listed clothing and headscarf purchases among their most frequent expenditures.

Young women in Shanlin today adopt one of two major clothing styles: a version of the traditional local dress worn by their mothers (which I call "young traditional") and a more generic style modeled on urban attire and fashions popular among youths in Taiwan and Hong Kong (what villagers term sin sik'e or the "new style"). Women who adopt local dress are commonly referred to by Shanlin and township residents as those "who wear the headscarf" (bao hoegin'e) or "who wear blue dress" (cng lam sna'e), terms that highlight the ubiquitous headcovering and the blue, cropped tops symbolic of Huidong attire (see Fig. 13). Although these two items were worn by all women who donned local dress, the generic nature of these expressions glossed over the many sartorial variations that were emerging in the reform era among different generations of Shanlin women.

In the mid-1990s, young women who adopted young traditional attire incorporated several sartorial and headscarf patterns that distinguished their dress habits from those of older women, a trend that encouraged additional (some argued excessive) expenditures. Unlike older women who continued to adhere to the standard blue- or green-colored headscarves made from cotton fabric, young traditionalists preferred longer headscarves of varying colors and patterns made from newer synthetics. Either individually or in groups, young women shopped continually for new material and varied their colors by seasons, regularly alerting one another to desirable fabrics that had appeared in one of the many dry goods shops scattered throughout the village. Through these shopping ventures they accumulated large stocks of headscarves, in some cases as many as one hundred headscarves per individual. Given that headscarf prices during my research averaged 13 *yuan* (including the material itself and the tailoring), multiple purchases over the course of a season could add up to a considerable sum.

The most striking difference between young traditional attire and that of older women was that many young traditionalists alternated between wearing the trademark blue, side-buttoned, cropped top and adopting urban-style turtlenecks, high-necked blouses, and jackets (see Fig. 14). These variations forced young women to expand their purchasing range and to invest both in traditional tops and in the ever-changing styles of urban dress found in village and township shops. Prices for such items ranged from 60 or 70 to as much as several hundred *yuan*, meaning that frequent expenditures to meet

FIG. 14: Young traditional dresser with new style shirt (photograph by the author, 1995)

the stylistic demands of different seasons often consumed a significant portion of a woman's earnings.

Aficionadas of the new style, however, shunned all aspects of traditional dress, choosing instead to wear a stylish mix of urban attire: jeans, trousers, sweaters, turtlenecks, and blouses (see Fig. 15). They did not wear the headscarf at all, leaving their hair long or cutting it fashionably short. Some women in this category had begun to attract public attention not because they shunned traditional dress per se but because their attire offered greater bodily exposure than local styles. Exposed necklines, bare arms, and closely fitted jeans contrasted sharply with the loose clothing and comparatively well-covered bodies of women in local attire. When coupled with a growing preference for skirts, shorts, and tight-fitting shirts or short-sleeved blouses in the summer months, these stylistic choices provided rich

FIG. 15: Young women in new style attire (photograph by the author, 1996)

ground for debates over both extravagant consumption practices and the potential sexual excesses lurking in young women's bodies.

This brief categorizing of clothing styles suggests that Shanlin women had specific standards for dress and were concerned that their appearance conform to such standards in order to keep up with ever-changing fashion trends. This concern was not linked to the desire for an individual style but for a collective dress that identified one with a particular social group—a dui pnua unit or even the village as a whole. Groups of young women wearing both young traditional and new style attire collectively changed styles within each category—from season to season and from one headscarf or top fashion to another.[3] They closely monitored the standards for appropriate dress within their peer group, from the desirable length of a cropped top or headscarf to the right fall of a pleat, the proper length of skirts and shorts, and the correct color combinations for tops and jackets. Precisely because much of this decision making was done collectively, it was not uncommon to see a group of dui pnua wearing the same headscarf fabric, jacket, or even top. These items constituted embodied symbols of dui pnua intimacy, blurring distinctions between individual women while reaffirming the cohesiveness of the dui pnua unit itself. Some styles could even be correlated by village, and Shanlin women were proud of their ability to set new fashions and display a chic appearance.

This concern with style was conveyed through the expression zng tik, roughly translated as "to be well outfitted" or "to dress stylishly." The importance of being able to zng tik was reinforced by peer-group sanctions (for instance, criticisms of poorly dressed dui pnua), village gossip, and a strong community emphasis on dressing well found among all generations of women and even some men.[4] Potential spouses were often evaluated on the basis of their physical appearance, reinforcing the status of stylish attire among young people of dating or marriageable age. Young women's ability to earn income also fed their ability to zng tik. The emphasis on maintaining a stylish appearance, coupled with the fact that many young women now had more money to spend on clothes, drove a self-perpetuating cycle of changing styles and fervent consumption.

Older villagers often criticized this obsession with being able to zng tik and the frequent clothing expenditures it encouraged, attributing it to pressure to follow popular trends, a reform-era tendency toward wasteful spending, and a desire to live well. Parents regularly complained that their children dressed fashionably while they themselves wore cast-off and patched clothing (usually men more often than women). Others highlighted the growing gap between image and material reality, attacking young women's inclination to spend beyond their means by succumbing to the pressure to zng tik even when they lacked the resources. As one retired cadre in Shanlin argued, "Even if young women do not earn enough, they see that [someone else] has [a new style] and they want it too." Having lived through the shortages of the Maoist decades, he criticized young women's efforts to accumulate social capital by creating a fashionable body image, even when doing so required going into debt (see also Freeman, 2000:222; Heath, 1992). Continuing his diatribe against such expenditures, this cadre added, "Those who wear blue dress are not extravagant, they maintain that same style. Those who change [who wear the new style] are extravagant, they change a lot." Ignoring the many transformations in local dress styles over the years, he openly censured young women who wore new style attire for instigating wasteful consumption trends.

I had originally planned to interview this retired cadre about his experiences during the Cultural Revolution when he had been stripped of his official position and even briefly imprisoned by the new revolutionary leadership. Whereas his wife was eager to lament about that period and the hardships they had experienced, he was more interested in reflecting on the changes that had taken place in the post-Mao era. Rather than focusing on the political excesses of the Cultural Revolution decade, he seized on the potential material and social excesses lurking in the bodies of young women who now dressed in the new style. Following his tirade against extravagance, he added, "The modernized [women] want to wear everything, even skirts. It's excessive." Critiques such as this one—of skirts, shorts, and sleeveless shirts—highlight the new style's excessive *exposure* of the body through revealing attire. Ironically, they operate in a fashion opposite to early Mao-era attacks on the gin'a that decried an excessive *covering* of the body, face, and head because it was seen to constrain free movement and limit productivity (constraints emphasized by this very same cadre in his recollections of such campaigns). In drawing attention to women's bodies, revealing clothing also inspired anxieties about the changing social mores reflected in young women's new social and sexual behavior, behavior that many villagers argued originated in the youth culture fostered by local factories. By articulating their anxieties in this manner, critics implicitly associated the popular clothing trends of the 1990s with production sites seen to spawn a similar kind of social and sexual excess.

Hosting, Ritual Impropriety, and Changing Social Mores

Whereas new clothing styles provided an embodied basis for reaffirming dui pnua bonds and enhancing heterosexual appeal (even as they aroused concerns among a more frugal and conservative older generation), celebratory meals expanded upon village ritual repertoires as they created new social contexts for fostering mixed-sex relationships. Adopting such occasions as birthdays, engagements, one-year wedding anniversaries, births, and a dui pnua's departure for work outside the village, young people have begun to host meals to which they invite an increasingly diverse range of guests. Unlike the same-sex arrangements that previously dominated village ritual celebrations, these new forms of hosting often included spouses, fiancés, work acquaintances, and dui pnua. As such, they reflected the socializing patterns emerging from mixed-sex workplaces like stone-carving factories.

Celebratory meals take place in a variety of spaces, including local restaurants, village homes, karaoke parlors (KTVs), and, more recently, dance halls. The expense of holding such an event varies by venue, with the home offering the most frugal option and a restaurant or KTV the most costly. As with women's clothing expenditures, however, attacks on extravagance and spending beyond one's means constitute only one element of villagers' responses to this new hosting trend. Here, questions of ritual and social propriety also come to the fore.

Birthday celebrations are the most prominent of these new events, popular among stone polishers, women who work in or own village shops, and even those in less profitable lines of work such as fishing-net repair and animal husbandry. The lack of a direct correlation between economic status and the hosting of birthday celebrations suggests that such events do not function exclusively as a marker of social distinction; instead, birthday meals produce another kind of symbolic capital for the women who host and participate in them: a display of sophistication as evidenced by their willingness to socialize with nonkin men in a public setting. By the same token, this very mixed-sex component also engenders expressions of ambivalence and insecurity among female participants themselves, for they fully recognize that such events are by no means an established feature of village social life.

Concerns about social impropriety were in many ways compounded by the debates over ritual impropriety that permeated many discussions about birthday celebrations. Ideally, village families aspired to celebrate the birthdays of (usually male) elders, beginning in their sixtieth year and often continuing for three consecutive years in order to insure good luck. Because of the expense incurred by this long-term ritual obligation, however, few Shanlin families had held such celebrations in the past, and few did so in the present.[5] Despite its absence in practice, the celebration of an elder's birthday nevertheless was seen to "increase good fortune" (tni hok) for the family and, therefore, to contribute both to the welfare of the individual honored and to that of the family as a whole.

Young people, by contrast, were not supposed to celebrate a birthday if their family had yet to honor the birthdays of its senior members.[6] This kind of ritual upstaging, villagers argued, would produce deleterious consequences for the welfare of all family members. When in 1996 nineteen-year-old Bbinghui announced aloud at a family dinner that she intended to celebrate her birthday that year, her paternal aunt reminded her that the last time she had made such arrangements, her mother fell ill. Her aunt reinforced this concern with generational protocol by openly criticizing the consumption patterns birthday celebrations encouraged. The very term for celebrating a birthday, literally "to eat birthday" (ziah sni lit), itself conveyed the act of consumption that defined the ritual. When Bbinghui's aunt sought to deter Bbinghui from participating in such celebrations, she would often say to her, "[You] don't need to go eat" (bbian ki ziah), thus highlighting her opposition to the consumption and expenditure that comprised the ritual itself.

Such critiques by parents and kin also underscored the increasingly burdensome social obligations created by a pervasive culture of youth hosting. Because of the growing popularity of treating others to meals, young people often found themselves pressured to host even when not personally inclined to do so or when they lacked sufficient resources. The example of A Den that I discussed in Chapter 3 powerfully conveys the force of this social pressure, for even though A Den was quite reluctant to treat guests in celebration of her engagement, she ultimately submitted to the urging of her peers and hosted a meal at a restaurant near her natal home. Like the burdensome gift-exchange obligations examined in the previous chapter, moreover, this culture of hosting also indebted those who accepted such invitations by obligating them to reciprocate at a later date so as to avoid accusations of parsimony and social parasitism. Because villagers found it shameful to constantly "eat off of others," they often praised an individual's moral character by noting that the person "did not like to be treated by others."[7]

It was the mixed-sex nature of many of these new celebratory meals, however, that aroused the greatest concerns among female participants. By examining the dynamics of specific birthday celebrations we can better understand how young women negotiated changing standards for social propriety given the growing prominence of integrated gatherings. Not all women responded to these pressures in the same way, nor did all perceive them as a potential threat to their reputations. Some experienced mixed-sex celebrations as a way to reaffirm dui pnua bonds as well as to assert open attitudes toward relations with men. Variations in experiences and anxieties suggest that the means available to create different kinds of intimate relationships were themselves changing rapidly, enhancing the risks felt by some women while opening up progressive possibilities for others.

The simple issue of seating arrangements offers some insights into how different women navigated these new social settings. When I attended 23-year-old A Hong's birthday celebration in 1996, she hosted guests in the common room on the second floor of her natal home located in the older section of the village. Her mother and younger sister had helped her arrange two round tables in the cramped but spotlessly clean space, taking care to leave as much room as possible between them. A Hong's female guests began arriving first, including members of her dui pnua and friends from other Huidong villages. The women all sat at the table farther from the staircase, and as the men straggled in they occupied the other. Among the male guests were A Hong's husband, several of the village men with whom she sold Amway products, one dui pnua's husband, and another's fiancé. Throughout much of the evening there was very little interaction between the occupants of the two tables. Only after most of the female guests had left did A Hong, weary from the men's constant urging, reluctantly agree to push the two tables together. The remaining women guests persisted in clustering at the far end of their table, however, as the men continued to play boisterous drinking games.

In contrast, the participants at twenty-year-old Ggiokhua's birthday celebration exhibited few of the spatial concerns that structured A Hong's party. Although Ggiokhua raised pigs for a living and therefore did not have access to a great deal of disposable income, she chose to host her guests at a newly opened restaurant down by the village harbor.[8] She had invited four young women who were members of her dui pnua, me, a neighbor in his thirties, her teenage brother, and one of his dui pnua. The restaurant owner ushered us into a small room almost fully taken up by a large round table and chairs. Without hesitation, the group sat down at the same table, with the three men in a row against the back wall. Such close proximity to members of the opposite sex did not appear to pose a problem for these young women as it had for the guests at A Hong's gathering, something that was particularly surprising given the presence of an older man among Ggiokhua's guests.

The consumption of food and drink in a mixed-sex environment also produced varying responses from participants. Again, at A Hong's celebration, the mood at the women's table remained subdued for much of the evening and conversation lagged. Even after restaurant workers brought in steaming platters of fish, seafood, and meat, only two or three women picked at the dishes. One late arrival made a point of turning her back to the men's table as she began to eat the food that A Hong had set aside for her. But she set down her bowl after only a few bites, complaining that it was too embarrassing to eat in front of so many men.

A Hong's female guests were also less likely to drink alcohol or to participate in drinking games, either among themselves or with their male counterparts. Early in the evening, A Hong called for her husband to bring a bottle of beer over to the women's table. She poured glasses for all the women and then went around the table, one by one, playing a simple drinking game. After she finished toasting her female guests, she moved to the men's table and toasted each one of them in turn. Although the men continued to engage in lively drinking games throughout the evening, the women drank little after A Hong's initial toast.

By contrast, Ggiokhua's guests eagerly offered suggestions as she gave the food order to the restaurant owner. The mood was relaxed and playful in comparison to the tension and restraint exhibited by the female guests at A Hong's party. Ggiokhua had ordered beer along with the food, and as soon as it arrived she and the men poured full glasses for everyone. Ggiokhua began with the obligatory round of toasts, followed by a series of drinking games in which her dui pnua participated along with the male guests. Platter upon platter of food appeared on the table, and everyone dug in with equal gusto. When one favorite dish was finished, Ggiokhua called for a second order. Her face began to turn red from the liquor, and the other young women repeatedly pulled out their pocket mirrors to check their complexions as they played one drinking game after another.

How can we account for these disparities in women's comportment at mixed-sex gatherings? The composition of the two parties in terms of age, marital status, work, and education did not vary dramatically. Yet it was obvious that for the women at A Hong's celebration, the presence of men—even husbands, fiancés, and friends—led them to suppress their usual lively banter and refrain from consuming delicious food. Ggiokhua's female guests, though, exhibited no such restraint, even participating avidly in drinking games with their male counterparts. One of Ggiokhua's dui pnua later told me that their crowd frequently engaged in drinking bouts with other young men, often to the point of drunkenness. By contrast, the day after A Hong's birthday I encountered one of her dui pnua who had left the party early the night before. When I asked her why, she replied, "I had eaten my fill and everyone began drinking so I left." In this case, it is clear that her sense of discomfort came not merely from the consumption of alcohol—itself somewhat of an exaggeration—but also from the fact that it took place in a mixed-sex social environment.

By leaving parties once drinking began or by insisting on separate tables on celebratory occasions such as birthdays, young women preserved a sense of social decorum even as they engaged in what were, from the older generation's perspective, radical challenges to traditional patterns of same-sex social interaction. Over the years I spent in Shanlin, young women and men repeatedly reminded me that five or ten years prior they could not have eaten or talked together in public places like they did in the mid-1990s, much less drunk alcohol together in restaurants or KTVs. Yet the fact that the female participants at A Hong's and Ggiokhua's celebrations monitored their behavior to such different degrees also suggests that the social liberalization of the 1990s was far from complete. In their efforts to negotiate a sense of propriety while participating in mixed-sex social events, some young women sought to minimize the potential for "chaos" so often attributed to newly integrated industrial work sites. For others, however, such activities constituted an established feature of an emerging social world that blended easily with stone-carving factories and with the increasingly relaxed forms of male-female interaction encouraged by such sites.

Contested Spaces: KTVs and Prostitution

In Chapter 3, I argued that the new kinds of social intimacy fostered by these socializing trends had also led to greater sexual intimacy between young women and men, as couples began to engage in sexual relations before holding a wedding ceremony and, in some cases, even prior to registering with the government. In the more open society of the 1990s, moreover, these trends were accompanied by a growing sex industry centered around restaurants, hotels, and, most prominently in Shanlin, KTVs. Young women's ambivalence about mixed-sex socializing was exacerbated by the presence of these controversial sites, for they worried that by spending leisure time with men, they might be associated with such spaces and the activities they were presumed to foster. As I turn first in this section to villagers' perceptions of how prostitution operated in their community and its connection to the stone-carving industry, I focus on the ways these representations shaped the limits of young village women's behavior by exemplifying the potential moral fall latent in their new interactions with men.[9] As prostitution formed the ultimate boundary of acceptability, public perceptions of prostitution also circumscribed young women's efforts to define themselves as open and progressive actors in the reform era.

On one of my first visits to Shanlin, I noticed women dressed in frilly, semi-translucent pajama outfits trailing behind men on village streets. When I inquired about who these women were, I was told quite brusquely that they were zui he, prostitutes, hired to bathe and massage their male clients. Although the customers were mostly middle-aged village men, the women performing these services came from outside the region, usually from poorer provinces in the interior such as Anhui, Sichuan, and Guangxi.

By the time I returned to Shanlin in 1995 for extended fieldwork, the booming stone-carving industry had led to a mushrooming of KTVs, restaurants, hotels, and dance halls across the township. With these enterprises came an expansion in commodified sex services. Shanlin itself had several KTVs clustered around the main village intersection and smaller establishments located in the market area. Villagers tended to identify KTVs as the main sites for prostitution, places where men went to sing, eat, and drink and where women purportedly could be hired for both company and sex.[10] The predominance of migrant women working in restaurants and KTVs, regardless of the actual nature of the work they performed, colored the image of all migrant women in the township. Villagers identified them by their speech (using Mandarin in public), their flashy, often figure-accentuating attire, and their places of employment.

It was not long, however, before villagers began to argue that prostitution had also attracted local women from the township seat and its surrounding villages. They attributed this expansion to the stone-carving industry and identified the men traveling to Chongwu to do business with local factories as the main consumers of hotel, restaurant, and KTV services, along with the factory owners, managers, and officials who feted them. The growing trend of hosting among Shanlin residents also encouraged village men to frequent such establishments—treating those who contributed labor to raising a roof, celebrating special events, or simply as a way of spending leisure time. The resulting increase in the demand for women's sexual services was coupled with a money-dominated social climate that, many villagers claimed, easily attracted young women to high-paying jobs, regardless of the cost to their reputations.

There were four terms used by Shanlin residents to describe different kinds of prostitutes. Zui he, the term I had heard in 1993, remained the general referent for all prostitutes. Three other terms had emerged since then, however, all of which were export codes for different types of stone used in the stone-carving industry. These codes distinguished women by their place-based identities and forms of dress. 603, the code designating a local black mica granite frequently used in headstone orders, referred to Shanlin women who wore the headscarf and local attire (young traditional dress). AG98, another stone category, identified women from outside the region, migrant women, who engaged in prostitution. Finally, some villagers employed code 604 to refer to women from the township seat who wore urban attire and worked as prostitutes. Whereas their use of stone classifications to identify purveyors of sexual services reflects the extent to which villagers perceived their lives as increasingly tethered to the fate of this one industry, it also reveals their considerable ambivalence about the larger social impact of that industry and of market reforms more generally.

603 was by far the most prevalent term I heard used by villagers—whether in jest or in seriousness—in large part because it directed attention specifically to the kind of prostitution most relevant to the community. From the outset, 603 identified young women "who wore the headscarf" as participants in commodified sex. As I discuss more fully in Chapter 7, this group occupied a particularly ambiguous position in village society. On the one hand, they were seen as more conservative than their counterparts who dressed in the new style, especially in their relations with men. This conservatism was exemplified by their reluctance to visit their husbands on their own initiative and to interact with nonkin men in social situations. On the other hand, this group was also singled out for being too open and casual in their heterosexual encounters, behavior critics attributed to their lack of education and, by extension, to their inability to assimilate the openness of the reform era in a healthy, balanced manner.[11] These conflicting characterizations meant that young women "who wore the headscarf" were simultaneously held to two competing standards of behavior: the purity and innocence of purportedly uneducated, nubile village women and the willingness to engage in mixed-sex interactions demanded by the socializing and consumption patterns of an open youth culture. Those who fell through the cracks and were accused of "doing 603" (zue liok kong sam) represented the antithesis of the first standard and the uncontrollable excess of the second.[12]

Not only were the young women accused of "doing 603" ostensibly engaging in prostitution in their own community or in the nearby township seat, thus potentially making their behavior known to other villagers, but they were simultaneously removing their sexuality from the realm of socially recognized reproduction. By using the export code 603 to name the local prostitute, villagers depicted prostitution as a form of commodification unrelated to biological or social reproduction (cf. White, 1990; Wolf, 1972). Like stone-carving factories, local prostitutes were exporting an indigenous resource, in this case female sexuality, and exchanging it simply for money. Moreover, by framing prostitution in the language of the stone-carving industry, villagers created an additional link between the social "chaos" critics attributed to the mixed-sex workplace and the social and moral dangers of commodified sex itself.

In general, then, villagers' accounts of prostitution depicted the prostitute as an embodiment of social disorder, immorality, and even vice. I heard only one story in my years in Shanlin of a young woman who had been forced into prostitution by her parents, a story that depicted them as greedy for the money she could earn by selling her body. Other tales of young women who had become prostitutes emphasized the woman's own desire to make money, despite the disgrace such work would bring to her and her family.[13] A Ping told me one such tale as she recounted for me the dui pnua history described in the previous chapter. Of the core group of dui pnua she had developed in her childhood, there was one she no longer spoke to or interacted with because, according to A Ping, the woman had "turned bad" (bian pai). When I asked her to explain what she meant by this phrase, A Ping added that when she and her dui pnua were teenagers, this woman's older brother had opened a KTV business, and she frequently spent time with him there. When she invited her fellow dui pnua out for meals, they began to notice that she had large sums of money to spend, money she claimed came from helping her brother at the KTV. One day she asked them to accompany her when another one of her "friends" was treating. The friend turned out to be a man in his thirties, a rather unsuitable companion for a teenage village woman. At this point, A Ping said, she realized that her dui pnua was working as a prostitute, and she cut off relations with her. She concluded, "Everyone knew what she was doing. We call it 603."

A Ping refused to interact with this woman because, she claimed, if other villagers saw them together, they would assume that she, too, was a prostitute. In order not to damage her own reputation, A Ping chose instead to end her intimate relationship with this woman and to restrict her own activities. Her decision reflects the extent to which young women in the 1990s often struggled to negotiate uncertain standards for proper behavior. Purported interactions with a man other than one's husband or with a woman of questionable morals might be sufficient to push one's own reputation over the edge through the force of the village gossip mill.

By the time I had come to know A Ping, however, she did venture out to KTVs and restaurants for celebratory meals. Although such changes in her behavior were partly a function of maturity, A Ping also remained concerned that she not engage in questionable socializing with village or township men, especially when she was still married to her first husband. When a village youth invited her to a meal at a restaurant in celebration of his wedding, she made a point of asking whether there would be separate tables for male and female guests. When a friend from the township seat asked her to run a shop he had just opened, she refused, despite rapidly declining sales in her own dry goods store, for fear that people would assume they were involved in an improper relationship. In 1998, while recounting for me how she and several dui pnua had been treated to a meal in a township restaurant by a man who worked at the Chongwu post office, A Ping described in great detail how she had hesitated before entering the restaurant, as if to suggest that a modest woman such as she did not generally visit such establishments or socialize with Chongwu men (an ironic statement in retrospect, given that she would soon marry a man from Chongwu). Following these portrayals of modest behavior, however, A Ping proceeded to update me on the celebration she had hosted for her birthday the previous year, emphasizing that she had decided to treat a group of dui pnua and male village friends at a restaurant in town specifically to escape the watchful eyes of Shanlin residents. Claiming that these activities were now more acceptable in the current village climate—"last year, this year, things are more developed [kah huatdian]. People don't talk as much"—A Ping sought to justify her mixed-sex socializing and entry into contested social spaces in ways that warded off potential questioning of her modesty and propriety.

It was not unheard of for groups of young women to visit a KTV to sing songs and enjoy a meal, although it was certainly more acceptable for them to do so in same-sex groups than in mixed-sex ones. Such outings were expensive, however, and thus they usually took place in conjunction with a celebratory hosting of some sort. Below, I discuss two occasions on which I accompanied roughly the same group of young women to a village KTV. On the first occasion we were treated by the owner of the KTV, an invitation held out to A Den, who had been his former business partner, and subsequently extended to her dui pnua. The second occasion followed the finalization of Bbizu's divorce and her receipt of the divorce settlement from her former conjugal family. In celebration, she treated a number of dui pnua (overlapping with the first group) to a meal and singing at the same KTV. In analyzing these two events, I highlight the shifts in the women's reactions to and perceptions of the KTV as a mixed-sex social space. I also examine their efforts to redefine their activities within such a space as legitimate and socially acceptable, efforts that sometimes foundered on the unstable terrain of sexual desire and moral uncertainty.

Around nine o'clock one fall night in 1995, five Shanlin women and I approached the neon glow emanating from the KTV sign near the main village intersection.[14] We hung back at the elaborately decorated door, hesitant to enter, until one member of the group pushed it open and strolled boldly into the first-floor room, furnished only with a bar and shelves stocked with liquor behind it. Our host greeted us at the entrance and then led us up a narrow, winding staircase to the second floor. Halfway up the stairs the group stopped abruptly, at an impasse because the women in front did not dare to be the first ones to enter. We stood still, each urging the other to lead the way, until A Den took charge and the rest of us followed. At the top of the staircase the group filed quickly into a room on the right, glancing only briefly at the main space where a few women and men gathered around a bar.

Our room was furnished with a set of black faux-leather couches arranged in a U-shaped formation facing a large-screen television. A low glass table sat in front of the couches, and two microphones lay on top of it. We sat timidly on the edge of our seats, looking uncomfortable and uncertain as to what to do next. Our host came bustling into the room and handed over a songbook, instructing us to begin selecting songs. After he left, the group began to look around, commenting on the furniture and decorations. A Den was the first to speak, remarking, "So, this is a KTV!" The music videos for the songs we had ordered began to appear on the television screen, and the mood relaxed a bit as we cautiously started to sing along and sip the drinks brought by a Mandarin-speaking waitress. The same waitress soon returned again, carrying platters of steaming food and a large bowl of soup. At first the group was too polite to eat, each woman urging food on her companions, passing bowls, and studiously avoiding taking any herself. Even at the end of the evening most of the food remained untouched.

The videos continued one after another, and the group slowly warmed up to singing. At one point, long after our host had left us to our own devices, two women moved to the open space and began to dance a waltz together while the rest of us continued to sing along with the videos, some reciting the words from memory and others haltingly following the stream of characters as they moved across the bottom of the television screen. After several hours of entertainment, we prepared to leave, thanking our host profusely for his generosity. We proceeded quickly down the stairs and into the dark, quiet street, talking in excited tones about the evening.

Six months later, one of the original participants, Bbizu, announced that she was going to treat the group to a meal and singing at the same KTV in honor of the long-awaited finalization of her divorce. The mood at this second celebration was much more lighthearted and self-assured than on our first visit. No one hesitated at the door; instead, we all walked directly in as if we frequented the place regularly. The group proceeded up the stairs and investigated all of the available rooms before settling on the room we had occupied previously. We immediately began to laugh and joke among ourselves, making for a festive air in contrast to the palpable unease that had characterized the prior occasion.

Bbizu stepped out to phone additional guests, and the rest of us ordered songs as the food arrived. We sat down and unabashedly began to eat, reaching eagerly with our chopsticks and filling our own bowl or that of the woman next to us. Little attention was paid to proper etiquette, and no one held back for fear of appearing too eager. The contrast with the first occasion was all too clear: not a morsel was left on the platters by the end of the night.

Bbizu soon returned to the room looking disturbed, however. While using the telephone, she had seen the husband of one of her dui pnua sitting in the lounge across from ours with a strange woman. Shortly afterward there was a knock at the door, and the young man opened it slightly, motioning for Bbizu to come out. She left briefly, and upon returning she explained that the man was embarrassed that she had seen him and urged her not to tell her dui pnua about the encounter. The incident put a slight damper on the exuberant mood, and members of the group began to muse aloud about what other people would think of their socializing in such a place. By encountering village men who had come to a KTV to escape the watchful eyes of wives or female kin, these young women were moving into a terrain marked by uncertain morality and the sexual desires of men. Confirming the male stamp on the KTV, one of the women later refrained from going out to the bathroom because there were "too many men out there."

As if to shore up their own claim to this space, however, members of the group then began to recount the number of times they had been to this specific KTV, who had treated them on each occasion, and which rooms they had occupied. By retelling the story of their physical occupation of the space and the consumption activities they had engaged in there, they asserted their own interpretation of the kind of socializing they enacted, framing a particular standard of behavior in KTVs that rejected the link between these leisure sites and prostitution. Their accounts reaffirmed their rightful participation in such consumption because of their access to independent income and their inclusion in a social economy organized around hosting. In response to concerns that villagers would talk about them for going to a KTV, Bbizu tossed her head defiantly and exclaimed that women could also visit KTVs to sing, eat, and have fun (and could do so more frugally than men, who would have drunk liquor as well). They were not doing anything wrong simply by socializing there, she contended; in fact, her response suggested that they were redefining both the space itself and the meanings it produced.

Despite the mainstream perception of KTVs and restaurants as sites frequented primarily by men and prostitutes, young women such as Bbizu and her dui pnua sought to reclaim them as leisure spaces available to all. They rejected the association of KTVs solely with prostitution, depicting their own activities as honest fun—singing and eating.[15] Yet their occasional displays of uncertainty also suggested that village opinion and the potential link to prostitution remained salient concerns. The image of the woman who had "turned bad" lurked in the background, and group members took care to monitor their own behavior so as to avoid overtly sexual interpretations of their activities.

Conclusion

The major consumption activities engaged in by young Shanlin women in the mid-1990s ranged from clothing purchases to birthday celebrations and the hosting of other celebratory meals. Despite the greater diversity of these consumption patterns, they have remained rooted both in young people's participation in wage labor and in the social networks and ritual expectations that structured village life. Precisely because of its embeddedness in the community, consumption has created additional burdens for young women as they have struggled to maintain standards of style and fashion adhered to by their peers and to fulfill expectations of reciprocity valued by villagers more generally. At the same time, young women have eagerly seized on the creative opportunities afforded by an expanding realm of village consumption, diversifying their appearance, modes of socializing, and even socializing venues. Such creative potential has come at a price, however, forcing young women to justify new standards and practices in ways that reaffirm their own adherence to modesty, morality, and frugality—the meanings of which are themselves very much in flux.

Young women's claims that access to wage income has brought them greater freedom to consume and engage in leisure activities exist in tension with the implicit and explicit constraints they faced when they attempted to exercise such freedoms. Villagers' reactions to these activities have varied dramatically, from the older generation's critiques of wasteful expenditure and unnecessary hosting to a more general perception of stone-carving factories and leisure sites as disorderly spaces that have produced social and sexual excesses among village youths, the extreme case being the figure of the local prostitute. We should not underestimate the economic and social significance of young women's entry into profitable, skilled wage labor, nor should we overlook the consequences of their participation in mixed-sex socializing and their efforts to claim social spaces previously stamped with male desires. Yet, as young women actively redefined the social landscape of rural Huidong, they also found themselves having to negotiate conflicting standards for acceptable social and sexual behavior.

By participating in new forms of leisure and consumption, young women have created opportunities for reaffirming their bonds with one another and for forging new kinds of intimacy with their male counterparts. Although celebratory meals, like the gift exchanges discussed in the previous chapter, reinforced a material basis for dui pnua obligation, they also provided dui pnua with an expanding array of settings and occasions through which to produce and strengthen forms of same-sex intimacy. When such socializing incorporated male peers, as in the birthday celebrations described above, it further broadened the scope of young people's intimate attachments, even as it redefined the very nature of that intimacy. Most of the young women I knew were reluctant to expand dui pnua bonds to encompass relationships with men, even though they were open to interacting with young men in casual social encounters and in the new forms of ritual hosting and entertainment that were becoming established features of a reform-era youth culture. Although intimate life was changing at a rapid pace, the ultimate outcome of such transformations remained very much a matter of community debate and contestation.

PART THREE The Production of Difference

CHAPTER SIX 🕮 Ethnicity in Drag: Mass Media, Tourism, and the Politics of Representation

Cross-dressing, appearing in drag, transvestism, and transsexualism emerge in a context where the notion of subjectivity is challenged, where identity is always perceived as capable of construction, invention, change. (hooks, 1992:145)

As I discussed in Chapter 2, beginning in the 1950s a diverse group of state actors created and promulgated a language of reform that represented the customs and people of eastern Hui'an as feudal and backward. These representations justified reformers' interventions in intimate practices as part of molding the local populace into enlightened, socialist citizens. My analysis of these early reform campaigns revealed how Huidong women were made to stand for something larger than themselves as exemplars of feudal thought and practice, oppressive marriage customs, sexual repression, and patriarchal inequality. In this chapter, I ask how dress, marriage, and labor now signify difference "differently" through a form of ethnicity made more flexible by the post-Mao market economy and related processes of commodification. Whereas under high socialism officials studiously avoided attributions of ethnic difference to support the aim of incorporating Huidong women into a Han socialist nation, by the 1990s entrepreneurs and cadres increasingly identified local women with ethnic minorities in order to better market the signs of regional difference. This goal of marketing ethnicity was not as straightforward as it might appear, however. Huidong residents' own commitment to their Han identity meant that they were not always willing to play the part of the exotic ethnic other crafted for them in media images and by tourism entrepreneurs and officials.

The concept of drag provides some guidelines for understanding how this contested process of ethnic hailing worked in the 1990s. I draw on feminist theories of gender and performativity to show how Huidong women's intimate practices, including the very surfaces of their bodies, have come to constitute an ethnicity that is itself imitative, lacking an originary essence. My analysis proceeds from a notion of drag as a performance that exposes cultural anxieties about categorical ephemerality, and it assumes that drag might not always be liberating for those who do the performing or are represented through it.[1] The repeated iterations of ethnic identity that appear in images of Huidong women simultaneously reinforce local women's ambiguous ethnic and civilizational status and reveal considerable anxiety about what their Han identity itself represents. Ironically, this categorical uncertainty also facilitates Huidong women's reincorporation into the post-Mao nation-state, not as the nation's unassimilable other but instead as a kind of categorical excess that must be contained in order to reaffirm existing identity structures and hierarchies. The process of crafting and contesting these representations of ethnicity subsequently creates new possibilities and constraints both for image producers and for the women and men who confront their contradictory effects in the mundane routines of their daily lives.

State mediation and construction of ethnic identity in post-1949 China are by now widely recognized. By seeking to create and preserve clear boundaries between groups, state ethnographers forced the amalgamation of peoples who failed to recognize one another as co-ethnics (Diamond, 1995; Harrell, 1995a; Hsieh, 1995; Litzinger, 1995; McKhann, 1995; Schein, 2000:84–86) and refused to grant separate ethnic status to groups that claimed a distinct identity (Gladney, 1994a; Oakes, 1998:102–106).[2] The category of ethnicity (*minzu*) was effectively defined, as Oakes astutely argues, "according to cultural distance from the Han" (Oakes, 1997:46).[3] By taking the Han as the standard of civilization to which all other groups should aspire (a hierarchy reinforced by the adoption of Morgan's evolutionary theory of stages of civilization), state ethnographers created a definition of ethnicity based on the presence of non-Han cultural markers (Oakes, 1997:46–48). This construction in turn delineated two categories of citizens in the People's Republic of China (PRC)—the "ethnic" (or national) minorities (*shaoshu minzu*) and the "nonethnic" Han (*Hanzu*)—despite the PRC's official definition of itself as a "multiethnic" state that purported to accord all groups the same standards of citizenship.

Although the residents of eastern Hui'an were incorporated into this socialist vision of ethnicity as members of the majority Han, their Han status has never been a wholly comfortable one, as attested to by the repeated state reform campaigns of the 1950s and 1960s that sought to bring them into conformity with "civilized" Han culture. This anxiety over the ethnic status of Huidong residents was reinforced in the early Mao years by Chinese scholars who posited a common origin for extended natal residence marriage in eastern Hui'an and similar customs of delayed postmarital cohabitation among non-Han and earlier Han groups in China's south and southwest.[4]

Xiamen University professor Lin Huixiang was introduced to the customs of eastern Hui'an when he was sent to assist with land-reform and Marriage Law campaigns in the county in 1951. In an article written not long after those experiences, Lin (1981) argued that the marital practices of Huidong residents were strikingly similar to those of the Buyi, Miao, and Li minorities, as well as to those found among some Han inhabitants of the Pearl River Delta region earlier in the century. Lin proposed that all of these examples of delayed postmarital coresidence represented remnants of an ancient transition from a matrilineal to a patrilineal society and that they derived from women's belated struggles to retain the power they had enjoyed in a matrilineal system.[5] Unlike non-Hans, however, Huidong women (like women in the delta) faced severe restrictions on extramarital sexual relations, a distinction Lin attributed to the fact that at some point the original inhabitants of those regions had assimilated into Han society. Because Han peoples had "become civilized" (1981:276) at an earlier time than most non-Hans, he argued, they had also progressed to the feudal stage sooner, meaning that they had experienced more extended exposure to feudalism's emphasis on female chastity and patriarchal control. Lin's historical reconstruction thus depicted Huidong women (together with their earlier delta counterparts) as living remnants of an ancient moment of evolutionary and ethnic transition; their suffering—evidenced in his view by sexual repression, conjugal discord, and high suicide rates—proved the aberrant status of such marriage practices given the current level of Han civilization.

In short, Lin's account emphasized the extent to which Hui'an women constituted temporal and ethnic hybrids. His Marxist-inspired evolutionary analysis, together with the writings and recollections of official reformers from the same period, defined this group as straddling the boundary between Han and non-Han, socialist and feudal, civilized and backward. In the post-Mao era, Chinese anthropologists and historians have returned to Lin's original thesis, reopening debates about Huidong residents' ethnic status. Some have concurred with Lin's argument that extended natal residence marriage represented a cultural remnant of an ancient transition from a matrilineal to a patrilineal society (Jiang, 1985, 1989); others have looked anew at the ethnic origins of the region's inhabitants (Chen, 1986; Guo, 1997); and still others have rejected the idea that local people were anything but Han (Chen, 1990).[6] By the early 1990s, a rough consensus had emerged among scholars from both the PRC and Taiwan who generally agreed that contemporary Huidong residents were descended from a combination of Han settlers migrating into the region and local peoples native to the area. Although who these local peoples had been remained open to debate (were they ancient Bai Yue, Li, Dan boat people, or others?), the conclusion of ethnic mixing successfully pushed the question of ethnic origins into the distant past.[7]

What influence, if any, have these debates had on Huidong residents' own sense of their identity? Throughout my time in Shanlin, I was struck by the extent to which official classification as Han had become intrinsic to villagers' self-definition, making them quite resistant to suggestions (scholarly or popular) that they were, to the contrary, descended from a minority group. This resistance has led me to question how ethnicity has become interwoven with intimate practices and relationships in China, yet in strikingly different ways across the country. Some groups, such as the Yi community in which Erik Mueggler (2002) worked, seek to reclaim the intimate relationship of bodies to place by defining that relationship in specifically ethnic terms. Huidong residents, by contrast, define local women's embodied practices as indexes of place through appealing to regional and gender differences that reaffirm what is for them an unquestioned Han status. Post-Mao image producers, many schooled in nationwide modes of representing ethnic difference, have struggled to contain these tensions as they create a new genre of representation centered on the mass-mediated figure of "the Hui'an woman."[8]

Mass Media and Ethnicity in the Reform Era

The economic reforms of the last two decades have sparked rapid growth in China's popular media, with new publications, television programs, and films emerging regularly and old ones repackaging themselves in order to compete in a market economy. A cursory perusal of this burgeoning media industry beginning in the late 1980s invariably turns up multiple images of "the Hui'an woman." Photographed, painted, or occasionally described through words, this figure appears again and again in all of her sartorial finery, gender-bending physical strength, and exotic splendor. She graces the pages of national pictorial magazines such as *Minsu huakan* (Folklore pictorial); provincial publications like *Fujian minzu* (Fujian ethnicity) and *Fujian qingnian* (Fujian youth); tourism promotional materials in both Chinese and English; and newspapers ranging from the local *Quanzhou wanbao* (Quanzhou evening news) to the national *Renmin ribao* (People's daily) and even the distant *Xinjiang jun ken bao* (Xinjiang military land reclamation news).

These images undermine a taken-for-granted association between Hui'an women and the Han majority by both exoticizing and eroticizing the women they represent. In so doing, media representations evoke a vaguely defined Hui'an ethnicity rooted both in a particular locale and in the bodies and practices of local women. Unlike the explicit eroticism that often suffuses images of official minority women, however, the eroticization of "the Hui'an woman" is held in check in these portrayals by rhetorical and visual returns to women's labor abilities and the feudal, repressive nature of their marriage customs.[9] By reinscribing "the Hui'an woman" within a Han-socialist order of labor and productivity, media representations reclaim some basis for asserting a Han identity for all Hui'an residents. And by highlighting the purportedly repressive aspects of local marriages and sexual relations, they distinguish Hui'an women from official minorities whose "primitiveness" ostensibly manifests itself in free, even promiscuous, sexuality.

Although these representational moves authorize the state's classification of eastern Hui'an residents as Han, they also unsettle any coherent understanding of what it means to be Han; they call into question the very essence of Han-ness itself (Gladney, 1994b). In the process they simultaneously reveal a host of other lines of difference based on place and gender that crosscut the ostensibly homogeneous Han majority. To date there has been very little dialogue between studies that explore diversity within an already established Han category (Cohen, 1993; Gladney, 1994a; Honig, 1992, 1996; Kipnis, 1997) and those that examine the construction of Han identity through its opposition to ethnic minorities (Gladney, 1994b; Harrell, 1995b; Schein, 1997). The contested nature of Hui'an identity, then, enables us to evaluate the force of state-defined categories and the role of a market-oriented media in diversifying ethnic classifications and unsettling their connection to a wide array of intimate practices. Media images of "the Hui'an woman," many of which rely on models to perform exotic ethnic difference, at once reaffirm categorical ethnic identities and struggle to contain them within recognized boundaries.

"Feudal Head, Democratic Belly, Frugal Top, Wasteful Pants"[10]

This rhyme from the early Maoist era succinctly encapsulates the vision of socialist liberation through frugality and simplicity repeatedly invoked by the government campaigns to reform pre-1949 features of Huidong women's attire. The saying also foreshadows the ways that Huidong women's appearance has been made to represent both the alluring "ethnic" side of Hui'an culture and its "repressive" Han elements. Women's bamboo hats and long headscarves, the cropped, side-buttoned tops that reveal their abdomens, and the low-waisted, flowing black pants reaching only to midcalf physically constitute a generic image of "the Hui'an woman." Visual depictions of this striking dress create a sensual, exotic figure, yet one whose allure is frequently undercut by textual ref-

FIG. 16: *Minsu huakan* cover (*Minsu huakan* 1 [1989])

erences to a pervasive "feudal backwardness" rooted in repressed sexuality.

The cover of the first 1989 issue of the national pictorial magazine *Minsu huakan* displays a "Hui'an woman" seated atop a pile of granite with the ocean in the background (see Fig. 16). The bright red of her pants and yellow of her bamboo hat are reflected in the colored borders that frame the picture and the deep blue of the sea blends with her blue cropped top. The viewer's gaze is drawn not only to her colorful attire but also to her matching red fingernail polish and lipstick. Her status as a model, confirmed by her cosmetic embellishments, ill-fitting dress, and short, loose headscarf, distances her sensual appeal from the portrayals of "real" Hui'an women found inside the magazine.

The magazine's two-page spread, titled "Hui'an Women's Attire," features the same model on the left-hand page, now standing and facing a set of black-and-white photos on the right-hand page (Figs. 17 and 18). The black-and-white shots contrast sharply with the vivid colors and full views of the model, the precise detail of the color shots blurring into a virtually indistinguishable mass of bodies in the black-and-white photos. Although the latter photos represent

FIG. 17: Black-and-white photo of "real" Hui'an women (*Minsu huakan* 1 [1989]:21)

"real" Hui'an women, only in one photograph does a single figure face the camera directly. We view the rest of the women either from the side or the back, their faces almost completely covered by elaborate headpiece decorations and long, close-fitting headscarves. This lack of visual access, particularly when contrasted with the clarity of the model shots, reinforces an image of "the Hui'an woman" as mysterious and inaccessible to outsiders.

The written text of the article initiates the reader into the world of "the Hui'an woman" by raising the issue of her ethnicity, only to defer the question to one of local identity and distinctive appearance. The article begins by addressing the reader as follows: "At first glance, you might assume that the young woman in these photos is an ethnic minority woman from the border regions. She is actually the universally known Huidong woman" (Liu and Lin, 1989:21). Without explicitly identifying Huidong women as Han, the authors locate them geographically as residents of the jagged coastline of eastern Hui'an county. Having raised but not resolved the question of ethnicity, the article then moves directly to a detailed description of Huidong women's attire, traversing their bodies from head to toe. At each step, the authors depict the bright colors and intricate patterns favored by Huidong women. These portrayals further reinforce Huidong women's conformity to Han stereotypes of colorful ethnic minority "costumes," creating a visual association with officially recognized minorities at the same time that the text itself

FIG. 18: Black-and-white photo of "real" Hui'an women (*Minsu huakan* 1 [1989]:21)

disavows such a connection.[11] Descriptions of various sartorial elements also alternate in emphasis between exposure and concealment of the body, a fluctuation that enacts Huidong women's status as simultaneously "open" ethnics and "controlled" Han (Diamond, 1988:18-19; Gladney, 1994b:103-108).

The color photos of the model mediate between the reader and the black-and-white photographs. They convey the sexual allure and exoticism of Huidong women's dress yet make such attire more appealing to an urban Han reader by locating both it and the wearer within a modern aesthetic of style and beauty. The model literally displays the colorfully exotic aspect of the ethnic Hui'an woman, whereas the black-and-white photos confirm the backward nature of Huidong womanhood.[12] The implicit dialogue between the sets of photographs enacts the categorical ambiguity embodied by Huidong women, positioning them at the crossroads of Han and ethnic, civilized and backward.

The very use of models suggests that such exotic cultural difference is most appealing to an urban Han readership when it is packaged and (re)presented by non-Huidong, presumably Han women—in other words, when it is portrayed "in drag."[13] Through her drag performance, the model creates an image of desirable Hui'an femininity that blends codes of ethnic exoticism with conventional Han feminine beauty. At the same time, her performance also destabilizes a sense of coherent ethnic identity; it creates what Marjorie Garber calls "category crisis," a crisis constituted by "a failure of definitional distinction, a borderline that becomes permeable, that permits of border crossings from one (apparently distinct) category to another" (1992:16). As a physical embodiment of this categorical ambiguity, the model subtly challenges any presumption of an original identity that underlies either her performance or the figure she represents. Instead, her modes of dress and bodily comportment simultaneously affirm and undermine distinct Han and minority identities, just as the very fact of her performance further weakens the links between embodied practices and a national population categorized according to ostensibly essential ethnic differences.

The Search for Authentic Difference

The didactic tone of the lead sentence in the *Minsu huakan* article, "At first glance, you might assume," reflects a widespread compulsion on the part of media producers to clarify the status of "the Hui'an woman," to determine the figure's authenticity as either ethnic or Han. In July 1994, the national television program *Zheng da zong yi* went in search of "the Hui'an woman" during a special segment on Fujian province. The variety show's national host, Cheng Qian, began the segment by expressing his lifelong fascination with Hui'an women and their distinctive attire. Yet he quickly cautioned the audience not to leap to assumptions: "Looking at this Huidong woman on the surface, people [*renmin*] think that they [*tamen*] are an ethnic minority. Actually, they are genuine Han."

The camera zooms in as Cheng utters this last sentence, focusing the viewing eye on his face as he assures the national audience that Huidong women are in fact authentic members of the Han majority. Cheng's use of the category "people" reflects the national body (the "people" in the "People's Republic of China"), ostensibly multiethnic yet in reality dominated by the 92-percent Han. His use of "they," in contrast, enacts the othering of Huidong women at the very moment that Cheng seeks to bring them inside, to reaffirm that "they" are really part of "us."[14] By distinguishing between surface impressions and some unidentified form of essential truth, Cheng assertively reincorporates Huidong women into the category of Han. Yet his very insistence on their Han authenticity bespeaks an underlying uncertainty about that status.

Cheng leaves it to the show's local host, the young, vivacious Ding Hong, to discern the true nature of Huidong women. As Ding walks down the main road of a Huidong village, she points out women's intriguing headscarves and invites the viewer to join her in getting beneath that mysterious facade. She enters the village market where she attempts unsuccessfully to speak with local sellers and buyers gathered around displays of vegetables, meats, and other foodstuffs. The camera pans across individual women dressed in local attire as the voice-over informs the viewer that some are lively and outgoing, drawing customers to their stands, whereas others are painfully shy and unwilling to face the camera. When Ding does finally discover a young woman willing to speak, she turns out to be dressed in typical urban attire. Responding to Ding's query about why she chooses not to wear local dress, the young woman asserts in Mandarin, "I don't want to wear it. . . . It's OK not to." Ding then echoes the woman's own words for the viewer, suggesting that the speaker's status as a Huidong woman (despite her nontraditional dress and use of Mandarin, the national language) reinforces an inscrutability that literally requires translation.[15]

Ding's inability to find a traditionally dressed Huidong woman who will speak on camera does not prevent her from inserting her own interpretations through repeated use of the voice-over technique.[16] The scenes of the village market end with a lengthy shot of two women dressed in local attire walking away from the camera. As the camera slowly zooms in on the silver belts dangling from their waists, one of the women looks back briefly. Noticing the camera, she nudges her companion, and the two engage in a moment of jostling and gesturing, after which the same woman glances back once again. Ding has no access to their words or thoughts, however. She can only reiterate her fascination with the image through her own voice-over: "In my heart, Huidong women still retain an element of mystery. My curiosity about their attire is similar to their [curiosity] about us."

By interpreting the woman's backward glance as an expression of curiosity similar to her own, Ding claims access to Huidong women's subjectivity despite the obstacles she encountered when filming the program. And by identifying her response with those of the two women, Ding reaffirms Cheng's initial assertion that Huidong women are "genuine Han," that beneath the facade they are "just like us." Yet such a claim further undermines any unified vision of what, precisely, "Han" or "us" are. Not only do the adventure-style tone of the program and Ding's repeated expressions of fascination with the "mystique" of Huidong women belie these attempts at incorporation, but they call into question what is being incorporated. Media producers' heavy-handed efforts to create a unitary ethnic identity for Huidong women—to mediate such women's elusive qualities for their viewers and readers—in effect reveal the performative nature of ethnicity or, to borrow Judith Butler's formulation, "the imitative structure of [Han-ness] itself—as well as its contingency" (1990:137). Images of "the Hui'an woman" expose the absence at the heart of Han identity, the lack of a clear referent for a coherent Han majority. By extension, these contested images also reinforce the contingent status of that powerful binary, Han versus ethnic minority.

Sensual Other or Hardworking Han?

The conditional nature of Huidong women's Han identity becomes even more apparent when we compare two types of images: those in which the sensuality and eroticism that characterize portrayals of official minority women find their way into depictions of "the Hui'an woman" and those that seek to de-exoticize "the Hui'an woman" by emphasizing her remarkable physical strength and labor abilities. These modes of representation at once edge "the Hui'an woman" into the category of ethnic minority and struggle to recuperate her definitive Han status.

The prominence of vividly sensual, and even sexual, representations of ethnic-minority women has sparked considerable debate in China's art and film circles, most often in response to works by

Han artists (Clark, 1987:20; Harrell, 1995b:8–13; Gladney, 1994b; Lufkin, 1990; Yau, 1989:122–123). Whereas fantasies of sexualized minority women potentially expose "civilized" Hans to the degeneration and danger of primitive backwardness (Diamond, 1988; Schein, 1997), such images also display the highly politicized gap between minority sensuality and Han sexual restraint and controlled fertility (Gladney, 1994b). Artistic renditions of Huidong women evoke a similar dialectic of fascination and fear with respect to the sexualized female form. In paintings of women from the region, artists often accentuate the curve of women's hips and buttocks set off by their low-waisted pants and silver waist belts.[17] The billowing effect of the wind on women's wide-legged trousers is used to draw attention to the shape of the thighs or a cocked hip contrasted with an exposed midriff.[18] In the oil painting *Spring*, the artist emphasizes the full shape of the woman's breasts beneath her blue cropped top as she sits primly looking out from the painting. In none of these cases do artists resort to nudity to convey sensuality and fecundity. Rather, they use the flowing lines of Huidong women's attire and the contrast between exposure and concealment to create a subtle sensuality that lies just below the surface.

The sensual appeal of the Huidong woman's body has become a recognizable trope available for adoption by the popular media as well. The signature introduction for the early 1990s' television serial *Xiamen xinniang* (Xiamen bride) offers a striking example of this mainstreaming process.[19] The show's plot revolves around a wealthy Taiwanese family seeking a Mainland wife for their mentally disabled eldest son. The unsuspecting future bride turns out to be a Hui'an woman who works as a waitress in urban Xiamen. The woman's natal family, still resident in Hui'an, is desperately poor and urges her to agree to the match so that they can benefit from her substantial bride-wealth. Although the female protagonist wears urban dress throughout the series, the betrothal photo sent to the family in Taiwan shows her dressed in traditional Huidong attire. In general, however, the connection to Hui'an is superfluous to the plot, virtually all of which takes place in Xiamen or Taiwan.

Despite this tenuous narrative link, an animated image of "the Hui'an woman" introduces each episode of the show, as well as the segments within the episode following commercial breaks. The lead-in begins by tracing the outline of a figure of "the Hui'an woman," starting with her bamboo hat and continuing downward, outlining her body. The figure then raises her arm and sweeps it down her body; and her gesture fills in her outline with color and traditional clothing features. She swivels her hips back and forth suggestively, drawing an awkward-looking man (her mentally disabled husband) into the frame. As he wraps his arms around her bare stomach, both figures point to the title of the show as it appears in the upper left-hand corner of the screen.

This brief lead-in is repeated several times over the course of each episode, creating a sensual image of "the Hui'an woman" defined by traditional clothing features. The irrelevance of the image and the Hui'an connection in general to the show's plot attests to the freeing up of such sensual imagery and its ready recognition by a general viewing audience. With her bamboo hat and headscarf, cropped top and exposed abdomen, and flowing pants that sit low on her waist, "the Hui'an woman" can be exoticized and even sexualized in images such as this one. The growing popularity of these exotic, sexualized representations creates a widely recognized link between "the Hui'an woman" and ethnic minority status, in effect undermining any certainty about her Han identity or what it might mean.

In contrast to the sensual images portrayed in shows like *Xiamen xinniang*, other media depictions avidly de-exoticize "the Hui'an woman" by embedding her in a Han-socialist framework of physical labor and self-sacrifice. Once again, however, this inscription as Han is far from stable, for it posits "the Hui'an woman" not as modern, but as an anachronism dating from an earlier period in which hard labor was valorized as part of building a socialist society. The market-reform era has witnessed the devaluation of worker and peasant identities, with heroic acts of labor and self-sacrifice increasingly derided for being excessively political, even primitive (Kipnis, 1997; Rofel, 1994, 1999). In this context, Huidong women's propensity to engage in demanding manual labor also undermines their smooth incorporation into the category of modern Han. Their anachronistic displays of physical exertion disrupt not only Confucian gender hierarchies but ostensibly modern work patterns as well.

At the outset of Ding's search for the "real Huidong woman" in the *Zheng da zong yi* episode, she encounters a group of young and middle-aged women, in all of their sartorial finery, straining to transport a long block of granite. The block hangs from ropes attached to bamboo carrying poles that the women balance across their shoulders, working in pairs to distribute the weight as they shuffle slowly toward their destination. After they have deposited the stone at a construction site, Ding tries to engage one of the bearers in conversation, asking why she, a woman, performs such heavy labor. The woman turns away laughing, her retort muffled by background noise. Ding's voice-over nonetheless reinforces the unusual nature of this gender division of labor: "Huidong women's labor intensity exceeded my expectations."

Representations showing Huidong women engaged in feats of heavy physical labor have become as constitutive of "the Hui'an woman" as portrayals that focus on their exotic dress. They grace the covers of publications like the Fujian workers' magazine *Shenghuo-chuangzao* (Life-creativity, February 1989; December 1990; September 1991).[20] They appear without identifying text of any kind in regional newspapers such as *Xiamen ribao* (July 2, 1998, p. 12) and *Quanzhou wanbao* (October 24, 1996, p. 3). The frequency with which young women from eastern Hui'an migrated to the coastal cities of Xiamen, Guangzhou, and Shenzhen in the 1980s to work on construction sites has undoubtedly strengthened urbanites' association of Huidong women with heavy manual labor. But this association cannot explain why such images have been produced and reproduced in a wide array of media long into the 1990s.

Despite the widespread post-Mao disdain for physical labor, the hardworking Huidong woman clearly has her own kind of appeal. Popular sayings reinforce Huidong women's widely proclaimed ability to work hard and endure suffering. The oft-repeated phrase "industrious, simple, frugal" transforms women's impressive physical strength into a model of the virtuous Confucian wife or daughter who subsumes her own desires in devotion to her family's welfare. Such tributes to women's commitment to hard work figure prominently in statements by men who are themselves native to Hui'an county but not to Huidong itself. Reflecting on the exotic images of Hui'an women that dot pictorial magazines, film screens, and stages, these authors distinguish between Hui'an the county and Huidong the sub-county region so as to salvage an image of all Hui'an women free from identification as exotic and ethnic. By appealing to women's self-sacrificing nature and their ability to perform heavy labor of all kinds, such authors seek to reclaim a specifically Han nativeplace identity for all Hui'an residents.

"The Mystery of the Hui'an Woman," by Hui'an native Zhuang Dongxian, appeared in the magazine *Fujian qingnian* (Fujian youth) in the late 1980s. Zhuang begins the piece with a depiction of Hui'an women's dress clearly intended to model the standard representation found in most media portrayals. Yet, rather than using this voyeuristic detail to exoticize "the Hui'an woman," Zhuang instead lambastes the genre for creating a "twisted image." Identifying himself as a fellow native, he proceeds to delineate the small percentage of the county's population that conforms to this image. He then concludes, "It is an error of common sense to [identify] this extremely small number of Huidong women as Hui'an women" (1988:26).

Zhuang goes on to recount the history of Hui'an women's awesome labor contributions, reminding his readers that in the 1950s and 1960s they were world renowned for their ability to endure pain and hardship, honored as "the paragon of Chinese national womanhood" (*Zhonghua minzu nüxing de dianfan*) (1988:26–27). Nowadays, however, "mention Hui'an women and people are only interested in the bizarre clothing of the 40,000 women from a marginal area, their exposed navels, and the silver waist belts crowning their pants, as well as their backward marriage customs [*hunyin louxi*] and the multiple legends derived from them" (1988:27). Zhuang identifies this shift as one basis for the contemporary depiction of Hui'an women as "eternally tragic."

In response, Zhuang the native takes it upon himself to "say a few fair, just words about our hometown women" (1988:27). At turns condemning and praising Hui'an women's spirit of self-sacrifice, Zhuang tries to salvage the image of "the Hui'an woman" by grounding the figure in her almost superhuman labor capacity. He expresses his respect for his hometown sisters by praising (both visually and textually) their hard work and devotion to labor. By shifting the focus of representation from women's exoticized bodies to their laboring bodies, he seeks to reintegrate them into dominant Han society and subsequently to achieve positive recognition for all

Hui'an women through appealing to nationwide cultural ideals. Yet Zhuang himself notes that Hui'an women's heyday as a model of hardworking Chinese womanhood has long passed; wholehearted manual labor and socialist devotion are no longer national ideals of the present. As a result, Zhuang is ultimately forced to conclude that, like the covered-up plaque that once honored Hui'an women's contributions to building the Wutan Reservoir, those ideals, too, have become merely "a relic of history" (1988:26).[21]

Diversifying Difference

Huidong residents were not immune to these contradictory images of local women or their consequences. As they actively engaged with and often contested popular images of local women that portrayed them in specifically ethnic, exotic terms, they sought to shift the axes of difference away from ethnicity as an all-encompassing marker to incorporate many of the divisions that undermine an illusion of Han homogeneity: native place and localism, rural versus urban residence, and backward versus civilized status. By asserting multiple bases for identity and by redefining the significance of women's bodies and intimate relationships, residents subsequently opened up possibilities for self-identification that went beyond the binary opposition between Han and ethnic minority. In other words, the Shanlin men and women I knew were actively engaged in a project of diversifying difference as it has been conceived within socialist China.

Although Shanlin women felt the effects of media images more immediately, men were more likely to engage in discussions about their own ethnic identity, their reactions to outsiders' depictions of local women, and their perceptions of one of the starkest signs of local difference, women's dress. When asked directly about their ethnic status, most men answered unequivocally that they were Han (the status marked on their state-issued personal identification cards). Although often aware of academic studies that claimed they were descended from ethnic minorities, male villagers disputed the relevance of such findings for their present state-defined status. Moreover, through a resurgence in lineage activities and the reproduction of lineage genealogies, Shanlin men implicitly contested as-

FIG. 19: Rebuilding a village ancestral home (photograph by the author, 1995)

sertions of an ethnic minority past as well. During my fieldwork, the two major surnames in the village devoted considerable time and resources to tracing ancestral genealogies that firmly rooted them in the core regions recognized as the birthplaces of the Han.[22] Through rebuilding and renovating lineage-branch halls, reinvigorating lineage-based worship and pilgrimage, and rewriting genealogies, lineage elders and members actively reproduced a communal history that reaffirmed their Han origins (see Fig. 19).

Yet, in general, ethnicity was not an overtly relevant marker of identity for village men. More salient lines of difference included the distinction between rural and urban status and the importance of native-place affiliation. Instead of framing the rural/urban divide in individual terms, most men looked to the macro level, criticizing the state for its lack of investment in local infrastructure and the rural economy.[23] When it came to place-based affiliation, however, village men were often quite specific about how they identified themselves. In response to my questions about ethnic status, a group of Mazu temple elders vehemently denied that they were members of an ethnic minority, instead claiming status as a "village people" (hniu zok), a people identified by their specific place of residence. As we gathered on the courtyard benches just outside the temple entrance, the temple elders painstakingly elucidated the differences in dress and local marriage customs that distinguished them from the residents of Chongwu, the nearby township seat. When they considered the status of those differences in ethnic terms, however, they concluded that the locales shared the same ethnic identity: "we are Han [and] Chongwu is also Han." Although this official category linked them through a national rubric of ethnic identification, on a day-to-day basis the place-based differences marked by dress styles and marriage practices mattered most to these long-time village residents.

When discussing local women's dress and its connection to their own status, this same group of elderly men recalled that in the past Shanlin men had worn styles similar to that found among women today—a top that buttoned on the side rather than down the middle and wide-legged trousers cropped above the ankle and tied at the waist with a belt. They described local women's contemporary attire not as specifically ethnic, then, but as a remnant from an earlier era. Because Shanlin men long ago had begun to interact with outsiders on fishing and trading expeditions, they had changed their style of dress earlier in the century. Women's lack of mobility meant that they faced no such impetus to change and therefore retained older styles into the present.

The gin'a, the elaborate headpiece worn by Shanlin women prior to the CCP reforms of the early 1950s, posed a problem in this configuration of dress and ethnic status, however. One of the temple elders argued that the gin'a resembled the garb of ethnic minorities. Using the civilizational scale espoused by state ethnographers, he then proceeded to define minorities as people who lived deep in the mountains and whose lives had not changed dramatically over time. Village women *had* changed their dress and headpiece styles, however, meaning that they could not, according to his definition, be affiliated with official minorities. The fact that the gin'a merely "resembled" ethnic minority attire enabled him to push the possibility of minority origins deep into the past while simultaneously recuperating a definitive Han status for the present.

Younger men who moved frequently and more freely in urban circles were less interested in refuting ethnic origins and more concerned with claiming a modern, civilized standing in the present. Many, having grown up with mothers and sisters who wore local attire, professed that they were "used to it" and found it attractive. In an urban context, however, they often saw such dress as a marker of backwardness. One village businessman in his thirties who prided himself on his stylish urban appearance (enhanced by a leather jacket and prominent gold wristwatch) refused to travel beyond Chongwu with his wife who wore local attire. Much like new urban officials in the early 1950s who sought to divorce their "backward" peasant wives because "'they did not want to be seen with them in public'" (Diamant, 2001:468), this young man claimed that he never ventured out in urban areas with his wife because city people stared at her as if she was "some kind of high-class animal" and this attention presumably reflected negatively on his own efforts to pass as a sophisticated urbanite. When I asked him to explain this fascination on the part of city residents, he used my foreign status as a basis for comparison. Chinese stare at foreigners, he argued, because they are curious; they stare at Hui'an women because they think the women are "bumpkinish" (*tu*).

Being seen together with his wife, then, posed a problem for this young man because it called into question his own status as modern and sophisticated. As a result, he did not describe the kind of difference marked by traditional women's dress as ethnic per se but instead as a product of the distinction between the countryside and the city. This absence of an ethnic identification among local men in large part explains their lack of a stake in women's attire such as one might find in honor-based societies where men more closely monitor women's bodily exposure or where men lobby actively to force women to alter their appearance. Although Shanlin men did view traditional women's dress as a reflection of their native place, that affiliation did not in itself exclude them from the promise of modernity (as, for instance, an ethnic identity might). Perhaps for this reason the young businessman did not force his wife to change her style of attire but chose to protect his sophisticated persona outside of the region simply by refusing to be seen with her in public.

The Negotiation of Difference

Shanlin women who chose to wear local dress could do little to escape the intrigued looks and curious inquiries they faced from outsiders, some of whom asked whether they really did marry as young as age twelve or thirteen (as portrayed in films and media articles) and whether their husbands beat them and otherwise treated them poorly (as was widely claimed). Local attire acted as a sign, in other words, of all that was perceived as backward and oppressive in Huidong society and it literally inscribed such signifiers on women's bodies. Shanlin women's reactions to such encounters differed according to whether they themselves wore local dress, had never worn it, or had made a conscious decision to change to an urban style at some point in their lives (usually in their teens or twenties). Those in the latter two groups did not face the same experience of heightened difference encountered by women who continued to wear traditional attire. As Ding's reaction to the stylishly dressed young shopkeeper revealed, these Huidong women were not seen as mysterious or exotic, although often the only thing separating them from their alluring sisters was their appearance.

Village women who wore local dress and traveled out of the immediate Huidong region faced the question of whether or when they should "change dress." Although on the surface it seemed an innocuous question, in fact it raised a host of issues concerning women's own self-image and the type of urban experience to which they aspired. Schein argues that rural Miao women who traveled to cities in core Han regions "experienced a strong ambivalence about the marking of their difference" (1997:80). Although Miao migrants sought to blend in with city residents so as to "avoid provoking attributions of backwardness" (Schein, 2000:209), they also recognized that they were there to earn money through performing their difference, the main signs of which were dress and hairstyle. Shanlin women, by contrast, did not go to cities as part of ethnic-minority performance troupes or as exotic showpieces for restaurants and hotels. They went to take care of business, visit relatives, shop, see a doctor, or even work. They knew, however, that wearing local dress in urban centers would attract a kind of attention that was not so different from that experienced by Miao women. By examining the points at which Shanlin women made the decision to change their appearance we can begin to understand what wearing local dress meant to them and how it positioned them with respect to other groups within the Chinese nation.

The dress decision usually varied by the length and purpose of a woman's intended stay outside of the village, her age, and the distance she would travel. Women of all ages who made short trips to the provincial cities of Quanzhou, Xiamen, or Fuzhou rarely changed out of local attire. When I asked them why, most responded that it was simpler to go as they were and that by now residents of those cities were so accustomed to seeing them that they did not pay them much notice. Yet virtually all could recount past incidents in which they had been singled out by urbanites because of their appearance, and, in some cases, the encounters went beyond the typical stares or laughter by raising the specific question of Huidong women's ethnic status.

A Lang, A Ping's elder sister-in-law, recalled for me in 1996 an incident that had occurred during a recent visit to Xiamen. She had gone by herself to the island of Gulangyu, a residential district and popular tourist destination a short boat ride from downtown Xiamen. While walking along the boardwalk she caught the attention of a group of domestic tourists and overheard them saying that she was a member of the Gaoshan nationality from Taiwan (*Gaoshanzu*). A Lang's voice shook with outrage as she recounted the story, interrupting her narrative in midstream to assert forcefully that she was Han, not an ethnic minority. She then described how the tour guide eventually disabused the group of its misconception, informing them that she was from Hui'an county in Fujian and that she was Han.

A Lang's strong reaction to her mistaken identity reveals much about her own deeply felt Han affiliation and the pervasive bias within China against ethnic minorities in general. Despite an official state rhetoric of ethnic equality, the very construction of Han as the pinnacle of civilization—a pinnacle toward which all other groups should aspire—places ethnic minorities lower down the civilizational hierarchy. Yet, when I asked A Lang whether she thought it was undesirable to be seen as an ethnic minority, she replied in the negative. She went on to explain that people often assumed Hui'an women were members of an ethnic minority because of their attractive, colorful attire. Without acknowledging any sense of contradiction, A Lang then repeated that this affinity did not mean they were minorities but instead definitively Han. The unstable coexistence of these two categories is reflected in A Lang's perception of the tourists' response as a form of misrecognition, one that she cannot help but respond to by reaffirming the majority-minority binary through angrily asserting her own identification as Han.

By the 1990s, most Shanlin women who migrated outside the county for long-term residence or work resolved this potential conflict by deciding to change their attire. These women argued that it was "more convenient" to wear urban dress because they would not attract stares or overtures from strangers as a result of their appearance. Those who went to polish stones in stone-carving factories in the nearby counties of Jinjiang and Tongan (located on the outskirts of Quanzhou and Xiamen) sometimes altered their appearance to a lesser degree, simply following factory requirements that they remove their headscarves during working hours so as to prevent accidents on the factory floor. Even middle-aged women who maintained temporary residence in Xiamen and other provincial cities (usually because of their husbands' jobs) typically modified their dress while living in the city, shedding their headscarves and wearing trousers instead of wide-legged, cropped pants.

One brisk March afternoon in 1996 I was walking down a side street in Shanlin when I ran into A Bbue and her 22-year-old daughter. They were off to worship at their family's ancestral home and invited me to join them. At first I had not recognized A Bbue's younger daughter because she was not wearing her usual headpiece and headscarf. Only when the two women began the worship for family safety and prosperity, arranging bowls of auspicious offerings around the paper tue sin figures that represented members of the family, did I discover that the daughter was scheduled to depart the next day for the distant northern province of Heilongjiang where she would spend the next seven months polishing stones in a factory managed by a Shanlin native. When I inquired as to why she had decided to change her dress, A Bbue's daughter explained that it would make her travels simpler. Although people in the village had laughed at her at first, she assured me that they would get used to it over time. Like other young women who had left the community to perform construction labor in Beijing or to look for work in booming Shenzhen, A Bbue's daughter had changed all features of her dress, from the headscarf to the cropped top.

In cases like that of A Bbue's daughter, however, the shift to urban attire was usually temporary. Once a woman returned to the village (and sometimes once she stepped off the airplane) she changed back to local dress. When I encountered A Bbue's daughter the following October, shortly after she had returned from Heilongjiang, I found her once again donning the headpiece and headscarf, together with the traditional cropped top. The women I talked to about this practice did not view their adoption of urban clothing as a betrayal of identity because, like A Lang, they did not associate their physical appearance with ethnic status (cf. Schein, 1997:81). Instead, for them local clothing, headscarves, and hairstyles connoted a tie to a place (Huidong, or specifically Shanlin). Taking up residence outside of that place necessitated changes in such bodily practices in order to facilitate integration into a new environment. At the same time, however, these women's responses to the dilemma of changing dress also redefined the significance of their attire in ways that reaffirmed their Han identity, tenuous though that identity might be. They would always be Huidong women, regardless of how they dressed. But they would not always be the exotic, ethnic Huidong women so often depicted in media images.

By the mid-1990s, some Shanlin women had begun to act on the appeal of local attire by marketing it to outsiders. Village seamstresses who made items of local dress and women engaged in the production of bamboo hats eagerly sold their wares to Japanese customers visiting stone-carving factories and to the township's growing numbers of domestic and foreign tourists. Huidong women living in urban centers also capitalized on the marketability of their difference. On one of my many bus trips from Xiamen to Shanlin, I encountered A Ha, a village woman in her mid-forties. A Ha's husband ran a business out of Xiamen, and I frequently saw her on the township bus as she traveled back and forth between her two homes, leaving her two sons in the care of their elderly grandparents in the village. A Ha usually wore urban attire when resident in Xiamen and then switched back to local dress once she returned to Shanlin. On this occasion, however, I found her already decked out in the full panoply of local attire. A Ha explained that she was now selling Hui'an specialty foodstuffs in a Xiamen market, regional products such as sweet potato flour and tiny dried shrimp. She wore local dress in order to appear more "authentic" to Xiamen consumers and enhance her sales. Once she finished selling in the market, she usually changed back to her city clothes.

Unlike village women who merely sold items of local dress, A Ha appeared willing to perform her Huidong identity in the marketplace as a sales ploy. The fact that she openly joked about her behavior with the other women on the bus also suggested to me that she was able to distance herself from her performance so that it did not conflict with her own sense of self, one rooted in a place and not an ethnic status. For this reason, A Ha was able to capitalize on her local identity by following in a long-standing tradition in China of marketing a place through its "specialty goods" (*techan*). By donning village attire, she enhanced her local affiliation, making both herself and her goods more authentic to urban consumers steeped in the mass-mediated imagery of "the Hui'an woman." That image for A Ha was not the exotic vision created by the model in the *Minsu huakan* spread or in other media portrayals. Instead, it was the hardworking Huidong woman who used the resources at her disposal to improve her own life and that of her family.

By the same token, the laughter of the other women on the bus as they listened to A Ha's account underscores the ambiguity that pervaded even local conceptions of Huidong identity. Whereas A Ha claimed that her dress made her more authentic to Xiamen shoppers, the other women argued that such efforts were lost on urban residents who had little understanding of what constituted "real" Hui'an foodstuffs. In a similar vein, consumers simply assumed that A Ha was a "real" Hui'an woman because of her attire. Yet her conscious performance of that role also calls into question what, in fact, A Ha was selling in the Xiamen market. Was there an essential Hui'an identity that underlay her performance? Or did her appeals to authenticity simply reveal the anxious desire to reaffirm something that was itself ephemeral? As I listened to A Ha's account of the market, I began to wonder whether her successful performance of Huidong identity was not itself contingent on urbanites' recognition of precisely the image she sought to counter, the exotic, mass-mediated image of "the Hui'an woman."

Local Tourism and Commodified Ethnicity

A Ha's donning of Huidong attire in the Xiamen marketplace represented the mere tip of the iceberg in a process of identity commodification and construction that was rapidly gathering steam within Hui'an itself. With the decline of local fishing and instability in the stone-carving industry, both the county and township governments began in the late 1990s to seek new avenues for economic development. Chongwu's historical status as an "ancient stone city" and the natural beauty of its beaches and mountains encouraged officials to promote tourism as one solution to the area's economic woes.[24] Such promotion inevitably included "the Hui'an woman" with her distinctive attire and folk customs as one such tourist attraction (see FJSZLYZ, 1997:133-134).

The representational history of "the Hui'an woman" outlined throughout this chapter shows how the popular media in reform-era China have often blurred the lines between ostensibly distinct categories of ethnic and Han, backward and civilized. Similarly contradictory images appear in the glossy tourism brochures, tourism policy initiatives, and promotional events of the latter half of the 1990s. Tourism ventures seek to capitalize on the folk appeal of local women, yet the adoption of full-scale ethnic marketing techniques poses considerable problems given both official state categorization and local identification as Han. Although tourism depictions of Huidong women persist in presenting ethnic images of exotic allure, they also struggle to represent Huidong women as modern Han participants in the reform-era economy. Shanlin women's own resistance to efforts to incorporate them as part of "the local scenery" suggests that the contradictions inherent in these marketing efforts may undermine the future of tourism as a cornerstone of the local economy.

Tourism publications target domestic audiences, overseas Chinese, and foreigners alike, promoting an exotic image of "the Hui'an woman" together with calls for outside investment in the county. The written texts offer detailed descriptions of women's attire and headpieces, defining such features as holdovers from an ethnic minority past. The 1994 English-language publication *Focus on Fujian* includes an entire section titled "The Stone City of Chongwu." The text recounts the history of the city itself and, in the same breath, describes the unique attire of the local women.[25] The author moves from this discussion of dress to address the ethnic origins of the city's residents, concluding, "The southern area of Fujian used to be inhabited by the ancient Bai Yue people, who, isolated by the area's unique geographical position, were never assimilated into Han culture. As a result, some aspects of their own particular lifestyle and customs have been preserved" (Xi, 1994:70–72).

A photo spread earlier in the volume also affirms these ethnic origins. The reader happens upon four photos of groups of women: each group represents the colorful attire and intricate hairstyles of one of four regions and peoples of Fujian (Fujian Tourism Bureau and Press, 1994:12–13). In addition to a shot of Hui'an women (whose awkward poses and ill-fitting headscarves again suggest that they are models), the photos also include women from Meizhou Island, whose dress purportedly imitates that of the goddess Mazu, women of Xunbu who decorate their hair with flowers and other ornaments, and She women, whose hairstyles and clothing depict phoenix symbolism. Although only the She are an officially recognized minority, the simultaneous display of distinctive attire and hair ornamentation incorporates all four groups into a continuum that conflates ethnicity and native-place identity. This conflation "ethnicizes" the women from Hui'an, Meizhou, and Xunbu, who are, at least officially, defined only by their place of residence, while it simultaneously undermines the coherence of ethnic categories by destabilizing their boundaries and defining features.

As the county and township governments began to promote tourism in the late 1990s, they adopted a range of representational strategies aimed at establishing "the Hui'an woman" as a tourist attraction. In November 1997, the county government, in conjunction with the Provincial Tourism Bureau, held a several-day-long Hui'an Fishing District Culture Festival (*Hui'an yu qu wenhua jie*).[26] The festival was intended both to promote local tourism and to attract business investment from overseas Chinese and domestic investors.[27] Much as in official minority areas, folk/ethnic appeal was employed as an "enticement," luring in outsiders who might invest in the county (Oakes, 1998:10). With this goal in mind, festival activities in Chongwu provided participants with an opportunity to enjoy the local flavor. In addition to holding a competition for the best photographs of Huidong women (which I was invited to judge), organizers also arranged a parade of Huidong women's attire with participants drawn from across the region. Older Shanlin women dressed in their pre-1949 finery: the gin'a, their hair brushed in the appropriate elaborate style, and the patchwork vest (tit bue) over their black silk tops (see also FJHB, 1998). A group of young women wore contemporary-style headscarves and blue tops, creating an image of traditional dress as at once malleable and persistent over time.

Unlike the Shanlin women who walked in the parade, other villages sent groups of young women dressed in their local best who rode shiny black mopeds with large red bows attached in front.[28] The juxtaposition of young women in traditional Huidong attire with the high-tech mopeds invokes the modernization impulse of the market economy—an impulse expressed in tourism development itself—at the same time that it packages such development in a traditional guise. Following on the heels of the moped brigade were middle-aged women in local dress who held long fishing nets stretched out between them as they walked along (see Lin, 1997). These two groups of women visually embodied the cornerstones of the local economy (stone carving and fishing), yet their very presentation was mediated by the region's new economic hope, local tourism.

Other tourism and promotional ventures also employ the traditional image of the Huidong woman as an exotic and alluring attraction for the region. Township businesses use her in packaging designs to authenticate local products (such as stuffed fish rolls [hi gng]), and she graces billboards along the main provincial highway that advertise the county's most successful consumer product, Huiquan beer. As part of a township makeover designed to attract greater numbers of tourists, Chongwu invested 21.4 million *yuan* in a stone statue park built in 1997 on one of the town's hills overlooking the ocean (FJNJ, 1998:187). The opening of the park was scheduled to coincide with the cultural festival—one more attempt to entice investors as well as tourists with the visual appeal of Huidong women. Upon

FIG. 20: Statue of "the Hui'an woman" in the Chongwu statue park (photograph by the author, 1998)

entering the statue park, visitors first encountered three larger-than-life sculptures of women in various poses, each displaying the trademark features of local dress in noticeably voluptuous detail (see Fig. 20). Similar sculptures were scattered throughout the grassy hilltop amid life-size carvings of historical personages, Buddhist iconography, and figures from Chinese mythology.

The statue park, like other theme parks throughout China, creates an idealized vision of the historical Chinese nation by erasing any reference to the more recent—and more disruptive—socialist past (Anagnost, 1997:164–165; Oakes, 1998:52–57). The site incorporates "the Hui'an woman" into a timeless display of cultural icons, thereby including her in a still powerful ideal of Han Chinese civilization. By doing so, however, the park eliminates any reference to this figure's contentious status in an evolving socialist vision of ethnicity and modernity. The tourist site recuperates "the Hui'an woman" by resituating her in a mythical past, yet it does so by displaying the figure in a form that resignifies her as exotically, even ethnically, alluring. In other words, in this commodified space of touristic display, "the Hui'an woman" is now identified not as a feudal remnant but as a desirable object of exotic allure. This signification is certainly not lost on the predominantly Han tourists who frequent the site. As they complete their voyeuristic journey through the park, tourists are given the opportunity to have their picture taken while wearing the attire of local women rather than the garb of mythical or historical figures from China's past. Like the cross-dressing models who populate many of the media images of Huidong women, locally adorned tourists perform, if only temporarily, the blurring of categorical boundaries so often enacted by the figure of "the Hui'an woman."

When I returned to Shanlin in the summer of 1998, I discovered a new image that further reinforced the ambiguous status of "the Hui'an woman" as representative of the region, the towering statue of a woman, which I discussed in Chapter 1. Carved by a local stone factory, the figure represented another of the new tourist sites built at the initiative of the township government. When I hiked up to view the statue, I found a figure that displayed the expected features of local women's dress—her cropped top cut short and her exposed abdomen marked by a prominently carved navel. She held a bamboo hat in one hand and a gathered fishing net in the other, and stood firm against the wind as an embodiment of strength and hard work. Like the anachronistic appeals to local women's laboring capacity found in Zhuang's piece, however, this figure represented Huidong women to the outside world on the basis of ideals no longer aspired to by most Chinese. Instead of her industry and ability to "eat bitterness," it was the visual impact of the statue that left the deepest impression on visitors. The exotic attire that draped the statue's muscled limbs reinforced an image of ethnic difference that left one wondering what, precisely, was being celebrated in this figure that now gazed out over the region, visible from both land and sea.

Unstable Coexistence

In villagers' reactions to the "Hui'an woman" statue and to the above-mentioned festival we begin to glimpse the future of Huidong women's place in an expanding market economy that includes local tourism as a widely promoted component. Given the unstable coexistence of categories based on ethnicity, place, and gender in the images of local women that populate the physical landscape and the mass media, Shanlin residents must struggle to make these images intelligible in ways that confirm their own perceived place in the post-Mao nation-state. Villagers' engagement with these portrayals can be classified according to two major modes: refusal of representation and questioning authenticity.

Already in Ding's failed attempts to convince Huidong women to speak on camera we witnessed women's reluctance to participate in the representational process. I observed this dynamic on numerous occasions over the course of my fieldwork, as the numbers of journalists (both Han Chinese and foreign) and curious tourists visiting Shanlin grew. Village women shied away from the camera, refusing to pose and even turning away from candid shots. A French television team that descended on the village in the fall of 1996 was forced to offer payment in exchange for on-camera interviews and shots of daily life, and even then they encountered substantial resistance. By agreeing to participate in photo shoots or to model for visiting artists, young women exposed themselves to potential accusations of moral and sexual impropriety. Even when asked to take part in events sponsored by the government, such as the tea ceremony held for visiting dignitaries attending the 1997 cultural festival, young Shanlin women (sometimes under pressure from their elders) were often loath to play their newly constructed role in wooing outsiders.

Schein (1997) has argued that the demand for monetary compensation constitutes an assertion of agency on the part of minorities and enables them to control the terms of their engagement with dominant Han cultural producers. In this case, the difference between Miao entrepreneurs and Shanlin residents lies in the latter's lack of self-identification as an ethnic minority. Local women have little incentive to represent themselves as ethnically alluring when they identify so stridently as Han. And yet the growing numbers of tourists and journalists streaming into the region might leave them little choice. The very presence of curious outsiders intent on capturing images of village life and local women forces residents to see themselves from the outside in by constituting their world as an object to be looked upon and vicariously consumed. Resistance within such a world, therefore, already presumes one's status as a marked category.

The questioning of authenticity represents another kind of effort to mediate the formation of a tourist landscape on villagers' own terms. This response emerges most prominently in reactions to the physical representations of Huidong women constructed as part of local tourism development. When I asked villagers who had visited the statue park in Chongwu about their impressions, most commented that the figures of local women were far from realistic. This reaction was even more pronounced in responses to the towering statue of "the Hui'an woman" erected in 1998. Men and women alike declared it coarse and crude, unrealistic, and out of proportion. One young woman who accompanied me to view the statue proclaimed that "the face is pretty, but the [overall] figure is unattractive." Women generally denounced the statue as an inaccurate representation of themselves, in much the same way that villagers in general denied the validity of representations that depicted Huidong women as exotic members of an ethnic minority. Unlike self-identified ethnic minorities who use and even internalize state discourses of authentic tradition in order to make themselves more marketable in an international tourist economy (Oakes, 1997), Shanlin residents have rejected state-sponsored tourism investments because they fail to conform to villagers' own understanding of authenticity, an authenticity that rejects their appropriation as "ethnic" objects of the Han tourist gaze.

At the same time, however, I caution against reading villagers' critiques as examples of straightforward resistance to the tourist project. When I returned to Shanlin in the summer of 1998, many eagerly told me about the new statue and urged me to visit it. Despite the statue's lack of authenticity, it also marked their position in an emerging tourist economy that offered the potential for greater infrastructure investment and tourist-oriented business, opportunities of great importance to rural Shanlin residents dissatisfied with their disadvantaged position in the national economic order. Like A Ha, they were receptive to the idea of marketing the local, if only that process could be separated from the exoticizing elements that characterized ethnic images of local women. The extent to which boundaries between "the local" and "the ethnic" blur in Huidong, however, leads me to conclude that such an ideal is not likely to materialize. As a result, the very basis on which villagers claim their identification with the Han nation will also remain unclear, for the images promoted as representative of the region are precisely those that call into question the fixity of identity boundaries and the original essences such boundaries purport to contain.

CHAPTER SEVEN 🌿 Symbolic Citizenship in a Civilized Nation

The images of "the Hui'an woman" found in the reform-era media and in the marks left on the local landscape in the aftermath of the 1997 cultural festival have heightened Shanlin residents' awareness of their own distance from Han cultural norms. Over the course of the 1990s, villagers' responses to this distance were also informed by a new understanding of civilization and culture promoted through President Jiang Zemin's campaigns to "build socialist spiritual civilization." These campaigns introduced their own vocabulary for evaluating villagers' standing in a changing socialist civilizational hierarchy through a language of quality, culture, and civilization. Rather than displacing the prior Maoist discourse of "feudal backwardness," the rhetoric of spiritual civilization has coexisted with it, feeding on its hierarchical premises while cultivating a vision of China as a rightful participant in an international community of civilized, productive nation-states.

In this final chapter, I examine how national-level civilizing aspirations have once again begun to take shape within Shanlin, producing contentious debates over a newly emerging figure in village society, the young woman "who wears the headscarf" (bao hoegin'e). The conjuncture of socialist spiritual civilization campaigns with Mao-era civilizing discourses has created a series of identifications that link residents' own unease about this figure and her intimate practices to broader concerns about China's status as a civilized nation. I analyze villagers' evaluations of the young woman "who wears the headscarf" in terms of the tropes of lack and excess that structure national debates on the civility and modernity of the Chinese nation. Given these national anxieties, I then ask whether it is possible for young Shanlin women today (those "who wear the headscarf" and those who do not) to lay claim to a modern, civilized status within the nation-state or whether they must look elsewhere for models of the future.

The figure of the young woman "who wears the headscarf" represents women in their teens and twenties who continue to don what I described in Chapter 5 as young traditional attire (headpiece and headscarf; cropped, side-buttoned top). In their reflections on this figure, villagers attributed to it many of the contradictory features of their own engagement with reform-era aspirations, specifically in regard to economic development, openness, progress, and civilization. Put another way, they defined the young woman "who wears the headscarf" as the weak link in their more general efforts to achieve these reform-era goals. For many, this figure constituted what Anagnost (1997:77), following Gyan Prakash, terms an "inappropriate other," both an internal embarrassment and an ever-present sign of how far villagers felt they still had to travel to escape their feudal past and achieve civilized status. Like "the Hui'an woman," moreover, this figure literally wore her difference on her body, embodying the connections between intimate practices and national civility that have repeatedly constituted Huidong residents as an uncomfortable anomaly within the socialist nation.

Socialist Spiritual Civilization

The post-Mao regime's concern with civilization (*wenming*) in both its material and spiritual forms first emerged at the Third Plenum of the Communist Party's Eleventh Central Committee in 1978, the meeting that launched market reforms across the nation. Campaigns to foster socialist ethics and eliminate spiritual pollution flourished briefly in the period from 1981 to 1984, but they were directed primarily at party members and intellectuals. Once the movement began to spread to other groups, it was squashed by the top leadership, who were now fearful of instigating another Cultural Revolution–type mass movement and slowing economic growth (Dirlik, 1982; Gold, 1984; Goldman, 1994:116–132; Schram, 1984:42–56). In 1986, however, at the Sixth Plenum of the Twelfth Central Committee, a new directive on spiritual civilization was issued, the "Resolution Regarding Guiding Directions for the Building of Socialist Spiritual Civilization." Yet even with this renewed commitment to cultivating a correct spiritual and moral atmosphere, concern persisted within the leadership that cadres continued to encourage economic growth at the expense of fostering socialist thought and behavior among the nation's citizens.

As China's economy grew rapidly in the early 1990s, the party leadership became increasingly anxious about emerging social and moral weaknesses in the population. From their perspective, morality was on the decline, materialism was on the rise; people were more concerned with pleasure and individual welfare than with social good; and "feudal superstitious" practices were spreading at a rapid rate, together with pornography, prostitution, gambling, and drug use. With his rise to power in the 1990s, Jiang Zemin spearheaded a reinvigoration of the Socialist Spiritual Civilization Movement. In 1995, at the Fifth Plenum of the Fourteenth Central Committee, a new document was passed, "[We] Must Raise the Building of Socialist Spiritual Civilization to an Even More Prominent Position." Momentum in support of the movement culminated at the Sixth Plenum in October 1996 with the widespread publication of the "Resolution by the Communist Party and the Central Government Concerning Some Major Problems in Strengthening the Building of Socialist Spiritual Civilization."[1]

This 1996 document reaffirmed the party's commitment to socialist spiritual civilization while at the same time it preserved economic development as the centerpiece of post-Mao governance. The widely reproduced image of two hands grasping firmly (*liang shou zhua, liang shou dou yao ying*) symbolized the party's assertion that economic agendas, although granted a primary position, were not to overshadow the cultivation of moral and social values. "At no time," the document asserted, "can [we] pay the price of sacrificing spiritual civilization for a brief period of economic development."[2] Simultaneous attention to both material and spiritual civilization, leaders argued, was critical to the achievement of the regime's ultimate goal, socialist modernization (*shehuizhuyi xiandaihua*). At least rhetorically, then, the party identified the building of spiritual civilization as a key element in its future development plan:

The major goal for the next fifteen years is to firmly establish and build a common ideal of socialism with Chinese characteristics throughout the entire nation; to firmly establish support for and unwavering confidence in the party's basic line; *to achieve clear improvement in the quality of citizens* [as seen in] the cultivation of thought and morality, the level of scientific education, [and] concepts of democratic rule of law; *to achieve clear improvement in the quality of cultural life* based on demands for active health, abundance and variety, and service to the people; *to achieve clear improvement in urban and rural civilization levels* according to the major markers of social atmosphere, public order, and living environment. ("Zhongguo gongchandang," 1996, p. 1; emphasis added)

The three key terms in the post-Mao regime's civilizing project appear prominently in this statement: quality (*suzhi*), culture (*wenhua*), and civility or civilization. The attention to quality refers directly to a rapidly growing population (particularly a rural population) that officials and intellectuals alike perceive as lacking the skills and discipline necessary to boost China's productive capacity without draining existing resources through uncontrolled (*luan*) consumption (see also Anagnost, 1995, 1997:86–97; "Zhongxuanbu nongyebu," 1995:1). The improvement of citizens' quality has come to be seen as essential to the modernization of the country and its successful incorporation of capitalist forces, goals that require rational (rather than uncontrolled) production and consumption. In other words, having initiated the process of market reforms, the post-Mao leadership has sought to foster the kinds of citizens who not only produce wealth but also know how to spend their wealth constructively while maintaining a commitment to collective welfare (Anagnost, 1997:91–92). Rather than replacing citizens defined by their relation to the state with those defined by their ties to the market (Miller, 1995:44), spiritual civilization campaigns strive to instill a proper commitment to both the market and the state, promoting an ethos of production and consumption that is market driven and yet collectively oriented.[3]

This discourse of quality, in short, is directed at a population perceived as ill prepared for an era that is simultaneously more progressive and more economically demanding. As something measurable (it can be "high" or "low") and qualifiable ("good" or "bad"), quality marks both bodies and minds; like Bourdieu's *habitus* (1977), it encodes embodied characteristics, inculcated ways of speaking and acting, and degrees of cultivation (moral, status-based, or urbane, for instance).[4] The discourse of quality reflects the subjective orientation of spiritual civilization campaigns that promote a mode of being that must be internalized through the didactic power of the state and then displayed through practice and speech (see Xue and Yuan, 1986; Xue, 1996). Particularly when combined with "culture" (as in *wenhua suzhi*), quality is deployed to refer to a diverse range of attributes, skills, and experiences.[5]

The linking of culture with quality reinforces the common view that China cannot improve the quality of its vast population without intensive efforts at education (see Jie, 1997:chap. 10).[6] Popular and scholarly discourses frequently employ culture as a stand-in for education, with those who "have culture" (*you wenhua*) being better educated than those who do not (see Kipnis, 1997:179, 182). This usage is perhaps too narrow, however. As I discuss below, Shanlin residents' references to the "low cultural quality" of the young woman "who wears the headscarf" encompass more than simply her level of education, already presumed to be quite minimal.[7] Cultural quality can also be read from behavior, particularly when it involves contested forms of intimate practice, such as marital or sexual relations. Furthermore, cultural quality is also determined by speech, including both manner of speaking (coarse versus cultivated) and the ability to speak Mandarin as opposed to only local dialect. In sum, both culture and quality mark patterns of behavior, ways of speaking, and personal attributes such as dependability, modesty, and diligence.[8] They evoke a practice-based understanding of civility that, when combined with both the subjective and pragmatic orientations of spiritual civilization campaigns, inspires new state interventions in Huidong villages as local officials draw on the language of spiritual civilization to justify efforts to remake both the human and physical face of their communities.

As a "contemporary *practice* of the state" (Anagnost 1997:85; emphasis in original), the building of spiritual civilization in Shanlin motivated a series of highly practical campaigns, with cadres organizing short-term adult literacy classes targeted at women, forcefully clearing the streets of obstructions, dredging the polluted village canal, planting trees, distributing trash receptacles, and building new, sanitary public bathrooms. The catchall nature of these campaigns reflected the diverse connotations of the very concept of spiritual civilization, its vagueness enabling local officials to subsume a wide range of goals under its rubric. Despite Shanlin officials' limited attention to improving the quality of village residents, they continued to appeal to the subjective dimensions of spiritual civilization discourse in order to justify their pragmatic—and, as many argued, overly intrusive—interventions in the community.

Toward the end of 1996, village officials, together with township-government representatives, initiated a widespread campaign to clean up the environment and create an orderly village atmosphere.[9] This initiative focused on removing trash, "beautifying" the face of the village, and eliminating the traffic snarls that plagued Shanlin's increasingly crowded streets. With these goals in mind, officials called for the removal of stone slabs and other valuable building materials that residents had stacked along roadsides for use in future house-building or renovation projects. After giving villagers twenty-four-hours' notice, cadres let loose hired gangs that smashed building materials remaining outside after the deadline. The village government also fined the owners of these materials for blocking traffic and cluttering the streets. When I asked one village official why such forceful methods were necessary, he responded by appealing directly to the discourse of spiritual civilization: "The people here, [their] quality is low [soozit ge]; they won't take the initiative." Hence "low quality," rather than motivating an expansion in the pedagogical scope of the campaign, instead justified punitive methods that forcefully remade the face of the community. In a strikingly Foucaultian twist, what this cadre identified as villagers' point of resistance to spiritual civilization campaigns (their "low quality") actually produced the state's own disciplinary intervention.[10]

The cadre's reference to the "low quality" of Shanlin residents reflects the extent to which the rhetoric of spiritual civilization (the triad of quality, culture, and civilization) has been adopted by both low-level officials and, as I show below, villagers themselves. This linguistic dissemination suggests that despite the often limited practical impact of spiritual civilization campaigns, like Mao-era reforms, the movement has been able to introduce a new language of distinction and value that shapes understandings of civilized behavior and socialist citizenship.[11] Shanlin villagers' discursive production of the young woman "who wears the headscarf" reveals how villagers integrated both Maoist and post-Mao civilizing discourses in ways that created new distinctions of civility within local society, often without the direct intervention of state actors.

The Young Woman "Who Wears the Headscarf"

The figure of the young woman "who wears the headscarf" has emerged in Shanlin at a time when styles of dress and adornment in the community have become increasingly diverse, producing greater distinctions among generations of women as well as between young women who have continued to wear local attire and growing numbers who have adopted the new style. Within the category of new style dressers, we find women who have never worn the headscarf and its accompanying attire and those who have decided to change their dress permanently, switching from local garb to urban styles, usually in their late teens or early twenties. The reflections of women who have made this change provide some insights into how they viewed the figure of the young woman "who wears the headscarf" and what that figure had come to represent in local society. I present here the comments of one young woman whose decision to alter her dress occurred during my stay in Shanlin but whose views are representative of the many members of her generation with whom I discussed this issue.

While passing through the village market one fall day in 1996 I walked blithely past Kingden, a young woman roughly twenty years of age, without recognizing her. For as long as I had known her, Kingden had always worn local dress, but that fall she had suddenly decided to change her attire. When confronted with the perplexed expression on my face, she quickly explained her decision by claiming that "it is more convenient to go out [of the village]" dressed in the new style than in traditional garb. She followed this allusion to convenience with a more specific reference to the stares and expressions of curiosity that women who wore local dress attracted when they ventured out of the Huidong region, an experience that she compared to the alienation faced by migrants who had come to Chongwu from elsewhere in China. Unlike the young and middle-aged women described in the previous chapter who temporarily altered their appearance for similar ease of travel, Kingden's appeals to convenience suggested more dramatic changes in the kinds of activities in which she sought to engage, those that would require social as well as geographical mobility.

As she continued with her explanation, Kingden suddenly justified her decision to change her dress by referring to activities of a very different order. "If you wear the headscarf and go out dancing, then everyone will laugh at you," she added. With this statement, Kingden associated dress with both social and personal images. Her explanation implied that a village woman who wore local attire was not the kind of woman expected to go dancing in a public place, nor would she be expected to *desire* to do so. Going dancing in public was a new and not yet fully accepted activity for young women in Shanlin; like singing karaoke in KTVs, it inevitably aroused suspicions about a young woman's modesty and sexual activities. Village gossip was even more incendiary if the young woman involved wore local attire, as I explain below. By changing her dress, Kingden opened up a new range of behavioral and subjective possibilities, potentially transforming the very image she projected to others and created for herself. In fact, after Kingden adopted new style attire, I noticed that she began to spend more time in public spaces such as the village market where she could be seen socializing in mixed-sex groups. She also opened a stylish clothing shop on a side street in the market area, a business that required her to travel outside of the county to purchase the newest urban fashions.

To argue that all of these changes were a product of Kingden's decision to switch her style of dress would be farfetched. The fact that she had recently been rejected by her boyfriend, with whom she had maintained a somewhat unconventional relationship, also played a major role in encouraging her lifestyle shift.[12] Nonetheless, she expressed her desire to transform her activities and self-image by altering her public presentation, as seen most vividly in her rejection of the headscarf and local attire and her adoption of new style dress. This decision reflects two connections between physical appearance and subjectivity. On the one hand, Kingden clearly perceived a strong link between her dress and the image she conveyed to others. On the other hand, she also attributed a disciplining role to sartorial styles, in that her mode of dress required conformity with patterns of behavior and desire deemed appropriate for that appearance. The figure of the young woman "who wears the headscarf" was associated in village discourse with qualities of (sometimes excessive) modesty, close-mindedness, and the inability to understand how to be progressive or open. Not only was such a figure expected not to visit sites like karaoke parlors or dance halls, but if she did it was assumed that she was up to no good. Villagers often asserted that such a visit would imply the woman was working as a prostitute, and they used one of the several terms discussed in Chapter 5 that identified prostitutes by their dress (traditional or new style) and place of origin (Huidong villager, town resident, or migrant). By changing her appearance, Kingden implicitly acknowledged the constraints engendered by the discursive production of this figure. As someone who no longer "wore the headscarf," she sought to legitimate her desire to go out dancing as both progressive and socially acceptable.

The figure of the young woman "who wears the headscarf" was also invoked by other groups of villagers, such as young women who had never worn local attire (usually because of higher levels of education or extended residence outside the village) and educated men. I have selected these two groups because they have the most at stake in reinforcing boundaries between "feudal" and "civilized" behavior or between those who "lack culture" or have "low cultural quality" and those who do not. Young women who wore urban dress and educated village men revealed in their reflections a creative appropriation of terms drawn from both Maoist and post-Mao civilizing campaigns. At the same time, their narratives implicitly expressed concerns that they, too, might be implicated in the very feudal practices or low quality that they were quick to criticize in others. Like Shanlin cadres who used the language of spiritual civilization to justify their intrusive interventions in the community, new style young women and educated village men employed socialist civilizing discourses to distance themselves from those they saw as outside the scope of civility. For both groups, these discourses "form[ed] a kind of symbolic fence, both marking a boundary and enclosing a category, and therefore avoiding dangerous categorical mixtures" (Caldeira, 2000:68–69).

In our many conversations over the years that I spent in Shanlin, A Hun, a stylish young mother in her early twenties, repeatedly sought to distinguish herself from childhood dui pnua "who wear the headscarf." She claimed that she had outgrown her relationships with these women because they were unable to understand her more progressive thinking inspired by several years of residence in the provincial capital Fuzhou and extended contact with urbanites such as her brother's wife. On other occasions, as I accompanied A Hun to visit her natal home or chatted with her as we worked together in a village fish-processing factory, she defined this disparity in terms of marital behavior. Whereas she had visited her husband voluntarily before they lived together, she claimed that young wives who wore local dress waited for their mothers-in-law to summon them for conjugal visits. "We who wear this kind of dress [the new style] don't need to be called," she exclaimed matter-of-factly. "Only those who wear the headscarf do."[13] In other words, A Hun posited a direct link between how a woman dressed and how she could be expected to behave in relation to changing marriage practices (of course those expectations need not conform to actual behavior). As someone who wore the new style, she depicted herself as open and progressive (she did not need to be called for conjugal visits). The woman "who wears the headscarf," however, was seen as inherently conservative and therefore less likely to visit her husband on her own.

Although A Hun contrasted the figure of the young woman "who wears the headscarf" with her own self-image as open and progressive, her bases for that opposition were somewhat shaky. She certainly looked the part of the sophisticated urbanite, dressed as she often was in stylish outfits with her face tastefully made up. Yet despite her quite passable Mandarin skills, A Hun frequently bemoaned her lack of education and minimal literacy, weaknesses that she argued prevented her from finding satisfying employment and from creating a lifestyle different from that of other village women. Although she had lived in urban Fuzhou for several years prior to marriage, she had spent her time there working in a factory like other rural migrants. Despite having married into one of the wealthiest families in Shanlin, she nonetheless continued to work as a stone polisher and later in the fish-processing factory (together with many young women who wore local attire), as well as to care for her son and perform household chores. Her appeal to marriage practices as the key marker of distinction enabled her to deflect attention away from these similarities and, as a result, to claim a more sophisticated status. In the process, however, A Hun also perpetuated the stereotypical construction of the young woman "who wears the headscarf" as a close-minded figure excessively modest in her marital behavior.

Other village women defined this form of modesty as explicitly feudal, reclaiming the term from the Maoist discourses discussed in Chapter 2 that had linked feudal practices to backwardness, restricted productivity, and oppression more generally. In early 1997, a young woman by the name of Sioklei returned to Shanlin to marry. She had been working as a stone carver in another township in the county and had come back rather unhappily to formalize an arranged match. In the days leading up to her wedding, Sioklei desperately avoided participating in any wedding preparations. One evening we sat chatting in a friend's shop where Sioklei had sought refuge, reluctant to fulfill her task of bringing some items to her future mother-in-law. She did not want to make the visit alone and asked another woman present to accompany her. When this woman agreed, Sioklei suggested that she take the items into the house, enabling Sioklei simply to wait outside. In response, the woman jumped up from her seat and loudly retorted, "Are you one who wears the headscarf or who [dresses] in the new style? Such embarrassment!" (Li si bao hoegin'e a si sin sik'e? Ziok pai se!).

Sioklei in fact did dress in the new style, but her unwillingness to enter her future conjugal home suggested to this woman—who herself wore local attire—the attitude of someone "who wears the headscarf." The connection to actual dress is clearly irrelevant in this case; instead, the figure of the woman "who wears the headscarf" is invoked as a sign of excessively shy, even feudal, marital behavior and attitudes. When I later asked a teenager who had observed this interaction to explain the woman's attack on Sioklei, she replied quite straightforwardly, "those who wear the headscarf are more feudal." This teenager did not herself dress in local garb, but like A Hun she associated those who did with overly modest and backward marital practices. It is precisely in the contemporary context of rapidly changing marriage and courtship practices that continued use of the term "feudal" produces powerful new social distinctions among village women. By accusing "reluctant" peers of being feudal, young women such as this teenager who socialize openly with boyfriends, fiancés, and husbands can justify their own radically new practices as being specifically "not feudal" and thus appropriate given China's new era of "reform and opening." In the process, however, some of the older connotations of feudal, such as its association with women's limited productivity and the need for class-based liberation, disappear. As they remove the term from a Maoist signifying chain, these women reveal in their statements the extent to which use of the signifier "feudal" no longer operates in village society as a state disciplinary strategy but functions as a popular tactic for insuring social distinction and acceptability. Although young women might "make sense of their own world and experience with the language by which they are discriminated against" (Caldeira, 2000:85), they nonetheless do so in ways that undermine the univocality of the state's authoritative discourse (Bakhtin, 1981:342–344; Litzinger, 2000:211).

When we turn to the comments made by educated village men, however, we find that the figure of the young woman "who wears the headscarf" did more than signify backward marriage practices. For these men, this figure generally represented precisely the opposite of extreme modesty or shyness: excessively liberal and chaotic (*luan*) marital and sexual behavior. In my discussions with different generations of village men about their perceptions of the current state of village society, I began to notice a common refrain among a minority who were somewhat better educated (meaning they had gone on to high school or junior vocational school). Without any prompting on my part, these men in their twenties through fifties often identified the figure of the young woman "who wears the headscarf" as the source of the chaotic behaviors and social disorder emerging in the market-reform era. In particular, they attributed to this figure unruly practices such as breaking off engagements, divorcing without cause, frequenting KTVs, and having extramarital affairs or dating multiple men (accusations not unlike those of prostitution mentioned above). This undisciplined behavior, educated men argued, was a product of this figure's "low cultural quality" (*wenhua suzhi di*), typically a reference to low levels of education and limited knowledge. They claimed that because of their low cultural quality, young women "who wear the headscarf" did not fully understand what it meant to be open or progressive; they were unable to adopt the liberating ideals of the reform era in a balanced, healthy manner. These men employed the new discourse of socialist spiritual civilization to formulate a critique that distinguished healthy or moderate mixed-sex interactions from those that were uncontrolled or promiscuous in their eyes.

Being "civilized," in other words, required controlled sexuality, not the chaotic interactions that educated men attributed to young women who continued to wear local attire. This association of unrestrained sexuality with traditional dress inverts a more commonplace image in China and elsewhere in Asia of women who wear Western or urban attire as being sexually promiscuous (see, for instance, Ong, 1987:179–186, 198–199). Although Shanlin villagers occasionally voiced such concerns about specific women who dressed in the new style (particularly because their attire tended to be more form fitting and revealing), accusations of promiscuity were hurled more frequently at the generic category of young women "who wear the headscarf" for whom the perceived transgression was even greater. Critics rarely specified who was actually engaging in these chaotic sexual interactions; as in accusations of prostitution, the very vagueness of the attacks enabled them to express uneasiness about rapidly changing social mores without accusing specific actors. The figure of the young woman "who wears the headscarf" served this purpose well, transforming Shanlin's experience of "reform and opening" into what many men in this group described as an "uncultured opening" (*meiyou wenhua de kaifang*). Their discomfort with this figure and her chaotic behavior also evoked a more diffuse sense of anxiety about economic reforms in general and the undisciplined consumer practices encouraged by new market forces.

The reflections of these two groups (young women who wore urban dress and educated men) generated the figure of the young woman "who wears the headscarf" out of the convergence of two discourses of civilization: one, a Maoist rejection under the sign of the "feudal" of all that had to be overthrown in order to construct a liberated socialist society (but a sign that functions somewhat differently today), and two, a post-Mao concern with quality and culture as the keys to forging the disciplined, productive citizens necessary for China to assume its rightful place in a global community of civilized nations. This discursive convergence produces a figure that, like its predecessor "the Hui'an woman," bridges multiple boundaries. The young woman "who wears the headscarf" brings the feudal past into what is purportedly an enlightened, civilized socialist present; at the same time, she is unprepared for this present, mired as she is in the chaos induced by "low cultural quality." The presence of lack and excess in the figure of the young woman "who wears the headscarf" illustrates the powerful social divisions civilizing discourses have engendered within Shanlin itself, divisions that shift as the state loses control over the very meaning of its own civilizing language. We begin to see how through these discourses officials and villagers alike produce figures of Huidong women that bridge multiple forms of difference, exposing tensions at the heart of the socialist civilizing project about how to define and foster civilized socialist citizens.

The Contradictions of Civilized Citizenship

The link between civilizing processes and citizenship ideals appears most prominently in a domain I have come to think of as "symbolic citizenship." Symbolic citizenship defines how a national community is imagined and sets the terms for identifying idealized citizens. It goes beyond characterizing "the nature of social membership within modern political collectivities" (Turner, 1993:3) by establishing what kinds of people are imagined as eligible for that membership in the first place. Moreover, symbolic citizenship shows how civilizing processes define citizenship through intimate, often embodied, practices that mark individuals and groups as appropriately or insufficiently civilized, thereby establishing their eligibility for inclusion in or exclusion from an ideal body politic.

The images of Huidong women discussed above and in previous chapters show how civilizing processes have produced figures whose very presence calls into question the homogeneity of China's Han majority. Unlike the non-Han woman who is defined by her "intractable otherness" (Schein, 2000:129), figures such as "the Hui'an woman" and the young woman "who wears the headscarf" are inherently ambiguous. To borrow Trinh Minh-ha's powerful formulation, each figure is an "inappropriate 'other' or 'same' who moves about with always at least two gestures: that of affirming 'I am like you' while persisting in her difference and that of reminding 'I am different' while unsettling every definition of otherness arrived at" (1997:418). This constant unsettling movement between sameness and difference is what motivates a civilizing response in eastern Hui'an and consequently makes the stakes involved in achieving civilization so high. For if ostensible members of the Han majority fail to conform to state-sponsored visions of civilized citizenship, then how can that majority justify a civilizational order premised on the "backwardness" of minority groups?

Symbolic citizenship rests on a particular conception of the ideal citizen as a figure who literally enacts the civility, progress, and productivity of the nation through specific kinds of embodied practices. As icons of uncivilized lack and excess within the nation, both "intractable" minority others and "inappropriate" figures such as "the Hui'an woman" and the young woman "who wears the headscarf" are excluded from this idealized position, yet for somewhat different reasons. As living examples of the past in the present, as theoretically Han but in practice not-quite-Han, the figures of Huidong women constitute not the far side of a boundary—as does the minority other—but instead a bridge.[14] "The bridge," Michel de Certeau suggests, "is ambiguous everywhere: it alternately welds together and opposes insularities. It distinguishes them and threatens them. It liberates from enclosure and destroys autonomy" (1984:128). In other words, the bridge modifies space by breaking down barriers between interior and exterior, by transporting the limits of the nation (defined here by ethnicity, gender, geography, and even class) into its very center. For instance, as part of China's burgeoning Han coastal core, the figure of the young woman "who wears the headscarf" resists affiliation with the stereotype of the poor, uncivilized peasant of the interior and the backward ethnic minority. Yet neither is she identified with the progressive urban Han. Moreover, both "the Hui'an woman" and the young woman "who wears the headscarf" integrate ostensibly disparate temporalities; they bring the past into the present by re-instantiating the feudal in moments imbued with the glimmerings of socialist civilization and modernization. Both spatially and temporally, then, these figures "bridge" the Chinese nation by confounding categorical divisions between civilized and backward, socialist and feudal, Han and non-Han, coastal and interior, economically comfortable (*xiaokang*) and poor—in short, between the space and time of the national self and that of the marginalized other.

What do these figures mean for the Shanlin women and men who struggle with and against them in their daily lives? If the images of local women produced by civilizing discourses fail to conform to widely touted expectations of civilized citizenship, then how does this failure affect the way Shanlin residents imagine their place in a national order? As an exclusionary practice, citizenship involves the drawing and maintaining of boundaries between one nation and another. Civilized citizenship, moreover, establishes boundaries within the space of the nation itself; it makes certain groups (Hans, urbanites, the educated, men) responsible for the civilizing of others (ethnic minorities, peasants, the uneducated, women). "The boundaries that define members [of a citizenry] are usually drawn around the geographical community," Dorothy Solinger tells us, "[b]ut they may also delineate only some of the groups within it" (1999:6). Although civilizing discourses appear to advocate the uplifting of all, they in effect privilege some groups over others. For those whose membership in any one group remains uncertain, the stakes in espousing and enacting standards of civilization assume even greater proportions. Thus various groups within Shanlin have engaged in a process of internal othering by appealing to different civilizing discourses, with local cadres, educated men, and young women with urban, progressive aspirations repeatedly displacing the markers of incivility onto others, such as young women who continue to wear local attire. As they symbolically construct a vision of the ideal body politic, civilizing discourses promote an understanding of citizenship that excludes not only "intractable" others within the nation-state but also those whose bodies and intimate practices resist the binary formulations on which such an imagined community rests.

Finally, the emergence of the young woman "who wears the headscarf" precisely at the height of China's market-reform era also raises specific questions about the viability of socialism and its broader appeal, for the citizen targeted by contemporary spiritual civilization campaigns is defined specifically as a socialist citizen. The emphasis on "building" (*jianshe*) in 1990s' spiritual civilization discourse exposes the gaps at the heart of the socialist endeavor, the anxious desire for something essential but still absent despite almost fifty years of party rule. The figure of the young woman "who wears the headscarf" is generated out of this moment of uncertainty; for diverse groups of Shanlin residents, she represents the locus of anxieties about their standing and abilities at a time when the very meaning of socialism is increasingly uncertain. Meanwhile, production of this figure also shifts villagers' attention away from the broader economic challenges and disparities that have long plagued community members, redirecting it to the gendered and embodied intimate practices that have distinguished Shanlin and the Huidong region from other parts of rural Han China. What is at stake in the figure of the young woman "who wears the headscarf," therefore, is not only the civility of the citizen but also potentially the form and future of Chinese socialism itself.

Conclusion

Anagnost has argued that civilization "encapsulates what has been called the 'Janus-facedness' of the national imaginary, looking toward the past to face the future; it marks simultaneously a place of plenitude and of lack" (1997:164). As products of different civilizing discourses in socialist and late-socialist China, the figures of "the Hui'an woman" and the young woman "who wears the headscarf" exemplify these contradictory impulses in national projects of civilization and modernization. During the Maoist high tide of socialist construction, local and regional state actors aspired to fix the terms of civility through acting on the bodies of Huidong women in order to mold them into liberated socialist citizens. By attacking distinctive features of women's dress, intervening in women's postmarital residence patterns, and struggling to dissolve all-female networks and collective suicide pacts, state actors also sought to solidify the status of all Huidong residents as members of the Han majority. The recent turn toward ethnic commodification in eastern Hui'an suggests that their efforts did not so much clarify that status as simply defer debate, thereby enabling the market forces of a more open era to seize on and commodify an ambiguous local identity.

In the post-Mao period, officials have retreated from many of these reformist actions directed at local women's bodies, turning instead to a new discourse of socialist spiritual civilization to justify their efforts to shape the contours of the civilized socialist nation. The terms of that discourse become intertwined with the anti-feudal orientation of earlier Maoist campaigns, making them available for a diverse array of projects. Young women who adopt urban attire deny cotemporality to their locally dressed counterparts by accusing them of feudal marital and dating practices; in the process they resignify a prior state civilizational discourse and apply it to newly defined progressive ends. Educated men appeal to the language of quality and culture in denying a rational progressiveness to young women "who wear the headscarf." Yet that denial also reveals considerable insecurity about both their own place in an emerging market economy and the post-Mao regime's commitment to insuring economic prosperity for all. In short, as the socialist state "loses its univocal grip on meaning" (Young, 1995:22), the very language of civilizing discourses can be made to serve local projects with goals quite distinct from the socialist civilizing aims of both Mao-era and post-Mao state actors.

These limits to socialist civilizing projects do not, however, necessarily weaken the power of symbolic citizenship. Despite their ability to resist some state interventions or redefine the terms of civilizing discourses, Shanlin women cannot fully escape the exclusionary forces that bar them from an idealized vision of civilized socialist citizenship. The fact that they are widely recognized as wearing their difference on their bodies—whether in their adornment styles or marital and sexual practices—means that they often find themselves already constituted as not-quite-Han, not-quite-civilized, and, hence, not-quite-citizens. The growth of the mass media and tourist commodification only enhances this recognition, spreading images of "the Hui'an woman" across the nation and making it more difficult for actual Huidong women (regardless of their attire) to avoid being identified with them.

Epilogue

I had just arrived back in Xiamen after a two-year hiatus, and I was sluggish with jet lag and irritated by the loss of my luggage. The hot summer air was oppressively familiar, and I retreated to the air-conditioned coolness of my hotel room where I contemplated the bus trip back to Shanlin. During my last visit in 2000 I had only managed to spend a few days in the village on either end of a conference I was attending in the city. With some trepidation, I picked up the phone and dialed a Shanlin number.

After several unsuccessful attempts in the spring of 2002 to reach my host family in Shanlin, I had finally tried a number scrawled on a back page of an old address book, next to which I had written "the shop." If I remembered correctly, this was the phone number for the telephone that Bbingden and Soelan had installed in their small fruit shop a few years prior. Hearing Bbingden's soft voice on the other end of the crackling trans-Pacific line, I breathed a sigh of relief. After the usual exchange of greetings, Bbingden brought me up to date on recent events in the family—her father's retirement, her youngest brother's job prospects, the ongoing conflicts between her mother and sisters-in-law, and her own birth to a baby boy. After hearing that I planned to return that summer, she peremptorily informed me that I would be staying with her this time, in the new house she was now occupying with her husband and two children.

It was Bbingden's story with which I began this book, and it seems a fitting way to draw it to a close. After all those years of avoiding her mother-in-law and husband and even after bearing her first child, Bbingden had stubbornly remained in her parents' home. On my return trips to Shanlin over the late 1990s and into the new millennium, I had often shared with her the room she maintained in their house. Her mother-in-law's house was old and dirty, Bbingden complained, and although her daughter usually spent the night there Bbingden preferred her parents' more spacious accommodations, especially when her husband was away. With her own limited income from the fruit shop and her husband's modest salary as a fisherman on a Taiwanese fishing boat, the couple had taken almost five years to build their own home. But now, in the summer of 2002, two of the three floors were completed and decorated in a simple fashion, sufficient for their nuclear family to move in. When I called Bbingden on that first evening in Xiamen, she excitedly proclaimed that the spare bedroom was ready and waiting for me.

Despite Bbingden's warm welcome, I was nervous about staying in her new home. I had never become well acquainted with her husband, Wilam, because he was often away from the village fishing and Bbingden herself had rarely spent much time with him until now. Since the lunar new year, however, the Chinese government had stopped issuing the papers local men needed to fish on Taiwanese boats; the decision was evidently an effort to better control the labor market and to pressure the Taiwanese government into improving labor and safety standards by granting PRC fishermen rights to come ashore in Taiwan during storms. Men like Wilam who were in Shanlin at the time the ban was enforced found that they were prevented from returning to work. As had other men over the years, they turned to the stone-carving industry for employment. During the month I spent with Bbingden and Wilam, he worked as a stone cutter in a local factory, leaving early in the morning and returning each evening tired and dusted with a thick covering of fine stone powder.

Only thirteen years into her marriage did Bbingden begin to live permanently with her husband. If I had entered her life at this point, I would have seen a typical village housewife, busily caring for her two children and new home, only peripherally involved in the business she still ran with her dui pnua, Soelan. I would have had little appreciation for the years in which Bbingden had avoided her mother-in-law and refused requests for conjugal visits; the period after the birth of her first child when she had remained in her natal home, returning to her mother-in-law's house only at night, and often not even then; or this last, and from all accounts quite difficult, pregnancy during which Soelan had cared for and fed her on a daily basis. Although Bbingden's early married years had differed dramatically from those of her younger sister A Den, by the summer of 2002 both women led similar lives, residing with their husbands in their own homes and taking care of small children. Moreover, looking around at younger women in the community, I would have seen little to remind me of the extended periods of postmarital natal residence common a mere decade earlier. By the new century, many wives moved in with their husbands shortly after they married and villagers generally accepted that a bride might be pregnant on her wedding day. As long as the couple had already registered their marriage with the government such practice was usually condoned. Certainly there was gossip and hushed talk if the bride was very pregnant, as Bbingden's paternal cousin had been just the year before, but I did not sense the kind of condemnation that had characterized so many of the conversations about similar circumstances in the mid-1990s. By contrast, I would now expect that it would be a bride who insisted on remaining in her natal home for several years after her wedding who would arouse concern, her pai se behavior indicating that something was very wrong indeed with the marriage.

This consolidation of conjugality was often, as in Bbingden's case, fostered by a couple's ability to live separately from the husband's parents and brothers. Yet persistently high population to land ratios in Shanlin and the substantial sums required to build a house meant that not all couples would be able to live in their own homes and residence in a stem (now rarely extended) family household was seldom a sufficient obstacle to joint residence. Regardless of a couple's housing situation, as long as a woman had married within Shanlin or into a nearby village she still visited her natal home on a frequent basis, certainly if her mother was alive, and her parents might visit her as well. On my circuits through the village that summer, as I stopped in to renew friendships with the many families who had welcomed me during years of research, I was surprised to find older couples babysitting their daughter's child or to discover the daughter herself, now married for several years and the mother of one child or even two children, chatting with her parents or helping with housework. Although the daughter now considered herself part of her husband's "own people," she remained a frequent presence in her parents' home.

As I took in these changes, I wondered what to make of the fact that extended periods of postmarital natal residence seemed to be gradually disappearing from the community. Young people were clearly much happier choosing their own spouse, and the kinds of mixed-sex socializing that had aroused such an uproar in the mid-1990s had settled into a pattern of interaction now accepted and even expected in village life. Lacking close ties with the generation then coming of age in Shanlin, I could not ascertain whether this pattern produced the same kinds of dilemmas and tensions faced by young women a few years earlier. It did not appear so on the surface, but of course one never knew what went on in the privacy of homes or in whispered conversations. At the very least, for the women I knew who had reached adulthood in the mid-1990s, interactions in mixed groups, even those including boyfriends and husbands, no longer generated expressions of anxiety or pai se reluctance as they so often had in prior years. Certainly, same-sex socializing remained a prominent feature of village life, and dui pnua ties continued to structure many of the activities engaged in by all villagers. But the social worlds now available to young women and men were much more flexible and inclusive than those of the past.

Did these changes mean that Shanlin had lost its contentious status and was fully absorbed into the Han mainstream? Some villagers thought so. One older mother, concerned that her son's fiancée would break off their match because she had become accustomed to life in the provincial capital, Fuzhou, claimed that there was now little difference between the village and the city; in Shanlin they had telephones and televisions just like city folks. In terms of material life, many Shanlin families were rapidly approaching urban living standards, if not overtaking them in housing stock, particularly those among the expanding nouveaux riches (see Fig. 21). On my visit in 2002, I could not help but notice the emerging class disparities within the community as well as the stark contrasts between the relatively comfortable lifestyles of many locals and the simple exis-

FIG. 21: Villa built to overlook the village harbor (photograph by the author, 2002)

tence led by the growing number of migrants in the township, men and women from poorer interior provinces who were becoming the major workforce in economic sectors ranging from construction to motorcycle taxis. Trucks ladened with huge blocks of granite piled precariously high lumbered down Shanlin's main streets all day long that summer. They were on their way to the harbor at the base of New Street where the government was building a protected, deepwater port in the hope that Taiwanese and other international vessels would soon be able to dock there. Unlike the enclosed harbor of the 1980s that was built almost exclusively by village women, this recent project involved only migrant workers. Locals were no longer willing to perform hard manual labor for the meager wages the government was able to pay.

Yet living standards and labor patterns were not the only things that had set Shanlin apart from other Han communities, either rural or urban. Shanlin women had also enacted local difference through their bodies and actions, most notably in their marriage and residence patterns and their dress and adornment styles. As I described above, postmarital separation periods were growing shorter as time went on, but what of dress? Although women of Bbingden's cohort still preferred local attire, their younger counterparts were increasingly "changing dress" or choosing never to wear the headscarf at all. This trend had begun in the latter half of the 1990s: between the time I first met A Ping in 1996 and when I left Shanlin in the spring of 1997, she had replaced her cropped top and headscarf with stylish urban attire, letting her long hair flow loose down her back or piling it up on her head in the hot summer months. Some women of her age group, like Kingden (introduced in the previous chapter), were following in her footsteps, whereas others chose to preserve local dress. For those reaching maturity in the new millennium, however, there was seldom a choice to be made. It was the rare teenager who adopted the headscarf. Now that most village children continued their education at least through junior middle school, local dress was rapidly becoming obsolete. Within a generation or two, I surmised, only elderly women would be found sporting traditional village attire.

On one of my regular visits to a retired local official, however, I was surprised to learn that the township government still had aspirations of preserving and marketing these sartorial signs of local difference. Tourism development remained a high priority for the region, and he claimed that plans were afoot to build a preservation district for Hui'an women's customs. The district, slated for Shanlin and neighboring Haibin, would include a tourist street where women would don local garb to entertain visitors while they shopped. As a means of drawing tourists down to the villages, this plan maintained the course of tourism development outlined in Chapter 6, using the appeal of "the Hui'an woman" and the persistent ambiguity of locals' ethnic status to market the region to outsiders. On this visit, the irony of the project struck me with full force: whereas it had been state reformers who had struggled for so many decades to eradicate these and other signs of difference in Huidong villages, it was now a new generation of market-oriented officials who were trying to preserve that difference so as to profit from it. As far as I could discern, however, the plan to develop the preservation district existed only on paper or in the minds of township officials. I saw no signs in Shanlin that summer that such "preservation" was being put into practice.

From a community that had attracted so much attention and intervention from socialist reformers in the 1950s and 1960s, Shanlin was gradually becoming a more typical Han village on China's burgeoning southeast coast. Did this mean, then, that state actors were ultimately successful in their efforts to make Shanlin residents into civilized, socialist citizens? As Derek Sayer reminds us, despite the contestations over power that have marked the twentieth century, "rule *is* accomplished, domination is secured much of the time, . . . whether or not this takes the form of imposing great arches" (1994:373; emphasis in original). But that securing of rule, Sayer (1994:374) continues, rarely takes place through simple consent or mystification; instead, a "knowing complicity" makes certain forms of social and political life hegemonic. In Shanlin, women and men were complicit in the reformist projects of the socialist regime to the extent they had to be to get by. And yet their cynicism about reformers' motivations showed through in both their acquiescence and resistance to Maoist campaigns, just as it did in their responses to the movement to build "socialist spiritual civilization." When intimate life is at stake, moreover, that acquiescence and resistance take place on the plane of bodily capacities and personal desires, interweaving state power with identities and aspirations that may conflict with espoused state aims. Shanlin residents have gradually absorbed state-sponsored messages about progress, liberation, and civility and then integrated them into the warp and weft of their own lives. In the process, they have also adapted those messages to address pressures and concerns often far removed from those of official actors. These contradictions suggest that struggles over intimate politics are likely to continue in communities such as Shanlin, even though they may look very different from the contests of the past.

Appendix

Propaganda Folk Songs and Protest Poetry

I. "Zap sang sio bbe gao Ng Dng" (Ten send-offs of little sister to Huangtang)

Yit sang sio bbe bbeh ki gnia	On the first send-off little sister sets out
zu sik ho diao lan dioh tnia	We must obey the Chairman's call
ki gao Ng Dng ho bbnia snia	Going to Huangtang [will bring] a good name
kng lin su siong dioh an dnia	[I] advise you to settle your thoughts.
Li sang sio bbe bbeh cut hniu	On the second send-off little sister departs from the village
ga li yit ce lin bbian sniu	Do not worry over family matters
wi liao bi zam ki gia lniu	Send back grain in preparation for battle
bbo gnia loo doo ziah lni hng	Do not fear the long distance en route.
Sna sang sio bbe gao gio tao	On the third send-off little sister reaches the bridge
bbeh ki m'tang sniu tao zao	On your way [you] must not think of running off
hok ziong lingdo tao zit diao	Obeying [your] leader is of utmost importance
yit ce gangzok dioh dai tao	Take the lead in all work.
Si sang sio bbe gao Loo Dan	On the fourth send-off little sister reaches Loodan [a place-name]
zu sik ying bbing gado lan	Chairman Mao wisely guides us
koo lan huan sin zue zu lang	Enabling us to turn over and become our own masters
m'tang bbue gi lan wun lang	[You] must not forget our benefactor.
Ggnoo sang sio bbe gao Ziong Mu	On the fifth send-off little sister reaches Chongwu
bi zam gia lniu si dng gu	Sending grain for the battle will take a long time
bbeh ki m'tang sniu lan cu	While there [you] must not miss our home
an sim ba lniu gia gao ciu	Keep your mind on sending grain into our hands.

Lak sang sio bbe gao cia zam haksip du zok tao zit hang zingdi gangzok m'bang sang sit hian ci Iniu lai wi gng	On the sixth send-off little sister reaches the bus station Studying Mao's works is of the utmost importance [You] must not ease off political work Raise grain to make into steel
Cit sang sio bbe bbeh zniu cia yit ce kun lan m'tang gnia bbeh wi gaihong zing bbing snia zing cu ggnoo ho tao zit gnia	On the seventh send-off little sister boards the bus Do not fear any difficulties Fight for [your] name for liberation Fighting for the "five goods" is the most important.
Bat sang sio bbe cia bbeh kui siong gip gi ci tolagi lai lai ki ki zin wu li koo lan wu long gah wu hi	On the eighth send-off of little sister the bus prepares to depart The higher-ups support tractors Back and forth [they] are quite beneficial So that we have agricultural [produce] and fish.
Gao sang sio bbe gao loo diong diong gok cut liao bbnoo dik dong ho diao zuan gok lai kui hong ciu diong wu Iniu sim bbo hong	On the ninth send-off little sister reaches mid-route China has produced a Mao Zedong [Who] calls upon the entire country to open up wastelands With grain in hand [our] minds are at rest.
Zap sang sio bbe gao Ng Dng kng bbe m'tang sniu bbeh dng an sim gangzok gao gia Iniu singli wansing hui lan hniu	On the tenth send-off little sister reaches Huangtang [I] advise you little sister do not think of returning Work contentedly to send [home] grain [Upon] successful completion return to our village.

II. "Znia ggeh hai dai" (Raising seaweed in the first month)[1]

Znia ggeh hai dai hooli bbang gian guat giat cut si lin bang gikbbing singsan limbbu dang daige hoosiong lai bangbbang	In the first month we are busy caring for the seaweed We must be determined in exposing the Gang of Four The responsibility for revolution and production is heavy Everyone must join together and help out.
Li ggeh hai dai lai hooli huai liam ging ai Ziu Zongli zuan gok lin bbin zuan sim yi	In the second month we come to tend the seaweed Remembering our esteemed Premier Zhou The entire nation offers their regards

goo gim diong ggua siang pingli?	From ancient times to the present, at home and abroad, who can compare?
Sna ggeh hai dai dioh siu sing	In the third month we must harvest the seaweed
Hua Zusik lingdo zin ying bbing	The leadership of Chairman Hua is so wise
sna diong di gok tng ha ding	The Third Plenum rules the country [and] all under heaven is stable[2]
zuan gok linbbin zin huan gging.	The entire nation welcomes [the reforms].

III. "Hulu hue huga" (Women, return to your husbands' homes)

Kng lan hulu dioh zingzue	I advise us women that we must put all in order
goh lin su siong dioh te hue	Each one of us must understand
dng kia lniuge si bbo due	Extended natal residence has no base
huga si lan e gun gu due	The husband's home is our base area [*genjudi*].
Kng lan zibbe dioh lin cing	I advise us sisters to recognize clearly
hue ki huga si gongying	Returning to [our] husbands' homes is glorious
lan dioh huzoo gah hooging	We must aid and respect one another
gianlip huce e gamzing	To build feelings between husband and wife.
Huce gongyok lang lang ding	Couples one after another make a pledge
bibbian cu lai ki doozing	To avoid conflict in the home
lam lu wanzuan lai bozing	Men and women fully guarantee
gianlip bbibbnuan e geding	To build a happy family
kng lan hulu zi gah bbe	I advise us women, sisters old and young
ying ying liat liat hue huge	Heroic and upright, return to [our] husbands' homes
bboohuan dai tao koo lang de	Lead the way as a model for others
bbinzu ziyiu wu gao bbe.[3]	Democracy and freedom are ours to enjoy till the end.

IV. Two anti-gin'a songs (untitled)

A.

Lin bbin zinghu zin ziah ggao	The People's Government is really something
ko lan dua ge bbo soe, soe ng tao	No longer do we comb up our hair but wear it in a bun
ko ggun gin'a hian dioh zin lilao	With our gin'a removed, we are free and easy
ko ggun hoe'a cah leh, zin yandao	With flowers in our hair, oh so pretty.

B.

Dngdue hongsiok zin bbo tong	Local customs are really no good

dua gin titbue ciu bbo long	The gin'a, titbue [long vest], no sleeves for one's arms
sen sidai a dioh gaizong	In this new era [we] must change our style [gaizong]
gin'a lai gao sna gi dik	Three bamboo sticks inside the gin'a
taogin ziap dioh gui zap sik	A headscarf made from an array of colors
bbo ho knua a dioh gaigik	It's unattractive and must be reformed.

V. "Kng lan hulu dioh kiam ze" (Advise our women that they must owe a debt)[4]

Man:

Kng lan hulu dioh kiam ze	[I] advise our women that they must owe a debt
hian si gaihong gai tao ge	Now with Liberation [they should] change their headpiece
Ina lai m'tang hong gian te	If they come [to their husbands' homes], none of that feudal style
cu bbni tao bbe lang e seh	The neighbors near and far will talk.

Woman:

Kng lin ling gun bbian goh te	[I] advise you, good sir, not to mention [this] again
ggun sin ziyiu zup gui he	Our persons are free at this young age
ggun hong siok ge si znia kuan le	Our customs are all this style
m'si ggun sin m'kiam ze	It's not that we don't owe a debt.

Man:

Li gian lang lueh'a di kam kam	You look at others with your bamboo hat drawn low
zing dioh bat lang long e cam	As if encountering them is misery
wi ho li lai dak am kia	Why do you spend each night here standing?
yin ho li sna dun m'gna ziah	Why three meals do you not dare to eat?

Woman:

Bbeh ziah m'ziah si ggun dai	Whether or not we eat is our own business
ggun ci gui ge wu ziaosiong lai	We come regularly every crab season.

Man:

Wi sim bbnih bban bbeh li bbo lai?	Why did you not come for the grain harvest?

Woman:

Ggun li ggeh lai dna too	We came in the second month to carry dirt
ggun sna ggeh lai zing too dao	We came in the third month to plant peanuts
li yao siu luan zi kao!	You bastard carrying on like this!

VI. "Bueh kng lan e ho A Zi" (Eight words of advice for our good older sister)

Yit kng lan e ho a zi	The first word of advice for our good older sister
tnia ggua lai gang doli	Listen to me speak reason
hong gian zu ggi zit diao gun	This root of feudalism
dik de lai buih ki	I have come especially to uproot.
Li kng lan e ho a zi	The second word of advice for our good older sister
wu koo dioh gin gi	Quickly record [your] bitterness
hong gian sok bok hai si lang	Feudal fetters bring great harm
gan koo tua zit si	Suffering drags on a lifetime.
Sna kng lan e ho a zi	The third word of advice for our good older sister
m'tang kao ti ti	Don't cry bitterly
yi hong yik siok si ho dai zi	Transforming established habits and customs is a good thing
sang lin gao huga ki	Sending you to your husband's home
Si kng lan e ho a zi	The fourth word of advice for our good older sister
bbian gnia bbo ziyiu	There is no need to fear that you won't be free
gao cu wu lan dong lingdo	Our Party leaders are everywhere
gao cu wu ho dong zi	Good comrades are everywhere.
Ggoo kng lan e ho a zi	The fifth word of advice for our good older sister
sna koo bbian goo li	There is no need to worry about what you wear
gan koo pok soo si ho tuan tong	It is a good habit to be hardworking and simple
Bbnoo zu sik e ho e li	Good child of Chairman Mao.
Lak kng lan e ho a zi	The sixth word of advice for our good older sister
wi lan sio hnia di	For us younger siblings
ziong cu hunyin wu ziyiu	From now on [we] have freedom in marriage
sio bbe gamsia li	Little sister thanks you.

[The speaker was unable to remember the seventh verse.]

Bat kng lan e ho a zi	The eighth word of advice for our good older sister
dua dna gao long cun ki	Boldly go to your [husband's] village
sia gao wun dong si cun hong	

262 APPENDIX: PROPAGANDA FOLK SONGS AND PROTEST POETRY

yong gam gnia ang gi	The Socialist Education Movement is [like] a spring wind Bravely carry forth the red flag.

VII. "Zap li ko lin" (The twelve miseries)

De yit ko lin di huan gan ong ggua cut si bbnia gan lan zit dang doo ge yiu zit dang pai bbnia bbo si leh dam ggnoo lang	The first misery is living in this troubled human world I was wronged at birth by a hard fate One winter passes and another comes I live on with this horrid fate, burdening others.
De li ko lin hun bueh li bbnia pai gah lang bbo ping bi ggua dioh tan za ki tue lang si [m'tang] dam ggnoo lang cing cun siao lian si	The second misery is those hateful eight characters[5] Nothing can compare with this horrid fate Long ago I should have died for him Thus not burdening his youth.[6]
De sna ko lin gnia bbnia gan lan wu si sniu dioh bbak koo ang bbo lang zai yna ggua kin dang koh ggua gan koo zit si lang	The third misery is this hard fate My eyes redden as I think of it No one knows my suffering Leaving me to bear the burden my entire life.
De si ko lin ko lin dai cian lai bban ki koh bbu hai ggua lna bbo seh bbo lang zai cin cniu soe zun zai dang zai	The fourth misery is this pitiful state So harmed have I been by my mother If I do not speak out, no one will know Like a small boat carrying a heavy load.
De ggoo ko lin bbnia cni cam sin te but si bbue bing an bing bbo zue dui ziao goo lan koh ggua gan koo zit si lang	The fifth misery is this wretched fate At times my body is not at peace There are no zue dui to care for us Leaving me to suffer my entire life.
De lak ko lin bbo loo ying cian lang bban lang knua ggua kin lna bbo koh lang lai hiao hing yin ho koh lang lai knua kin	The sixth misery is uselessness All hold me in contempt If my good intentions had not been wronged I would not be scorned by others.
De cit ko lin ko lin dai cian lai bban ki koh bbnia hai ggua lna bbo seh bbo lang zai wan sim ciat bbnia gnia lang zai	The seventh misery is this pitiful state I have been so harmed by this fate If I do not speak out, no one will know I do not want others to learn of the enmity in this short life.
De bueh ko lin too dua kui	At the eighth misery I sigh deeply

dam ggua bbnua sin e loo zui	My whole body is damp with morning dew
Ina bbo be bbu lai gua lui	If it was not for my attachment to my parents
za za gah se gan lai hun kui	I would have left this world long ago.[7]

De gao ko lin ggua gan koo	The ninth misery is my suffering
ong ggua cut si zue zabbo	Wronged by being born a woman
wu bni bbo lang lai knua goo	No one cares for me when I fall ill
zap sin si liao bbai lip too	[No matter] how many times I die, I lie forgotten beneath the earth.

De zap ko lin koo pai bbnia	The tenth misery is this bitter fate
sim gnua but si e tang tnia	It pains my heart at times
ggua dioh ki si goh wu yna	It is only right that I die
kia di se gan bbo bbnia snia	In this world I have no name [reputation].

Zap it hun ggua bbue za si	Eleven hates me for not dying sooner
sniu dioh ggua bbnia ko siong bi	I grieve when I think of my fate
Ina bbo koh lang lai koo ki	If I had not been so embittered by others
yin ho e sit hioh gah li gi	They would not have become such a diminished family.[8]

Zap li ko lin koo wan wan	The twelfth misery is bitterness without end
bbo lang kng ggua sim hue zuan	No one admonishes me to turn my resolve
sim gnua Ina sniu Ina m'gguan	The more I think the more I hesitate
sniu ggua snibbnia gui hongzuan	Imagining my life returning to the grave.

VIII. "Znia ggeh sng lai" (What the first month brings)

Znia ggeh lao liat m'ai ki	The first month [dawns] lively and bustling [but I] do not want to go
cng'a zit sin ang si si	
bbak sai lao lok si liam lui	Decked out all in red
ka dah cu diong too dua kui	The tears stream down pitifully
	Stepping into the house, [I] sigh deeply.

Li ggeh sng lai cih gui dang	The second month brings the wintry crab season
ki gao lin ge zue dng gang	Arriving at their home to perform long labor
bbak sai lao lok bbak ziu ang	Tears stream down and my eyes redden
bing bbo zue dui ziao goo lan	There are no zue dui to care for us.

Sna ggeh sng lai zing too dao	The third month brings the peanut planting
lin ge lai gio si gue zao	The family comes calling [and I] scatter
lan Ina bbo ki lang e kao	If we do not go, they will make a fuss
sniu bbeh gah bbu hun loo tao	[I] think of separating from my mother at the road's end.

Si ggeh sng lai lang tua lue	The fourth month brings the plowing
zinghu boo diao si han ze	The government has announced restrictions
soo yi ggun zit Ini ki zit geh	Therefore we go once a year
bbo sna bbo koo m'gna seh	No clothing to wear, [but we] do not dare speak [out].
Ggoo ggeh sng lai diam an zi	The fifth month brings sweet potato fertilizing
lit tao cut lai pak bbnua si	The sun comes out, baking [us until we] are half dead.
Iniu li goh knia zit lit ki	Wife, why don't you stay one more day before leaving?
ho bit anne gua si si	There is no need to rush so.
Lak ggeh cit ggeh ggun a lai	We come in the sixth and seventh months as well
cu bbin zim m lang a zai	The neighbors and aunts[9] also know.
Iniu li Ina lai ggua hua hni	Wife, when you come I am happy
ge ding e lang a bbnua yi	Everyone in the family is content.
Bueh ggeh sng lai bueh diong ciu	The eighth month brings the Mid-Autumn Festival
a goo lai gio m'ziap siu	Our sister-in-law comes to call [but] we refuse [to go]
ga goo Ina seh Ina bbeh liu	The more we talk with her the more we want to stay
gio goo Ina gnia ziah bbue giu	[So] we send her on her way before it grows too late.
Gao ggeh sng lai so zi ko	The ninth month brings the drying of the sweet potatoes
du dioh zit puah sai bak hoo	Encountering a sudden downpour
da ge teh sna koo lan boo	[Our] mother-in-law brings clothing for us to mend
bbue hiao zim'a bbeh lu ho	[But we] don't know how to use a needle.
Zap ggeh sng lai si poo si	The tenth month brings Pudu[10]
da ge lai gio ggun m'ki	Our mother-in-law comes to call [but] we refuse to go
ziah bbnih m'ki si ko yi	It is fine not to go [when called] to feast[11]
dioh koo da ge liu bbin zi	We have to allow our mother-in-law some face.
Zap yit ggeh sng lai ggeh ang hun	The eleventh month brings red clouds
ping iu hnia di zue zit gun	Friends and siblings gather together
knua gni a Iniu cng diong kun	Look at wife sleeping on the bed
cin cniu suat m leh sniu gun	Like Zhu Yingtai thinking of her gentleman.[12]

Zap li ggeh sng lai si Ini dao	The twelfth month brings the new year
gua'a ka lan ciu Ina gao	With cold that freezes the feet and turns hands numb
Iniu li m'kun koo siang kao?	Wife, why are you crying and not sleeping?
lin be kun'a poo lai gao.	For god's sake, [I] am sleeping on the very inside of the bed.[13]

Reference Matter

Notes

Introduction

1. The Mandarin expression *chang zhu niangjia* is not an emic category among eastern Hui'an residents. I have found it used in government documents and scholarly articles dating from the early twentieth century to the present. Villagers themselves do not have an overarching term to describe their marital practices, in large part because they are the norm in this area, the unmarked category. Thus a villager might say that a woman "has not yet gone" or "has not yet given birth" as a way of indicating her continued natal residence. Older women often described their shift to conjugal residence as "owing a debt" (kiam ze), a phrase that emphasizes their loss of freedom and their obligation to contribute labor to their conjugal families.

2. The classification of China's vast population into a mere 56 different nationalities/ethnicities (*minzu*) was the result of a state-sponsored program of "nationality identification" (*minzu shibie*). Teams of researchers were sent to frontier areas and other regions with apparently non-Han populations in order to distinguish majority Han from non-Han, and different non-Han groups from one another (Fei, 1981; Guldin, 1994:105–108; Yang, 1992).

3. According to official documents, the process of ethnic identification was initially undertaken in Hui'an county in 1952. At first ignoring the eastern part of the county, the county government sent cadres to investigate the possibility of Hui (Moslem) ethnicity among residents in a southern district (Hui'an Xian Difangzhi Bianzuan Weiyuanhui, 1998:799). In April 1954, officials carried out investigations in districts and administrative villages throughout the county, and they delineated an ethnic minority population of 5,337, all of whom were classified as Hui (1998:183). By the end of 1985, ethnic minorities officially constituted 3.81 percent of

the total county population. They were predominant Hui, followed by She, Mongolian, and a sprinkling of other groups, including Zhuang, Miao, Dong, Li, and Gaoshan (1998:183-184). According to the results of the fourth national census in 1990, Han comprised 99.9 percent of the population in Chongwu township where I conducted research (Hui'an Xian Renkou Pucha Bangongshi, 1991:12-19).

4. Stalin's criteria included common language, common territory, common economic life, and a common psychological makeup or culture. Investigators also considered traditional folk categories and indigenous ethnic consciousness (Harrell, 1995b:22-24). For a discussion of the problems Chinese researchers faced in applying Stalinist categories, see Harrell (1995b) and Guldin (1994:106-107).

5. The emergence of marriage resistance in the delta was facilitated by a vibrant silk industry dependent on female labor. In compensation marriage a wife used her earnings to purchase a concubine for her husband, thereby retaining her status as first wife but effectively avoiding all conjugal obligations. Sworn or popular spinsterhood took conjugal refusal one step further by providing a culturally accepted institution for unmarried women who aspired to an alternative mode of adulthood. By taking a vow of spinsterhood, a woman proclaimed herself an adult outside of marriage. Spinsters then formed communities around spinster houses, supporting themselves and caring for one another as they aged (Sankar, 1978, 1985; Stockard, 1989).

6. I have not been able to document for the Pearl River Delta socialist reform campaigns similar to those carried out in eastern Hui'an. There are accounts of Nationalist-era (1927-1949) government reform efforts (see FSGGCK, 1930), but there is very little information available on the early socialist period. Stockard (1989:115-116) briefly mentions efforts after 1949 to force nonresident wives and spinsters who remained in the delta back to their "proper" homes, but she does not provide details on how these efforts came about. C. K. Yang (1959a:15, 85-86) describes the presence of four "old maid houses" in a village outside of Guangzhou in 1948, but he does not discuss the plight of these 60 women (who included "separated wives" as well as widows and unmarried women) after 1949.

7. Due to space constraints, I have chosen not to discuss here China's many minority nationalities that have long-established traditions of delayed conjugal residence (often paired with sexual freedom) and institutionalized same-sex bonds. See Chapter 6 for a brief discussion of the Chinese-language scholarship that seeks to establish the ethnic origins of Huidong residents based on such customary affinities.

8. This approach diverges from a Marxist concern with unveiling the

oppressive relations between the state and society by showing how power is never exclusively fixed in a single agent or institution; instead, state apparatuses are part of a broader circulation of power throughout the social body (see Anagnost, 1994; Gupta, 1995; Mitchell, 1991). In fact, as Mitchell argues, the appearance of a boundary between state and society is itself the effect of a modern political order (Mitchell, 1991; see also Gordon, 1991). For arguments against a strict separation between state and society in China, see Perry (1994) and Zhang (2001a).

9. Benjamin is ultimately concerned with how this mutual recognition of subject-subject is all too readily transformed into a subject-other relationship of domination and submission. Whereas she draws on feminism to critique this tendency in psychoanalysis, Giddens appeals to the emancipatory power of democracy as the source of egalitarian transformations in intimate life.

10. This hierarchy of intimate bonds resembles what Povinelli (2002b:232) describes in a postcolonial context as an uneven distribution of "the intimacy grid."

11. Dui pnua refer to same-sex ties formed among both women and men. Although some scholars have translated dui pnua using the kinship-based expressions "sisterhood" or "brotherhood," the term in Minnan dialect has no kinship- or gender-specific component. To avoid this confusion, I retain the Minnan term throughout the book.

12. The distinction between the subject and the person or self features prominently in both Lacanian psychoanalysis and poststructuralist theory more generally, but I do not have the space here to address it adequately. For more detailed discussions of this relationship, see Hall (1985), Moore (1994:25), and Smith (1988).

13. In other words, individuals are not necessarily free to pick and choose among available subject positions because some positions bear more polit-ical weight than others (Moore, 1994:4). Works by feminists of color in the contemporary United States have made this point repeatedly by illustrating how we are never simply "women," defined exclusively by our gender, but instead are constituted contextually by a shifting intersection of race, class, gender, ethnicity, nationality, and sexuality. See Anzaldua (1987, 1990), Collins (1990, 1998), Crenshaw (1993), and Moraga and Anzaldua (1983).

14. The exception here would be women in certain minority communities who face contradictory desires to renew traditional sexual practices banned during the Maoist era (often for being "feudal and licentious") and to claim a modern gender and sexual identity in an increasingly commodified sexual market. Makley (2002, 2003) offers a powerful example of

this tension in a Tibetan community in Gansu. See also Schein (2000) and Mueggler (2001).

15. John and Jean Comaroff make this point quite nicely with regard to colonial society in southern Africa: "the symbolic politics of dualism and difference here were a refraction of the general tendency of colonial encounters to force ever deeper conceptual wedges into ever more articulated, indivisible orders of relations" (1997:26).

16. There is some debate among feminist scholars as to whether difference always "smuggle[s] in hierarchy" (Abu-Lughod, 1991:146). Elliston (1997) calls for attention to cultural and historical variability before assuming that all differences are inherently unequal. By contrast, Moore (1994:26) argues, "Difference is, of course, a relational concept, and it is always experienced relationally in terms of political discrimination, inequalities of power and forms of domination."

17. This experience is not unlike that of indigenous groups in liberal democracies, where an ostensibly egalitarian multiculturalism requires that they enact an original, pre-contact state. As Povinelli (2002a) convincingly argues, this is an impossible demand yet one that indigenous peoples must struggle to satisfy if they are to effectively press for land claims and other benefits from the liberal welfare state.

18. This shifting of otherness oscillates beyond the village as well, for villagers also argued that it was the inhabitants of *other* Huidong communities (specifically Xiaozuo and Jingfeng townships located across the bay) who were *truly* feudal and backward in their customs, marrying off their daughters at the young ages of nine or ten (or so I was told). However, the few Xiaozuo residents I knew engaged in the very same process, pointing out "those Chongwu people" (the township in which Shanlin is located) as being the most feudal and backward.

19. Han settlers had begun moving into the area as early as the late Tang dynasty (618–907), and several temples and nunneries in the township date to the southern Song dynasty (1127–1279) (Chen and Wang, 1992:20–21).

20. I use pseudonyms for all of the villages but have retained the real name of the township. According to the 1990 census, the villages in the township ranged in size from roughly 2,000 to 11,000 persons, whereas the population of the township seat was 25,657. The total township population was 63,802 (CWZZ, 1996:271).

21. Shanlin is technically a multisurname village, although it is numerically dominated by one surname group that divides itself into nineteen lineage branches. The second largest surname comprises three lineage branches dominated by the powerful third branch, and the remaining two surnames have been reduced to one lineage branch each.

22. Prior to construction of the village harbor (an endeavor that had been attempted several times in the past, with no success), village boats were forced to weather storms in the sheltered harbor of a neighboring community.

23. Older residents preferred to remain in the upper village for the community and familiarity it offered them. Despite efforts by their children to convince them to move down to live in newer homes, many of the elderly stubbornly continued to reside in increasingly run-down ancestral homes or in their families' original residences.

24. Only in 1997 was a new junior middle school built on the border between Shanlin and the neighboring village to serve students from the two communities. Prior to that time, Shanlin students attended the township seat's junior middle school. At the time of my research, students who went on to high school had to board at one of the four schools located closer to the county seat. When I returned to Shanlin in the summer of 2002, however, I found that the township junior middle school was being converted into a high school.

25. Most of these kin were men who had been captured by Nationalist forces while fishing in the Taiwan Strait in the early 1950s. They were forcibly conscripted into the Nationalist army and lost all contact with their families in Shanlin until the 1980s. Some married Taiwanese women; others remained single their entire lives. Those still alive live mostly in Jilong, Taiwan's northern port city, where they have established a native-place association and built their own Mazu temple, an offshoot of Shanlin's village temple.

26. My experience during these difficult months affirmed for me the power of Abu-Lughod's insights into the multilayered position of the anthropologist as an outsider. As she writes so lucidly, "What we call the outside, or even the partial outside, is always a position *within* a larger political-historical complex" (Abu-Lughod, 1993:40; emphasis in original).

Chapter 1

1. In Chapter 6 I discuss in greater detail the context in which the statue was erected.

2. I borrow the expression "gender divisions of labor" from Jacka (1997:1–2). I find it more precise than "gendered division of labor" and less biological than the traditional phrase "sexual division of labor." The plural form also emphasizes that there is not one overarching division of labor between men and women but that multiple divisions exist at any one

moment and that they change over time in response to social, political, and technological shifts.

3. Buck's surveys appear not to have included areas in which fishing dominated over agriculture, a fact that might account for the anomalous status of Huidong women's labor participation (Buck, 1956). Huidong women's ability to perform heavy manual labor was due partially to a general reluctance in the villages of eastern Hui'an to bind women's feet. Although elderly villagers recalled that wealthy women in the township seat had bound feet, they claimed that village women generally came from families too poor to handicap women in a manner that would inhibit their ability to perform labor.

4. Among Shanlin residents, three families were designated rich fishermen and one was denounced as a fishing capitalist. These two groups lost their fishing property and later were banned from participating in collective fishing altogether, or, in rare instances, were assigned to the worst boats. In the township as a whole, poor fishermen accounted for 45 percent of all fishing households, middle fishermen 15 percent, and rich fishermen 0.5 percent (CWZZ, 1996:91).

5. In some cases the original boat owner(s) retained ownership of the vessel, whereas in other cases men purchased joint ownership shares or received proceed shares depending on work point distribution. Fishing gear such as nets and lines was all collectively owned.

6. The shift to collective ownership required that the cooperative convert all private property—most importantly boats—to an accepted local value that was then paid out to the owner over a fixed period of time (usually three to five years). The cooperative also began to subtract a share of earnings for the "three funds" (*san jin*). These included a depreciation charge to cover boat upkeep and the building of new boats; a public welfare fund to aid poor families, the ill, and those faced with emergencies; and a public accumulation fund to supplement income in lean years. According to former cadres who had presided over this transition, the three funds deducted 8, 3, and 15-20 percent, respectively, from the cooperative's earnings.

7. Those left behind were cadres, older men too weak to withstand the harsh conditions, or those with poor political status; the latter two groups survived by fishing in coastal waters for crabs or small fish, activities that provided only the barest means of survival at the time.

8. Basic grain rations (also known as *jiben kouliang*) were a fixed allotment granted to individuals based on their membership in the collective (Oi, 1989:33-38). In Shanlin, basic rations varied significantly by the type of labor performed (see Chen and Shi, 1990:118-119, for a comparable

case). By the initial period of the Great Leap Forward, women no longer earned work points or received grain rations; instead, all of the harvest went to the collective and villagers ate in public canteens. Following the nationwide famine brought on by the excesses of the Great Leap and the subsequent closing of the canteens, production teams resumed a fifty-fifty distribution of work points and basic grain rations.

9. The only Shanlin men sent to labor on public works projects during this period were members of the "five black classes." Their participation represented a mass political deportation of politically suspect individuals and families during the late 1950s when conflicts with the Nationalists on Taiwan appeared to threaten the political integrity of the new socialist republic. Because of Shanlin's coastal location, it was seen as particularly susceptible to Nationalist infiltration. In order to reduce the risk ostensibly posed by these individuals, they were sent to farm unsettled lands in the interior of the county or to build irrigation works.

10. Work on the Wutan Reservoir lasted from July 1958 until March 1963, although the dam itself was completed in February 1960. The project employed 15,000 workers from four different communes, 80 to 90 percent of whom were women.

11. Renewed tensions in the Taiwan Strait and difficulties in finding sufficient fishing work for men quickly put an end to women's engagement in fishing. Outcries against the "inconvenience" of men and women fishing together and the inability to maintain modesty in such cramped quarters also led to its demise. See "Guanyu ge qu funü gongzuo hui bao zhai yao" (Summary report concerning woman-work in each district), 1957.

12. The women assigned to public works projects during the post–Great Leap famine at least had access to minimal rice rations, and many recalled saving portions of these meager rations to send to younger siblings back in their home villages. Those who remained in Huidong villages during the famine (primarily married women with children, the elderly, political outcasts, and young children) survived by eating the leaves from sweet potato plants.

13. Irrigation projects within the village, in contrast, employed the labor of married women who had already given birth and taken up residence with their husbands' families. From 1959 to 1964, married women in Shanlin built a reservoir that supplied the central village canal and dug several small ponds to irrigate surrounding fields.

14. The daughter-in-law's quick retort might just have easily reflected her own motives for ending her first arranged marriage. Only after her divorce did she marry A Di's son (who himself had been divorced by his first wife).

15. In 1972, however, the name was changed again to Hui'an Reservoir, and in 1973 it reverted back to the original name of Wutan Reservoir (Zeng and Cai, 1992:34–42; Zhong Gong Hui'an Xian Weiyuanhui and Hui'an Xian Renmin Weiyuanhui, 1960).

16. One *jin* equals 0.5 kg.

17. Villagers purchased these allotments at reduced prices from the Supply and Marketing Cooperative in the village. Extremely poor villagers (usually members of one of the five black types) were forced to make ends meet by buying their rice quota at the discounted price and then selling it on the black market for a higher market price. This left them with virtually no rice for their own consumption.

18. In this sense, we might see these women as similar to rural migrant domestic workers in the 1970s who Yan Hairong describes as "fragments of socialism, whose presence was somewhat incongruent with the grand view of socialism and women's liberation" (2003:582).

19. In 1961, Shanlin and Haibin dissolved their joint structure, and each formed a separate production brigade under the leadership of the renamed Chongwu People's Commune.

20. In 1964, the brigade established a Fishing Industry Middle School (*Yuye zhongxue*) that operated on a work-study model. Young men were trained in technical and basic education skills for a period of three years, after which time the brigade assigned them work on a fishing boat or in a relevant work unit. The school was disbanded in 1967 by the Cultural Revolution leadership.

21. The weight of 1 *dan* equals 50 kg.

22. Building the sea embankment was the one project in which Shanlin men participated in significant numbers. Because the site was close to the village, men could be sent for short work periods during the fishing off-season. This case fits most clearly into the model espoused by Davin who argues that public works projects absorbed surplus labor during lull periods (1979:138). Studies of rural Guangdong also describe joint male and female participation in local irrigation and flood-control projects (Parish and Whyte, 1978:169–170; Potter and Potter, 1990:76–78).

23. See the Appendix for a full transcription and translation of the folk song.

24. This line refers to the Third Plenum of the Eleventh Central Committee that in 1978 introduced market reforms and decollectivization policies. See the Appendix for the first two stanzas of the song.

25. According to township figures, in 1983 Shanlin women cultivated 529 *mu* of land and produced 1,106 *dan* of sweet potatoes, less than half the yield of five years prior. By 1987, total land cultivation in the village

had fallen to 300 *mu*, and by the time of my research plots were largely restricted to land high up on the mountain. The area of 1 *mu* equals approximately 1/15 of a hectare.

26. The need to assist fathers who fished in coastal waters was frequently cited as the major reason why girls dropped out of school in the past. Even in the mid-1990s, I encountered young teenage girls who had virtually no education for this very reason.

27. Other lines of work for women included operating a restaurant or karaoke parlor, again often with one's husband. Women also filled the lowest ranks of the village government and were responsible for family planning work. Young women who had gone on to receive a higher education (by which I mean completion of junior middle school or above) had the skills to move into more professional positions, such as teachers, health workers, accountants, or factory cashiers. Because of consistently low levels of female education in Shanlin, however, this group remained very much a minority.

28. Historically Hui'an county was renowned for its skilled stone masons who carved figures and relief plaques for temples, public buildings, and monuments, as well as stone slabs for housing construction. Stone carving in the area west of the Chongwu township seat dates back as far as the late Ming dynasty. Prior to the 1990s, the trade was organized on a master-apprentice basis, and all workers were male (F. Wang, 2000).

29. In a survey of 41 village households that I conducted in 1996, I found that the majority of men in their teens and twenties worked in some branch of stone carving. Although the older men in this cohort might have fished briefly before switching to factory work, teenagers typically went directly from school into a stone-carving apprenticeship and had no experience whatsoever with fishing.

30. This was out of a total number of 342 stone-carving and stone-material processing factories in the township (CWZZ, 1996:124). The majority of stone-carving factories are export oriented, with the largest customer bases located in Japan, Taiwan, and Southeast Asia. By 1996, virtually all of the major factories had attracted some form of overseas investment, qualifying them to export directly (CWZZ, 1996:129). In the township alone, foreign currency earnings from the stone-carving industry exceeded 2 billion *yuan* in 1999 (F. Wang, 2000:4).

31. This 1996 figure comes from a township government worker who also moonlighted as a local historian. It was confirmed in a 1998 newspaper article that found over 4,000 township women working in some form of stone carving, out of a total female township population of more than 16,000 (Zheng and Huang, 1998).

32. Because of increasingly unstable work demand by the latter half of the 1990s, however, stone polishers began to move frequently from one factory to another in search of steady work. Some left the township for stone-carving factories that had emerged in counties closer to Xiamen such as Jinjiang, Zhangzhou, and Tongan. Women returning from these factories claimed that work demand was more reliable there, and thus that they could count on earnings of over 1,000 *yuan* per month.

33. Shanlin opened to the Taiwanese fishing labor market in 1989. Fishermen go through a labor-introduction bureau for assignment on a Taiwanese boat, often using one of the six or seven such bureaus run by village men with relatives living in Taiwan. These labor exchanges have resolved labor shortages in the Taiwanese fishing industry and absorbed surplus labor from Shanlin.

Chapter 2

1. Prasenjit Duara contends that the *fengjian* tradition was revitalized in the late Qing dynasty (1644–1911) by intellectuals such as Liang Qichao who sought to modernize China through strengthening the role of local elites and integrating *fengjian* principles with Western law (1995:153–155). As Fitzgerald (1996) shows, however, this approach was rapidly replaced by a focus on nation-building under a strong, central government.

2. The year 1939 witnessed the initiation of a series of campaigns in Fujian to eradicate underage marriage, linking it explicitly to the deteriorating quality of the national race. Well into the 1940s, the provincial government urged counties to ban marriage below the legal age and to institute preventive measures such as premarital physical exams and marriage registration in order to enforce popular compliance with the law (see Friedman, 2002:162–169).

3. "Qudi hunyin lousu banfa."

4. This communication can be found in Fujian Provincial Party Archive file 11-6-4254(1).

5. A popular media account of collective suicide among Hui'an women from the 1930s, by contrast, identifies the loss of spousal affection, marital dissatisfaction, and family discord as the primary motivations behind young women's decision to take their own lives; no mention is made of the distinctive nature of marriage practices in the region ("Hui'an funü tongmeng zisha," 1935). I am grateful to Elizabeth Remick for sharing this article with me.

6. "Fujian sheng chajin minjian bu liang xisu banfa shixing xize," Nov. 11, 1948.

7. In 1926, students in eastern Hui'an's Jingfeng township organized a customs-reform troupe that traveled from village to village speaking out against such practices. The troupe obtained county government support in 1931 but failed to spread its message beyond Jingfeng and neighboring Xiaozuo township, dying out by 1937 (Zhuang, 1992, 1996). Elderly Shanlin residents could recall no such reform movements in their area during the Nationalist period.

8. Further comparative research is necessary to determine the importance of sartorial changes in marking the shift from the old society to the new. For instance, Erik Mueggler argues that members of a Yunnan Yi community described Liberation not as "turning over" (*fan shen*) but as "changing dress" (*huan yi*). Although such transformations were the result of improved economic conditions that enabled villagers to replace homespun hemp cloth with cotton, it is striking that they characterized Liberation in explicitly sartorial terms (Mueggler, 1998:986–987).

9. "Dong Zhou jidian guanche hunyinfa qingkuang baogao" (Report on the situation implementing of the Marriage Law in the Dong Zhou base area), rough draft, 1952, hereafter cited in the text as "Dong Zhou."

10. Prior to marriage, young girls simply combed their hair in a long braid and then coiled it on the top of their head. Married women resident in their natal homes and widows did not wear the gin'a or comb their hair in the elaborate style, nor did they use silver ornaments or decorative flowers (Chen and Shi, 1990:200).

11. By simplifying hair- and headpiece styles, the government also erased visible signs of marital status. Prior to these reforms, such styles distinguished in-married daughters-in-law from married daughters living in their natal homes. After the gin'a was banned and hairstyles were simplified, one could not necessarily determine a woman's residence status from her headpiece and hairstyle alone.

12. Part of this effort involved encouraging women to actually give up their silver and gold ornaments and jewelry. In the mid-1950s, the government collected silver hairpins, silver waist belts, and other jewelry as part of a campaign to encourage thrift. Villagers were purportedly compensated for the value of the items. As evidence of the different treatment of Huidong residents and officially recognized minorities, in one Guangxi minority region in the early 1950s, local cadres were criticized for "compelling" minorities to turn over their silver ornaments, offering insufficient compensation, and, in some cases, "branding anyone wearing jewelry as 'feudalistic and backward.'" All of these actions were attacked as examples of Han chauvinism and disrespect for minority customs and traditions (Dreyer, 1976:122–123).

13. The Marriage Law itself prohibited arranged and forced marriages, bigamy, concubinage, adopting a little daughter-in-law, interfering with widows' marital freedom, and using marriage to exact property. It required complete self-determination on the part of the man and woman to be married and banned third-party intervention in marital decisions. The legal marriage age was set at twenty for men and eighteen for women (ZRGH, 1950:2–3). See Johnson (1983:235–239) for an English translation of the law.

14. "Hui'an xian guanyu hunyin wenti baogao" (Report from Hui'an county regarding marriage problems), Sept. 15, 1950, hereafter cited in the text as "Report."

15. Susan Glosser has also argued that the CCP was more effective than Nationalist-era reformers in merging the conjugal family ideal (*xiao jiating*) with state-building goals, "successfully pushing the state deeper into the interior of the family unit" (2003:171). A subtle difference in our arguments lies in how we conceptualize the connection between the family and the nation-state. Whereas Glosser focuses on the CCP's injunction that nation-building be included as part of marital responsibilities, I suggest that the socialist nation required citizens whose liberation was marked by an array of intimate practices, including the specific manner in which citizens married.

16. "Hui'an xian guanche hunyinfa gongzuo zongjie" (A summary of work implementing the Marriage Law in Hui'an county), 1952, hereafter cited in the text as "Summary." According to this document, the judicial-reform movement in Fujian was enacted in response to a directive issued by the Central Committee of the East China Region. Johnson (1983:140) describes a nationwide rectification movement in 1952 that was designed to make the judicial institutions implementing the Marriage Law more responsive to central government policy. This Fujian movement was likely part of the national campaign, as it focused on both policy implementation and a rectification of mediation organs and personnel in the countryside.

17. In his 1927 report on the peasant movement in Hunan, Mao called for the overthrow of the feudal and patriarchal authority systems. Men, he argued, were subject to three systems: political authority, clan authority, and theocratic authority. Women, in addition to these three, were also dominated by the authority of the husband. In order to successfully destroy clan, theocratic, and male authority, however, peasants had to first overthrow the political authority of the landlords (Mao, 1954:45–49). Here we see early signs of Mao's privileging of class struggle over all other liberatory struggles (cf. Evans, 1998:3).

18. In fact, as Neil Diamant has shown for the 1950s and early 1960s, the absence of feelings was often cited by couples who sought approval for divorce, a rationale that officials and courts were likely to recognize and sanction (2000:276). Only in the 1980 Marriage Law, however, was "the breakdown of affection" officially recognized as a valid reason for divorce (Evans, 1997:23).

19. "Hui'an xian guanche hunyinfa gongzuo de chubu zongjie" (An initial summary of work implementing the Marriage Law in Hui'an county), 1953.

20. "Wajie funü zisha jituan gongzuo baogao" (Report on the work of disbanding women's collective suicide groups), 1952, hereafter cited in the text as "Disbanding."

21. The use of the inclusive Minnan dialect form of "us/we" (lan) throughout the song identifies the speaker herself as a married woman. See the Appendix for the full text of this song.

22. See Sankar (1978:43–48) for a discussion of collective suicides among nineteenth-century sisterhood members in the Pearl River Delta region. She argues that women employed collective suicide as a form of resistance in the face of efforts by local elites and officials to disband sisterhoods and abolish delayed residence marriage. Lee and Kleinman (2000) make a similar argument about individual suicides as a form of social resistance in contemporary China.

23. "Guanyu ben sheng Hui'an xian zai guanche hunyinfa yundong yihou zisha shijian de jiancha baogao" (An investigative report regarding suicide incidents following the movement to implement the Marriage Law in Hui'an county), Aug. 6, 1953. The role of ENR in promoting high suicide rates was not always so clear in these reports, however. Conflicts with both natal and conjugal kin were frequently listed as causes for suicide, along with illness and economic hardship. When marital dissatisfaction and conflict were mentioned, they were often paired with a woman's inability to request or acquire a divorce. These latter obstacles, seen as proof of incomplete implementation of the Marriage Law, were directly linked to suicide. See "Guanyu guanche hunyinfa yundong qian hou siren shijian de baogao" (A report concerning deaths prior to and following the movement to implement the Marriage Law), 1953; and "Gedi guanyu hunyin wenti siren de baogao tongjibiao" (A report and statistical chart on deaths related to marital problems in each district), 1953.

24. In fact, different recordings of the same death might claim altogether different reasons for the suicide or confuse important elements of a woman's experience (for instance, whether her marriage was freely chosen or arranged). Compare "Guanyu guanche hunyinfa yundong qian hou

siren shijian de baogao" and "Gedi guanyu hunyin wenti siren de baogao tongjibiao."

25. Across Hui'an the county government initiated classes in the winter of 1949-1950 that taught basic literacy and educated peasants on current policies. The classes sought to integrate study, production, and improved sanitation and health knowledge. In 1952, the winter class format was changed to People's Schools that met nightly and focused on eradicating illiteracy (Hui'an Xian Difangzhi Bianzuan Weiyuanhui, 1998:900).

26. Mao first advocated this approach in his draft resolution for the 1929 Gutian Conference, and it became party doctrine with his well-known Yan'an "Talks" of May 1942 (Holm, 1984:6; Wong, 1984:126). In the early 1950s, the Fujian provincial government and Women's Federation urged work teams and local governments to use folk songs, operas, and local expressions to spread knowledge of the Marriage Law and encourage popular compliance. See "Fujian sheng xuanchuan guanche hunyinfa yundong yue gongzuo zongjie" (Work summary of the movement month to propagandize and implement the Marriage Law in Fujian province), June 15, 1953, hereafter cited in the text as "Work Summary."

27. See the Appendix for a transcript of this and other anti-gin'a songs.

28. Work team reports from across Hui'an enumerate a number of propaganda tools, such as broadcasts, bulletin boards, slide shows, cartoons, and explanatory charts. Individual reports itemize the number of times people were exposed to Marriage Law propaganda over the course of a particular campaign (Summary, 1952; see also Yang, 1959b:chap. 12).

29. See the Appendix for a full transcript of this folk song.

30. The Summary report described three "fears" and three "don't dares" among women considering returning to their husbands' homes: "They feared excessive labor, they feared that their sisterhoods would laugh at them for having good relations with their husbands, and they feared the gossip of older women. . . . They didn't dare to eat their fill, to sleep enough, or to speak" (Summary, 1952).

31. "You guan ben sheng hunyin wenti de jidian cailiao" (Some materials regarding marriage problems in the province), 1957.

32. "Hui'an xian funü zisha qingkuang jianbao" (A brief report on the situation of female suicide in Hui'an county), 1957.

33. Information on this campaign comes from three documents: "Wu buzhang guanyu guanche hunyinfa yundong de zhishi" (Directive from Department Head Wu regarding the movement to implement the Marriage Law), Feb. 21, 1953; "Basic Summary"; and "Work Summary."

34. See, for instance, "Cong Hui'an xian shehui gaige yundong zhong kan chu" (A view from the Social Reform Movement in Hui'an county), 1952.

35. [Lin Bin] Youth, Letter to Hui'an County Women's Federation, dated July 24, 1959.

36. "Hui'an di san pi 'si qing' yundong funü gongzuo zongjie baogao" (A summary report on woman-work during the third phase of Hui'an's "four cleans" movement), Nov. 23, 1966, hereafter cited in the text as "Woman-Work."

37. Study classes also taught women to sing folk songs imbued with the messages of the movement. One song adopted the voice of a young girl urging her older sister to free herself from feudal suffering by following the party's call to go to her husband's village. See the Appendix.

38. The unspoken assumption being that when a woman slept at her conjugal home she was more likely to engage in sexual relations with her husband and become pregnant. This resolved two perceived problems: men's sexual needs and the need for wives to become pregnant to fully consolidate their residence shift.

39. When I asked whether this would mean that they would be cut off from their grain rations (now distributed through their conjugal brigades), Soehua replied that their mothers-in-law would periodically bring the grain rations to their natal homes. Thus it seems that conjugal kin themselves were not wholly invested in enforcing the movement.

40. Note that this elderly woman uses the verb "to come," reflecting her own conjugal residence and position as a mother-in-law. Unlike work team reports or campaign propaganda, she does not employ the verb "to return."

41. Nor did they use this language solely in dialogue with me, but also in their own conversations with one another.

Chapter 3

1. In my own research, I encountered no cases of Cultural Revolution divorces. Although some must have occurred, villagers who admitted to considering divorce because of their spouse's bad political status ultimately decided against it because of the considerable social stigma divorce was seen to incur.

2. Scholars working in communities across China have documented a similar incidence of underage marriage in the 1980s, attributing it to increased economic prosperity, village endogamy, and the impact of the family responsibility system (Davis and Harrell, 1993:10; Greenhalgh, 1993:233–235; Selden, 1993:159–160; Yan, 1997; Zheng, 1995:133–134).

3. Shanlin's shift to village endogamy in the 1980s is rather late when compared with patterns elsewhere in rural China (see Chan et al., 1984:188–

191; Parish and Whyte, 1978:171; Potter and Potter, 1990:200–201 for southern cases; and Johnson, 1983:202–203; Selden, 1993:152–157; Wolf, 1985:167–168; Yan, 1996:39–42 for northern cases). Certainly the gender divisions of labor in eastern Hui'an prevented the regular contact between young men and women found in predominant agricultural areas. By the 1980s, however, the village population had grown sufficiently to make genealogically distant, same-surname marriages more feasible. Villagers also attributed this trend to mothers who sought to protect their daughters from the suffering they had experienced by being forced to marry out of their natal villages (see also Chan et al., 1984:190). Unlike in the North China village studied by Liu (2000:53–56), comparative poverty and the unwillingness of outside women to marry into the community did not appear to be relevant factors.

4. Prior to passage of the county resolution in July 1985, a letter to the editor from a *Peasant Daily* reporter expressed outrage at the widespread practice in eastern Hui'an of engaging young children and marrying them off before the legal age. Now in the national limelight, provincial authorities made Hui'an a model case for vigorously eradicating this "feudal backward custom" (Chen, 1985, 1987). Much of the subsequent media coverage proclaimed high levels of campaign success, in some cases claiming that the practice had been eliminated after a year of intensive work. Ironically, in none of these articles (except Li and Sun, 1986) was there any mention of women's postmarital extended natal residence; instead, underage marriage was presented as a problem of persistent feudal influences and economic underdevelopment, combined with rising pressures on parents from mounting betrothal and wedding costs (Liu, 1986; "Qingchu fengjian," 1986; Wu 1985).

5. Like other women who married before 1949, Sutgoo emphasized that she was carried in a sedan chair on her wedding day, as compared to brides after 1949, who were forced to walk but who often had fellow dui pnua to accompany them. Most brides only remained in their conjugal homes for three days following the wedding; Sutgoo was forced to stay for five, she surmised, because her mother-in-law was widely known as a virtuous widow who single-handedly raised her son following her husband's untimely death. After a bride's initial wedding stay, she made two more trips back and forth between her two homes before settling once again with her natal family.

6. In Shanlin, time is often calculated according to the Chinese lunar calendar. The fourth month usually falls in May.

7. A refusal to participate in wedding and funeral processions was a clear sign that a young wife was pregnant, as it was considered inauspicious for

a pregnant woman to join in these ritual events. Female kin or dui pnua in the know might request two strips of mourning cloth for a pregnant woman asked to attend a funeral, thus signaling the fact that she was carrying a child.

8. Beneath this pragmatic concern lay the less openly articulated reproductive uncertainty produced by frequent changes in the government's population policy. The desire to have children now bespoke a fear that the government might begin to regulate births even more stringently in the future (see also Greenhalgh, 1993:232).

9. These differences between A Den and her mother and older sister appear prominently in the length of their postmarital separations. Whereas A Den lived apart from her husband for only a year and a half after they married, her mother waited four years before moving to Shanlin from neighboring Haibin, and her sister did not bear a child until six years after her marriage, although she, too, was held to her father's requirement that she not marry until reaching the legal age.

10. Married women rarely distinguished lexically between natal and conjugal kin; listeners grasped the distinction based on context or familiarity with the speaker. Having little training in such nuances, I often found myself confused at first and resorted to asking outright which family a woman was referring to.

11. According to A Ping, her mother agreed to break off the match because she did not want A Ping to suffer, as she had, by marrying out of her natal village. A Ping's father had been adopted by her grandparents, who began to mistreat him after they had three sons of their own. A Ping claimed that this abusive relationship also extended to her mother and intensified after her mother's first child, a son, died as an infant. Her grandmother regularly cursed her mother for bearing only girls (she had five daughters, two of whom she gave up for adoption) until she finally gave birth to A Ping's younger brother.

12. A Ping accused her conjugal family of linguistically excluding her through their use of the exclusive form of the first person plural pronoun. She claimed that when talking with her, they always referred to their family as "ggun" (the exclusive "our" or "we"), never "lan" (the inclusive form). So of course she responded by using "lin" (the plural "you") or "yin" ("they" or "their"). This usage upset her mother-in-law, for it suggested that A Ping did not consider herself a part of the family. When later recounting this incident to a group of dui pnua, A Ping retorted angrily, "If you're going to distinguish [yourselves from me] in that way, then I will follow you and do the same!" (Lin anIni hun, ggua ziu deh lin anIni hun!).

13. Village practice required that the initiator of the divorce compensate the other party. In the period from 1995 to 1997, compensation ranged from 5,000 to as much as 15,000 *yuan*, approximately USD 600 to 1800.

14. Yan also notes that in the 1990s karaoke machines became common items in marital gifts, although in the North China village where he worked they were included as part of bride-wealth, not dowry (2002:51).

15. Regional folktales provided similar romantic resources. The popular third-century story of Liang Shanbo and Zhu Yingtai was consumed widely in Shanlin through opera performances and folk songs. The tale depicts a thwarted love affair, ending with the woman, Zhu, forced to enter an arranged match and Liang, her lover, dying of grief. Yet rather than submitting to her fate, Zhu leaps from her bridal sedan at the very moment that it passes Liang's grave. The grave opens to receive her, reuniting the two lovers in death.

16. Lu ping iu is itself a loanword from Mandarin, a direct transliteration of *nü pengyou*.

17. Articles 12 and 24 of the 1994 Regulations on the Administration of Marriage Registration stated that cohabiting underage couples would not be recognized as married, nor would couples who had reached the legal age but had not registered their marriage (www.china.org.cn/chinese/funv/228104.htm). The Supreme People's Court followed with an opinion stating that such relationships would not receive legal protection, and the Ministry of Civil Affairs issued a document requiring local administrative units to actively implement the new regulations (www.china.org.cn/chinese/funv/227411.htm; www.china.org.cn/chinese/funv/230978). The 1994 enforcement of the legal age and marital registration in Shanlin was in part a response to these new laws (see also Shi, 2004). Yet given enforcement failures in the 1980s (when similar regulations were in place), it was likely the combination of the 1994 Regulations with a renewed population-control campaign that finally forced local officials to crack down on underage and unregistered marriages. I thank Ethan Michelson for sharing his thoughts on the 1994 Regulations with me.

18. It appears that Shanlin residents generally faced such restrictions much later than villagers in other parts of the country. In her study of rural Shaanxi, Greenhalgh found that couples systematically registered their marriages as early as 1979 and that virtually all married at or above the legal age (1993:234–235). Prior to 1994, Shanlin officials periodically enforced population controls by requiring married women who had not yet reached the legal marriage age to have an abortion if they became pregnant.

19. On the 1980s, see Hui'an County Government Circular 1 (1988). In Shanlin, the monetary component of bride-wealth was comparatively

low in the mid-1990s. Over the course of my research it remained at only a little more than 2,800 *yuan*, one of the lowest figures in the township. However, other components of bride-wealth, such as gold jewelry, gifts of foodstuffs, or a new house, were rising in value over the 1990s, as were elements of dowry, including household appliances and consumer electronics. Other scholars have documented intensive state efforts to regulate wedding rituals and exchanges as part of larger modernizing projects. See Kim (2001) for such campaigns in North China and Kendall (1996) for an extensive discussion of weddings and state modernization efforts in South Korea.

20. In addition to relationships among teenagers, this category also included other nonmarital relationships, such as those involving divorcées. If a divorce had not been officially registered with the village government, however, birth-planning officials would continue to monitor a divorced woman's fertility.

21. A Ping's decision to reside with her husband immediately after registering with the government was not necessarily a result of her marriage to a man from Chongwu. Older Shanlin women who had married into the township seat generally maintained postmarital natal residence, even though the practice was not observed in Chongwu itself. Thus A Ping's decision reflected the dramatic changes in extended natal residence marriage taking place in the late 1990s as young wives significantly reduced the length of (or abandoned altogether) postmarital residence in their natal homes.

22. The causes of Bbizu's divorce, which I discuss in Chapter 5, were explained to me in this manner.

23. My discussion here of private and public intimacy is inspired by Berlant's analysis of the "intimate public" in the contemporary United States. According to Berlant, "the intimate public sphere of the U.S. present tense renders citizenship as a condition of social membership produced by personal acts and values, especially acts originating in or directed toward the family sphere" (1997:5). Berlant is concerned with how an active public sphere and national politics have been eviscerated by conservatives' reinvigoration of a core nation defined by traditional white, heterosexual concepts of home and family. My use of public intimacy highlights a similar kind of contradiction, whereby the personal nature of conjugal intimacy is overwritten by state and community goals that might appear less overt but are in fact no less coercive.

24. This saying plays on a Minnan-language tonal change in the middle character of the expression for romantic love, turning the first character for love into the term for chaos or disorder. The Minnan saying is "m'si dam luan ai, si dam luan ai."

Chapter 4

1. Although the chapter concentrates mostly on female dui pnua ties, some of the arguments I make below apply to male dui pnua networks as well. Social constraints made it difficult for me to study male dui pnua networks in action as I did with young women. Moreover, I surmise that the constancy of men's relationship to patrilineal kinship networks over their life cycle means that dui pnua provide them with a supplementary, as opposed to substantively different, kind of community.

2. Lin (1981:256, 258) provides two accounts from pre-1949 Hui'an of women forming groups that monitored members' sexual relations with their husbands, and in one case he notes that membership required a contribution of either five silver dollars or ten *jin* of eels. Although Lin does not describe these groups specifically as sisterhoods (the term he uses for dui pnua), it is likely that they included women who we would today recognize as dui pnua.

3. As one young married woman asserted to me in no uncertain terms, "being married or unmarried is the same thing. It is only when [we] have a child that we count as 'one's own people.'" In this case, the category of "one's own people" to which she referred was that of her husband's patriline. The ambiguity of women's kinship status between marriage and childbirth is also reflected in ritual and worship. A nonresident wife is always included in the domestic ancestor worship conducted by her natal family, but she may or may not be included in that of her conjugal family. Once she gives birth and shifts residence, however, her conjugal family always includes her in their worship, and in the first few years after residence shift her natal family may continue to include her as well.

4. The Mandarin cognate for cin is *qin*, as in *qinqi* for relative or kin, *qin'ai* for beloved, or *qinqie* for close or intimate. In her discussion of sworn sisters in the *nüshu* region of southern Hunan, Cathy Silber also notes the polysemous quality of *qin* and the difficulty in establishing its precise meaning when used to describe intimate nonkin relationships (1994:53 n. 25).

5. Along similar lines, family division (such as when a married son sets up a household separate from that of his parents) is often described as establishing separate stoves.

6. Stockard (1989) and Siu (1990) also describe how natalocally resident delta women in the late imperial era and early Republic refused to eat in their conjugal homes. Wealthy women even brought their own food and cooks with them on conjugal visits.

7. Stafford argues that the sharing of food among nonkin in rural Taiwan can be interpreted in terms of status contests based on the concept of

"face" or *mianzi*. He contends that accepting a gift of food symbolizes an inability to feed oneself adequately, just as urging others to eat with you demonstrates your ability to care successfully for your own needs (Stafford, 1995:108). By interpreting commensality as both indicative and productive of intimacy, I suggest that dui pnua perhaps are more willing than others to minimize this element of face.

8. In Minnan dialect it is common to use the plural form (we, us) to refer to oneself. Zue dui and dui pnua have the same meaning. See the Appendix for the full transcription of this song.

9. It was one such group suicide in the 1980s that inspired Hui'an native Lu Zhaohuan (1986) to pen the short story "Shuang zhuo" (Twin bracelets) about the relationship between two female dui pnua in a Huidong village.

10. When I asked young women to explain the reasons behind suicides (collective or individual), some attributed them to malevolent spirits that lured pretty young women into the afterworld to serve as wives.

11. The fact that the women had died young might also have determined this otherwise unorthodox practice. Members of a senior generation did not participate in funerary or burial rituals in cases of premature death. Thus dui pnua, being of the same generation as the deceased, could step into a role typically played by siblings or patrilateral cousins.

12. For an in-depth discussion of this form of worship in the Minnan region, see Shi (1997).

13. Several scholars have documented the increasing elaborateness of life cycle rituals in the post-Mao era, as the government relaxed many of its prior restrictions on religious and ritual life (Dean, 1993; Siu, 1989; Whyte, 1988). As these and other works show, however, these developments have not been without conflict, particularly when local cadres respond to central government demands that they crack down on "feudal superstition" and "wasteful" rituals (see Anagnost, 1987; Feuchtwang, 1989; Feuchtwang and Wang, 1991; Kim, 2001; Yang, 2000). During my time in Shanlin, by contrast, I witnessed little inclination on the part of local officials to intervene in either life cycle rituals or popular religious practice, except in the case of banning earth burials, which I discuss below.

14. Throughout the 1990s these funerals were mostly earth burials, and the procession was headed by the coffin born on the shoulders of male patrilineal kin. By my return visits in 2000 and 2002, however, villagers had been forced to comply with national regulations requiring cremation. Funeral participants accompanied the corpse to the crematorium located in the western part of the county, and the ashes were either stored there or brought back to the village. Some families continued to hold funeral processions in which male mourners carried the urn containing the deceased's

ashes to a resting place on the mountain above the village. How long they would be allowed to continue this practice was not clear.

15. At the time of my research, dui pnua of sons contributed 50 *yuan*, those of daughters 20 to 30 *yuan*, those of grandsons 10 *yuan*, and dui pnua of granddaughters only 5 *yuan*. This declining scale of monetary contributions reflects the gender and generational features determining the closeness of an individual's relationship to the deceased.

16. Funeral attire varies by an individual's gender, generation, and relation to the deceased. In general, dress and paraphernalia follow a continuum from most filial to most peripheral, with hemp as the material assigned to the most filial (i.e., to direct male descendants), continuing through coarse muslin, and green and then red colors. Dui pnua of sons wear muslin mourning jackets identical to those worn by sons, but distinguished by the absence of hemp and by a piece of red cloth in the center of the headband. Daughters' dui pnua carry strips of muslin with pieces of red and green yarn tied around them, whereas daughters wear only green yarn. The additional red for dui pnua in these cases might serve prophylactic purposes, protecting nonkin from death pollution (Watson, 1982:167–168; Wolf, 1970). However, both granddaughters and their dui pnua carry red and green, whereas grandsons and their dui pnua have only red. Funeral paraphernalia also distinguishes categories of agnatic and affinal kin.

17. When a young wife was required to give a gift to kin in the category of "one's own people," however, her mother-in-law was expected to cover the cost.

18. Chongwu custom required a gift of 200 *yuan* for men and 100 *yuan* for women, bringing A Ping's total gift obligation to 800 *yuan* for this group alone.

Chapter 5

1. This process of displacement might operate differently among China's many populations, as seen in Dorothy Solinger's argument that urban residents "[blame] peasants in their midst for the social ills induced by the market" (1999:10). Unlike urbanites who displace their anxieties onto rural outsiders, however, Shanlin villagers tend to focus their concerns on the members of their community whose lives have been most profoundly transformed by market reforms, namely young village women.

2. Working women who had already shifted to conjugal residence typically kept their earnings for personal use or for their children's needs, regardless of whether they had formed an independent nuclear family unit or remained part of a stem or extended family.

3. There are cases of women who actually change from one category to another, usually from young traditional to the new style. I discuss the significance of these cases in Chapter 7.

4. Even middle-aged women performing manual labor dressed in the full panoply of local dress, although they substituted cotton or polyester pants for silk trousers. They took care to dress in their best clothes and headscarves when visiting other villages or making trips to the township or county seat. At the same time, these women who had lived through the poverty and the profrugality campaigns of the pre- and post-1949 periods condemned those who spent beyond their means and regularly proclaimed the value of being thrifty (kiam).

5. The only birthday celebration for an elder that I witnessed during my research was for a local schoolteacher in his late eighties who had been persecuted for decades as a rightist. He had six sons who pooled their resources to fund the event and even hired a car to drive their father to a well-known restaurant in the township seat to which they had invited guests from all over the township.

6. Watson argues that the opening of McDonald's restaurants across East Asia has promoted the celebration of children's birthdays in countries where they had previously not been marked ritually (1997a:19, 1997b:103-104). Although such global consumer sites had not yet been introduced into Shanlin or the township seat, family-owned restaurants and KTVs were having a similar impact.

7. Here, Stafford's (1995) interpretation of the sharing of food among nonkin as a means of creating indebtedness seems more apposite.

8. Nor did Ggiokhua have familial resources that she could draw on in funding her celebration. Whereas A Hong's father was a village cadre, Ggiokhua's father fished for a living; and whereas A Hong had older brothers who contributed to the family's income, Ggiokhua had only a younger brother who was still apprenticed to a stone carver. Her mother had died, moreover, leaving her with no close female kin to help in hosting a party.

9. Social protocol in my research setting prevented me from interviewing the women who worked in establishments identified with prostitution; hence, I limit my discussion here to how the practice of sex work and the individuals understood to participate in it were perceived and portrayed by Shanlin residents. See Hershatter (1997) for both a historical and a contemporary analysis of prostitution in China. Jeffreys (1997a, 1997b) examines the criminalization of prostitution in the reform era, focusing specifically on police eradication campaigns that centered on karaoke halls and hotels.

10. This depiction of KTVs as sites for prostitution is not unique to Shanlin. In her documentary on Shanghai women, Yang interviews several

professional women who complain about the lack of acceptable places for after-work socializing. They claim that KTVs are not frequented by "proper" women (Yang, 1997b). The factory women studied by Lee in Shenzhen also attributed a "dubious moral status" to lounges, restaurants, and beauty parlors, arguing that "'women don't spend their hard-earned money that way'" (1998:133). Jeffreys (1997a) illustrates how karaoke halls in Beijing have become synonymous with prostitution, both in the eyes of the police and among city residents.

11. It should be noted that young men's behavior was not scrutinized by villagers in the same way.

12. Such dual forms of young female subjectivity and the social and self-discipline they produce are not unique to the Shanlin case. Ong cogently argues that Malay factory women also faced conflicting images of themselves as simultaneously pleasure seekers during off-work hours and childlike dependents on the factory floor (1990:412–413). The experience of Shanlin women who wear young traditional attire, however, shows how these dual images might coexist within a single context.

13. The question of motivation is quite complex and one that I do not have the space to address here. In villagers' depictions, women took up prostitution for economic reasons, put simply as "to make money" (either for themselves or others). Although Hershatter refutes a simple "markets produce sex work" equation, she does suggest that a wide range of economic motivations often encourage prostitution, motivations that are frequently ignored or minimized in official and scholarly writings on China's prostitution "problem" (1996, 1997:350–357, chap. 14).

14. The women who attended this outing ranged in age from nineteen to twenty-two. They worked in a variety of occupations within the village and dressed in both young traditional attire and the new style.

15. By the same token, redefining KTVs as leisure sites does not necessarily eradicate their connection to prostitution. As Hart (1998:90–93) argues in her study of sex workers and their male clients in urban Spain, visiting sex workers and the neighborhoods they inhabit can itself be seen as a form of leisure that involves not only sex but also conversation and company.

Chapter 6

1. There are some tensions among feminist theorists regarding the ontological status of drag. For Marjorie Garber (1992) and bell hooks (1992), drag represents a liberating movement, a breaking out of established categories that exposes deep-seated cultural anxieties about gender and sexual

identity. For Judith Butler (1990), however, drag does not presume an existing original form of identity but instead enacts the very lack of an interior essence. In other words, drag highlights the role of social performances in creating the *appearance* of that essence (see also Butler, 1997).

2. Of the more than 400 ethnic groups that applied for state recognition, only 54 (including the Han) were initially recognized by the 1960s; 2 were added later to bring the total number to 56 (Fei, 1981:60–61; Gladney, 1991:17; Harrell, 1995b:23–24).

3. The term *minzu* encapsulates two meanings: ethnicity and nationality. The Chinese usage is itself vague, perhaps intentionally so given Mao Zedong's withdrawal of the CCP's earlier promise of national self-determination for non-Han minorities. Scholars working with officially recognized minority groups tend overwhelmingly to adopt the translation "minority nationalities" or to retain the original Chinese so as not to privilege one sense of the term over the other. I generally translate *minzu* as ethnicity because it best corresponds to the position of Huidong residents within the Chinese nation-state. Having never been officially classified as a "minority nationality" and refusing to identify themselves as such, Huidong residents instead are merely likened to such groups through reference to ethnic-cum-cultural difference.

4. One of the earliest examples of this approach is a 1930 piece by Xiamen University historian and folklorist Ye Guoqing in which he compared the customs of the Miao, Yao, and Zhuang peoples of the southwest with those of the southern Fujian region. Ye noted the striking similarities between delayed postmarital cohabitation in Hui'an county and the marriage customs of the Miao and Zhuang. Based on the many convergences between the customs of these disparate groups (despite the vast distances that separated them), Ye contended that they had originally derived from the same race (*shi tong zhongzu de*) (1990 [1930]).

5. This theory of primitive or matrilineal residualism pervades Han ethnological accounts of ethnic minorities throughout the post-1949 period, implicitly reinforcing a vision of the Han as the pinnacle of modernity and civilization (see Gladney, 1994b:101–102; McKhann, 1995). Moreover, this formulation also appears in the writings of minority ethnologists themselves, men and women fully steeped in the evolutionary principles of Marxist social science (Litzinger, 2000:207).

6. There were some scholars who rejected an ethnic or evolutionary explanation for the distinctive cultural configuration in Huidong, offering instead functionalist arguments that rested on natal family desire to retain a daughter's labor (Qiao, 1990, 1992). As Lan (1995:20) convincingly argues, however, a functionalist approach cannot explain the origins of local

customs (only their persistence) nor why similar practices have not been found in communities with comparable economic bases.

7. Moreover, most scholars supported Lin's original thesis that local marriage practices were outdated and oppressive for women, in part because Han feudal influences had enshrined an ideal of female chastity (Jiang, 1989; Lu, 1992; Shi, 1992; Zhuang, 1994:31–32). None questioned why markers of ethnic difference were identified exclusively with women, nor did they ask why Huidong women had remained committed to these practices through decades of state-sponsored reform campaigns. In other words, despite reopening the ethnicity debate, post-Mao intellectuals and Taiwanese scholars ignored what were clearly equally compelling issues of state intervention, cultural commitment, and female agency.

8. Once again, I use the term "the Hui'an woman" to indicate a particular subject position created, in this case, by the homogenizing effects of mass media images. Although some media depictions employ the more geographically specific term, "the Huidong woman," they too create a stereotypical figure against which "real" Huidong women are compared.

9. See the following works for analyses of the exoticization and eroticization of ethnic minority women in post-1949 art, film, and mass media: Clark, 1987; Gladney, 1994b; Lufkin, 1990; Schein, 1997; Yau, 1989. Although official minorities are not represented exclusively by their women, men usually serve as the background to women's more striking otherness and sensual appeal (Lufkin, 1990:29–36; Schein, 1997:87).

10. "*Fengjian tou, minzhu du, jieyue yi, langfei ku.*"

11. The black-and-white photos, in contrast, display the repressed, literally weighted-down quality of Huidong womanhood, features emphasized in the article through attention to the heavy silver earrings, bracelets, and waist belts favored by women of all ages. The authors argue that Huidong women's affinity for silver waist belts far exceeds urban, "modern" women's love of gold necklaces. The text thus sets up a clear contrast between the exotic, yet weighted-down, appearance of Huidong women and the simpler, lighter adornment favored by modern, urban, Han Chinese women. The transition from heavy to light parallels a process of cultural development (*wenhua fazhan*) that further affirms the status of urban Hans as civilized and modern (Oakes, 1998:136–138).

12. The entire layout of the magazine follows this format. Photo articles on minorities within China or on "primitive" ethnic groups outside of China are juxtaposed with shots of presumably Han urbanites modeling stylish modern attire and of foreign Caucasian models, as well as interior shots of modern homes and decorating. Unlike other ethnicity publications in which the Han are only depicted as urban and modern (see Gladney,

1994b:97), *Folklore* intersperses minority articles with historical accounts of Han society and stories of traditional Han culture reenacted in the present. By so doing, it reinforces an image of present-day ethnic minorities as living relics of the Han past.

13. I would like to thank Smita Lahiri for suggesting to me this concept of culture in drag. A similar example appears in the case of Han women who don minority dress when working as prostitutes in predominantly minority regions (Hyde, 2001).

14. Blum (1998) argues that Han Chinese use of the third person pronoun when referring to ethnic minorities objectifies minorities as an inanimate, taxonomic category, particularly in cases where the singular form of the pronoun is used (see also Benveniste, 1971). Here Cheng employs the plural pronoun "they" (*tamen*), which grants agency and personhood despite its othering power. In the first part of the original sentence, however, he uses an awkward singular form, "this Huidong woman" (*zhege Huidong nü*), a usage that reinforces the construction of Huidong women as a categoric type that lacks agency and, as Blum suggests, that is implicitly backward and powerless in comparison with the dominant Han.

15. In this case, Spivak's question *"Can* the subaltern speak?" (1988; emphasis added) seems less appropriate than asking whether, on the rare occasion *when she speaks*, her subaltern status makes her words incomprehensible, literally *in need of* translation?

16. Nor is it clear that the women who did speak directly to Ding knew that they were being filmed. An interview with the cameraman for the segment and an article later published about its filming confirm that the crew failed to convince any village women to be interviewed on camera (the sole exception being the village Women's Association representative). The shots included in the program were filmed secretly from a distance (Chen, 1994; Guo, 1994).

17. For examples of published reproductions of such artwork, see Wei Jiangqiong's *Ocean Road*, Chen Wuxing's *Hui'an Woman*, and Li Xiaowei's *Spring* (*Zhongguo-Chongwu*, 1997:59); Wu Jiachuan's *Flood* (FJQH, 1982:17); and Xu Ruizhen's *Lantern Festival* (*Quanzhou wanbao*, Oct. 31, 1996, p. 7).

18. The visual effect of outlining lines of a clothed body strongly resembles Yuan Yunsheng's use of tightly wrapped sarongs to accentuate Dai women's hips and buttocks in his controversial Beijing airport mural (Lufkin, 1990:29–36).

19. This series was filmed jointly by Xiamen Television and a Taiwan television station and aired in both China and Taiwan. It was shown in 45 episodes in the early 1990s. I watched tapes of the show housed at Xiamen

Television in 1996 after hearing about it from numerous friends in Xiamen and Taiwan. The plot is based on the novel of the same title by the Taiwanese author Wang Benhu (1992).

20. This magazine was originally titled *Fujian gongren* (Fujian worker).

21. Zhuang (1988:26) refers here to the commemorative plaque "Long Live Hui'an Women," which was erected in the county seat under the auspices of a Hui'an native serving in the central government. Following this official's fall from power, the plaque was smeared over with lime, although the stone itself was left standing. Zhuang also notes that the name of the county reservoir built largely through the efforts of Hui'an women was later changed from "Hui'an Women's Reservoir" to "Wutan Reservoir," Wutan being the name of the locale in which it was built (see Chapter 1).

22. The largest surname group claimed to be descended from an official who had migrated from present-day Henan province; the second largest group claimed descent most proximally from Anhui and through that ancestor also from Henan. See Wigen (1999:1190) for an account of similar claims to Han origins under the Qing.

23. Anagnost also argues, based on interviews in 1989, that "the inhabitants of the hinterland do not necessarily place the causal factors of their poverty and backwardness within themselves but point instead toward their distance from a government that disvalues and excludes them from the selective and highly circumscribed locations of special economic processing zones" (1997:122).

24. According to Oakes (1998:47), China first included tourism in its seventh five-year plan (1985–1990), under the auspices of the "National Social and Economic Development Plan." A 1998 Fujian source claimed that over 200,000 tourists had begun to visit Hui'an each year and that the county was preparing to invest almost 100 million *yuan* in Chongwu's basic infrastructure and tourist facilities over the next two years (FJHB, 1998). Little of this investment seemed to have been realized when I returned to Shanlin in 2002.

25. The article consistently confuses female residents of the township seat with women from the surrounding villages. The photos accompanying the article also fail to distinguish between the two groups with their very different clothing styles and marriage customs.

26. Although I was not present for the festival itself, I followed its early planning stages in 1997 and conducted interviews with officials from the Provincial Tourism Bureau, township, and village when I returned in 1998. I also canvassed Shanlin residents about their participation in and reactions to the festival. One of the main supporters of the festival was the vice-director of the Fujian Provincial Tourism Bureau, himself a native of Shanlin.

Several other cultural festivals were held in the province that year, marketing everything from Hakka culture to local delicacies (FJNJ, 1998:187).

27. Articles in the local newspaper reinforced this association between the festival and outside investment by listing the number and size of investment deals signed during the festival (e.g., *Quanzhou wanbao*, Nov. 14, 1997). *Zhongguo-Chongwu*, the glossy publication that accompanied the festival, included diagrams of investment channels and lists with contact information for relevant government offices. See also Oakes (1998:125–130) on the role of ethnic tourism and festivals in promoting province-wide investment in Guizhou in the early 1990s.

28. Among the photos included in the section on Huidong women's attire in the accompanying promotional brochure *Zhongguo-Chongwu* there is a picture of a young woman wearing a headscarf and cropped top sitting astride a shiny black moped (1997:57). Photos of Hui'an women in the Fujian workers' magazine *Shenghuo-chuangzao* depict a transition from manual to skilled labor through the use of technology. The cover of the Feb. 1997 issue portrays a Hui'an woman seated on a motorcycle, dialing a mobile phone, and wearing a beeper on her belt. The photo is titled "The modern Hui'an woman." A 1998 cover displays a young Hui'an woman adjusting her headpiece in the mirror of a motorcycle; the caption for this photo reads "New Hui'an Woman." The colorful blouse peeking out from beneath the woman's cropped top in the first photo and the loose-fitting headscarf in the second suggest that models were used for both shots.

Chapter 7

1. See "Zhongguo gongchandang shi si jie liu zhong quan hui zai jing juxing" (The Sixth Plenum of the Fourteenth Central Committee of the Chinese Communist Party is held in Beijing), *Fujian ribao*, Oct. 11, 1996, p. 1 (Xinhua News Bureau Beijing, Oct. 10, 1996); and "Zhong gong zhongyang guanyu jiaqiang shehuizhuyi jingshen wenming jianshe ruogan zhongyao wenti de jueyi" (Resolution by the Communist Party and the central government concerning some major problems in strengthening the building of socialist spiritual civilization), *Quanzhou wanbao*, Oct. 14, 1996, pp. 1–2 (Xinhua News Bureau Beijing, Oct. 13, 1996).

2. "Zhongguo gongchandang," p. 1. The slogan about two hands grasping firmly was painted prominently on the outer wall of the Chongwu township government building, easily viewed by all who passed by on the main road between the township and the county seat.

3. This tension between constructive and excessive consumption is not unique to socialist or late-socialist societies, although, as I argued in Chap-

ter 5, the role of centralized economies as what Verdery (1996) calls "redistributive regimes" has historically made consumption a contested domain of practice across the socialist world.

4. I would like to thank Li Zhang for suggesting to me these parallels between *suzhi* and *habitus*. She makes a similar argument in her analysis of rural migrants in Beijing and their "migrant *suzhi*" (Zhang, 2001b).

5. In a volume devoted exclusively to analyzing the problem of quality in contemporary China, Jie Sizhong (1997) outlines eight different categories of *suzhi*, ranging from personality (*ren'ge*), spirit (*jingshen*), morality (*daode*), and culture (*wenhua*) to science (*kexue*), health (*jiankang*), profession (*zhiye*), and aesthetics (*shenmei*). He ultimately offers a rather pessimistic portrayal of the current quality of China's citizens in all of these forms.

6. This concern with education coalesced in the mid-1990s into two nationwide policies: a campaign to eradicate illiteracy and a commitment to enforcing nine years of compulsory education. In Shanlin, attention to the first policy was only cursory (as evidenced by the short-lived nature of the adult literacy classes sponsored by the village government). The second inspired a greater commitment as seen in the building of a new junior middle school to serve Shanlin and neighboring Haibin.

7. When I began teaching a basic literacy class to Shanlin women in their teens and twenties, other villagers assumed that my students had to be women "who wear the headscarf." In fact, most did not wear local attire, confirming the arbitrary nature of the link between dress and level of education.

8. Compare with Yang's depiction of classes in "culture and etiquette" (*wenhua liyi*) attended by young Shanghai women where they learn such skills as speaking graciously and skillfully, socializing at banquets, appreciating music and art, and dressing fashionably (1999:49–50). For other discussions of quality and culture as they have been used by intellectuals in regard to peasants, see Bodman and Wan (1991:169–170), Flower (1997), and Kipnis (1997:chap. 9).

9. In November 1996, the Shanlin village government issued a 23-point Environmental Sanitation Compact ([*Shanlin*] *cun huanjing weisheng gongyue*) in which it outlined its plan for improving the physical and social environment of the village. These actions were taken during a period in which Chongwu township as a whole was striving to obtain "civilized township" status. The Quanzhou city party secretary had issued an ultimatum to the township government and had provided a detailed list of improvements to be accomplished within a 50-day period if the township

was to receive this honor. It accomplished enough of them to be designated a civilized township by the winter of 1997 (Lin and Lin, 1997).

10. Accusations of "low quality" have also been directed against rural officials themselves, for instance as a rationale for favoring urban over rural representatives in the composition of the people's congresses. As Kevin O'Brien notes, such discrimination is justified by claims that "equal weighting of urban and rural residents [in people's congresses] . . . would produce large majorities of low quality (*suzhi*) rural deputies, which might diminish the vitality of representative assemblies" (2001:413). Rural officials' willingness to use the discourse of quality against their fellow villagers might very well reflect their own insecurity about their standing in a national political hierarchy organized around both place and civilizational markers.

11. When I returned to Shanlin for visits in the summers of 1998, 2000, and 2002, I found streets and paths once again littered with garbage and traffic halted by piles of building materials. When I pressed them about the decline in sanitation and public order, village officials offered little comment; their attention had turned to new demands from higher authorities despite the grumbling and complaints from community members.

12. During the day I often found Kingden at her boyfriend's home where she was engaged in the activities typical of married women, such as cooking, washing clothes, and caring for her boyfriend's son by his first marriage. Her boyfriend's first wife, one of Kingden's dui pnua, had committed suicide. Although Kingden's situation was not typical in Shanlin, it did reflect the growing prominence of nonmarital relationships between young women and men, not all of which ultimately culminated in marriage.

13. Recall that prior to the mid-1990s, young wives did not visit their husbands unless they were called for by their mothers-in-law or other female conjugal kin. Even when summoned, moreover, many refused to visit or stayed for only a few hours or one night.

14. As Schein reminds us, the exoticized figure of the ethnic minority "never quite [fits] with the pace and standards of the nation, but always somehow [signifies] its limits, its margins, its feminized other" (2000:11).

Appendix

1. The woman who recited this song could recall only the first three of five stanzas.

2. This line refers to the Third Plenum of the Eleventh Central Committee, which in 1978 introduced market reforms and decollectivization policies.

3. This line was the original ending when the song was coined in the 1950s. According to the women who recited the song for me, a work team that entered the community in the 1960s made them change the last line so that it praised Mao Zedong. One clear sign of the alteration was the fact that the revised ending did not rhyme with the rest of the stanza.

4. "Owing a debt" refers to a married woman's shift to conjugal residence.

5. The eight characters are the four pairs of characters indicating the year, month, day, and hour of one's birth that are used in fortune-telling and matchmaking.

6. The sarcasm in this sentence suggests that although her own fate is terrible she still is not willing to die and free her husband from their tragic marriage.

7. It is considered extremely unfilial for a child to die before his or her parents.

8. "Sit hioh gah li gi" translates literally as "like a leafless tree with broken branches," meaning that the family has been destroyed by illness and death.

9. These aunts are specifically the wives of the father-in-law's brothers, reinforcing the fact that a woman marries into her husband's extended patrilineal family.

10. Pudu is a festival appeasing wandering spirits and hungry ghosts.

11. "To feast" refers to eating the holiday meal.

12. The line alludes to the "snow plum" genre of song, which retells the tale of the tragic love affair between Zhu Yingtai and Liang Shanbo.

13. Here the husband indicates that the wife has the rest of the bed to herself and he will not try to touch her.

Character List

1. Since I have not been able to confirm the precise characters for this expression, these should be taken as merely suggestive. Translated literally as "water goods," these characters capture both the commodified nature of prostitution and historical references to the pleasure boats that housed courtesans and common prostitutes (Hershatter, 1997:36; Mann, 1997:128–130, 137–138).

Works Cited

Abrams, Philip. 1988. "Notes on the Difficulty of Studying the State." *Journal of Historical Sociology* 1(1):58–89.
Abu-Lughod, Lila. 1986. *Veiled Sentiments: Honor and Poetry in a Bedouin Society*. Berkeley and Los Angeles: University of California Press.
———. 1990. "The Romance of Resistance: Tracing Transformations of Power Through Bedouin Women." *American Ethnologist* 17(1):41–55.
———. 1991. "Writing Against Culture." In *Recapturing Anthropology: Working in the Present*, ed. Richard G. Fox, pp. 137–162. Santa Fe, N.Mex.: School of American Research Press.
———. 1993. *Writing Women's Worlds: Bedouin Stories*. Berkeley and Los Angeles: University of California Press.
Anagnost, Ann. 1987. "Politics and Magic in Contemporary China." *Modern China* 13(1):40–61.
———. 1994. "The Politicized Body." In *Body, Subject, and Power in China*, ed. Angela Zito and Tani E. Barlow, pp. 131–156. Chicago: The University of Chicago Press.
———. 1995. "A Surfeit of Bodies: Population and the Rationality of the State in Post-Mao China." In *Conceiving the New World Order: The Global Politics of Reproduction*, ed. Faye D. Ginsburg and Rayna Rapp, pp. 22–41. Berkeley and Los Angeles: University of California Press.
———. 1997. *National Past-Times: Narrative, Representation, and Power in Modern China*. Durham, N.C.: Duke University Press.
Andors, Phyllis. 1975. "Social Revolution and Woman's Emancipation: China During the Great Leap Forward." *Bulletin of Concerned Asian Scholars* 7(1):33–42.
Anzaldua, Gloria. 1987. *Borderlands/La Frontera: The New Mestiza*. San Francisco: Spinsters/Aunt Lute Books.

———, ed. 1990. *Making Face, Making Soul/Haciendo Caras: Creative and Critical Perspectives by Women of Color*. San Francisco: Aunt Lute Books.

Austin, J. L. 1975. *How To Do Things with Words*. Oxford: Clarendon Press.

Bakhtin, M. M. 1981. *The Dialogic Imagination: Four Essays*. Transl. Caryl Emerson and Michael Holquist. Austin: University of Texas Press.

Baum, Richard, and Frederick C. Teiwes. 1968. *Ssu-Ch'ing: The Socialist Education Movement of 1962–1966*. Berkeley: Center for Chinese Studies, University of California.

Benveniste, Emile. 1971. "The Nature of Pronouns." In *Problems in General Linguistics*, pp. 217–222. Coral Gables, Fla.: University of Miami Press.

Benjamin, Jessica. 1988. *The Bonds of Love: Psychoanalysis, Feminism, and the Problem of Domination*. New York: Pantheon Books.

Berlant, Lauren. 1997. *The Queen of America Goes to Washington City: Essays on Sex and Citizenship*. Durham, N.C.: Duke University Press.

———. 1998. "Intimacy: A Special Issue." *Critical Inquiry* 24:281–288.

Berlant, Lauren, and Michael Warner. 1998. "Sex in Public." *Critical Inquiry* 24:547–566.

Bloch, Maurice, and Jonathan Parry. 1982. "Introduction: Death and the Regeneration of Life." In *Death and the Regeneration of Life*, ed. Maurice Bloch and Jonathan Parry, pp. 1–44. Cambridge: Cambridge University Press.

Blum, Susan D. 1998. "Pearls on the String of the Chinese Nation: Pronouns, Plurals, and Prototypes in Talk About Identities." *Michigan Discussions in Anthropology* 13 (special issue on "Linguistic Form and Social Action"):207–237.

Bodman, Richard W., and Pin P. Wan, eds. 1991. *Deathsong of the River: A Reader's Guide to the Chinese TV Series Heshang*. Ithaca, N.Y.: Cornell University East Asia Program.

Bourdieu, Pierre. 1977. *Outline of a Theory of Practice*. Transl. Richard Nice. Cambridge: Cambridge University Press.

Buck, John Lossing. 1956. *Land Utilization in China*. New York: The Council on Economic and Cultural Affairs.

Butler, Judith. 1990. *Gender Trouble: Feminism and the Subversion of Identity*. New York: Routledge.

———. 1997. "Gender is Burning: Questions of Appropriation and Subversion." In *Dangerous Liaisons: Gender, Nation, and Postcolonial Perspectives*, ed. Anne McClintock, Aamir Mufti, and Ella Shohat, pp. 381–395. Minneapolis: University of Minnesota Press.

Caldeira, Teresa P. R. 2000. *City of Walls: Crime, Segregation, and Citizenship in Sao Paulo*. Berkeley and Los Angeles: University of California Press.

Chan, Anita, Richard Madsen, and Jonathan Unger. 1984. *Chen Village: The Recent History of a Peasant Community in Mao's China*. Berkeley and Los Angeles: University of California Press.

Chen Guohua. 1986. "Huidong nü zuyuan chu tan" (A preliminary discussion of the ethnic origins of Huidong women). *Quanzhou xuekan* (Quanzhou college journal) 4.

Chen Guoqiang. 1990. "Chongwu de yishi yu zushu shi tan" (A preliminary discussion of Chongwu attire and ethnic affiliation). In *Chongwu yanjiu* (Chongwu research), ed. Chen Guoqiang, pp. 251–261. Hui'an: Zhongguo Shehui Kexue Chubanshe.

Chen Guoqiang, and Shi Yilong, eds. 1990. *Chongwu Dazuo cun diaocha* (An investigation of Chongwu's Dazuo village). Fuzhou: Fujian Jiaoyu Chubanshe.

Chen Qingfa, and Wang Feng. 1992. "Huidong Chongwu zhen de lishi dili huanjing ji dui wai guanxi" (The environment, geography, and history of Huidong's Chongwu township and its outside relations). In *Huidong ren yanjiu* (Research on Huidong people), ed. Qiao Jian, Chen Guoqiang, and Zhou Lifang, pp. 19–31. Fuzhou: Fujian Jiaoyu Chubanshe.

Chen, Tina Mai. 2001. "Dressing for the Party: Clothing, Citizenship, and Gender-Formation in Mao's China." *Fashion Theory* 5(2):143–172.

Chen Xiangrong. 1994. Interview with author. Xiamen, China. August 4.

Chen Yonghui. 1985. "Zheli de zaohun xianxiang ling ren chijing" (The phenomenon of early marriage here is truly astonishing). *Nongmin ribao* (Peasant daily), February 8, p. 3.

———. 1987. "Hui'an zaohun lousu jiben xiaochu" (Hui'an's backward custom of early marriage is basically eliminated). *Nongmin ribao* (Peasant daily), January 2, p. 3.

Chongwu Township Government. n.d. *Chongwu zhen li nian yuye chanliang tongji ziliao* (Yearly statistical material on Chongwu township fishing production).

Clark, Hugh R. 1991. *Community, Trade, and Networks: Southern Fujian Province from the Third to the Thirteenth Century*. Cambridge: Cambridge University Press.

Clark, Paul. 1987. "Ethnic Minorities in Chinese Films: Cinema and the Exotic." *East-West Film Journal* 1(2):15–31.

Cohen, Myron L. 1993. "Cultural and Political Inventions in Modern China: The Case of the Chinese 'Peasant.'" *Daedalus: Journal of the American Academy of Arts and Sciences* 122(2):151–170.

Collier, Jane Fishburne. 1997. *From Duty to Desire: Remaking Families in a Spanish Village.* Princeton, N.J.: Princeton University Press.

Collins, Patricia Hill. 1990. *Black Feminist Thought: Knowledge, Consciousness, and the Politics of Empowerment.* New York: Routledge.

———. 1998. *Fighting Words: Black Women and the Search for Justice.* Minneapolis: University of Minnesota Press.

Comaroff, John L., and Jean Comaroff. 1997. *Of Revelation and Revolution.* Vol. 2, *The Dialectics of Modernity on a South African Frontier.* Chicago: The University of Chicago Press.

"Cong Hui'an xian shehui gaige yundong zhong kan chu" (A view from the Social Reform Movement in Hui'an county). 1952. Fujian Provincial Party Archive, file 134-1-33.

Connell, R. W. 1990. "The State, Gender, and Sexual Politics: Theory and Appraisal." *Theory and Society* 19:507–544.

Corrigan, Philip. 1994. "State Formation." In *Everyday Forms of State Formation: Revolution and the Negotiation of Rule in Modern Mexico,* ed. Gilbert M. Joseph and Daniel Nugent, pp. xvii-xix. Durham, N.C.: Duke University Press.

Corrigan, Philip, and Derek Sayer. 1985. *The Great Arch: English State Formation as Cultural Revolution.* Oxford: Basil Blackwell.

Cott, Nancy F. 2000. *Public Vows: A History of Marriage and the Nation.* Cambridge, Mass.: Harvard University Press.

Crenshaw, Kimberle Williams. 1993. "Beyond Racism and Misogyny: Black Feminism and 2 Live Crew." In *Words That Wound,* ed. Robert W. Gordon and Margaret Jane Radin, pp. 111–132. Boulder, Colo.: Westview Press.

Croll, Elisabeth. 1981. *The Politics of Marriage in Contemporary China.* Cambridge: Cambridge University Press.

Croll, Elisabeth J. 1997. *Desires and Destinies: Consumption and the Spirit of Confucianism.* London: School of Oriental and African Studies, University of London.

CWZZ. 1996. *Chongwu zhen zhi* (Chongwu Township gazetteer). Chongwu: Chongwu township Government.

Davin, Delia. 1979. *Woman-Work: Women and the Party in Revolutionary China.* Oxford: Oxford University Press.

Davis, Deborah, and Stevan Harrell. 1993. "Introduction: The Impact of Post-Mao Reforms on Family Life." In *Chinese Families in the Post-Mao Era,* ed. Deborah Davis and Stevan Harrell, pp. 1–22. Berkeley and Los Angeles: University of California Press.

Davis, Deborah S. 2000. "Introduction: A Revolution in Consumption."

In *The Consumer Revolution in Urban China*, ed. Deborah S. Davis, pp. 1–22. Berkeley and Los Angeles: University of California Press.

de Certeau, Michel. 1984. *The Practice of Everyday Life*. Transl. Steven Rendall. Berkeley and Los Angeles: University of California Press.

Dean, Kenneth. 1993. *Taoist Ritual and Popular Cults of Southeast China*. Princeton, N.J.: Princeton University Press.

Diamant, Neil J. 2000. *Revolutionizing the Family: Politics, Love, and Divorce in Urban and Rural China, 1949–1968*. Berkeley and Los Angeles: University of California Press.

———. 2001. "Making Love 'Legible' in China: Politics and Society During the Enforcement of Civil Marriage Registration, 1950–1966." *Politics and Society* 29(3):447–480.

Diamond, Norma. 1975. "Collectivization, Kinship, and the Status of Women in Rural China." In *Toward an Anthropology of Women*, ed. Rayna R. Reiter, pp. 372–395. New York: Monthly Review Press.

———. 1988. "The Miao and Poison: Interactions on China's Southwest Frontier." *Ethnology* 27(1):1–25.

———. 1995. "Defining the Miao: Ming, Qing, and Contemporary Views." In *Cultural Encounters on China's Ethnic Frontiers*, ed. Stevan Harrell, pp. 92–116. Seattle: University of Washington Press.

Dirlik, Arif. 1982. "Spiritual Solutions to Material Problems: The 'Socialist Ethics and Courtesy Month' in China." *The South Atlantic Quarterly* 81(4):359–375.

———. 1989. "Revolutionary Hegemony and the Language of Revolution: Chinese Socialism Between Present and Future." In *Marxism and the Chinese Experience: Issues in Contemporary Chinese Socialism*, ed. Arif Dirlik and Maurice Meisner, pp. 27–39. Armonk, N.Y.: M.E. Sharpe.

"Dong Zhou jidian guanche hunyinfa qingkuang baogao" (Report on the situation implementing the Marriage Law in the Dong Zhou base area). 1952. Fujian Provincial Party Archive, file 134-1-33.

Dreyer, June Teufel. 1976. *Minority Nationalities and National Integration in the People's Republic of China*. Cambridge, Mass.: Harvard University Press.

Duara, Prasenjit. 1995. *Rescuing History from the Nation: Questioning Narratives of Modern China*. Chicago: The University of Chicago Press.

Elliston, Deborah. 1997. "En/Gendering Nationalism: Colonialism, Sex, and Independence in French Polynesia." Ph.D. diss., New York University.

Engels, Friedrich. 1972. *The Origin of the Family, Private Property, and the State*. New York: Penguin Books.

Erwin, Kathleen. 2000. "Heart-to-Heart, Phone-to-Phone: Family Values, Sexuality, and the Politics of Shanghai's Advice Hotlines." In *The Consumer Revolution in Urban China*, ed. Deborah S. Davis, pp. 145–170. Berkeley and Los Angeles: University of California Press.

Evans, Harriet. 1997. *Women and Sexuality in China: Female Sexuality and Gender Since 1949*. New York: Continuum.

———. 1998. "The Language of Liberation: Gender and *Jiefang* in Early Chinese Communist Party Discourse." *Intersections* 1; available at http://wwwsshe.murdoch.edu.au/hum/as/intersections.

Farrer, James. 2002. *Opening Up: Youth Sex Culture and Market Reform in Shanghai*. Chicago: The University of Chicago Press.

Fei, Hsiao Tung. 1981. "Ethnic Identification in China." In *Toward a People's Anthropology*, ed. Fei Hsiao Tung, pp. 60–77. Beijing: New World Press.

Feuchtwang, Stephan. 1989. "The Problem of 'Superstition' in the People's Republic of China." In *Religion and Political Power*, ed. Gustavo Benavides and M. W. Daly, pp. 43–68. Albany: State University of New York Press.

Feuchtwang, Stephan, and Ming-ming Wang. 1991. "The Politics of Culture or a Contest of Histories: Representations of Chinese Popular Religion." *Dialectical Anthropology* 16(3/4):251–272.

Fitzgerald, John. 1996. *Awakening China: Politics, Culture, and Class in the Nationalist Revolution*. Stanford, Calif.: Stanford University Press.

FJHB. 1998. "Hui'an zhi lü tiandi kuan" (The broad expanse of Hui'an tourism). *Fujian huabao* (Fujian pictorial); available at http://www.fujian-window.com/Fujian_w/news/huabao/hb9801/c-fp36.html.

FJNJ. 1998. *Fujian nianjian* (Fujian yearbook). Fuzhou: Fujian Renmin Chubanshe.

FJQH. 1982. *Fujian qihua* (Fujian lacquer painting). Fuzhou: Fujian Renmin Chubanshe.

FJSZLYZ. 1997. *Fujian sheng zhi lüyou zhi* (Fujian province tourism gazetteer). Fuzhou: Fangzhi Chubanshe.

Flower, John Myers. 1997. "Portraits of Belief: Constructions of Chinese Cultural Identity in the Two Worlds of City and Countryside in Modern Sichuan Province." Ph.D. diss., University of Virginia.

Foucault, Michel. 1978. *The History of Sexuality*. Vol. 1, *An Introduction*. Transl. Robert Hurley. New York: Vintage Books.

———. 1983. "The Subject and Power." In *Michel Foucault: Beyond Structuralism and Hermeneutics*, ed. Hubert L. Dreyfus and Paul Rabinow, pp. 208–226. Chicago: The University of Chicago Press.

———. 1991. "Governmentality." In *The Foucault Effect: Studies in Govern-

mentality, ed. Graham Burchell, Colin Gordon, and Peter Miller, pp. 87-104. Chicago: The University of Chicago Press.

Freeman, Carla. 2000. *High Tech and High Heels in the Global Economy: Women, Work, and Pink-Collar Identities in the Caribbean.* Durham, N.C.: Duke University Press.

Friedman, Edward, Paul G. Pickowicz, and Mark Selden. 1991. *Chinese Village, Socialist State.* New Haven, Conn.: Yale University Press.

Friedman, Sara L. 2000. "Spoken Pleasures and Dangerous Desires: Sexuality, Marriage, and the State in Rural Southeastern China." *East Asia*, special issue on East Asian Sexualities 18(4):13-39.

———. 2002. "Civilizing the Masses: The Productive Power of Cultural Reform Efforts in Late Republican-Era Fujian." In *Defining Modernity: Guomindang Rhetorics of a New China, 1920-1970*, ed. Terry Bodenhorn, pp. 151-194. Ann Arbor: Center for Chinese Studies, The University of Michigan.

———. 2004. "Embodying Civility: Civilizing Processes and Symbolic Citizenship in Southeastern China." *The Journal of Asian Studies* 63(3):687-718.

———. 2005. "The Intimacy of State Power: Marriage, Liberation, and Socialist Subjects in Southeastern China." *American Ethnologist* 32(2):312-327.

FSGGCK. 1930. *Fengsu gaige cong kan* (A collected volume on customs reform). Guangzhou: Guangzhou Tebie Shi Dangbu Xuanchuan Bu.

"Fujian sheng chajin minjian bu liang xisu banfa shixing xize" (Detailed regulations for implementation procedures to prohibit undesirable customs among the people). 1948. Fujian Provincial Party Archive, file 11-6-4254(2), November 11.

"Fujian sheng xuanchuan guanche hunyinfa yundong yue gongzuo zongjie" (Work summary for the movement month to propagandize and implement the Marriage Law in Fujian province). 1953. Fujian Provincial Party Archive, file 134-1-44, June 15.

Fujian Tourism Bureau, and Hong Kong China Tourism Press, eds. 1994. *Focus on Fujian.* Hong Kong: Hong Kong China Tourism Press.

Gal, Susan, and Gail Kligman. 2000. *The Politics of Gender After Socialism.* Princeton, N.J.: Princeton University Press.

Gao Xiaoxian. 1994. "China's Modernization and Changes in the Social Status of Rural Women." In *Engendering China: Women, Culture, and the State*, ed. Christina K. Gilmartin, Gail Hershatter, Lisa Rofel, and Tyrene White, pp. 80-97. Cambridge, Mass.: Harvard University Press.

Garber, Marjorie. 1992. *Vested Interests: Cross-Dressing and Cultural Anxiety*. New York: Routledge.

"Gedi guanyu hunyin wenti siren de baogao tongjibiao" (A report and statistical chart on deaths related to marital problems in each district). 1953. Fujian Provincial Party Archive, file 144-1-17.

Giddens, Anthony. 1992. *The Transformation of Intimacy: Sexuality, Love, and Eroticism in Modern Societies*. Stanford, Calif.: Stanford University Press.

Gillette, Maris. 2000. "What's in a Dress? Brides in the Hui Quarter of Xi'an." In *The Consumer Revolution in Urban China*, ed. Deborah S. Davis, pp. 80-106. Berkeley and Los Angeles: University of California Press.

Gladney, Dru C. 1991. *Muslim Chinese: Ethnic Nationalism in the People's Republic*. Cambridge, Mass.: Council on East Asian Studies, Harvard University.

———. 1994a. "Ethnic Identity in China: The New Politics of Difference." In *China Briefing, 1994*, ed. William A. Joseph, pp. 171-192. Boulder, Colo.: Westview Press.

———. 1994b. "Representing Nationality in China: Refiguring Majority/Minority Identities." *Journal of Asian Studies* 53(1):92-123.

Glosser, Susan L. 2003. *Chinese Visions of Family and State, 1915-1953*. Berkeley and Los Angeles: University of California Press.

Gold, Thomas B. 1984. "'Just in Time!' China Battles Spiritual Pollution on the Eve of 1984." *Asian Survey* 24(9):947-974.

———. 1993. "Go with Your Feelings: Hong Kong and Taiwan Popular Culture in Greater China." *China Quarterly* 136:907-925.

Goldman, Merle. 1994. *Sowing the Seeds of Democracy in China: Political Reform in the Deng Xiaoping Era*. Cambridge, Mass.: Harvard University Press.

Gordon, Colin. 1991. "Governmental Rationality: An Introduction." In *The Foucault Effect: Studies in Governmentality*, ed. Graham Burchell, Colin Gordon, and Peter Miller, pp. 1-52. Chicago: The University of Chicago Press.

Grayson, Deborah R. 1998. "Mediating Intimacy: Black Surrogate Mothers and the Law." *Critical Inquiry* 24:525-546.

Greenhalgh, Susan. 1993. "The Peasantization of the One-Child Policy in Shaanxi." In *Chinese Families in the Post-Mao Era*, ed. Deborah Davis and Stevan Harrell, pp. 219-250. Berkeley and Los Angeles: University of California Press.

"Guanyu ben sheng Hui'an xian zai guanche hunyinfa yundong zisha shijian de jiancha baogao" (An investigative report regarding suicide incidents following the movement to implement the Marriage Law in Hui'an county). 1953. Fujian Provincial Party Archive, file 144-1-8, August 6.

"Guanyu ge qu funü gongzuo hui bao zhai yao" (Summary report concerning woman-work in each district). 1957. Hui'an County Party Archive, file 12-1.1-33.

"Guanyu guanche hunyinfa yundong qian hou siren shijian de baogao" (A report concerning deaths prior to and following the movement to implement the Marriage Law). 1953. Fujian Provincial Party Archive, file 144-1-8.

Guldin, Gregory Eliyu. 1994. *The Saga of Anthropology in China: From Malinowski to Moscow to Mao.* Armonk, N.Y.: M.E. Sharpe.

Guo Feng. 1994. "Hui'an nü: yu zhe haixiu shang jingtou" (The Hui'an woman: On television despite her shyness). *Xiamen guangbo dianshi bao* (Xiamen broadcast television news), July 13, p. 1.

Guo Zhichao. 1997. "Tianye diaocha yu wenxian jikao: Huidong wenhua zhi mi shijie" (Fieldwork and documentary research: A preliminary explanation of the secret of Huidong culture). *Xiamen daxue xuebao* (The journal of Xiamen University) 3:109–114.

Gupta, Akhil. 1995. "Blurred Boundaries: The Discourse of Corruption, the Culture of Politics, and the Imagined State." *American Ethnologist* 22(2):375–402.

Hall, Stuart. 1985. "Signification, Representation, Ideology: Althusser and the Poststructuralist Debates." *Critical Studies in Mass Communication* 2:91–114.

———. 1996. "The Problem of Ideology: Marxism Without Guarantees." In *Stuart Hall: Critical Dialogues in Cultural Studies*, ed. David Morley and Kuan-Hsing Chen, pp. 25–46. London and New York: Routledge.

Hansen, Thomas Blom, and Finn Stepputat. 2001. "Introduction: States of Imagination." In *States of Imagination: Ethnographic Explorations of the Postcolonial State*, ed. Thomas Blom Hansen and Finn Stepputat, pp. 1–38. Durham, N.C.: Duke University Press.

Harrell, Stevan. 1995a. "The History of the History of the Yi." In *Cultural Encounters on China's Ethnic Frontiers*, ed. Stevan Harrell, pp. 63–91. Seattle: University of Washington Press.

———. 1995b. "Introduction: Civilizing Projects and the Reaction to Them." In *Cultural Encounters on China's Ethnic Frontiers*, ed. Stevan Harrell, pp. 3–36. Seattle: University of Washington Press.

Hart, Angie. 1998. *Buying and Selling Power: Anthropological Reflections on Prostitution in Spain.* Boulder, Colo.: Westview Press.

Heath, Deborah. 1992. "Fashion, Anti-Fashion, and Heteroglossia in Urban Senegal." *American Ethnologist* 19(1):19–33.

Hershatter, Gail. 1996. "Chinese Sex Workers in the Reform Period." In *Putting Class in Its Place: Worker Identities in East Asia*, ed. Elizabeth J. Perry, pp. 199–224. Berkeley: Institute of East Asian Studies, University of California.

———. 1997. *Dangerous Pleasures: Prostitution and Modernity in Twentieth-Century Shanghai*. Berkeley and Los Angeles: University of California Press.

———. 2000. "Local Meanings of Gender and Work in Rural Shaanxi in the 1950s." In *Re-Drawing Boundaries: Work, Households, and Gender in China*, ed. Barbara Entwisle and Gail E. Henderson, pp. 79–96. Berkeley and Los Angeles: University of California Press.

———. 2002. "The Gender of Memory: Rural Chinese Women and the 1950s." *Signs: Journal of Women in Culture and Society* 28(1):43–70.

Herzfeld, Michael. 1997. *Cultural Intimacy: Social Poetics in the Nation-State*. New York: Routledge.

Hinton, William. 1966. *Fanshen: A Documentary of Revolution in a Chinese Village*. New York: Vintage Books.

Holm, David. 1984. "Folk Art as Propaganda: The *Yangge* Movement in Yan'an." In *Popular Chinese Literature and Performing Arts in the People's Republic of China, 1949–1979*, ed. Bonnie S. McDougall, pp. 3–35. Berkeley and Los Angeles: University of California Press.

Honig, Emily. 1985. "Burning Incense, Pledging Sisterhood: Communities of Women Workers in the Shanghai Cotton Mills, 1919–1949." *Signs: Journal of Women in Culture and Society* 10(4):700–714.

———. 1992. *Creating Chinese Ethnicity: Subei People in Shanghai, 1850–1980*. New Haven, Conn.: Yale University Press.

———. 1996. "Native Place and the Making of Chinese Ethnicity." In *Remapping China: Fissures in Historical Terrain*, ed. Gail Hershatter, Emily Honig, Jonathan N. Lipman, and Randall Stross, pp. 143–155. Stanford, Calif.: Stanford University Press.

Honig, Emily, and Gail Hershatter. 1988. *Personal Voices: Chinese Women in the 1980's*. Stanford, Calif.: Stanford University Press.

Hoodfar, Homa. 1997. *Between Marriage and the Market: Intimate Politics and Survival in Cairo*. Berkeley and Los Angeles: University of California Press.

hooks, bell. 1992. *Black Looks: Race and Representation*. Boston: South End Press.

Hsieh, Shih-chung. 1995. "On the Dynamics of Tai/Dai-Lue Ethnicity: An Ethnohistorical Analysis." In *Cultural Encounters on China's Ethnic Frontiers*, ed. Stevan Harrell, pp. 301–328. Seattle: University of Washington Press.

Huang Shu-min. 1989. *The Spiral Road: Change in a Chinese Village Through the Eyes of a Communist Party Leader.* Boulder, Colo.: Westview Press.

Huang Xiyi. 1992. "Changes in the Economic Status of Rural Women in the Transformation of Modern Chinese Society." *Social Sciences in China* 13(1):83-105.

"Hui nü song" (Ode to Hui'an women). 1963. *Fujian ribao* (Fujian daily). Reprinted in *Hui'an xian zhi* (Hui'an county gazetteer), 1998, ed. Hui'an Xian Difangzhi Bianzuan Weiyuanhui, pp. 1268-1269. Beijing: Fangzhi Chubanshe.

Hui'an County Government Circular 1. 1988. "Hui'an xian renmin zhengfu guanyu jinzhi jie hunyin suoqu caiwu, fandui gao pinjin, gao caili de tonggao" (Hui'an county government circular regarding using marriages to extort wealth, opposing high bride-wealth [and] wedding gifts). In *Hui'an xian zhi* (Hui'an county gazetteer), 1998, ed. Hui'an Xian Difangzhi Bianzuan Weiyuanhui, p. 1283. Beijing: Fangzhi Chubanshe.

Hui'an County Government Resolution 303. 1985. "Hui'an xian renmin zhengfu guanyu yanjin zaohun wenti de jueding" (Hui'an county people's government resolution concerning strict prohibition of early marriage). In *Hui'an xian zhi* (Hui'an county gazetteer), 1998, ed. Hui'an Xian Difangzhi Bianzuan Weiyuanhui, pp. 1273-1275. Beijing: Fangzhi Chubanshe.

"Hui'an di san pi 'si qing' yundong funü gongzuo zongjie baogao" (A summary report on woman-work during the third phase of Hui'an's "four cleans" movement). 1966. Fujian Provincial Party Archive, file 123-1-69, November 23.

"Hui'an funü tongmeng zisha" (Hui'an women make a pact to commit suicide). 1935. *Funü yue bao* (Women's monthly) 1(10):20.

Hui'an Xian Difangzhi Bianzuan Weiyuanhui, ed. 1998. *Hui'an xian zhi* (Hui'an county gazetteer). Beijing: Fangzhi Chubanshe.

"Hui'an xian funü zisha qingkuang jianbao" (A brief report on the situation of female suicide in Hui'an county). 1957. Fujian Provincial Party Archive, file 138-2-775.

"Hui'an xian guanche hunyinfa gongzuo de chubu zongjie" (An initial summary of work implementing the Marriage Law in Hui'an county). 1953. Fujian Provincial Party Archive, file 134-1-44.

"Hui'an xian guanche hunyinfa gongzuo zongjie" (A summary of Hui'an county's work implementing the Marriage Law). 1952. Fujian Provincial Party Archive, file 134-1-33.

"Hui'an xian guanyu hunyin wenti baogao" (Report from Hui'an county regarding marriage problems). 1950. Fujian Provincial Party Archive, file 138-2-57, September 15.

Hui'an Xian Renkou Pucha Bangongshi, ed. 1991. *Fujian sheng Hui'an xian 1990 nian renkou pucha ziliao* (1990 census materials, Hui'an county, Fujian Province). Hui'an: Hui'an Xian Renkou Pucha Bangongshi.

"Hui'an xian xuanchuan guanche hunyinfa yundong jiben zonglun" (Basic summary of the movement to propagandize and implement the Marriage Law in Hui'an county). 1953. Fujian Provincial Party Archive, file 144-1-22, May 14.

Hyde, Sandra Teresa. 2001. "Sex Tourism Practices on the Periphery: Eroticizing Ethnicity and Pathologizing Sex on the Lancang." In *China Urban: Ethnographies of Contemporary Culture*, ed. Nancy N. Chen, Constance D. Clark, Suzanne Z. Gottschang, and Lyn Jeffery, pp. 143–162. Durham, N.C.: Duke University Press.

Jacka, Tamara. 1997. *Women's Work in Rural China: Change and Continuity in an Era of Reform*. Cambridge: Cambridge University Press.

Jeffreys, Elaine. 1997a. "'Dangerous Amusements': Prostitution and Karaoke Halls in Contemporary China." *Asian Studies Review* 20(3):43–54.

———. 1997b. "Guest Editor's Introduction." *Chinese Sociology and Anthropology* 30(1):3–27.

Jiang Bingzhao. 1985. "Fujian Hui'an funü changzhu niangjia hunsu de tedian ji qi canliu de lishi yuanyin" (Distinctive features of extended natal residence marriage customs among women in Hui'an Fujian and historical reasons for their survival). *Renleixue yanjiu* (Anthropology research), *Shi kan hao* (Trial volume):112–119.

———. 1989. "Hui'an diqu changzhu niangjia hunsu de lishi kaocha" (A historical investigation of extended natal residence marriage customs in the Hui'an region). *Zhongguo shehui kexue* (China social science) 3:193–203.

Jie Sizhong. 1997. *Guomin suzhi you si lu* (Worried musings on the quality of citizens). Beijing: Zuojia Chubanshe.

Johnson, Kay Ann. 1983. *Women, the Family, and Peasant Revolution in China*. Chicago: The University of Chicago Press.

Judd, Ellen R. 1989. "*Niangjia*: Chinese Women and Their Natal Families." *Journal of Asian Studies* 48(3):525–544.

Kendall, Laurel. 1996. *Getting Married in Korea: Of Gender, Morality, and Modernity*. Berkeley and Los Angeles: University of California Press.

Kim, Kwang-Ok. 2001. "Politics of 'Backwardness': An Ethnographic Study of the Socialist Spiritual Civilization Movement in Contemporary Rural North China." Paper presented at the conference "Civilizing

Discourses and the Politics of Culture in Twentieth-Century China," Harvard University, Cambridge, Massachusetts.
Kipnis, Andrew B. 1997. *Producing Guanxi: Sentiment, Self, and Subculture in a North China Village*. Durham, N.C.: Duke University Press.
Lan Daju. 1995. "Lishixue yu renleixue de dui hua: Huidong renwen yanjiu" (A dialogue between history and anthropology: Research on Huidong human culture). *Xiamen daxue xuebao* (The journal of Xiamen University) 4:19–24.
Lee, Ching Kwan. 1998. *Gender and the South China Miracle: Two Worlds of Factory Women*. Berkeley and Los Angeles: University of California Press.
Lee, Sing, and Arthur Kleinman. 2000. "Suicide as Resistance in Chinese Society." In *Chinese Society: Change, Conflict, and Resistance*, ed. Elizabeth J. Perry and Mark Selden, pp. 221–240. London and New York: Routledge.
Lefebvre, Henri. 1991. *The Production of Space*. Transl. Donald Nicholson-Smith. Oxford: Blackwell.
Lefort, Claude. 1986. *The Political Forms of Modern Society: Bureaucracy, Democracy, Totalitarianism*. Cambridge, Mass.: The MIT Press.
Li Jian and Sun Shan. 1986. "Ai shen, jiang lin zhekuai tudi" (The spirit of love arrives on this patch of land). *Quanzhou wanbao* (Quanzhou evening news), December 2, p. 3.
Li, Tania Murray. 1999. "Compromising Power: Development, Culture, and Rule in Indonesia." *Cultural Anthropology* 14(3):295–322.
[Lin Bin] Youth. 1959. Letter to Hui'an County Women's Federation, July 25. Hui'an County Party Archive, file 12-1.1-63.
Lin Huixiang. 1981. "Lun changzhu niangjia fengsu de qiyuan ji muxi zhi dao fuxi zhi de guodu" (A discussion of the origins of extended natal residence customs and the transition from matrilineal to patrilineal society). In *Lin Huixiang renleixue lunzhu* (Lin Huixiang's anthropological works), ed. Xiamen Daxue Renlei Bowuguan, pp. 254–288. Fuzhou: Fujian Renmin Chubanshe.
Lin Jiahuang and Lin Ruifeng. 1992. "Huidong diqu changzhu niangjia hunsu de yanxi yu gaige" (Continuity and reform in the extended natal residence marriage customs of the Huidong region). In *Huidong ren yanjiu* (Research on Huidong people), ed. Qiao Jian, Chen Guoqiang, and Zhou Lifang, pp. 248–257. Fuzhou: Fujian Jiaoyu Chubanshe.
Lin Shuikun. 1997. "Ying ge yan wu song yu qu" (In praise of a prosperous fishing district). *Quanzhou wanbao* (Quanzhou evening news), November 21, p. 8.

Lin Yingming and Lin Yaoping. 1997. "Wenming xin feng huan gu zhen" (A new civilized wind enlivens an ancient township). *Quanzhou wanbao* (Quanzhou evening news), January 6, p. 1.

Litzinger, Ralph A. 1995. "Making Histories: Contending Conceptions of the Yao Past." In *Cultural Encounters on China's Ethnic Frontiers*, ed. Stevan Harrell, pp. 117–139. Seattle: University of Washington Press.

———. 2000. *Other Chinas: The Yao and the Politics of National Belonging.* Durham, N.C.: Duke University Press.

Liu Qinghe and Lin Ruqiu. 1989. "Fujian Hui'an chuantong nüfu" (Hui'an Fujian traditional women's attire). *Minsu huakan* (Folklore pictorial) 1:20–21.

Liu, Xin. 2000. *In One's Own Shadow: An Ethnographic Account of the Condition of Post-Reform Rural China.* Berkeley and Los Angeles: University of California Press.

Liu Zhongyi. 1986. "Kaituo wenming zhi lu" (Opening up a civilized path). *Zhongguo funü bao* (China women's news), September 26, pp. 1–2.

Lu Zhaohuan. 1986. "Shuang zhuo" (Twin bracelets). *Fujian wenxue* (Fujian literature) 4:4–18.

———. 1992. "Man tan 'Huidong nü xianxiang'" (An informal discussion of "the image of the Huidong woman"). In *Huidong ren yanjiu* (Research on Huidong people), ed. Qiao Jian, Chen Guoqiang, and Zhou Lifang, pp. 234–247. Fuzhou: Fujian Jiaoyu Chubanshe.

Lufkin, Felicity Anne. 1990. "Images of Minorities in the Art of the People's Republic of China." M.A. thesis, University of California, Berkeley.

Makley, Charlene E. 2002. "On the Edge of Respectability: Sexual Politics in China's Tibet." *Positions: East Asia Cultures Critique* 10(3):575–630.

———. 2003. "Gendered Boundaries in Motion: Space and Identity on the Sino-Tibetan Frontier." *American Ethnologist* 30(4):597–619.

Mann, Susan. 1997. *Precious Records: Women in China's Long Eighteenth Century.* Stanford, Calif.: Stanford University Press.

Mao, Zedong. 1954. "Report of an Investigation Into the Peasant Movement in Hunan." In *Selected Works of Mao Tse-Tung,* Vol. 1, pp. 21–59. London: Lawrence and Whishart.

Mauss, Marcel. 1990. *The Gift: The Form and Reason for Exchange in Archaic Societies.* Transl. W. D. Halls. New York: W.W. Norton.

McKhann, Charles F. 1995. "The Naxi and the Nationalities Question." In *Cultural Encounters on China's Ethnic Frontiers,* ed. Stevan Harrell, pp. 39–62. Seattle: University of Washington Press.

Meisner, Maurice. 1986. *Mao's China and After: A History of the People's Republic.* New York: The Free Press.

Miller, Daniel. 1994. *Modernity, An Ethnographic Approach: Dualism and Mass Consumption in Trinidad.* Oxford: Berg.
——. 1995. "Consumption as the Vanguard of History: A Polemic by Way of an Introduction." In *Acknowledging Consumption: A Review of New Studies*, ed. Daniel Miller, pp. 1–57. London: Routledge.
Min Tu-Ki. 1989. *National Polity and Local Power: The Transformation of Late Imperial China.* Cambridge, Mass.: The Council on East Asian Studies, Harvard University and The Harvard-Yenching Institute.
Mitchell, Timothy. 1991. "The Limits of the State: Beyond Statist Approaches and their Critics." *American Political Science Review* 85(1):77–96.
Mohanty, Chandra Talpade. 1997. "Women Workers and Capitalist Scripts: Ideologies of Domination, Common Interests, and the Politics of Solidarity." In *Feminist Genealogies, Colonial Legacies, Democratic Futures*, ed. M. Jacqui Alexander and Chandra Talpade Mohanty, pp. 3–29. New York: Routledge.
Moore, Henrietta L. 1994. *A Passion for Difference: Essays in Anthropology and Gender.* Bloomington: Indiana University Press.
Moraga, Cherrie, and Gloria Anzaldua, eds. 1983. *This Bridge Called My Back: Writings by Radical Women of Color.* New York: Kitchen Table, Women of Color Press.
Morgan, Lewis Henry. 1964. *Ancient Society.* Cambridge, Mass.: Harvard University Press.
Mueggler, Erik. 1998. "The Poetics of Grief and the Price of Hemp in Southwest China." *Journal of Asian Studies* 57(4):979–1008.
——. 2001. *The Age of Wild Ghosts: Memory, Violence, and Place in Southwest China.* Berkeley and Los Angeles: University of California Press.
——. 2002. "Dancing Fools: Politics of Culture and Place in a 'Traditional Nationality Festival.'" *Modern China* 28(1):3–38.
Oakes, Tim. 1998. *Tourism and Modernity in China.* London: Routledge.
Oakes, Timothy S. 1997. "Ethnic Tourism in Rural Guizhou: Sense of Place and the Commerce of Authenticity." In *Tourism, Ethnicity, and the State in Asian and Pacific Societies*, ed. Michel Picard and Robert E. Wood, pp. 35–70. Honolulu: University of Hawai'i Press.
O'Brien, Kevin J. 2001. "Villagers, Elections, and Citizenship in Contemporary China." *Modern China* 27(4):407–435.
Oi, Jean C. 1989. *State and Peasant in Contemporary China: The Political Economy of Village Government.* Berkeley and Los Angeles: University of California Press.
Ong, Aihwa. 1987. *Spirits of Resistance and Capitalist Discipline: Factory Women in Malaysia.* Albany: State University of New York Press.

———. 1990. "Japanese Factories, Malay Workers: Class and Sexual Metaphors in West Malaysia." In *Power and Difference: Gender in Island Southeast Asia*, ed. Jane Monnig Atkinson and Shelly Errington, pp. 385–422. Stanford, Calif.: Stanford University Press.
Parish, William L., and Martin King Whyte. 1978. *Village and Family in Contemporary China*. Chicago: The University of Chicago Press.
Perry, Elizabeth J. 1994. "Trends in the Study of Chinese Politics: State-Society Relations." *China Quarterly* 139:704–713.
Potter, Sulamith Heins, and Jack M. Potter. 1990. *China's Peasants: The Anthropology of a Revolution*. Cambridge: Cambridge University Press.
Povinelli, Elizabeth A. 2002a. *The Cunning of Recognition: Indigenous Alterities and the Making of Australian Multiculturalism*. Durham, N.C.: Duke University Press.
———. 2002b. "Notes on Gridlock: Genealogy, Intimacy, Sexuality." *Public Culture* 14(1):215–238.
Putonghua Minnan fangyan zidian (Mandarin Minnan dialect dictionary). 1982. Ed. Xiamen Daxue Zhongguo Yuyan Wenxue Yanjiusuo Hanyu Fangyan Yanjiushi (Xiamen University Chinese Language and Literature Research Institute, Chinese Dialect Research Office). Fuzhou: Fujian Renmin Chubanshe.
Qiao Jian. 1990. "Wei 'bu luo fujia' she yi jie" (Putting forth an explanation for "delayed transfer marriage"). In *Chongwu yanjiu* (Chongwu research), ed. Chen Guoqiang, pp. 261–264. Hui'an: Zhongguo Shehui Kexue Chubanshe.
———. 1992. "Huidong diqu changzhu niangjia hunsu de jieshi yu zai jieshi" (Explanation and reexplanation of extended natal residence marriage customs in the Huidong region). In *Huidong ren yanjiu* (Research on Huidong people), ed. Qiao Jian, Chen Guoqiang, and Zhou Lifang, pp. 258–265. Fuzhou: Fujian Jiaoyu Chubanshe.
"Qingchu fengjian louxi, kaituo wenming zhi lu" (Eradicating feudal backward customs, opening up a civilized path). 1986. *Fujian ribao* (Fujian daily), October 18, pp. 1–2.
"Qudi hunyin lousu banfa" (Procedures for prohibiting backward marriage customs). 1943. Fujian Provincial Party Archive, file 6-1-999.
Rebhun, L. A. 1999. *The Heart Is Unknown Country: Love in the Changing Economy of Northeast Brazil*. Stanford, Calif.: Stanford University Press.
Rofel, Lisa. 1994. "Liberation Nostalgia and a Yearning for Modernity." In *Engendering China: Women, Culture, and the State*, ed. Christina K. Gilmartin, Gail Hershatter, Lisa Rofel, and Tyrene White, pp. 226–249. Cambridge, Mass.: Harvard University Press.

———. 1999. *Other Modernities: Gendered Yearnings in China After Socialism*. Berkeley and Los Angeles: University of California Press.
Ruf, Gregory A. 1998. *Cadres and Kin: Making a Socialist Village in West China, 1921-1991*. Stanford, Calif.: Stanford University Press.
Sangren, P. Steven. 1987. *History and Magical Power in a Chinese Community*. Stanford, Calif.: Stanford University Press.
Sankar, Andrea. 1978. "The Evolution of the Sisterhood in Traditional Chinese Society: From Village Girls' Houses to Chai T'angs in Hong Kong." Ph.D. diss., University of Michigan.
———. 1985. "Sisters and Brothers, Lovers and Enemies: Marriage Resistance in Southern Kwangtung." *Journal of Homosexuality* 11(3/4):69-81.
Sayer, Derek. 1994. "Everyday Forms of State Formation: Some Dissident Remarks on 'Hegemony.'" In *Everyday Forms of State Formation: Revolution and the Negotiation of Rule in Modern Mexico*, ed. Gilbert M. Joseph and Daniel Nugent, pp. 367-377. Durham, N.C.: Duke University Press.
Schein, Louisa. 1997. "Gender and Internal Orientalism in China." *Modern China* 23(1):69-98.
———. 2000. *Minority Rules: The Miao and the Feminine in China's Cultural Politics*. Durham, N.C.: Duke University Press.
Schoenhals, Michael. 1992. *Doing Things with Words in Chinese Politics: Five Studies*. Berkeley: Institute of East Asian Studies, University of California.
Schram, Stuart. 1984. *Ideology and Policy in China Since the Third Plenum, 1978-1984*. London: Contemporary China Institute, School of Oriental and African Studies.
Scott, James C. 1998. *Seeing Like a State: How Certain Schemes to Improve the Human Condition Have Failed*. New Haven, Conn.: Yale University Press.
Selden, Mark. 1993. "Family Strategies and Structures in Rural North China." In *Chinese Families in the Post-Mao Era*, ed. Deborah Davis and Stevan Harrell, pp. 139-164. Berkeley and Los Angeles: University of California Press.
Shi Huifen. 2004. "Tongju liu nian wei dengji, neng fo suan shishi hunyin? Jian tan xin 'hunyin fa' shishi hou de jizhong fei hun zhuangtai" (Does cohabiting for six years without registering count as de facto marriage? A discussion of several types of nonmarital status following implementation of the new "Marriage Law"). *Zhongguo bao'an* (China security service) 6:29-30.
Shi Yilong. 1992. "Hui'an Dazuo ren de hunyin" (Marriage among the residents of Dazuo, Hui'an). In *Huidong ren yanjiu* (Research on Huidong

people), ed. Qiao Jian, Chen Guoqiang, and Zhou Lifang, pp. 96–113. Fuzhou: Fujian Jiaoyu Chubanshe.

———. 1997. "Cong gu hun ye gui dao shen ling de zhuanhua: Minnan 'si ren fo'a' de chubu yanjiu" (The transition from lonely souls and wild ghosts to gods: An initial study of Minnan region "private Buddhas"). *Mintai minsu* (Customs of Minnan and Taiwan), *Chuang kan hao* (Inaugural issue):1–32.

Shorter, Edward. 1977. *The Making of the Modern Family.* New York: Basic Books.

Shue, Vivienne. 1988. *The Reach of the State: Sketches of the Chinese Body Politic.* Stanford, Calif.: Stanford University Press.

Silber, Cathy. 1994. "From Daughter to Daughter-in-Law in the Women's Script of Southern Hunan." In *Engendering China: Women, Culture, and the State,* ed. Christina K. Gilmartin, Gail Hershatter, Lisa Rofel, and Tyrene White, pp. 47–68. Cambridge, Mass.: Harvard University Press.

Silverstein, Michael. 1976. "Shifters, Linguistic Categories, and Cultural Description." In *Meaning in Anthropology,* ed. Keith H. Basso and Henry A. Selby, pp. 11–55. Albuquerque: University of New Mexico.

———. 1985. "Language and the Culture of Gender: At the Intersection of Structure, Usage, and Ideology." In *Semiotic Mediation: Sociocultural and Psychological Perspectives,* ed. Elizabeth Mertz and Richard J. Parmentier, pp. 219–259. Orlando, Fla.: Academic Press.

Siu, Helen F. 1989. "Recycling Rituals: Politics and Popular Culture in Contemporary Rural China." In *Unofficial China: Popular Culture and Thought in the People's Republic,* ed. Perry Link, Richard Madsen, and Paul G. Pickowicz, pp. 121–137. Boulder, Colo.: Westview Press.

———. 1990. "Where Were the Women? Rethinking Marriage Resistance and Regional Culture in South China." *Late Imperial China* 11(2):32–62.

Smith, Paul. 1988. *Discerning the Subject.* Minneapolis: University of Minnesota Press.

Smith-Rosenberg, Carroll. 1975. "The Female World of Love and Ritual: Relations Between Women in Nineteenth-Century America." *Signs: Journal of Women in Culture and Society* 1(1):1–29.

So, Alvin. 1986. *The South China Silk District: Local Historical Transformation and World-System Theory.* Albany: The State University of New York Press.

Solinger, Dorothy J. 1999. *Contesting Citizenship in Urban China: Peasant Migrants, the State, and the Logic of the Market.* Berkeley and Los Angeles: University of California Press.

Spivak, Gayatri Chakravorty. 1985. "The Rani of Sirmur." In *Europe and Its Others*, Vol. 1, *Proceedings of the Essex Conference on the Sociology of Literature*, ed. Francis Barker, Peter Hulme, Margaret Iversen, and Diana Loxley, pp. 128-151. Colchester, Eng.: University of Essex.

———. 1988. "Can the Subaltern Speak?" In *Marxism and the Interpretation of Culture*, ed. Cary Nelson and Lawrence Grossberg, pp. 271-313. Urbana and Chicago: University of Illinois Press.

Stacey, Judith. 1983. *Patriarchy and Socialist Revolution in China*. Berkeley and Los Angeles: University of California Press.

Stafford, Charles. 1995. *The Roads of Chinese Childhood: Learning and Identification in Angang*. Cambridge: Cambridge University Press.

Stockard, Janice E. 1989. *Daughters of the Canton Delta: Marriage Patterns and Economic Strategies in South China, 1860-1930*. Stanford, Calif.: Stanford University Press.

Thornborg, Marina. 1978. "Chinese Employment Policy in 1949-78 with Special Emphasis on Women in Rural Production." In *Chinese Economy Post-Mao*, Vol. 1, *Policy and Performance*, ed. Joint Economic Committee of Congress, pp. 535-604. Washington: U.S. Government Printing Office.

Tong Enzheng. 1989. "Morgan's Model and the Study of Ancient Chinese Society." *Social Sciences in China* 10(2):182-205.

Topley, Marjorie. 1975. "Marriage Resistance in Rural Kwangtung." In *Women in Chinese Society*, ed. Margery Wolf and Roxane Witke, pp. 67-88. Stanford, Calif.: Stanford University Press.

Trinh, T. Minh-ha. 1997. "Not You/Like You: Postcolonial Women and the Interlocking Questions of Identity and Difference." In *Dangerous Liaisons: Gender, Nation, and Postcolonial Perspectives*, ed. Anne McClintock, Aamir Mufti, and Ella Shohat, pp. 415-419. Minneapolis: University of Minnesota Press.

Turner, Bryan S. 1993. "Contemporary Problems in the Theory of Citizenship." In *Citizenship and Social Theory*, ed. Bryan S. Turner, pp. 1-18. London: Sage Publications.

Verdery, Katherine. 1991. "Theorizing Socialism: A Prologue to the 'Transition.'" *American Ethnologist* 18(3):419-439.

———. 1996. *What Was Socialism, And What Comes Next?* Princeton, N.J.: Princeton University Press.

"Wajie funü zisha jituan gongzuo baogao" (Report on the work of disbanding women's collective suicide groups). 1952. Fujian Provincial Party Archive, file 134-1-33.

Wang Benhu. 1992. *Xiamen xinniang* (Xiamen bride). Taizhong: Chen Xing Chubanshe.

Wang Feng, ed. 2000. *Chongwu shi wenhua* (Chongwu stone culture). Hui'an: Hui'an Xian Wenxue Yishujie Lianhehui.

———, ed. 2002. *Tian feng hai tao hua Chongwu* (Wind and waves: talking about Chongwu). Chongwu: Chongwu Gucheng Fengjing Qu Guanlichu.

Wang Zheng. 2000. "Gender, Employment and Women's Resistance." In *Chinese Society: Change, Conflict, and Resistance*, ed. Elizabeth J. Perry and Mark Selden, pp. 62–82. London and New York: Routledge.

Watson, James L. 1982. "Of Flesh and Bones: The Management of Death Pollution in Cantonese Society." In *Death and the Regeneration of Life*, ed. Maurice Bloch and Jonathan Parry, pp. 155–186. Cambridge: Cambridge University Press.

———. 1997a. "Introduction: Transnationalism, Localization, and Fast Foods in East Asia." In *Golden Arches East: McDonald's in East Asia*, ed. James L. Watson, pp. 1–38. Stanford, Calif.: Stanford University Press.

———. 1997b. "McDonald's in Hong Kong: Consumerism, Dietary Change, and the Rise of a Children's Culture." In *Golden Arches East: McDonald's in East Asia*, ed. James L. Watson, pp. 77–109. Stanford, Calif.: Stanford University Press.

Weston, Kath. 1991. *Families We Choose: Lesbians, Gays, Kinship*. New York: Columbia University Press.

White, Luise. 1990. *The Comforts of Home: Prostitution in Colonial Nairobi*. Chicago: The University of Chicago Press.

Whyte, Martin K. 1988. "Death in the People's Republic of China." In *Death Ritual in Late Imperial and Modern China*, ed. James L. Watson and Evelyn S. Rawski, pp. 289–316. Berkeley and Los Angeles: University of California Press.

Wiegman, Robyn. 2002. "Intimate Publics: Race, Property, and Personhood." *American Literature* 74(4):859–885.

Wigen, Karen. 1999. "Culture, Power, and Place: The New Landscapes of East Asian Regionalism." *American Historical Review* 104(4):1183–1201.

Williams, Brackette F. 1989. "A Class Act: Anthropology and the Race to Nation Across Ethnic Terrain." *Annual Review of Anthropology* 18:401–444.

Wolf, Arthur. 1970. "Chinese Kinship and Mourning Dress." In *Family and Kinship in Chinese Society*, ed. Maurice Freedman, pp. 189–208. Stanford, Calif.: Stanford University Press.

Wolf, Margery. 1972. *Women and the Family in Rural Taiwan*. Stanford, Calif.: Stanford University Press.

———. 1975. "Women and Suicide in China." In *Women in Chinese Society*, ed. Margery Wolf and Roxane Witke, pp. 111–141. Stanford, Calif.: Stanford University Press.

———. 1985. *Revolution Postponed: Women in Contemporary China*. Stanford, Calif.: Stanford University Press.

———. 1992. *A Thrice-Told Tale: Feminism, Postmodernism, and Ethnographic Responsibility*. Stanford, Calif.: Stanford University Press.

Wong, Isabel K. F. 1984. "*Geming Gequ*: Songs for the Education of the Masses." In *Popular Chinese Literature and Performing Arts in the People's Republic of China, 1949–1979*, ed. Bonnie S. McDougall, pp. 112–143. Berkeley and Los Angeles: University of California Press.

"Wu buzhang guanyu guanche hunyinfa yundong de zhishi" (Directive from Department Head Wu regarding the movement to implement the Marriage Law). 1953. Fujian Provincial Party Archive, file 134-1-44, February 21.

Wu Jieling. 1985. "Fujian Hui'an xian gebie xiang zaohun yanzhong" (Early marriage is serious problem in a few villages in Fujian's Hui'an county). *Zhongguo funü bao* (China women's news), May 15, p. 1.

Xi Xi. 1994. "The Stone City of Chongwu." In *Focus on Fujian*, ed. Fujian Tourism Bureau and Hong Kong China Tourism Press, pp. 69–73. Hong Kong: Hong Kong China Tourism Press.

Xue Dezhen. 1996. "Jingshen wenming jianshe shi ren zishen de xiandaihua jianshe" (The building of spiritual civilization is the building of the modernized self). *Renmin ribao* (The people's daily), June 13, p. 13.

Xue Dezhen and Yuan Zhiming. 1986. "Jingshen wenming jianshe shi yizhong zhuti xing de jianshe" (The building of spiritual civilization is a subjective building). *Renmin ribao* (The people's daily), November 14, p. 5.

Yan Hairong. 2003. "Spectralization of the Rural: Reinterpreting the Labor Mobility of Rural Young Women in Post-Mao China." *American Ethnologist* 30(4):578–596.

Yan Yunxiang. 1996. *The Flow of Gifts: Reciprocity and Social Networks in a Chinese Village*. Stanford, Calif.: Stanford University Press.

———. 1997. "The Triumph of Conjugality: Structural Transformation of Family Relations in a Chinese Village." *Ethnology* 36(3):191–212.

———. 2001. "Practicing Kinship in Rural North China." In *Relative Values: Reconfiguring Kinship Studies*, ed. Sarah Franklin and Susan McKinnon, pp. 224–245. Durham, N.C.: Duke University Press.

———. 2002. "Courtship, Love, and Premarital Sex in a North China Village." *The China Journal* 48:29–53.

———. 2003. *Private Life Under Socialism: Love, Intimacy, and Family*

Change in a Chinese Village, 1949–1999. Stanford, Calif.: Stanford University Press.

Yang, C. K. 1959a. *A Chinese Village in Early Communist Transition*. In *Chinese Communist Society: The Family and the Village*. Cambridge, Mass.: The MIT Press.

———. 1959b. *The Chinese Family in the Communist Revolution*. Boston: The Technology Press, Massachusetts Institute of Technology.

Yang, Kun. 1992. *Minzuxue diaocha fangfa* (Methods of ethnological investigation). Beijing: Zhongguo Shehui Kexue Chubanshe.

Yang, Mayfair Mei-hui. 1997a. "Mass Media and Transnational Subjectivity in Shanghai: Notes on (Re)Cosmopolitanism in a Chinese Metropolis." In *Ungrounded Empires: The Cultural Politics of Modern Chinese Transnationalism*, ed. Aihwa Ong and Donald Nonini, pp. 287–319. New York: Routledge.

———, dir. 1997b. *Through Chinese Women's Eyes*. Documentary film.

———. 1999. "From Gender Erasure to Gender Difference: State Feminism, Consumer Sexuality, and Women's Public Sphere in China." In *Spaces of Their Own: Women's Public Sphere in Transnational China*, ed. Mayfair Mei-hui Yang, pp. 35–67. Minneapolis: University of Minnesota Press.

———. 2000. "Putting Global Capitalism in Its Place: Economic Hybridity, Bataille, and Ritual Expenditure." *Current Anthropology* 41(4):477–509.

Yau, Esther. 1989. "Is China the End of Hermeneutics? Or, Political and Cultural Usage of Non-Han Women in Mainland Chinese Films." *Discourse* 11(2):115–136.

Ye Guoqing. 1990 [1930]. "Dian Qian Yue de Miao Yao Zhuang su yu Min su zhi bijiao" (A comparison of the customs of the Miao, Yao, and Zhuang of Yunnan, Guizhou, [and] Guangdong with Minnan customs). *Zhangzhou shi minsu fangyan xuehui* (Zhangzhou city folk customs and dialect learned society), October 25, p. 4.

"You guan ben sheng hunyin wenti de jidian cailiao" (Some materials regarding marriage problems in the province). 1957. Fujian Provincial Party Archive, file 138-2-775.

Young, Robert J. C. 1995. *Colonial Desire: Hybridity in Theory, Culture, and Race*. London and New York: Routledge.

YXGMM. 1934. "Yang xianzhang guanxin min mo" (County Magistrate Yang is concerned about the people's suffering). *Haifeng* (Sea breeze) 1(2):5–6.

Zeng Wenfa and Cai Sicheng, eds. 1992. *Hui'an xian shuili dianli zhi* (Records of Hui'an county water and electrical power). Hui'an: Hui'an Xian Shuili Dianli Ju.

Zhang, Li. 2000. "The Interplay of Gender, Space, and Work in China's

Floating Population." In *Re-Drawing Boundaries: Work, Households, and Gender in China*, ed. Barbara Entwisle and Gail E. Henderson, pp. 171–196. Berkeley and Los Angeles: University of California Press.

———. 2001a. "Migration and Privatization of Space and Power in Late Socialist China." *American Ethnologist* 28(1):179–205.

———. 2001b. *Strangers in the City: Reconfigurations of Space, Power, and Social Networks Within China's Floating Population*. Stanford, Calif.: Stanford University Press.

Zheng da zong yi (Zheng da variety). 1994. China Central Television. July 31.

Zheng Xiaoying, ed. 1995. *Zhongguo nüxing renkou wenti yu fazhan* (Issues and development among China's female population). Beijing: Beijing Daxue Chubanshe.

Zheng Xiuhua and Huang Bingfa. 1998. "Chongwu nong chao nü" (Chongwu women creating a trend). *Fujian ribao* (Fujian daily), May 6, p. 5.

Zhi Wei. 1949. "Tan shuage jixi lougui: bing yuqi Chen juzhang shuage de chenggong" (A discussion of cleaning away deep-rooted habits and bad practices: Predicting the success of Bureau Chief Chen's cleansing). *Luoyang daobao* (The Luoyang guide) 11:8–9.

Zhong Gong Hui'an Xianwei Bangongshi. 1964. "Hui'an funü gaizao ziran de weida chuangju: ji Huinü shuiku de jianshe" (Hui'an women's great undertaking of transforming nature: Commemorating the construction of the Hui'an Women's Reservoir). Fujian Provincial Party Archive, file 134-1-428.

Zhong Gong Hui'an Xian Weiyuanhui and Hui'an Xian Renmin Weiyuanhui. 1960. "Zhi shan zhi shui jinian bei bei wen" (Harnessing the mountains and rivers commemorative tablet inscription). Reprinted in *Hui'an xian zhi* (Hui'an county gazetteer), 1998, ed. Hui'an Xian Difangzhi Bianzuan Weiyuanhui, p. 1263. Beijing: Fangzhi Chubanshe.

"Zhong gong zhongyang guanyu jiaqiang shehuizhuyi jingshen wenming jianshe ruogan zhongyao wenti de jueyi" (Resolution by the Communist Party and the central government concerning some major problems in strengthening the building of socialist spiritual civilization). 1996. *Quanzhou wanbao* (Quanzhou evening news), October 14, pp. 1–2.

Zhongguo-Chongwu (China-Chongwu). 1997. Hong Kong: Xianggang Minnan Ren Chuban Youxian Gongsi.

"Zhongguo gongchandang shi si jie liu zhong quan hui zai jing juxing" (The Sixth Plenum of the Fourteenth Central Committee of the Chinese Communist Party is held in Beijing). 1996. *Fujian ribao* (Fujian daily), October 11, p. 1.

"Zhongxuanbu, nongyebu guanyu shenru kaizhan nongcun shehuizhuyi jingshen wenming jianshe huodong de ruogan yijian" (Some suggestions from the Central Propaganda Department, Agricultural Department regarding the intensified development of activities to build socialist spiritual civilization in the countryside). 1995. *Renmin ribao* (The people's daily), November 30, p. 1.

Zhou Lifang. 1992. "Dazuo nan nü laodong fen gong ji funü de diwei" (The division of labor among men and women in Dazuo and women's status). In *Huidong ren yanjiu* (Research on Huidong people), ed. Qiao Jian, Chen Guoqiang, and Zhou Lifang, pp. 87–95. Fuzhou: Fujian Jiaoyu Chubanshe.

Zhuang Dongxian. 1988. "Hui nü zhi mi" (The mystery of the Hui'an woman). *Fujian qingnian* (Fujian youth) 1:26–28.

Zhuang Lianfu. 1992. "Dui 'Huidong gailiang fengsu tuan' de hui yi" (A recollection of the "Huidong customs-reform troupe"). *Hui'an wenshi ziliao* (Hui'an literary and historical materials) 8:48–49.

———. 1996. Interview with author. Xiaozuo, Hui'an. November 30.

Zhuang Yingzhang. 1994. "Huidong hunyin zhidu chu tan: yi Shanxia dong cun wei lie" (A preliminary discussion of the Huidong marriage system: The case of Shanxia's East Village). In *Hua nan hunyin zhidu yu funü diwei* (The South China marriage system and women's status), ed. Ma Jianzhao, Qiao Jian, and Du Ruile, pp. 10–44. Guangxi: Guangxi Renmin Chubanshe.

ZRGH. 1950. *Zhonghua renmin gongheguo hunyinfa* (Marriage Law of the People's Republic of China). Beijing: Renmin Chubanshe.

Character List

NOTE: Characters in parentheses indicate Mandarin equivalents.

aizing	爱情	love
bao hoegin'e	包花巾的	those who wear the headscarf
bbesen	迷信	superstition
bbian ki ziah	免去食 (吃)	[to] not need to go eat, it is not necessary to go eat
bbin bing	民兵	People's Militia
bbin hao	民校	People's School
bbnia snia e sunsit	名声的损失	the loss to one's reputation
bbo diong yong	无重用	useless
bbo kaihong	无开放	closed, not progressive (as in one's thinking)
bbo kaihuat	无开发	not progressive, backward
bbo kohak	无科学	unscientific
bbue tong	不会通	closed, blocked (as in one's thinking)
bian pai	变否 (坏)	to turn bad
bu cheng yangzi	不成样子	it won't do
bueyong gamzing	培养感情	to cultivate feelings
bu luo fujia	不落夫家	delayed transfer marriage (literally, to not remain in the husband's home)

chan zhi	产值	production value
chang zhu niangjia	长住娘家	extended natal residence marriage
chuji hezuoshe	初级合作社	lower producers' cooperative
cin	亲	close, intimate, affection, love
cindong	亲堂	patrilineal kin who share the same ancestral home
cng lam sna'e	穿蓝衫 (衣服) 的	those who wear blue dress
cut gang	出工	to put out labor
cut ki gnia gnia ze	出去行行者 (走一走)	to go out and walk around (also used to refer to dating)
da bao gan	大包干	contracting everything to the household
da dui	大队	production brigade
daibiaohui	代表会	representative committee
dam luan ai	谈恋爱	to be in love, to have a romance
dan	担	measure of weight (equal to 50 kg)
daode	道德	morality
deh dnia	(定亲)	ritual confirmation of a betrothal (follows kit)
deh lang	(跟着人)	to follow, go along with, to participate in gift exchanges
di sim'e	知心的	one who knows your heart
ding hun	订婚	to get engaged, to register one's marriage with the government
dui pnua; zue dui	对伴; 做对	institutionalized same-sex, nonkin bonds
e xi	恶习	evil custom
fan shen	翻身	"turning over," liberation
fengjian	封建	feudal
fengjian jiemei qingyi	封建姐妹情谊	feudal sisterly affection

fengjian tou, minzhu du, jieyue yi, langfei ku	封建头, 民主肚, 节约衣, 浪费裤	feudal head, democratic belly, frugal top, wasteful pants
funü	妇女	woman
Funü hui fujia	妇女回夫家	Women, return to your husbands' homes
fuquan de tongzhi	夫权的统治	the rule of the husband's authority
fu yu	富渔	rich fisherman
gagi'e lang	自己的人	one's own people, patrilineal kin
gai zong	改装	changing dress
gaige kaifang	改革开放	reform and opening
gamzing	感情	feeling
gang iu	厂友	factory friend
gankoo	艰苦	bitter, difficult
ganqing	感情	feeling
gaoji hezuoshe	高级合作社	advanced producers' cooperative
Gaoshanzu	高山族	Gaoshan ethnicity
genjudi	根据地	base area
Ggua ziok'e lang luan'a!	我这个人乱啊!	I'm such a mess!
ggun	阮	we, our (exclusive form)
giat hun	结婚	to marry
gin'a	巾仔	the elaborate headpiece worn by Huidong women until the reforms of the early 1950s
gio sin lniu	叫新娘	to call for the bride
gnia	惊 (怕)	to fear, to be afraid
gnia pai se	惊 (怕) 否势 (不好意思)	to fear being embarrassed or ashamed
gongdik	功德	a death ritual that guides the deceased's soul on its journey to the underworld
Hanzu	汉族	Han ethnicity, the Han
hi gng	鱼卷	stuffed fish rolls

hniu zok	乡族	village people
hoegin	花巾	headscarf and frame
honggian	封建	feudal
honggian sokbok	封建束缚	feudal constraints
huan yi	换衣	to change dress
huatdian	发展	developed, progressive
hui fujia	回夫家	return to the husband's home
Hui'an nü	惠安女	"the Hui'an woman"
Huinü shuiku	惠女水库	Hui'an Women's Reservoir
hukou	户口	official residence, village register
hulin	夫人	a form of worship performed by married women who have given birth and shifted residence
hulu ban	妇女班	women's class
hunyin louxi	婚姻陋习	backward marriage customs
ji	集	collective
jiben kouliang	基本口粮	basic grain ration
jiankang	健康	health, healthy
jianli aiqing	建立爱情	to build love
jianli ganqing	建立感情	to build feelings
jianshe	建设	building, construction
jiebaizimei	结拜姊妹	sworn sisters
jieban wei fei zhi niantou	结伴为非之念头	to band or get together and form inappropriate thoughts
jiefang	解放	Liberation, to liberate
jiehun zheng	结婚证	marriage license
jin	斤	measure of weight (equal to 0.5 kg.)
jingshen wenming	精神文明	spiritual civilization
jiti zisha	集体自杀	collective suicide
kah huatdian	比较发展	more developed, progressive
kaihong	开放	open, liberal

kexue	科学	science, scientific
kiam	俭	thrifty, frugal
kiam ze	欠债	to owe a debt (a wife's assumption of conjugal residence)
kit	乞(订)	initial betrothal (usually made in childhood)
kit'e m'si lu ping iu; lu ping iu si gagi gnia'e	乞的(订的)不是女朋友;女朋友是自己行的(找的)	someone you've been betrothed to is not a girlfriend; a girlfriend is someone you find on your own
koo gua	苦歌	bitterness song
ku	苦	bitter, bitterness
kue	契	a sworn relation, usually modeled on the parent-child bond
lan	(咱们)	we, our (inclusive form)
Li si bao hoegin'e a si sin sik'e? Ziok pai se!	你是包花巾的或是新式的? 这么否势(不好意思)!	Are you [one] who wears the headscarf or who [dresses] in the new style? Such embarrassment!
liang shou zhua, liang shou dou yao ying	两手抓,两手都要硬	both hands must grasp and grasp firmly
lin	你们	you (plural)
Lin anlni hun, ggua ziu deh lin anlni hun.	你们那样分,我就跟着你们那样分.	If you're going to distinguish [yourselves from me] in that way, then I will follow you and do the same.
laotong	老同	old sames
ling	灵	powerful, potent, efficacious
lolik	劳力	labor power
lu ping iu	女朋友	girlfriend
luan	乱	chaotic, disorderly, uncontrolled
luan ai	恋爱	romantic love
lueh'a	笠仔 (斗笠)	broad-rimmed bamboo hat

meiyou wenhua de kaifang	没有文化的开放	an uncultured or uneducated opening or liberalization
mianzi	面子	face, reputation
minzu	民族	ethnicity, nationality
minzu shibie	民族识别	ethnic identification
m'si dam luan ai, si dam luan ai	不是谈恋爱是谈乱爱	it's not romantic love, it's chaotic love
mu	亩	measure of area (approximately 1/15 of a hectare)
nü pengyou	女朋友	girlfriend
nüshu	女书	women's script
oo hun	乌(黑)婚	underage (literally, black) marriage
pin yu	贫渔	poor fisherman
ping iu	朋友	friend
pai se	否势(不好意思)	embarrassed, shy, ashamed
Po si jiu li si xin	破四旧立四新	Destroy the four olds, establish the four news
poodiong lionghui	铺张浪费	wasteful extravagance
qin	亲	close, intimate, affection, love
qin'ai	亲爱	beloved
qing ming jie	清明节	Tomb Sweeping Festival
qinqi	亲戚	relative, kin
qinqie	亲切	close, intimate
ren kouliang	人口粮	basic grain ration
renge	人格	personality
renmin	人民	people
sang'geng	送庚	a baby's one-month birthday celebration
shaoshu minzu	少数民族	national minorities
Shehui chu	社会处	Social Affairs Bureau
shehuizhuyi xiandaihua	社会主义现代化	socialist modernization
shen nü miao	神女庙	goddess temple
shenmei	审美	aesthetics
shi gong jia de	是公家的	to belong to the state

sio gang	细(小)工	little (manual) labor
soozit ge	素质低	low quality
suku	诉苦	speaking bitterness
suzhi	素质	quality
tamen	她们, 他们	they
tao loo	头路	occupation, profession
techan	特产	specialty product
teshu lousu	特殊陋俗	especially backward customs
tiah	拆	to tear, to rip off
tifa	提法	formulation
tit bue	(背心)	patchwork vest worn by elderly women
tni hok	添福	to increase good fortune
tu	土	coarse, country bumpkinish
tue sin	替身	a paper figure used in domestic worship to represent a family member
weiyuanhui	委员会	steering committee
wenhua fazhan	文化发展	cultural development
wenhua liyi	文化礼仪	culture and etiquette
wenhua suzhi	文化素质	cultural quality
wenhua suzhi di	文化素质低	low cultural quality
wenming	文明	civilization, civilized, civility
wu yan'e	有缘的	to be fated to be with
xiang	乡	administrative village
xiao jiating	小家庭	conjugal/nuclear family
xiaokang	小康	economically comfortable
xu sui	虚岁	age according to the Chinese reckoning system
yang	阳	the positive, light, and masculine in nature; opposing principle to *yin*
Yi feng yi su	移风易俗	Transform established habits and social customs
yin	他们	they, their

yin	阴	the negative, dark, and feminine in nature; opposing principle to *yang*
yuan	元	unit of Chinese currency
yu gong	渔工	fishing laborer
yuye zibenjia	渔业资本家	fishing capitalist
zhege Huidong nü	这个惠东女	this Huidong woman
zhong yu	中渔	middle fisherman
Zhonghua minzu	中华民族	the Chinese nation
Zhonghua minzu nüxing de dianfan	中华民族女性的典范	the paragon of Chinese national womanhood
zhousui	周岁	age calculated by precise birthdate
zhunsheng zheng	准生证	birth-permission certificate
ziah sni lit	食(吃) 生日	to celebrate a birthday
zhiye	职业	profession
ziyou lian ai	自由恋爱	free love
ziyou jiehun	自由结婚	free marriage
zng tik	装漂亮	to dress attractively and fashionably
zoh sit	作穑 (做事)	to work
zoocu	祖厝	ancestral home
zue gang	做工	to labor
zue gueh	做活	to do manual labor
zue liok kong sam	做六〇三	to do 603 (to engage in prostitution)
zui he	水货[1]	prostitute
zuo huo	做活	to do manual labor
zuo shi	做事	to work

Index

Note: Page numbers with an *f* indicate figures; those with a *t* indicate tables; those with an *n* indicate endnotes. Minnan entries are printed in the Franklin Gothic font, as in the text, to distinguish them from Mandarin terms in italics.

Abu-Lughod, Lila, 132–133, 273*n*26
adoption practices, 37–38, 46–47, 79, 113–114, 280*n*13
"Advise Our Women That They Must Owe a Debt" (song), 91, 260
affection: marriage and, 79, 108–117, 126–128, 281*n*18; intimacy and, 110–117, 132–134; romantic love and, 126–128, 134, 136, 286*n*15; terms for, 127–128, 134, 287*n*24, 288*n*4. *See also* "cultivating feelings"
agriculture, 32, 35–41, 49, 80; collectivization of, 43, 50, 77, 95–96, 152; decline of, 56, 276*n*25
alcohol, 80, 114, 182–184, 192, 224. *See also* substance abuse
All China Women's Federation, 40

Amway sales representatives, 119, 182
Anagnost, Ann, 231, 246
ancestor worship, 22, 140, 142, 147–149, 219; Tomb Sweeping Festival and, 147, 155; hulin case for, 148–152, 149*f*; genealogies and, 214, 288*n*3. *See also* rituals
arranged marriages, 73, 79, 94, 116, 118, 121–128, 240
Austin, J. L., 69
authenticity, 206–208, 227–229
authoritative discourse, 101–102

Bai Yue people, 223
Bakhtin, Mikhail, 101–102
bamboo hat (lueh'a), 33, 88*f*, 111, 202, 203*f*, 205*f*
bbin bing (People's Militia), 86, 90, 152
bbin hao (People's School), 85, 90, 152

Benjamin, Jessica, 10, 271*n*9
Benveniste, Emile, 295*n*14
Berlant, Lauren, 10, 136–137, 287*n*23
birth celebrations: gifts for, 137–138, 162, 163; hosting of, 179–180
birthday celebrations, 140, 179–185; of elders, 180–181, 291*n*5; of young people, 181, 291*n*6
birth-permission certificate (*zhun sheng zheng*), 130
"bitterness songs" (koo gua), 85
"black marriages" (oo hun), 110–111, 129
Bloch, Maurice, 149
Blum, Susan D., 295*n*14
Bourdieu, Pierre, 163, 234
bride-wealth, 123, 131, 286*n*14
Buck, John, 36, 274*n*3
Buddhism, 149, 225
bueyong gamzing ("cultivating feelings"), 108–109, 118, 121, 123–124; dangers of, 127, 132–134. *See also* affection
bu luo fujia ("delayed transfer marriage"), 7
Butler, Judith, 293*n*1

"call for the bride," 1–2, 14–15, 89, 125, 239, 248–249
chang zhu niangjia, see extended natal residence
chastity, 7, 82, 84, 270*n*5
Chen, Tina, 77
Chen Xinxing, 59
Cheng Qian, 206
child care, 61
Chinese New Year, *see* New Year holiday
cholera, 37

Chongwu, 21, 24, 25, 75, 164, 272*n*18, 290*n*18; tourism and, 4, 18, 223–225, 253; map of, 20*f*; extended natal residence in, 287*n*21
cin ("intimacy"), 142–143, 288*n*4
cindong, *see* gagi'e lang
citizenship: Foucault on, 10; ethnicity and, 198–199, 230–231, 293*n*2; "symbolic," 243–246. *See also* state power
"civilization" (*wenming*), 231, 233, 242–246. *See also* socialist spiritual civilization campaigns
collectivization: of fishing, 40–43, 55; of agriculture, 43, 50, 77, 95–96, 152; public works projects and, 43–48; extended natal residence in, 93, 95–101
Comaroff, Jean, 272*n*15
Comaroff, John, 272*n*15
commodification, 4, 185–187, 197; of ethnicity, 16, 17, 222–226, 225*f*, 246–247; of sex, 271*n*14
communes, 13, 42, 88–89
Confucianism, 11, 211
conjugality, 109, 132–133
conjugal residence, 2, 62, 77, 95–101; women's classes and, 110; intimacy and, 113–117, 119. *See also* extended natal residence
construction jobs, 21–24, 32–33, 43–48, 52, 57, 58*f*, 60, 64, 154–155
consumerism, 15–16, 57–58, 233; fashion and, 173–179; celebrations and, 180–185. *See also* market reforms
Corrigan, Philip, 10
Cott, Nancy, 67

"counterintimacies," 136–137, 166. *See also* intimacy
crabbing, 56, 274n7
Croll, Elisabeth, 173
cross-dressing, *see* drag
"cultivating feelings" (bueyong gamzing), 107–109, 118, 121, 123–124; dangers of, 127, 132–134. *See also* "feelings"; intimacy
Cultural Revolution, 22, 26, 51–54, 100–101, 231; Revolutionary Committee of, 51–52, 110; divorces during, 283n1
"culture" (*wenhua*), 233, 234, 242–243

Davin, Delia, 276n22
de Certeau, Michel, 244
"delayed transfer marriage" (*bu luo fujia*), 7
Deng Yingchao, 40
"Destroy the four olds, establish the four news" campaign, 97–98
Diamant, Neil, 99, 281n18
difference: negotiation of, 5–9, 16, 217–222; power of, 16–19; binary, 17; "authentic," 206–208, 227–229; diversifying of, 213–216
Ding Hong, 207–209
divorce: motives for, 46, 121, 123–124, 132, 171, 241; Marriage Law reforms and, 92, 94; social acceptance of, 110, 133, 283n1; compensation for, 123–125, 286n13; meal preparation and, 143–144; celebrations of, 191. *See also* marriage

domestic violence, 50, 79
Dong Zhou report, 74–75, 77–79
drag, 197; ethnic identity and, 198, 206, 226
dress, 33, 74–77, 173–179, 237–243; socialist reforms of, 74–77, 88–89, 202–203, 230–231, 245; work points for, 88–89; funeral, 158*f*, 164–165, 290n16; "young traditional," 174–176, 174*f*, 186–187, 231; "new style," 175–179, 176*f*, 177*f*, 216, 224, 236, 239–243; among dui pnua, 177, 239; male, 178, 215; of migrant women, 186; of prostitutes, 186–187; media depictions of, 202–210, 203*f*–205*f*, 226–229; choice of, 217–222, 236–243, 253–254; of She nationality, 223; Western, 242
drinking games, 182–184. *See also* alcohol
Duara, Prasenjit, 278n1
dui pnua ("same-sex ties"), 11, 35, 136–167, 251; chastity and, 7, 84, 270n5; intimacy and, 7, 142–156, 162, 164; "feelings" and, 11, 82–83, 136, 143, 153; socialist reforms and, 13; work assignments and, 47, 50; ENR and, 100; wedding ceremonies and, 121, 123, 137–138, 156, 159–165, 160*f*; gift exchanges among, 133, 137, 147–148, 156–165; definition of, 138–142, 164–165, 271n11; male, 140, 141, 159, 165, 180–184, 271n11, 288n1; siblings and, 141–142; spirits of, 147–151; extent of, 155–156, 161–162; funerals and, 157–159,

158*f*, 164-165; rituals among, 157-165; collective attire of, 177, 239

"eating bitterness," 48-51, 62, 226
education, 97, 234-236, 239, 262, 273*n*24, 276*n*20; literacy, 72, 85, 90, 152, 153, 234, 239, 298*n*6. *See also* socialist spiritual civilization campaigns
"Eight Words of Advice for Our Good Older Sister" (song), 261-262
elders, 57, 80, 275*n*12; hairstyles of, 87-88, 87*f*; filial care of, 114, 119-120, 300*n*7; birthday celebrations of, 180-181, 291*n*5; houses of, 273*n*23; funeral customs and, 289*n*11
Elliston, Deborah, 272*n*16
engagement photographs, 110, 129, 209
Engels, Friedrich, 5, 40
ENR, *see* extended natal residence
environmental concerns, 54-56, 234-235
Environmental Sanitation Compact, 298*n*9
ethnicity: state identification of, 4-5, 198-201, 269*nn*2-4; gender and, 5-9, 17, 271*n*13; mass media and, 8-9, 18, 201-213, 203*f*-205*f*, 221-222, 226-229; commodification of, 16, 17, 222-226, 246-247; as performance, 197-198, 206; citizenship and, 198-199, 230-231, 293*n*2; origin myths and, 199-200; difference and, 206-208

extended natal residence (ENR), 2, 94-95, 248-251; origins of, 7, 199-200; adoptions and, 37; women's work assignments and, 45-47, 50-51; socialist reforms and, 67, 69-70, 75-81, 84, 110; Nationalist reforms and, 68, 71-74, 78; terms for, 69-70, 269*n*1; Dong Zhou report on, 74-75, 77-79; folk song about, 81, 97, 107, 259; suicides and, 82-83; collectivization and, 95-101; dui pnua and, 100; average length of, 112*t*, 119-120. *See also* conjugal residence

family planning, *see* population policy
Farrer, James, 15-16
fashion, 173-179. *See also* dress
"feelings" (*ganqing*), 95-96, 126-128, 131-135, 143-144, 281*n*18; dui pnua and, 11, 82-83, 136, 143, 153; arranged marriages and, 79, 123-124; socializing and, 107-108, 118. *See also* "cultivating feelings"
"feudal constraints" (honggian sokbok), 6, 46, 69-70; socialist ideals and, 3-4, 116-117; suicide pacts as, 13, 147; marriage and, 15; extended natal residence and, 69-70, 78-79; Mao on, 70, 230; sartorial, 74-75, 240-243; dui pnua and, 82-84
feuds, lineage, 73
fishing industry, 21, 36-39, 48-49, 95, 122, 152; Taiwanese, 25, 37, 62, 249, 278*n*33;

collectivization of, 41–43, 55, 95; women on, 45, 275*n*11; modernization of, 51–52; decline of, 52, 55–56, 61, 222; wages from, 52, 62; net repair for, 56, 57f, 60, 98, 180
Fishing Industry Middle School, 276*n*20
fish-processing plants, 26
Fitzgerald, John, 70, 278*n*1
folk songs, 8–9, 11–12, 67, 85–86, 257–265; "Ten Send-offs of Little Sister to Huangtang," 53, 257–258; about Mao Zedong, 53–54, 300*n*3; "Raising Seaweed in the First Month," 54–55, 258–259; "Women, Return to Your Husbands' Homes," 81, 97, 107, 259; "Twelve Miseries," 83, 145, 262–263; "Advise Our Women That They Must Owe a Debt," 91, 260; popular music and, 126; "What the First Month Brings," 146, 263–265; "Eight Words of Advice for Our Good Older Sister," 261–262; romantic folktales and, 286*n*15
foot-binding, 274*n*3
Foucault, Michel, 10, 130, 235
Fujian province, 24; map of, 2f, 20f; tourism and, 4, 18, 223, 253
funeral customs: cost of, 73, 158, 290*n*15; dui pnua and, 157–159, 158f, 164–165; attire at, 158f, 164–165, 285*n*7, 290*n*16; regulations for, 289*n*13, 289*n*14
Fuzhou (city), 24–25, 218, 239, 251

gagi'e lang ("one's own people"), 140–141, 147, 251, 288*n*3, 290*n*17. *See also* ancestor worship
gaige kaifang, *see* "reform and opening" policies
gai zong ("changing dress"), 74
Gal, Susan, 69
gambling, 73, 79, 80, 114, 133, 232
Gang of Four, 54, 258
ganqing ("feelings"), 95–96, 126–128, 131–135, 143–144, 281*n*18; dui pnua and, 11, 82–83, 136, 143, 153; arranged marriages and, 79, 123–124; socializing and, 107–108, 118. *See also* "cultivating feelings"
Gansu province, 271*n*14
Gaoshan nationality, 270*n*3
Garber, Marjorie, 292*n*1
gender, 26; ethnicity and, 5–9, 17, 271*n*13; division of labor and, 34–36, 39–44, 47–49, 56–66, 96–101, 273*n*2; class and, 39, 271*n*13; social reforms and, 76–77; education and, 277*n*26, 277*n*27; Mao Zedong on, 280*n*17; drag and, 292*n*1
"ghosts," 148, 300*n*10
gift exchanges: hosting obligations and, 121, 181; wedding ceremonies and, 131, 286*n*14; among dui pnua, 133, 137, 147–148, 156–165; Bourdieu on, 163; among "one's own people," 290*n*17
gin'a (headpiece), 6, 75–77, 76f, 204f, 215, 224; banning of, 67, 73, 86–88, 87f; folk songs about, 86, 259–260; "new style" dress and, 179, 224

gio sin lniu, see "call for the bride"
Glosser, Susan, 280n15
gongdik ceremonies, 158
grain rations, 43, 49–51, 96–97, 274n8, 283n39
Gramsci, Antonio, 10
gravestones, see stone-carving factories
Great Leap Forward, 22, 52, 96; public works projects during, 43–48, 57; famine after, 51, 97, 275n12; environmental concerns with, 54
Greenhalgh, Susan, 286n18
Guangdong, 7
Guanyin (deity), 13

habitus, 234
hair styles, 87f, 89, 176, 177f, 217; marriage reforms and, 74–76; of She nationality, 223; of unmarried women, 279n10, 279n11
Hall, Stuart, 12, 17, 69
Hart, Angie, 292n15
headpiece, see gin'a
headscarf, see hoegin
headstones, see stone-carving factories
Heilongjiang province, 62, 219–220
Henan province, 296n22
Hershatter, Gail, 40–41, 134, 292n13
hniu zok ("village people"), 215
hoegin (headscarf), 13–14, 34f, 88–89, 88f, 111, 174f, 175; cost of, 175; prostitution and, 186–187, 238; media depictions of, 202–203, 203f; as safety hazard, 219; tourism and, 223, 253; socialist spiritual civilization and, 230–231, 236–246; as educational marker, 234, 298n7; modern dress versus, 236–243, 253–254
Hokkien, see Minnan dialect
honggian sokbok, see "feudal constraints"
Hong Kong, 7, 25, 36, 61, 126
Honig, Emily, 134
hooks, bell, 197, 292n1
hosting, celebratory, 159, 179–185, 189–194
"household contracts" (*da bao gan*): fishing and, 55; agriculture and, 56
housing, Shanlin, 21–24, 23f, 24f, 32–33, 252f
Hui'an county, 2, 146; map of, 20f; Women's Federation of, 95–96; ethnic origins of, 200
Hui'an Fishing District Culture Festival, 223–224, 227, 230
Hui'an Socialist Education Working Group, 97
"Hui'an woman," 8–9, 16–17, 33–34; tourism and, 4, 18, 222–229, 253; media representations of, 8–9, 18, 201–213, 203f–205f, 221–222, 226–229; subjectivity and, 11–16, 19, 294n8; eroticization of, 18, 201–202, 208–210; statue of, 31, 33–34, 224–226, 225f, 228; physical strength of, 32–33, 210–213; modernization and, 244–245
Hui'an Women's Reservoir, 44–47, 213, 296n21
Huidong, see Hui'an county
Hui nationality, 269n3
hulin worship case, 148–152, 149f. *See also* ancestor worship

hulu ban ("women's night classes"), 85, 98, 100, 110
Hunan province, 280n17
Hu Zhu (village), 90

identity, ethnic: tourism and, 4, 18, 222–229, 253; socialist reforms and, 4–9; drag and, 197–222, 226
illiteracy, see literacy classes
Indonesia, 93
intimacy: state power and, 3, 9–11, 133–134, 287n23; dui pnua and, 7, 136–137, 142–156, 162, 164, 166; affection and, 110–117, 132–134; fear of, 113–114, 117; premarital, 119–121, 131, 185, 241. See also "cultivating feelings"

Jacka, Tamara, 273n2
Japan: invasion of China by, 7, 37; exports to, 25, 59, 61
Jeffreys, Elaine, 292n10
Jiang Bingzhao, 146–147
Jiang Zemin, 230, 232
Jiangxi province, 40, 44
Jie Sizhong, 298n5
Johnson, Kay Ann, 92, 280n16

karaoke parlors, 125, 167, 180; prostitution and, 185–193; social concerns about, 188–189, 191–192, 237–238, 241
kiam ze ("owing a debt"), 91, 269n1
Kleinman, Arthur, 149, 281n22
Kligman, Gail, 69
koo gua ("bitterness songs"), 85–86
Korea, South, 287n19
KTVs, see karaoke parlors

labor: division of, 33–34, 39–44, 47–49, 56–66, 96–101, 271n13; unskilled, 39, 49, 62–65, 291n4; work points for, 51, 88–89, 275n8; family demands for, 115
Lacan, Jacques, 271n12
Lahiri, Smita, 295n13
Lan Daju, 293n6
Lee Ching Kwan, 292n10
Lee Sing, 149, 281n22
Lefebvre, Henri, 170
Lefort, Claude, 53–54
Li, Tania, 93
Liang Qichao, 278n1
Lin Huixiang, 199–200, 288n2
literacy classes, 72, 85, 90, 152, 153, 234, 239, 298n6. See also education
Litzinger, Ralph, 17
lueh'a (bamboo hat), 33, 88f, 111, 202, 203f, 205f

Makley, Charlene, 271n14
Malaysia, 36, 61, 292n12
Mandarin dialect, xv–xvi, 126, 288n4, 295n14, 325–332
Mao Zedong: folk songs about, 53–54, 300n3; on feudal constraints, 70; on propaganda, 85; on non-Han minorities, 293n3
market reforms, 3–4, 15–16, 56–65, 57f–60f; decollectivization and, 55–56; gender divisions of labor and, 56–65; manual labor and, 61–65; marriage and, 107–117 passim, 133–135, 283n2; gift exchanges and, 159–165; youth socializing and, 169–173, 179–185, 189–193, 241–242; ethnic commodification and, 197–198,

208–209, 220–226, 228–229, 253; mass media and, 201–202. *See also* consumerism
marriage, 107–135; socialist reforms and, 4–9, 14–15, 77–81, 89–91, 93–95, 110; underage, 71, 79, 94, 110–111, 129, 278*n*2; arranged, 73, 79, 94, 116, 118, 121–128, 240; affection and, 79, 108–117, 126–128, 281*n*18; patrilocal, 94, 110; average age for, 111, 112*t*, 129, 163; adoption and, 113–114; legal age for, 118, 119, 280*n*13; registration of, 119–121, 128–131, 185, 250; bride-wealth and, 123; ritual concerns of, 130–131, 300*n*5; choice of attire and, 239–242; compensation, 270*n*5. *See also* divorce; wedding ceremonies
Marriage Law (1950), 41, 68; campaigns in support of, 77–84, 89–93, 110; suicides and, 82, 92; implementation of, 84–93; outcomes of, 93–96
Marx, Karl, 5, 40, 70
mass media: ethnicity and, 8–9, 18, 201–213, 203*f*–205*f*, 221–222, 226–229; television and, 9, 25, 126, 209, 227, 251, 295*n*19; Nationalist reforms and, 73; romantic love in, 126
matrilineal residualism, 199–200, 293*n*5
May Fourth Movement (1919), 73
Mazu (deity), 13, 150–151; temples of, 22, 72, 214–215, 273*n*25; attire of, 223
Meizhou Island, 223

Miao nationality, 199, 217, 227, 270*n*3, 293*n*4
Michelson, Ethan, 286*n*17
Micronesia, 62
migrants, 15–16, 21; dress of, 186, 217; jobs of, 186–187; *suzhi* and, 298*n*4
Ming dynasty, 21, 277*n*28
Minnan dialect, xv–xvi, 25, 126, 128, 281*n*21, 285*n*12, 287*n*24, 289*n*8, 325–332
minzu ("ethnicity"), 198–199, 293*n*3
Mitchell, Timothy, 271*n*8
mixed-sex socializing, 107–108, 113, 117–121, 125–126, 181–184, 189–193, 241–242, 251
modernization: tourism and, 4, 18, 224, 225, 227, 253; socialist spiritual civilization and, 230–236, 245, 254
Moore, Henrietta, 272*n*16
Morgan, Lewis Henry, 5, 198
Moslems, 269*n*3
Mueggler, Erik, 200–201, 279*n*8
music videos, 126, 190–191. *See also* karaoke parlors

Nationalist reforms, 68, 71–74, 78, 82
nationality: ethnicity and, 198–199, 230–231, 293*n*3; state identification of, 198–201, 269*n*2; citizenship and, 243–246
negotiation of difference, 5–9, 16, 217–222
nets, fishing, 56, 57*f*, 60, 98, 180
New Year holiday, 2, 14, 42, 108, 168

Oakes, Timothy, 198, 296*n*24

O'Brien, Kevin, 299n10
"occupation" (tao loo), 63, 65
"one's own people," *see* gagi'e lang
Ong, Aihwa, 292n12
oo hun ("black marriages"), 110–111, 129
opium, 73
Origin of the Family (Engels), 5, 40
otherness: Benjamin on, 10; "mobile," 18; marginalized, 19, 245; "inappropriate," 231, 243; "intractable," 243–244. *See also* subjectivity
"owing a debt" (kiam ze), 91, 260, 269n1

pai se ("shy") behavior, 111–117, 119–121, 125, 128, 132–136, 250
Parry, Jonathan, 149
People's Militia (bbin bing), 86, 90, 152
People's Schools (bbin hao), 85, 90, 152
population policy, 128–131, 133–134, 285n8, 286n17, 286n18, 287n20; adoption and, 37; age at marriage and, 112t, 128–129; marriage registration and, 118–119, 129–130; youth sexuality and, 131
pornography, 18, 232
Po si jui li si xin campaign, 97–98
Povinelli, Elizabeth, 271n10, 272n17
pregnancy: superstitions about, 115, 121, 284n7; marriage registration and, 129, 132, 250
premarital sex, 119–121, 131, 185, 241

"Procedures for Prohibiting Backward Marriage Customs," 71
"promiscuity," 242, 271n14
propaganda: folk songs and, 8–9, 11–12, 67, 81, 85–86, 257–265; marriage reforms and, 67, 81, 90–93; language of reform and, 68–70, 85, 101–103; Mao on, 85
prostitution, 79–80, 185–193, 232; motives for, 7, 188, 292n13; social concerns about, 125, 188–189, 191–192, 238, 241, 242; terms for, 185, 186; minority dress and, 295n13
public works projects, 43–48, 52, 57, 95
Pudu festival, 300n10
purchasing power, 7, 173–178, 290n2

qin ("intimacy"), 288n4
Qing dynasty, 278n1, 296n22
"quality" (*suzhi*), 233–235, 242–243, 299n10
Quanzhou (prefecture), 21, 25, 44, 218

"Raising Seaweed in the First Month" (song), 54–55, 258–259
Rebhun, L. A., 134–135
"reform and opening" policies, 3, 24
registration, marriage, 119–121, 128–131, 185, 250
Remick, Elizabeth, 278n5
"Resolution Regarding Guiding Directions for the Building of Socialist Spiritual Civilization," 232
rice, *see* grain rations
rituals, 72, 73; cultural festivals

and, 4, 223–224, 227, 230; socialist reforms and, 13, 289n13; pregnancy superstitions and, 115, 121, 284n7; marriage, 130–131, 300n5; Tomb Sweeping, 147, 155; hulin worship case for, 148–152, 149f; birthdays of elders and, 180–181. *See also* ancestor worship; Mazu

Romania, 68–69

romantic love, 126–128, 134, 136, 286n15. *See also* affection

same-sex ties, *see* dui pnua

Sangren, P. Steven, 148

Sankar, Andrea, 281n22

sartorial customs, *see* dress

Sayer, Derek, 10, 254

scarf, *see* hoegin

Schein, Louisa, 18, 217, 227, 244, 299n14

Schoenhals, Michael, 69, 101–102

seaweed cultivation, 51, 54–55, 98, 152, 153

sexually transmitted diseases (STDs), 80

Shaanxi province, 41

Shanlin, 19–25; maps of, 20f, 22f; housing in, 21–24, 23f, 24f, 32–33, 252f

She nationality, 223, 270n3

Silber, Cathy, 288n4

silk factories, 7, 270n5

Singapore, 7, 36

Sino-Japanese War (1937–1938), 7, 37

Siu, Helen, 288n6

socialism, 3–4, 116–117, 232, 253–254; intimacy and, 3, 9–11, 133–134, 287n23; ethnic categories and, 4–5, 198–201, 269nn2–3; marriage reforms and, 4–9, 14–15, 77–81, 89–91, 93–95, 110; language of, 53–54, 68–69, 101–103; extended natal residence and, 67, 69–70, 75–81, 84, 110; dress reforms and, 74–77, 88–89, 202–203, 230–231, 245; citizenship and, 198–199, 230–231, 243–246, 293n2. *See also* state power

Socialist Education Movement, 97, 234, 262

socialist spiritual civilization campaigns, 15, 17, 19, 68, 230–236, 245, 254

Solinger, Dorothy, 245, 290n1

Song dynasty, 21, 272n19

Song Lin (village), 92–93

"speaking bitterness" (*suku*), 38–39, 48–51, 85

Spivak, Gayatri, 295n15

Stafford, Charles, 288n7, 291n6

Stalin, Joseph, 5

state power, 3–4, 8–11, 27, 93, 270n8; language of, 53–54, 68–69, 101–103; intimacy and, 109, 128–134, 287n23; education and, 234–236; modernization and, 246–247, 253–254. *See also* citizenship

Stockard, Janice, 270n6, 288n6

stone-carving factories, 21, 23–25, 59–63, 60f, 66; wages at, 59–60, 62, 171–172; as mixed-sex environment, 169–173, 185, 188; prostitution and, 186–188; attire at, 219; economic instability and, 222, 249

stone quarries, 57

subjectivity, 11–14, 271n12,

271n13, 292n12; language and, 53–54, 68–69, 101–103; public presentation and, 207–208, 237–238. *See also* otherness
substance abuse, 73, 114, 232. *See also* alcohol
suicide, 6, 13, 81–84, 147–151; socialist concerns with, 6, 13, 68, 83–84, 101, 152, 200; Nationalist concerns with, 71–73, 82; gin'a ban as cause of, 88; prevention of, 91–92
suku, see "speaking bitterness"
superstitions, 13, 72, 73; about pregnancy, 115, 121, 284n7; restrictions on, 289n13, 289n14. *See also* rituals
surnames, 45–46; marriage among, 94, 110, 284n3; genealogies of, 214, 272n21, 296n22
suzhi ("quality"), 233–235, 242–243, 298n5, 299n10
"symbolic citizenship," 243–246

Taiwan, 21, 61, 86, 218; map of, 2f; fishing industry of, 25, 37, 62, 249, 278n33; television programs from, 25, 209, 295n19; 1996 elections in, 25–26; United States and, 25–26; marriage beliefs in, 124; popular singers from, 126; food sharing in, 288n7, 291n6
Taiwanese, romanization of, xvi
Tang dynasty, 272n19
tao loo ("occupation"), 63, 65
taxis, 59, 63–64
television, 9, 25, 126, 209, 227, 251, 295n19. *See also* mass media
temples, 22, 72, 214–215, 273n25

"Ten Send-offs of Little Sister to Huangtang" (song), 53, 257–258
Titanic (movie), 126
tni hok ("increase good fortune"), 180–181
Tomb Sweeping Festival, 147, 155
tourism, 4, 18, 222–229, 253
"Transform established habits and social customs" movement, 97–98, 101
transvestism, *see* drag
Trinh Minh-ha, 244
tuna fishing, 122
Tuzhai township, 90
"Twelve Miseries" (song), 83, 145, 262–63

underage marriage, 71, 79, 94, 110–111, 129, 278n2
United States, 25–26, 86
unskilled labor, 39, 49, 62–65
urban culture, 18–19; attire and, 294n11; political discrimination and, 299n10

venereal diseases, 60
Verdery, Katherine, 15, 68–69, 101–102, 298n3
village endogamy, 94, 283n3
"village people" (hniu zok), 215
violence: "representational," 17; domestic, 50, 79
voyeurism, 18, 232

wage labor, 39, 49, 59–60, 62–65
Wang Benhu, 296n19
Warner, Michael, 136–137
Watson, James, 291n6
wedding ceremonies: cost of, 73, 123, 131, 160–161, 284n4; sex before, 119–121, 132, 133, 185,

250; dui pnua and, 121, 123, 137–138, 156, 159–165, 160*f*; gift exchanges at, 157, 159–165, 286*n*14. *See also* extended natal residence; marriage
"We Must Raise the Building of Socialist Spiritual Civilization to an Even More Prominent Position," 232
wenhua ("culture"), 233, 234, 242–243
wenming ("civilization"), 231, 233, 242–246
"What the First Month Brings" (song), 146, 263–265
Wolf, Margery, 124
"Women, Return to Your Husbands' Homes" (song), 81, 97, 107, 259
Women's Association, 72
Women's Federation, All China, 40
Women's Federation of Hui'an County, 11, 78, 95–96
"women's night classes" (hulu ban), 85, 98, 100, 110
Women's Representative Committee, 86, 90
work, *see* labor
work points, 51, 88–89, 275*n*8

Wutan Reservoir, 44–47, 213, 296*n*21

Xiamen (city), 24, 44, 57, 218, 220–221, 248
Xiamen University, xv, 73, 146
Xunbu, 223

Yang, C. K., 270*n*6
Yang, Mayfair, 160–161, 291*n*10, 298*n*8
Yan Yunxiang, 109
Ye Guoqing, 293*n*4
Yi feng yi su movement, 97–98, 101
Youth League, 86, 97–100

Zhang, Li, 298*n*4
Zhejiang province, 36, 42
Zhou Enlai, 54–55
Zhuang Dongxian, 212
Zhuang nationality, 270*n*3, 293*n*4
zhun sheng zheng (birth-permission certificate), 130
ziah sni lit ("celebrate a birthday"), 181
zng tik ("dress stylishly"), 173, 178
zoh sit (*zuo shi*), 63
zue gang, 63
zue gueh (*zuo huo*), 39, 49, 62–65
zui he ("prostitutes"), 185, 186

Harvard East Asian Monographs
(* out-of-print)

*1. Liang Fang-chung, *The Single-Whip Method of Taxation in China*
*2. Harold C. Hinton, *The Grain Tribute System of China, 1845–1911*
3. Ellsworth C. Carlson, *The Kaiping Mines, 1877–1912*
*4. Chao Kuo-chün, *Agrarian Policies of Mainland China: A Documentary Study, 1949–1956*
*5. Edgar Snow, *Random Notes on Red China, 1936–1945*
*6. Edwin George Beal, Jr., *The Origin of Likin, 1835–1864*
7. Chao Kuo-chün, *Economic Planning and Organization in Mainland China: A Documentary Study, 1949–1957*
*8. John K. Fairbank, *Ching Documents: An Introductory Syllabus*
*9. Helen Yin and Yi-chang Yin, *Economic Statistics of Mainland China, 1949–1957*
10. Wolfgang Franke, *The Reform and Abolition of the Traditional Chinese Examination System*
11. Albert Feuerwerker and S. Cheng, *Chinese Communist Studies of Modern Chinese History*
12. C. John Stanley, *Late Ching Finance: Hu Kuang-yung as an Innovator*
13. S. M. Meng, *The Tsungli Yamen: Its Organization and Functions*
*14. Ssu-yü Teng, *Historiography of the Taiping Rebellion*
15. Chun-Jo Liu, *Controversies in Modern Chinese Intellectual History: An Analytic Bibliography of Periodical Articles, Mainly of the May Fourth and Post-May Fourth Era*
*16. Edward J. M. Rhoads, *The Chinese Red Army, 1927–1963: An Annotated Bibliography*
*17. Andrew J. Nathan, *A History of the China International Famine Relief Commission*
*18. Frank H. H. King (ed.) and Prescott Clarke, *A Research Guide to China-Coast Newspapers, 1822–1911*
*19. Ellis Joffe, *Party and Army: Professionalism and Political Control in the Chinese Officer Corps, 1949–1964*

*20. Toshio G. Tsukahira, *Feudal Control in Tokugawa Japan: The Sankin Kōtai System*
*21. Kwang-Ching Liu, ed., *American Missionaries in China: Papers from Harvard Seminars*
*22. George Moseley, *A Sino-Soviet Cultural Frontier: The Ili Kazakh Autonomous Chou*
23. Carl F. Nathan, *Plague Prevention and Politics in Manchuria, 1910–1931*
*24. Adrian Arthur Bennett, *John Fryer: The Introduction of Western Science and Technology into Nineteenth-Century China*
*25. Donald J. Friedman, *The Road from Isolation: The Campaign of the American Committee for Non-Participation in Japanese Aggression, 1938–1941*
*26. Edward LeFevour, *Western Enterprise in Late Ching China: A Selective Survey of Jardine, Matheson and Company's Operations, 1842–1895*
27. Charles Neuhauser, *Third World Politics: China and the Afro-Asian People's Solidarity Organization, 1957–1967*
*28. Kungtu C. Sun, assisted by Ralph W. Huenemann, *The Economic Development of Manchuria in the First Half of the Twentieth Century*
*29. Shahid Javed Burki, *A Study of Chinese Communes, 1965*
30. John Carter Vincent, *The Extraterritorial System in China: Final Phase*
31. Madeleine Chi, *China Diplomacy, 1914–1918*
*32. Clifton Jackson Phillips, *Protestant America and the Pagan World: The First Half Century of the American Board of Commissioners for Foreign Missions, 1810–1860*
*33. James Pusey, *Wu Han: Attacking the Present Through the Past*
*34. Ying-wan Cheng, *Postal Communication in China and Its Modernization, 1860–1896*
35. Tuvia Blumenthal, *Saving in Postwar Japan*
36. Peter Frost, *The Bakumatsu Currency Crisis*
37. Stephen C. Lockwood, *Augustine Heard and Company, 1858–1862*
38. Robert R. Campbell, *James Duncan Campbell: A Memoir by His Son*
39. Jerome Alan Cohen, ed., *The Dynamics of China's Foreign Relations*
40. V. V. Vishnyakova-Akimova, *Two Years in Revolutionary China, 1925–1927*, tr. Steven L. Levine
41. Meron Medzini, *French Policy in Japan During the Closing Years of the Tokugawa Regime*
42. Ezra Vogel, Margie Sargent, Vivienne B. Shue, Thomas Jay Mathews, and Deborah S. Davis, *The Cultural Revolution in the Provinces*
43. Sidney A. Forsythe, *An American Missionary Community in China, 1895–1905*

*44. Benjamin I. Schwartz, ed., *Reflections on the May Fourth Movement.: A Symposium*
*45. Ching Young Choe, *The Rule of the Taewŏngun, 1864–1873: Restoration in Yi Korea*
46. W. P. J. Hall, *A Bibliographical Guide to Japanese Research on the Chinese Economy, 1958–1970*
47. Jack J. Gerson, *Horatio Nelson Lay and Sino-British Relations, 1854–1864*
48. Paul Richard Bohr, *Famine and the Missionary: Timothy Richard as Relief Administrator and Advocate of National Reform*
49. Endymion Wilkinson, *The History of Imperial China: A Research Guide*
50. Britten Dean, *China and Great Britain: The Diplomacy of Commercial Relations, 1860–1864*
51. Ellsworth C. Carlson, *The Foochow Missionaries, 1847–1880*
52. Yeh-chien Wang, *An Estimate of the Land-Tax Collection in China, 1753 and 1908*
53. Richard M. Pfeffer, *Understanding Business Contracts in China, 1949–1963*
*54. Han-sheng Chuan and Richard Kraus, *Mid-Ching Rice Markets and Trade: An Essay in Price History*
55. Ranbir Vohra, *Lao She and the Chinese Revolution*
56. Liang-lin Hsiao, *China's Foreign Trade Statistics, 1864–1949*
*57. Lee-hsia Hsu Ting, *Government Control of the Press in Modern China, 1900–1949*
*58. Edward W. Wagner, *The Literati Purges: Political Conflict in Early Yi Korea*
*59. Joungwon A. Kim, *Divided Korea: The Politics of Development, 1945–1972*
60. Noriko Kamachi, John K. Fairbank, and Chūzō Ichiko, *Japanese Studies of Modern China Since 1953: A Bibliographical Guide to Historical and Social-Science Research on the Nineteenth and Twentieth Centuries, Supplementary Volume for 1953–1969*
61. Donald A. Gibbs and Yun-chen Li, *A Bibliography of Studies and Translations of Modern Chinese Literature, 1918–1942*
62. Robert H. Silin, *Leadership and Values: The Organization of Large-Scale Taiwanese Enterprises*
63. David Pong, *A Critical Guide to the Kwangtung Provincial Archives Deposited at the Public Record Office of London*
*64. Fred W. Drake, *China Charts the World: Hsu Chi-yü and His Geography of 1848*
*65. William A. Brown and Urgrunge Onon, translators and annotators, *History of the Mongolian People's Republic*
66. Edward L. Farmer, *Early Ming Government: The Evolution of Dual Capitals*
*67. Ralph C. Croizier, *Koxinga and Chinese Nationalism: History, Myth, and the Hero*

*68. William J. Tyler, tr., *The Psychological World of Natsume Sōseki*, by Doi Takeo

69. Eric Widmer, *The Russian Ecclesiastical Mission in Peking During the Eighteenth Century*

*70. Charlton M. Lewis, *Prologue to the Chinese Revolution: The Transformation of Ideas and Institutions in Hunan Province, 1891–1907*

71. Preston Torbert, *The Ching Imperial Household Department: A Study of Its Organization and Principal Functions, 1662–1796*

72. Paul A. Cohen and John E. Schrecker, eds., *Reform in Nineteenth-Century China*

73. Jon Sigurdson, *Rural Industrialism in China*

74. Kang Chao, *The Development of Cotton Textile Production in China*

75. Valentin Rabe, *The Home Base of American China Missions, 1880–1920*

*76. Sarasin Viraphol, *Tribute and Profit: Sino-Siamese Trade, 1652–1853*

77. Ch'i-ch'ing Hsiao, *The Military Establishment of the Yuan Dynasty*

78. Meishi Tsai, *Contemporary Chinese Novels and Short Stories, 1949–1974: An Annotated Bibliography*

*79. Wellington K. K. Chan, *Merchants, Mandarins and Modern Enterprise in Late Ching China*

80. Endymion Wilkinson, *Landlord and Labor in Late Imperial China: Case Studies from Shandong by Jing Su and Luo Lun*

*81. Barry Keenan, *The Dewey Experiment in China: Educational Reform and Political Power in the Early Republic*

*82. George A. Hayden, *Crime and Punishment in Medieval Chinese Drama: Three Judge Pao Plays*

*83. Sang-Chul Suh, *Growth and Structural Changes in the Korean Economy, 1910–1940*

84. J. W. Dower, *Empire and Aftermath: Yoshida Shigeru and the Japanese Experience, 1878–1954*

85. Martin Collcutt, *Five Mountains: The Rinzai Zen Monastic Institution in Medieval Japan*

86. Kwang Suk Kim and Michael Roemer, *Growth and Structural Transformation*

87. Anne O. Krueger, *The Developmental Role of the Foreign Sector and Aid*

*88. Edwin S. Mills and Byung-Nak Song, *Urbanization and Urban Problems*

89. Sung Hwan Ban, Pal Yong Moon, and Dwight H. Perkins, *Rural Development*

*90. Noel F. McGinn, Donald R. Snodgrass, Yung Bong Kim, Shin-Bok Kim, and Quee-Young Kim, *Education and Development in Korea*

*91. Leroy P. Jones and Il SaKong, *Government, Business, and Entrepreneurship in Economic Development: The Korean Case*
92. Edward S. Mason, Dwight H. Perkins, Kwang Suk Kim, David C. Cole, Mahn Je Kim et al., *The Economic and Social Modernization of the Republic of Korea*
93. Robert Repetto, Tai Hwan Kwon, Son-Ung Kim, Dae Young Kim, John E. Sloboda, and Peter J. Donaldson, *Economic Development, Population Policy, and Demographic Transition in the Republic of Korea*
94. Parks M. Coble, Jr., *The Shanghai Capitalists and the Nationalist Government, 1927–1937*
95. Noriko Kamachi, *Reform in China: Huang Tsun-hsien and the Japanese Model*
96. Richard Wich, *Sino-Soviet Crisis Politics: A Study of Political Change and Communication*
97. Lillian M. Li, *China's Silk Trade: Traditional Industry in the Modern World, 1842–1937*
98. R. David Arkush, *Fei Xiaotong and Sociology in Revolutionary China*
*99. Kenneth Alan Grossberg, *Japan's Renaissance: The Politics of the Muromachi Bakufu*
100. James Reeve Pusey, *China and Charles Darwin*
101. Hoyt Cleveland Tillman, *Utilitarian Confucianism: Chen Liang's Challenge to Chu Hsi*
102. Thomas A. Stanley, *Ōsugi Sakae, Anarchist in Taishō Japan: The Creativity of the Ego*
103. Jonathan K. Ocko, *Bureaucratic Reform in Provincial China: Ting Jih-ch'ang in Restoration Kiangsu, 1867–1870*
104. James Reed, *The Missionary Mind and American East Asia Policy, 1911–1915*
105. Neil L. Waters, *Japan's Local Pragmatists: The Transition from Bakumatsu to Meiji in the Kawasaki Region*
106. David C. Cole and Yung Chul Park, *Financial Development in Korea, 1945–1978*
107. Roy Bahl, Chuk Kyo Kim, and Chong Kee Park, *Public Finances During the Korean Modernization Process*
108. William D. Wray, *Mitsubishi and the N.Y.K, 1870–1914: Business Strategy in the Japanese Shipping Industry*
109. Ralph William Huenemann, *The Dragon and the Iron Horse: The Economics of Railroads in China, 1876–1937*
*110. Benjamin A. Elman, *From Philosophy to Philology: Intellectual and Social Aspects of Change in Late Imperial China*
111. Jane Kate Leonard, *Wei Yüan and China's Rediscovery of the Maritime World*

112. Luke S. K. Kwong, *A Mosaic of the Hundred Days:. Personalities, Politics, and Ideas of 1898*

*113. John E. Wills, Jr., *Embassies and Illusions: Dutch and Portuguese Envoys to K'ang-hsi, 1666–1687*

114. Joshua A. Fogel, *Politics and Sinology: The Case of Naitō Konan (1866–1934)*

*115. Jeffrey C. Kinkley, ed., *After Mao: Chinese Literature and Society, 1978–1981*

116. C. Andrew Gerstle, *Circles of Fantasy: Convention in the Plays of Chikamatsu*

117. Andrew Gordon, *The Evolution of Labor Relations in Japan: Heavy Industry, 1853–1955*

*118. Daniel K. Gardner, *Chu Hsi and the "Ta Hsueh": Neo-Confucian Reflection on the Confucian Canon*

119. Christine Guth Kanda, *Shinzō: Hachiman Imagery and Its Development*

*120. Robert Borgen, *Sugawara no Michizane and the Early Heian Court*

121. Chang-tai Hung, *Going to the People: Chinese Intellectual and Folk Literature, 1918–1937*

*122. Michael A. Cusumano, *The Japanese Automobile Industry: Technology and Management at Nissan and Toyota*

123. Richard von Glahn, *The Country of Streams and Grottoes: Expansion, Settlement, and the Civilizing of the Sichuan Frontier in Song Times*

124. Steven D. Carter, *The Road to Komatsubara: A Classical Reading of the Renga Hyakuin*

125. Katherine F. Bruner, John K. Fairbank, and Richard T. Smith, *Entering China's Service: Robert Hart's Journals, 1854–1863*

126. Bob Tadashi Wakabayashi, *Anti-Foreignism and Western Learning in Early-Modern Japan: The "New Theses" of 1825*

127. Atsuko Hirai, *Individualism and Socialism: The Life and Thought of Kawai Eijirō (1891–1944)*

128. Ellen Widmer, *The Margins of Utopia: "Shui-hu hou-chuan" and the Literature of Ming Loyalism*

129. R. Kent Guy, *The Emperor's Four Treasuries: Scholars and the State in the Late Chien-lung Era*

130. Peter C. Perdue, *Exhausting the Earth: State and Peasant in Hunan, 1500–1850*

131. Susan Chan Egan, *A Latterday Confucian: Reminiscences of William Hung (1893–1980)*

132. James T. C. Liu, *China Turning Inward: Intellectual-Political Changes in the Early Twelfth Century*

*133. Paul A. Cohen, *Between Tradition and Modernity: Wang T'ao and Reform in Late Ching China*

134. Kate Wildman Nakai, *Shogunal Politics: Arai Hakuseki and the Premises of Tokugawa Rule*
*135. Parks M. Coble, *Facing Japan: Chinese Politics and Japanese Imperialism, 1931–1937*
136. Jon L. Saari, *Legacies of Childhood: Growing Up Chinese in a Time of Crisis, 1890–1920*
137. Susan Downing Videen, *Tales of Heichū*
138. Heinz Morioka and Miyoko Sasaki, *Rakugo: The Popular Narrative Art of Japan*
139. Joshua A. Fogel, *Nakae Ushikichi in China: The Mourning of Spirit*
140. Alexander Barton Woodside, *Vietnam and the Chinese Model.: A Comparative Study of Vietnamese and Chinese Government in the First Half of the Nineteenth Century*
*141. George Elison, *Deus Destroyed: The Image of Christianity in Early Modern Japan*
142. William D. Wray, ed., *Managing Industrial Enterprise: Cases from Japan's Prewar Experience*
*143. T'ung-tsu Ch'ü, *Local Government in China Under the Ching*
144. Marie Anchordoguy, *Computers, Inc.: Japan's Challenge to IBM*
145. Barbara Molony, *Technology and Investment: The Prewar Japanese Chemical Industry*
146. Mary Elizabeth Berry, *Hideyoshi*
147. Laura E. Hein, *Fueling Growth: The Energy Revolution and Economic Policy in Postwar Japan*
148. Wen-hsin Yeh, *The Alienated Academy: Culture and Politics in Republican China, 1919–1937*
149. Dru C. Gladney, *Muslim Chinese: Ethnic Nationalism in the People's Republic*
150. Merle Goldman and Paul A. Cohen, eds., *Ideas Across Cultures: Essays on Chinese Thought in Honor of Benjamin L Schwartz*
151. James M. Polachek, *The Inner Opium War*
152. Gail Lee Bernstein, *Japanese Marxist: A Portrait of Kawakami Hajime, 1879–1946*
*153. Lloyd E. Eastman, *The Abortive Revolution: China Under Nationalist Rule, 1927–1937*
154. Mark Mason, *American Multinationals and Japan: The Political Economy of Japanese Capital Controls, 1899–1980*
155. Richard J. Smith, John K. Fairbank, and Katherine F. Bruner, *Robert Hart and China's Early Modernization: His Journals, 1863–1866*
156. George J. Tanabe, Jr., *Myōe the Dreamkeeper: Fantasy and Knowledge in Kamakura Buddhism*

157. William Wayne Farris, *Heavenly Warriors: The Evolution of Japan's Military, 500–1300*
158. Yu-ming Shaw, *An American Missionary in China: John Leighton Stuart and Chinese-American Relations*
159. James B. Palais, *Politics and Policy in Traditional Korea*
*160. Douglas Reynolds, *China, 1898–1912: The Xinzheng Revolution and Japan*
161. Roger R. Thompson, *China's Local Councils in the Age of Constitutional Reform, 1898–1911*
162. William Johnston, *The Modern Epidemic: History of Tuberculosis in Japan*
163. Constantine Nomikos Vaporis, *Breaking Barriers: Travel and the State in Early Modern Japan*
164. Irmela Hijiya-Kirschnereit, *Rituals of Self-Revelation: Shishōsetsu as Literary Genre and Socio-Cultural Phenomenon*
165. James C. Baxter, *The Meiji Unification Through the Lens of Ishikawa Prefecture*
166. Thomas R. H. Havens, *Architects of Affluence: The Tsutsumi Family and the Seibu-Saison Enterprises in Twentieth-Century Japan*
167. Anthony Hood Chambers, *The Secret Window: Ideal Worlds in Tanizaki's Fiction*
168. Steven J. Ericson, *The Sound of the Whistle: Railroads and the State in Meiji Japan*
169. Andrew Edmund Goble, *Kenmu: Go-Daigo's Revolution*
170. Denise Potrzeba Lett, *In Pursuit of Status: The Making of South Korea's "New" Urban Middle Class*
171. Mimi Hall Yiengpruksawan, *Hiraizumi: Buddhist Art and Regional Politics in Twelfth-Century Japan*
172. Charles Shirō Inouye, *The Similitude of Blossoms: A Critical Biography of Izumi Kyōka (1873–1939), Japanese Novelist and Playwright*
173. Aviad E. Raz, *Riding the Black Ship: Japan and Tokyo Disneyland*
174. Deborah J. Milly, *Poverty, Equality, and Growth: The Politics of Economic Need in Postwar Japan*
175. See Heng Teow, *Japan's Cultural Policy Toward China, 1918–1931: A Comparative Perspective*
176. Michael A. Fuller, *An Introduction to Literary Chinese*
177. Frederick R. Dickinson, *War and National Reinvention: Japan in the Great War, 1914–1919*
178. John Solt, *Shredding the Tapestry of Meaning: The Poetry and Poetics of Kitasono Katue (1902–1978)*
179. Edward Pratt, *Japan's Protoindustrial Elite: The Economic Foundations of the Gōnō*
180. Atsuko Sakaki, *Recontextualizing Texts: Narrative Performance in Modern Japanese Fiction*

181. Soon-Won Park, *Colonial Industrialization and Labor in Korea: The Onoda Cement Factory*
182. JaHyun Kim Haboush and Martina Deuchler, *Culture and the State in Late Chosŏn Korea*
183. John W. Chaffee, *Branches of Heaven: A History of the Imperial Clan of Sung China*
184. Gi-Wook Shin and Michael Robinson, eds., *Colonial Modernity in Korea*
185. Nam-lin Hur, *Prayer and Play in Late Tokugawa Japan: Asakusa Sensōji and Edo Society*
186. Kristin Stapleton, *Civilizing Chengdu: Chinese Urban Reform, 1895–1937*
187. Hyung Il Pai, *Constructing "Korean" Origins: A Critical Review of Archaeology, Historiography, and Racial Myth in Korean State-Formation Theories*
188. Brian D. Ruppert, *Jewel in the Ashes: Buddha Relics and Power in Early Medieval Japan*
189. Susan Daruvala, *Zhou Zuoren and an Alternative Chinese Response to Modernity*
*190. James Z. Lee, *The Political Economy of a Frontier: Southwest China, 1250–1850*
191. Kerry Smith, *A Time of Crisis: Japan, the Great Depression, and Rural Revitalization*
192. Michael Lewis, *Becoming Apart: National Power and Local Politics in Toyama, 1868–1945*
193. William C. Kirby, Man-houng Lin, James Chin Shih, and David A. Pietz, eds., *State and Economy in Republican China: A Handbook for Scholars*
194. Timothy S. George, *Minamata: Pollution and the Struggle for Democracy in Postwar Japan*
195. Billy K. L. So, *Prosperity, Region, and Institutions in Maritime China: The South Fukien Pattern, 946–1368*
196. Yoshihisa Tak Matsusaka, *The Making of Japanese Manchuria, 1904–1932*
197. Maram Epstein, *Competing Discourses: Orthodoxy, Authenticity, and Engendered Meanings in Late Imperial Chinese Fiction*
198. Curtis J. Milhaupt, J. Mark Ramseyer, and Michael K. Young, eds. and comps., *Japanese Law in Context: Readings in Society, the Economy, and Politics*
199. Haruo Iguchi, *Unfinished Business: Ayukawa Yoshisuke and U.S.-Japan Relations, 1937–1952*
200. Scott Pearce, Audrey Spiro, and Patricia Ebrey, *Culture and Power in the Reconstitution of the Chinese Realm, 200–600*
201. Terry Kawashima, *Writing Margins: The Textual Construction of Gender in Heian and Kamakura Japan*
202. Martin W. Huang, *Desire and Fictional Narrative in Late Imperial China*

203. Robert S. Ross and Jiang Changbin, eds., *Re-examining the Cold War: U.S.-China Diplomacy, 1954–1973*
204. Guanhua Wang, *In Search of Justice: The 1905–1906 Chinese Anti-American Boycott*
205. David Schaberg, *A Patterned Past: Form and Thought in Early Chinese Historiography*
206. Christine Yano, *Tears of Longing: Nostalgia and the Nation in Japanese Popular Song*
207. Milena Doleželová-Velingerová and Oldřich Král, with Graham Sanders, eds., *The Appropriation of Cultural Capital: China's May Fourth Project*
208. Robert N. Huey, *The Making of 'Shinkokinshū'*
209. Lee Butler, *Emperor and Aristocracy in Japan, 1467–1680: Resilience and Renewal*
210. Suzanne Ogden, *Inklings of Democracy in China*
211. Kenneth J. Ruoff, *The People's Emperor: Democracy and the Japanese Monarchy, 1945–1995*
212. Haun Saussy, *Great Walls of Discourse and Other Adventures in Cultural China*
213. Aviad E. Raz, *Emotions at Work: Normative Control, Organizations, and Culture in Japan and America*
214. Rebecca E. Karl and Peter Zarrow, eds., *Rethinking the 1898 Reform Period: Political and Cultural Change in Late Qing China*
215. Kevin O'Rourke, *The Book of Korean Shijo*
216. Ezra F. Vogel, ed., *The Golden Age of the U.S.-China-Japan Triangle, 1972–1989*
217. Thomas A Wilson, ed., *On Sacred Grounds: Culture, Society, Politics, and the Formation of the Cult of Confucius*
218. Donald S. Sutton, *Steps of Perfection: Exorcistic Performers and Chinese Religion in Twentieth-Century Taiwan*
219. Daqing Yang, *Technology of Empire: Telecommunications and Japanese Expansionism, 1895–1945*
220. Qianshen Bai, *Fu Shan's World: The Transformation of Chinese Calligraphy in the Seventeenth Century*
221. Paul Jakov Smith and Richard von Glahn, eds., *The Song-Yuan-Ming Transition in Chinese History*
222. Rania Huntington, *Alien Kind: Foxes and Late Imperial Chinese Narrative*
223. Jordan Sand, *House and Home in Modern Japan: Architecture, Domestic Space, and Bourgeois Culture, 1880–1930*
224. Karl Gerth, *China Made: Consumer Culture and the Creation of the Nation*

225. Xiaoshan Yang, *Metamorphosis of the Private Sphere: Gardens and Objects in Tang-Song Poetry*
226. Barbara Mittler, *A Newspaper for China? Power, Identity, and Change in Shanghai's News Media, 1872–1912*
227. Joyce A. Madancy, *The Troublesome Legacy of Commissioner Lin: The Opium Trade and Opium Suppression in Fujian Province, 1820s to 1920s*
228. John Makeham, *Transmitters and Creators: Chinese Commentators and Commentaries on the Analects*
229. Elisabeth Köll, *From Cotton Mill to Business Empire: The Emergence of Regional Enterprises in Modern China*
230. Emma Teng, *Taiwan's Imagined Geography: Chinese Colonial Travel Writing and Pictures, 1683–1895*
231. Wilt Idema and Beata Grant, *The Red Brush: Writing Women of Imperial China*
232. Eric C. Rath, *The Ethos of Noh: Actors and Their Art*
233. Elizabeth Remick, *Building Local States: China During the Republican and Post-Mao Eras*
234. Lynn Struve, ed., *The Qing Formation in World-Historical Time*
235. D. Max Moerman, *Localizing Paradise: Kumano Pilgrimage and the Religious Landscape of Premodern Japan*
236. Antonia Finnane, *Speaking of Yangzhou: A Chinese City, 1550–1850*
237. Brian Platt, *Burning and Building: Schooling and State Formation in Japan, 1750–1890*
238. Gail Bernstein, Andrew Gordon, and Kate Wildman Nakai, eds., *Public Spheres, Private Lives in Modern Japan, 1600–1950: Essays in Honor of Albert Craig*
239. Wu Hung and Katherine R. Tsiang, *Body and Face in Chinese Visual Culture*
240. Stephen Dodd, *Writing Home: Representations of the Native Place in Modern Japanese Literature*
241. David Anthony Bello, *Opium and the Limits of Empire: Drug Prohibition in the Chinese Interior, 1729–1850*
242. Hosea Hirata, *Discourses of Seduction: History, Evil, Desire, and Modern Japanese Literature*
243. Kyung Moon Hwang, *Beyond Birth: Social Status in the Emergence of Modern Korea*
244. Brian R. Dott, *Identity Reflections: Pilgrimages to Mount Tai in Late Imperial China*
245. Mark McNally, *Proving the Way: Conflict and Practice in the History of Japanese Nativism*

246. Yongping Wu, *A Political Explanation of Economic Growth: State Survival, Bureaucratic Politics, and Private Enterprises in the Making of Taiwan's Economy, 1950–1985*
247. Kyu Hyun Kim, *The Age of Visions and Arguments: Parliamentarianism and the National Public Sphere in Early Meiji Japan*
248. Zvi Ben-Dor Benite, *The Dao of Muhammad: A Cultural History of Muslims in Late Imperial China*
249. David Der-wei Wang and Shang Wei, eds., *Dynastic Crisis and Cultural Innovation: From the Late Ming to the Late Qing and Beyond*
250. Wilt L. Idema, Wai-yee Li, and Ellen Widmer, eds., *Trauma and Transcendence in Early Qing Literature*
251. Barbara Molony and Kathleen Uno, eds., *Gendering Modern Japanese History*
252. Hiroshi Aoyagi, *Islands of Eight Million Smiles: Idol Performance and Symbolic Production in Contemporary Japan*
253. Wai-yee Li, *The Readability of the Past in Early Chinese Historiography*
254. William C. Kirby, Robert S. Ross, and Gong Li, eds., *Normalization of U.S.-China Relations: An International History*
255. Ellen Gardner Nakamura, *Practical Pursuits: Takano Chōei, Takahashi Keisaku, and Western Medicine in Nineteenth-Century Japan*
256. Jonathan W. Best, *A History of the Early Korean Kingdom of Paekche, together with an annotated translation of* The Paekche Annals *of the* Samguk sagi
257. Liang Pan, *The United Nations in Japan's Foreign and Security Policymaking, 1945–1992: National Security, Party Politics, and International Status*
258. Richard Belsky, *Localities at the Center: Native Place, Space, and Power in Late Imperial Beijing*
259. Zwia Lipkin, *"Useless to the State": "Social Problems" and Social Engineering in Nationalist Nanjing, 1927–1937*
260. William O. Gardner, *Advertising Tower: Japanese Modernism and Modernity in the 1920s*
261. Stephen Owen, *The Making of Early Chinese Classical Poetry*
262. Martin J. Powers, *Pattern and Person: Ornament, Society, and Self in Classical China*
263. Anna M. Shields, *Crafting a Collection: The Cultural Contexts and Poetic Practice of the* Huajian ji 花間集 (*Collection from Among the Flowers*)
264. Stephen Owen, *The Late Tang: Chinese Poetry of the Mid-Ninth Century (827–860)*
265. Sara L. Friedman, *Intimate Politics: Marriage, the Market, and State Power in Southeastern China*

HQ 1236.5 .C6 F75 2006
Friedman, Sara.
Intimate politics

MAR 0 7 2008